The Campaign Manager

FOURTH EDITION

The Campaign
Manager

Running and Winning Local Elections

CATHERINE SHAW

**WESTVIEW
PRESS**
A Member of the Perseus Books Group

Designed by Brent Wilcox

Library of Congress Cataloging-in-Publication Data
Shaw, Catherine M. (Catherine Marie), 1955–
    The campaign manager : running and winning local elections /
Catherine Shaw. — 4th ed.
        p.   cm.
    Includes bibliographical references and index.
    ISBN 978-0-8133-4451-5 (alk. paper)
    1. Local elections—United States—Handbooks, manuals, etc.   2. Campaign
management—United States—Handbooks, manuals, etc.   I. Title.
    JS395.S43 2010
    324.70973—dc22

                                                                2009031172

10 9 8 7 6 5 4 3 2 1

Dedicated to my children,
Daniel Booker and Sarah Beth

Contents

Preface

Running for local office can be one of the most demanding and yet exhilarating experiences of your life. Your house will be a wreck, your children ignored, and your partner, whether involved in the campaign or not, will be stressed. And yet, seeking office or pushing through an issue-based campaign gives you an opportunity to be a leader, to effect change in your community, and to repay something to the city, county, state, or country you love. The campaign experience also offers you an opportunity to grow personally. You will be challenged and stretched as never before. When it's all over, win or lose, you will be a different person, with a different outlook on our political process and a new respect for those who run and serve.

When I first ran for mayor of Ashland, Oregon, in 1988, I had little prior government or management experience. Many felt I should start at the council level and work my way up before taking on the position of CEO of a multimillion-dollar municipality. However, having so little experience allowed me to view things with a fresh eye.

> "You have to be smart enough to understand the game and dumb enough to think it's important."
> **GENE MCCARTHY,**
> on how politics is like coaching football

After three terms and twelve years at that post, the council, the city staff, the community, and I implemented dozens of programs, including open space, water conservation, community composting and recycling, voter-approved air quality standards, wetland and floodplain preservation, wastewater treatment plant upgrades, forest management, and restoration and expansion of the library, fire station, and city offices. We also worked closely with our public school system to find ways to ease its financial burden in the wake of state budget cutbacks. We divested our hospital, helped save a ski resort, and acquired an ambulance service. We installed a dark fiber ring in our city, providing direct-connect, high-speed Internet access and cable TV services. By having community and government work in partnership, we've been able to create and act on opportunities normally available only to large metropolitan areas.

There are over a half million elective offices in the United States. If you have an inclination to serve and a desire to be a leader in your community, do it. Being in a position where you can have a positive impact on your community and bring about change is more rewarding and fun than you can imagine. Ultimately, the only real credentials you need are integrity, a caring heart, and a strong work ethic.

Since 1985 I have worked on or run many campaigns in my region. Through years of experimentation and collaboration with other seasoned campaigners, I found organizational techniques that worked in political campaigns, and I began to apply them to the campaign process. This book is the culmination of campaign trial and error and will give you the tools you need to organize the efforts of others on your behalf. Whether you are a novice or a seasoned campaigner, you will find information here that will make your efforts more organized and effective.

> "Politics—good politics—is public service. There is no life or occupation in which a man can find a greater opportunity to serve his community or his country."
> — **HARRY TRUMAN**

Good luck, and enjoy the process.

How to Use This Handbook

Running an effective local election is more work than you can possibly imagine. It involves recruiting volunteers, raising money (lots of it), running phone banks, creating media presentations, canvassing, and getting out the vote. The candidate or issue must be "packaged" in a believable and compelling way, and resources must be effectively allocated.

This handbook breaks a campaign down into manageable units for easy implementation. If you are the candidate, you will find the necessary tools to coordinate your efforts with those of your campaign manager and committee. If you're the campaign manager, either for a candidate or for an issue-based campaign, this handbook will organize and guide you and your team through the campaign process.

Because implementing each of the components of a winning campaign is easier if you have an understanding of the complexity of the whole process, take time to read this entire handbook before you design your campaign flow-chart or draft your campaign plan. Nevertheless, for those who came to this book late in the process, each chapter is designed to stand alone. If you have lawn sign installation in a week, you can go straight to that chapter and, following the instructions, implement that portion of the campaign.

The Framework

In local politics, there are generally three types of political campaigns:

- Partisan candidate
- Nonpartisan candidate
- Issue-based

Although some states allow a primary winner who receives more than 50 percent of the vote to take office with no runoff, a partisan race typically has a primary, with party winners squaring off in a general election.

A nonpartisan race usually has only one election, the general election, in which the winner takes all. However, some nonpartisan races, including judicial elections, require a candidate to receive 50 percent of the votes cast or face a general election runoff; this book includes strategies for winning 50 percent of the vote to avoid a runoff.

An issue-based campaign, like a nonpartisan race, takes place in one election cycle, but unlike candidate races, depending on the state and locality, the campaign can occur in any election. Issue-based campaigns may either be brought to the voters by the governing body (referral) or, in some states, be brought to the voters through the citizen initiative process.

> "Behind all political success is attention to detail."
> — **LARRY O'BRIEN**, adviser to John F. Kennedy

Within this handbook are field-tested systems designed to establish an organizational framework for campaign activities such as phone banks, clerical teams, brochure development, media, fund-raising, lawn sign dispersal and maintenance, canvassing, and the get-out-the-vote (GOTV) effort. Underlying each of these is the framework for systematically organizing other people's efforts on your behalf through the campaign committee, the campaign team, and extended volunteer organization in the field.

Also included are tips for building theme and message as well as disciplines to stay on your message whether you are in debates, facing the media, or creating campaign literature media production.

By breaking a campaign down into manageable units and organizing the activities within each component, you will never overload your workforce. Once you have decided what you can or want to do in organizing your campaign, you will need to plot these activities on a campaign flowchart, calendar, or plan. Campaign plans are probably the most widely accepted blueprint design for a campaign. However, I prefer a more visual campaign flowchart because it presents a campaign timeline that can be understood at a glance. Any campaign flowchart or calendar can be converted to a plan; immediately after the book's instructions on creating a flowchart, there are directions for a conversion to a campaign plan.

The Layout

Chapter 1, "Precinct Analysis," looks at voter behavior based on social context. Although the actual process for conducting a precinct analysis is located in the appendix, Chapter 1 explains the importance of, and reasoning behind, the many aspects of a precinct analysis. Conducting a precinct analysis will focus campaign time and resources for the biggest return. Further, it will reveal if a candidate or an issue has a fighting chance.

A precinct analysis is the foundation for finding support, swing voters, persuadable voters, and the votes needed to win, all while avoiding voters who are opposed to your efforts. Precinct analysis can and should be done long in advance of the campaign kickoff.

After conducting your precinct analysis and determining your chances, the remainder of the book targets organizational systems.

Chapter 2, "The Campaign Team," covers both the small, select group that will develop campaign strategies (the campaign committee) and the greater force behind activity implementation. The team includes volunteers, the media team, the treasurer, and the campaign chairs or co-chairs.

Chapter 3, "The Campaign Brochure," details the single most important thing the campaign committee will do in the campaign: develop a theme and message. Within this chapter, you will also find detailed information on benchmark polling, slogans, logo design, and the voters' pamphlet as well as tips on drafting an effective brochure.

Chapter 4, "The Volunteer Organization," gives you the structure for organizing your phone banks and clerical workers and provides sample scripts for their many activities.

Although this manual has many field-tested systems to save money in the political process, without a certain threshold of money, efforts to get your message to the voters will be hobbled. Chapter 5, "Fund-Raising," outlines the many ways a campaign can raise money through events, direct mail, and candidate and volunteer solicitation calls. Raising money on the Internet is also covered in this chapter.

Chapter 6, "Lawn Signs," covers logo design, finding locations, establishing structure for volunteer systems for placement, and maintenance and removal of both lawn and field signs. Also included are examples of signs that work.

Targeting voters, the topic of Chapter 7, builds on the precinct analysis to help you to find likely voters. The chapter also outlines how to communicate with such voters through direct mail and canvassing.

Chapter 8, "Media," provides examples of how to get the most out of your media dollars while effectively communicating with voters. Through the media, candidates and issue-based campaigns gain credibility. Given the expense and the power of this campaign line item, the more you know, the more effective you will be in getting the most out of each media dollar.

Chapter 9, "The Candidate," outlines how best to package the candidate to project as positive an image as possible. It also covers negative campaigning, attacks, debates, and dealing with the press in detail.

Chapter 10, "The Issue-Based Campaign," covers initiative, referendum, recall, and school and library money issues, along with a couple of "monsters in the night": the double majority and the super majority.

Chapter 11, "Getting Out the Vote," encompasses the all-important voter activation effort that is critical to a winning campaign. This chapter offers tips for last-minute voter persuasion, dealing with the hybrid campaign— that is, the election with both absentee mail voting and poll voting—and tried-and-true methods for the elections that are conducted partly or entirely through vote by mail. With over a decade of vote-by-mail experience, Oregon has this system down. Further, all the systems I share in the GOTV chapter have been perfected after decades of implementation. They arguably represent the best GOTV organizational system in the state.

> "Play for more than you can afford to lose and you will learn the game."
> —— **WINSTON CHURCHILL**

Chapter 12, "The Campaign Flowchart," puts in chronological order all that you will need to do to win. Although creating a flowchart is one of the first things you will do to organize your campaign, without the baseline knowledge of the first eleven chapters, a flowchart would be more difficult. Also included in this chapter is a campaign calendar, yet another alternative to the campaign plan, which works equally well for organizing campaign efforts.

Finally, Chapter 13, "After the Ball," is simply about winning and losing gracefully, putting your campaign to bed, election night, and retiring a campaign debt (should you have one).

Know the Law

First things first: Visit the county clerk, election office, or city recorder to become familiar with state and local election laws. For example, in my city, you are not allowed to place lawn signs more than six weeks before an election. You are also not allowed to place them on the strip between the sidewalk and the street. Although the homeowner may plant, mow, water, and care for this area, it is in fact part of the public right-of-way. To place a lawn sign here could be interpreted in one of two ways: Either you feel you're above the law, or you don't know the law. Either interpretation is a problem if you hope to be in government.

It is against federal law to place campaign literature in and around mailboxes. Even though you bought and installed your mailbox, the federal government dictates how it can be used. The same goes for the little boxes on the side of your home. Publicly owned buildings are maintained, lit, and owned by the taxpayers and so should not be used for campaign purposes, either. And on and on.

> "One thing I know: The only ones among you who will be really happy are those who will have sought and found how to serve."
> **ALBERT SCHWEITZER**

The county clerk or city recorder will also draw attention to filing dates that you and your treasurer must know. Missing a campaign expenditure filing deadline will almost always get you media coverage, but not the kind you need or want. Also missing the voters' pamphlet deadline can unnecessarily hobble your efforts.

Other than the legal materials from the county clerk, the city recorder, or the secretary of state, everything you need to run a successful campaign is included in this handbook.

THE TEN COMMANDMENTS OF CAMPAIGNING

Honor thy base

Stay on message

Money is thy savior

Never tell a lie

Aim at the souls that can be saved

Never waste donors' money

Do not commit adultery

Start early

Be prepared in all things

Know who you are

THE CARDINAL SINS OF CAMPAIGNING

Being caught in a provable lie

Committing a crime

Having a relationship with a member of your staff

Committing adultery

Declaring bankruptcy

1

Precinct Analysis

The Sinners, the Saints, and the Savables

IN THIS CHAPTER
- Context of Neighborhood
- Independents
- The Undervote
- Finding Swing Voters

In twenty years of working on campaigns, I have found that a precinct analysis is the single best tool in the campaign tool kit. A precinct analysis will tell you some important information:

- Votes needed to win
- Undervote attribution
- Location of your base and your opposition's base
- How to find swing voters
- Registration trends
- Issues voters care about
- Predicted base party vote
- Predicted voter turnout
- If there's any hope of a win

A precinct analysis gives you accurate direction on where best to spend time and campaign resources to have the greatest impact. It is the best road map you can use to get to a win, and it will save your campaign money, lots of money.

Unlike some campaign activities, a precinct analysis may be conducted months or even years before the campaign, because it is based on voting history. Take

> "Aim at the souls that can be saved."
> **BILL MEULEMANS**

advantage of this fact and get it out of the way. It's also cheap. Using this handbook and a few dollars, anyone can conduct a precinct analysis. Although election offices charge a nominal fee for past election records, the information you need is public, relatively easy to obtain, and inexpensive. The only exception would be in counties that do not keep records broken down by party, turnout, undervote, or precinct. For such counties, you may have to go elsewhere to get your data, such as a voter contact service, your party, or a political action committee (PAC) that has endorsed you and tracks voting history. If it is a voter contact service, be prepared to pay, but your party or an endorsing PAC will usually provide some voter contact information as an in-kind donation to your campaign. If your campaign is too local for PAC or party support, go to a candidate who has such support and offer to include him or her in a precinct analysis if the person's campaign can get you what you want.

> "Phyllis Schlafly speaks for all American women who oppose equal rights for themselves."
> — ANDY ROONEY

Nearly all county clerks or election offices will have past voting records. Some keep the information electronically; some have only abstracts and full printed reports. Some counties will allow you to check out the full reports of an election, but if they don't, pack a lunch and be prepared to spend a few hours down at the election office.

In addition to voting history from election offices, you may also use U.S. Census data (www.uscensus.gov) to further profile your voters with demographic and economic data. The census database will give you demographic information by state, county, and city. This information is often a great help for local elections, because data are presented separately for each city, apparently irrespective of size. So if your area of concern includes one or more small cities, you're in luck.

> "More than any other time in history, mankind faces a crossroads. One path leads to despair and utter hopelessness, the other, to total extinction. Let us pray we have the wisdom to choose correctly."
> — WOODY ALLEN

Whereas your polling data will tell you who supports your cause by gender, race, age, income, education, and party affiliation, a precinct analysis will give you an idea of how neighborhoods vote on issues and candidates that parallel your campaign. For example, if you are working on a countywide election and your polling data show that 60 percent of women support your cause, you do not know whether that is 60 percent across the board or 70 percent in one city and 30 percent in another. To make your polling work better for your purposes, ask the polling firm to break down your data by region—or better yet, by zone. While a poll may tell you where you are on an issue at a given moment, a precinct analysis will give you more of a continuum of voter tendencies.

There will be times, however, when a precinct analysis is of minimal help: for example, if you are running a partisan race in an area with a huge registration disadvantage and no voter history of a win from anyone in your party. In this example, a precinct analysis will tell you where your voters are lazy— that is, those in your party who tend to be nonvoters—and it may provide some information on swing voters, depending on the quality of the candidates in the previous elections, but

> "If you would persuade, you must appeal to interest, rather than intellect."
> **BENJAMIN FRANKLIN**

that's about it for candidate history information. Nevertheless, knowing where your lazy support lives can improve your odds come Election Day. These potential voters can be activated through voter contact, direct mail, canvassing, and phone bank calling. Still, unless your opposition is running his or her campaign from prison, if the voter registration difference is more than 15 percent, you are about to launch into an unwinnable race.

Basically, there are two kinds of voters: those with their minds made up and those who are undecided. Voters with their minds made up are either for you ("saints") or against you ("sinners"). Those who are undecided are the "savables." For precinct analysis purposes, we have to understand the first two groups—the sinners and the saints—but we focus on the third group, the savables.

I used to believe saints and sinners would cross the aisle if their candidate was profoundly compromised. Now I know better: In 2008, a Republican candidate for the Oregon House maintained a five-point registration advantage even after court documents surfaced alleging he force-fed his unwilling child to the point of vomiting, locked the child in a dark closet to help him get over his fear of the dark, squeezed him so tight that bruising resulted, and pleaded guilty to a misdemeanor assault charge after beating the child over the head with a screwdriver. The candidate was running against a mother of three, and a school budget committee member who had lots of political experience as a legislative assistant.

The Sinners. Sinners will not cast a vote your way, no matter what you say or do. You never want to give sinners a reason to vote: Don't canvass them, call them, or send direct mail to them. Nothing you say or do will convince these voters to support your candidate or issue. Sinners will vote against you if they vote in your election; they will never cross the aisle. If they do not stay home altogether on Election Day, the best you can hope for is an undervote. Remember, when it comes to sinners, apathy is your friend.

The Saints. Saints will vote for you, no matter what. They will not cross the aisle, but they can, and do, undervote. That means you do not want to completely ignore these voters, but you also do not want to waste valuable campaign resources on them.

The Savables. Savables are registered voters who are neither saints nor sinners, as they do not adhere to party lines. These are the voters you're looking for in a precinct analysis. They tend to be undecided, may be moved by hot-button issues, and often pay little or no attention to politics. Sometimes, they are partisans of one party, hiding from their neighbors by registering in another party.

With precinct analysis, you can determine where the savables live and then, by further analysis of education, age, and voting history, determine the likely numbers of those who will actually get out and vote. While a precinct analysis will give you important information for canvassing purposes, you must also persuade the likely voters with direct mail and phoning.

Election offices, political parties, and PACs often track voters by turnout. Voting frequency typically will be listed next to the registered voter's name as 4/4, 3/4, 2/4, 1/4, that is, people voting in four out of four of the last elections, three out of four, and so on. They're referred to as fours, threes, twos, and ones. Fours will take very little prodding to get to the polls. The others can be a little trickier to pin down, because some of the occasional voters vote only in presidential elections, some only in general elections, and others in their own individual pattern. However, with a little push, threes and often twos can be activated to get to the polls. This is where your precinct analysis is so critical: You never want to activate voters who are in your low-priority precincts, or you will turn out votes for the opposition. Your goal is to activate likely voters in high-priority precincts who will support your candidate or issue-based campaign.

> "Democracy is the worst form of government except for all the others that have been tried."
> — **WINSTON CHURCHILL**

People who went to the polls only once in the last four elections are pretty tough, and courting those who have never voted is a waste of time and money.

By conducting your precinct analysis early and studying who is most likely to vote, based on issues and past elections, you gain information that helps you shape your campaign theme and message. Obviously, if your message is focused on the large group of voters who are either undecided or disengaged, and you know where they live, you have a better chance of activating them and pulling them over to your cause.

Context of Neighborhood

In 2004, I was stuffing envelopes with a volunteer who lived in an area with a Republican-registration advantage of eighteen points. I told him that two years before, I had worked a campaign in his area and, during the GOTV, discovered that many Democrats believed they were registered Republicans. He said, "I have a confession to make: I'm a registered Republican—always have been, but I've never voted for a Republican in my life."

I began to wonder: How many Republicans or Democrats *never* vote party? Where do they live, and what do they look like? Those questions were the genesis of the survey outlined below in "Closet Partisans."

Precinct analysis looks at past voting patterns and the dynamic of party affiliation within the context of neighborhood. It is based on the premise that people who share similar values, politically and otherwise, live near each other. It looks for voting trends, specifically precinct-by-precinct voting trends, to give a geographic location of your core supporters. And, using data from past elections, it will reveal where to find support, swing, and undervote for similar candidates or causes. In this way, your efforts may be directed to activate and engage likely support. This is fundamental to a win: You want to invest effort where it will do the most good.

Social Context, Individual Traits, and Microtargeting

Pollsters and political consultants dismiss social context as old school, and indeed, few of us out here continue to center campaign strategy around it. But, after twenty-five years of tracking registration trends both by precinct and zone in my county and state, I find social context is more reliable today than ever. Further, its patterning dates back to the very founding of the nation. In *1776,* David McCullough highlights the adversity the British troops suffered during the siege of Boston, a city sympathetic to the revolution, and how anxious they were to move on to New York, where they would enjoy a warmer welcome. Even then, Americans segregated themselves by political ideology.

But it goes back even further. The genesis of our nation was the coupling of religious devotees with those seeking financial opportunity untethered to bloodlines. Not much has changed.

The fracturing within each of the voting blocs on a continuum of time is the essence of a precinct analysis. Indeed, not all whites vote the same, not all Chinese, not all women, not all men, not all eighteen- to twenty-five-year-olds, not all white women between eighteen and twenty-five. What we do today, and have done since getting on ships to cross the Atlantic, is pack up and move next door to people who share core values and think and vote like we do. As Bruce Oppenheimer of Vanderbilt University said, "A lot of this has to do with self-selection. Democrats tend to live next to Democrats. Republicans tend to live next to Republicans"[1]

Microtargeting

Microtargeting, which determines voter patterns according to lifestyle and consumptive behavior, absolutely works. Stores with member or discount cards capture information each time the card is swiped at the checkout counter; every time you charge on your credit card, information is captured. Information about the community in which you live, the car you drive, the cell phone you use, the movies you rent, the books you buy, and the television you watch is captured through sales and polling data. And all that captured information is worth something, and that something gets sold to campaigns and other marketers, who can accurately determine whether you will vote and, if so, whom you will vote for. Further, the data can profile people just like you all over the nation and come up with a precise picture of voting behavior based on age, residency, and buying patterns. It works. And for a price, you can buy this information.

> "No self-respecting woman should wish or work for the success of a party who ignores her sex."
> — **SUSAN B. ANTHONY**

Practitioners of microtargeting suggest that the failing of precinct analysis is that "geography, party registration and electoral turnout alone leaves some of your best voters stranded and untouched."[2] This is absolutely accurate; precinct analysis is about mining for gold in the veins rather than spending time going after the dust, and does so using data that are relatively easy to find and cheap to acquire. And because precinct analysis places the voter in a social context, it is indispensable to a winning strategy.

Precinct analysis shows which neighborhoods and communities are trending where, and more important, it will tell you where the greatest numbers of swing voters live. Once you're in the gold veins, precinct analysis behaves and looks very much like microtargeting because neighborhoods get profiled; that's why it has worked for two hundred years in some form or another.

Social Context

Knowing the social context of cities within a county is just as important as knowing the social context of neighborhoods within a city. This fine-grained knowledge allows the campaign to profile voters within a context of historic voting and registration trends.

For example, when I first began tracking voter registration in 1984, my county was fairly evenly mixed in registration, with a 2 percent countywide Republican registration advantage. Over the course of twenty-five years, this advantage moved from 2 percent to 11 percent and back to 2 percent in 2008. In 1986, the registration difference between Democrats and Republicans in my city was 16 percent; now it's 60 percent. Some communities completely flipped in registration, moving from a twenty-point Democratic advantage to a twenty-point Republican advantage. During the period between the last census and 2008, one boom city had one Democrat move in for every thirty Republicans.

> "Children must not be wholly forgotten in the midst of public duties."
> **JOHN ADAMS**

And the same profile that is flipping here is also flipping in small communities in other parts of the state that I've tracked. Although this profile may not hold where you live, in my corner of the world the new Republicans are landed poor, Roosevelt Democrats, blue-collar workers, undereducated people, truck owners, the religious right, survivalist militia, and people deeply suspicious of government. They also have a real resentment for public education and the educated. Where the Democrats are gaining ground is with the educated, the wealthy, business owners, Reagan Democrats, McCall Republicans (http://en.wikipedia.org/wiki/Tom_McCall), secular people, the youth, minorities, and unmarried women.

> "The larger the mob, the harder the test."
> **H. L. MENCKEN**

Nearly every sector of my county has become extreme in registration and voting pattern.

When areas become extreme in registration, attitudes and voting will also be extreme. For example, a Republican living in a heavily registered Democratic area will be left (liberal) of most in the party. A Democrat in a very Democratic area may have trouble getting blue enough.

> "There are times in politics when you must be on the right side and lose."
> **JOHN KENNETH GALBRAITH**

In 2008, the wife of a Democratic county commission candidate was chased out of the yard of a registered Democrat in a heavily registered Republican precinct. As she left, he yelled, "We don't want your kind up here." Tolerance is low out there right now, very low.

Individual Traits

Polling uses individual traits in conjunction with issue questions to target direct mail and television. For our purposes, individual traits include gender, ethnicity, education, economic standing, age, and other similar demographics. Although individual traits are important and will be thoroughly covered in Chapter 7, exclusively targeting voters using individual traits, without social context, can lead to missteps. Counties with many small cities, a mix of urban and rural voters, and multiple school districts are the stuff of down-ballot races. In these races, a strategy that treats all female, nonaffiliated voters—or all those within a certain gender, age, education, or income—as though they were one and the same, irrespective of where they live, is deeply flawed. On the other hand, a strategy based on individual traits among homogeneous populations is very effective.

Precinct analysis accepts the premise that a campaign should expend the bulk of time and resources in areas of the most persuadable voters, moderately acknowledge the party faithful, and virtually ignore areas of overwhelming opposition; the analysis puts this premise to work with the tools available within the public domain. This approach provides a campaign with the best outcome-to-money ratio of any other political strategy. However, should your campaign have the resources to run a poll or purchase information about voters' lifestyle and consumer habits, the book covers how to incorporate these data in your precinct analysis. For example, the shortcoming of a poll centered on individual traits can be mitigated by assigning precincts to geographic zones and then looking at similarities of voters within those zones.

Independents

Independent voters are registered voters who are not affiliated with a political party. In the twenty-seven states and District of Colombia where voters register by party, the ranks of independents have swelled in the last twenty years. Independents now occupy a third of the voter rolls. In the twenty-three states whose voters do not register by party, polls report similar numbers.[3]

Traditionally, a *swing vote* comes from a Democrat who votes Republican or a Republican who votes Democrat. However, political pundits, the media, and polling firms have elevated the status of independents (nonaffiliated voters, or NAVs) by heralding them as the swing vote and often credit them in postelection analysis for a particular win or loss. Further, in the face of substantive and credible research to the contrary, independents are presented in news and television dramas, side by side with Democrats and Republicans, as though they were a political party with a shared ideology.

A Misnomer

Polling conducted by the *Washington Post* and ABC in July 2002 and other polling by the *Washington Post*, Harvard University, and the Kaiser Family Foundation in 2007 indicate that independents are anything but. In the 2007 study, independents were assigned to one of five categories, with the "disguised partisans" and the "disengaged" comprising 48 percent of the polled independents. The "dislocated" (the socially liberal/fiscally conservative) were 16 percent of these voters, with the "disillusioned" (angry voters) and "deliberators" (true swing voters) evenly divided among the remaining 36 percent. Much of this study mirrors the conclusions drawn in the 1992 book, *The Myth of the Independent*, by Bruce E. Keith.

When the disengaged are combined with the disillusioned, who are less inclined to vote, the study highlights that 42 percent are unlikely to participate in elections. Indeed, in the states that keep election returns by party and turnout, nonaffiliated voters consistently underperform registered Democrats and Republicans by twenty points.

Nevertheless, with nonaffiliated voters occupying one-third of the registration, a campaign must know who these voters are, where they live, and how to effectively predict voting behavior.

Closet Partisans

In politics, voters generally must choose between a Democrat and a Republican when casting a vote. While each party maintains a baseline of guaranteed votes, reflected by registration percentages, can an equally predictable percentage of nonaffiliated and third-party registrants be ascribed to partisan candidates?

In 2004, after ten years of observing that NAVs consistently tracked party registration, precinct by precinct, I tested this assertion. To do so, I removed all third-party and nonaffiliated voters from registration totals and determined percentages of party registrants according to the new total.

Let me explain by way of example: Two actual precincts are listed in table 1.1. Precinct 2 has a total registration of 3,613 voters, of which 2,383 are

Democrats (66 percent), 407 are Republicans (11 percent), and 823 are non-affiliated voters and third-party registrants (23 percent). To determine if registered voters outside the major parties track like their partisan neighbors in party performance, I generated a new percentage for each of the parties by omitting NAVs plus third-party registrants from the total registration. Calculating the percentage of the combined total that Republicans and Democrats each hold generates a new percentage amazingly close to actual percentages of votes cast for each of the parties. So, in Precinct 2, the Democratic registration of 2,383 is added to the Republican registration of 407, totaling 2,790 voters. The new registration percentage for either Democrats or Republicans is calculated by dividing each party registration by the combined Democratic and Republican registration numbers.

Precinct	Reg	TO	Dem Reg	% D Reg	Rep Reg	% R Reg	others	% otr Reg	D+R	% owed Ds	% owed R's
Pct 2	3613	3325	2383	0.66	407	0.11	823	0.23	2790	0.85	0.15
Pct 27	4366	3637	1139	0.26	2156	0.49	1071	0.25	3295	0.35	0.65

TABLE 1.1 Tale of Two Precincts

Collapsing other registrants (third-party registrants and nonaffiliated voters) into Democratic (D) and Republican (R) registration yields a predictable percentage of votes owed candidates according to party affiliation.

That means if all those registered outside the two parties tracked their partisan neighbors, a Democratic candidate in Precinct 2 would receive 85 percent of the votes cast, and a Republican would receive 15 percent.

Similarly, in Precinct 27, out of the 4,366 registered voters, 1,139 are Democrats (26 percent), and 2,156 are Republicans (49 percent), and 1,071 are NAVs plus others (25 percent) (table 1.1). Exercising the same computation as done for Precinct 2, if NAVs and all others were to track the parties by the same percentages, the votes owed Democrats in Precinct 27 would be 35 percent, and the votes owed Republicans would be 65 percent.

And within a percentage point or two, that is exactly what they do: In eight out of ten precincts, NAVs plus others exactly track party. The remaining 20 percent who deviate from "votes owed" percentages are where the swing voters live.

Once you have calculated a percentage of votes owed, that number is multiplied by the turnout to get a votes-owed number. By subtracting the number of votes owed from the actual votes received by candidates, swing vote is revealed. Some precincts come in on votes owed within 1 percent; others consistently depart and do so always in the same direction, giving hundreds of votes to the other party's candidate. Those that consistently differ, or swing, are the focus of winning campaigns.

Expanding the Test

To determine if this model worked outside my county, I reviewed election outcomes of two very different counties in Oregon: Jackson and Lane. I examined both issue-based and partisan elections from 2002 to 2006 to determine if nonaffiliated voters performed predictably in concert with their partisan neighbors.

Jackson County, located in southern Oregon, with a 2006 Republican-registration advantage of eleven points, and Lane County, home of University of Oregon, with a 2006 Democratic-registration advantage of eighteen points, offered a wide array of voters and voting history for comparison. I began by assigning each precinct in each county with a new percentage owed partisan candidates solely on the basis of the registration of Republicans and Democrats. I then multiplied these percentages by the voter turnout to determine the votes owed to each of the partisan candidates. In this way, NAVs and third-party registrants collapsed into the Republican and Democratic registration in the same percentages as party registrants.

> "A citizen of America will cross the ocean to fight for democracy, but won't cross the street to vote in a national election."
>
> **BILL VAUGHAN**

Votes owed the partisan candidates, determined by the new registration percentage, was repeated for each election year and for all partisan candidates from 2002 through 2006. Issue-based campaigns were also charted to determine if they too tracked predictably, precinct by precinct. I also looked back at returns between 1986 and 2000 in Jackson County, where data were more easily accessed than in Lane County.

In both counties, the outcome was the same. Partisan candidates received the votes they were owed in better than 80 percent of the precincts. In precincts where voters did not follow the new party-registration percentages, some gave more votes to the Democratic candidates than were owed (left-leaning), and some gave more votes to the Republican candidates than were owed (right-leaning).

To determine which voters, partisans or independents, moved, a massive three-month volunteer effort was launched in Jackson County to systematically call through and identify all precincts where candidates were not getting the votes they were owed. Where precincts leaned right, all Democrats and independents were called, and where precincts leaned left, all Republicans and independents were called. In all, 23,356 voters were called, and 5,206 participated in the survey.

We asked only three questions in the survey:

1. In general, do you think the state is headed in the right or wrong direction?
2. In general, do you think the county is headed in the right or wrong direction?
3. In general, do you vote Republican or Democrat?

While it was our hope to force the voter to answer "Republican" or "Democrat" in the last question, many simply offered up "both," and that information was recorded.

The Outcome

Irrespective of whether a precinct moved left or right, a similar percentage of partisan voters confessed to never voting for a candidate in his or her party and a similar percentage of nonaffiliated voters evenly divided among Republicans and Democrats, confessed to always voting for one party or the other.

However, what distinguished the precincts that deviated from votes owed was the percentage of partisans and nonaffiliated voters who confessed to mixing their ballots—that is, voting for candidates in both parties on the same ballot, or split-ticket voting. Sixteen to 18 percent of all surveyed voters in the selected precincts—whether their precinct leaned left or right, and whether they were nonaffiliated, Republican, or Democrat—offered that they split their ticket. In short, in precincts where Republicans moved left and others where Democrats moved right, the independents directly mirrored the partisan registrants in the percentage of split-ticket voting. In other words, the swing vote among independents mirrored party swing in exactly the same percentages, precinct by precinct.

> "Americans know how to find the voting booth when something important is at stake."
>
> **N. DON WYCLIFF,**
> editor, *Chicago Tribune*

Knowing where nonaffiliated voter support predictably falls provides a roadmap for campaign targeting, saving money in mail and time in canvassing, and offers an opportunity to alter registration disparity through the GOTV effort. A campaign does this by avoiding nonaffiliated voters along with the registrants of the opposing party in precincts that are leaning away from their efforts.

Polarized Populations, Skewed Registration, and Independents

If independents mirror partisan voters, then they should continue to do so even as registration percentages shift. Voter-registration shifts often occur as economies change, churches arrive, or development reshapes an area. Indeed, voters relocate to a neighborhood near their place of worship and move to find work, better schools, or less congestion. For example, in one city in southern Oregon, the Republican-registration advantage increased 38 percent between 1986 and 2006. In another city thirty miles away, the Democratic registration advantage increased 44 percent in the same period. Clearly, voters are choosing to locate near like-minded neighbors, selecting a state, a region within a state, a community within a region, and a neighborhood within a city. It's a self-selecting process: Voters identify who they are

> "The art of being wise is the art of knowing what to overlook."
> **WILLIAM JAMES**

and how they will vote by where they choose to live. That's true with Democrats and Republicans and no less so with independents.

In the above study, independents in both Lane and Jackson Counties continued to track party affiliation as registration shifted. This is good news for political campaigns: As voters segregate themselves with like-minded people, targeting becomes easier and campaigns become more efficient and economical. If independents mirror the voting behavior of their neighbors, then within any given voting region with a large Republican voter-registration advantage, independents will actually be Republicans just as independents living in areas with skewed Democratic-registration advantage will actually be Democrats.

Implications for a Campaign

Because vendors (those who provide mail, television, radio, and other communications services for a campaign) are often the same people who provide targeting strategies, it is not in their best economic interest to determine how communication can be fine-tuned to avoid activating voters for the opposition. Furthermore, because vendors tend to live and work in large metropolitan areas, they're often unaware of the unique voting patterns of small cities in a given region and apply a one-size-fits-all approach. Campaigns that cover both rural and urban areas, as well as small and large cities, and that treat all independent voters as the same, ignoring the registration of their neighbors, do so at their peril.

Polling firms will typically contact Republicans, Democrats, and NAVs to test message and issues that may resonate with voters. They then present findings within each of these categories. But when a nonaffiliated voter is polled, the campaign cannot be certain if that voter is actually a Democrat or a Republican. This can result in unreliable information for the campaign.

After the Jackson-Lane study, I reviewed four polls for state and county races where preelection polls predicted a very different outcome than what eventually materialized. In each, once the nonaffiliated voters were removed, the preelection poll results fell within the margin of error. Granted, this is a small sample of the thousands of polls that are conducted each campaign season, but is still food for thought.

> "Illegal aliens have always been a problem in the United States. Ask any Indian."
>
> — ROBERT ORBEN

Indeed, in one race in 2004, a tracking poll showed the Democratic candidate winning by twenty points. Given that the district enjoyed a Republican registration advantage of six points and that it had been held by a Republican for twenty-eight years, the projection was suspect. After the election, which the Democrat won by two points, I removed the NAVs from the tracking poll and again found the poll fell within the margin of error, showing the Democrat winning by only five points.

Important to campaigning is the understanding that when news teams, pollsters, or strategists report where so-called independents fall within a targeted question, they are sharing meaningless information. Independents should be omitted from polling and targeted with campaign efforts only in precincts where partisan registrants are supportive of the candidate or cause.

The Undervote

Undervotes occur when voters skip a particular candidate or issue on their ballot. Generally, this happens for one of three reasons: Don't know. Don't like. Don't care. Voters who have not been paying attention to a particular race will "leave it up to those who do know" and typically skip a race.

In a primary in which candidates are running unopposed, much of the undervote can be attributed to "don't care." A high undervote in a primary is a potential problem in the general election, and your campaign should work to understand the undervote and avoid it.

Unopposed candidates or campaign teams who think they will save money for the general election by not running a primary are misguided. The primary is your opportunity to curry your base, amass volunteers, establish an organization, build name recognition, and test your campaign and volunteer team. If you are running for a state legislative office, it is an opportunity to show the lobby that your campaign is organized and means business. It is also an opportunity to lock your base while getting your message out—all without attacks from the opposition that could cause damage in the general.

Running a campaign in an unopposed primary may entail no more than securing locations for lawn and field signs, printing them, and organizing volunteers to put them up, maintain them, and pull them down after the election. Add to this one mailing to your party plus a couple of print ads in the local newspaper, and you're out the door. Given that your campaign must print signs, secure locations, and organize volunteers for the general, there is simply no reason not to conduct a primary. If you do not run a primary and your undervote comes in over 50 percent, you have a lot of work to do on your base that could have been managed with a modest primary campaign. If your undervote is over 60 percent, you're in trouble. Save yourself the heartache: Run a primary.

Your undervote and the undervote of your opposition provide important information for your campaign.

Your Undervote

Hotly contested general elections usually have undervotes in the 3 percent to 5 percent range, depending on the type of ballot. (Punch-card ballots have an undervote about three points higher than do scanned ballots.) However, unopposed primaries are very different from hotly contested general elections.

Coming out of an unopposed primary, you want as low an undervote as possible, but even if you run a primary campaign, be prepared for undervotes in the 20 to 30 percent range. Should high-priority precincts come in with significant undervotes (40 percent or more), you must determine why, so that the problem can be fixed in time for the general election. If a high undervote comes in where your saints live, don't worry, but in precincts with potentially high percentages of swing voters, it should be dealt with. Consider sending a persuasion piece to your party. Look for opportunities within those precincts for coffees and other social gathering. At the very least, send the candidate in for the canvass. A high undervote in a primary means additional work for you in the general, so put your team on notice.

I once worked for a candidate who ran uncontested in the primary and, to save money, did no campaigning for it. When I came on board for the general, I conducted a precinct analysis on the primary for each candidate and found that the opposition, which ran a modest primary campaign, had a relatively small undervote compared with my candidate, who had undervotes that went as high as 60 percent. The high undervote may have been the result of the voters' perception that the candidate was aloof and somehow thought he was too good to campaign. His invisibility during the primary only fed this belief.

The Opposition's Undervote

If both you and your opponent ran unopposed primaries, you now have some great information on your opposition for the general.

After a primary, spend some time with the results published by the elections office. Abstracts often do not list undervotes, but these can be easily calculated by adding votes received by a candidate and subtracting that total from the total turnout for the party. You will sweep in a few overvotes, but don't worry about that. When it comes to the opposition's undervote, you are looking for high undervotes in areas where there is a high swing voter potential.

After completing your precinct analysis (see appendix), look for any precincts previously considered off limits and that have both a modest swing voter potential and a high primary undervote in the opposing party, and put them back on the table. Your job is to determine whether some of the undervotes in these precincts resulted from voters in the don't-like category—they didn't like the candidate of their party. It is these voters the campaign should identify. Too often, campaigns take time conducting voter identification on members of their own party in precincts that historically vote for their party. Assume you have this support, and instead go behind enemy lines and pull votes from your opposition's base. Identify them, mail literature to them, and canvass them. With a little effort, you can move these voters.

Undervotes and Negative Campaigning

Your precinct analysis will tell you where a party is consistently undervoted in past elections. Abdicating registration strength by undervoting is helpful in close elections. Indeed, I consistently win issue-based and candidate races by the undervote. But sometimes a campaign can add to their problems.

Because the undervote can help win races, I study them. In the beginning of this chapter, I referenced a race in which a Democrat lost a legislative race to a Republican who pleaded guilty to misdemeanor assault charges on his child. The Democrat had out-raised and outspent the Republican by over two to one. In my research, I looked at the television spots of the Democratic candidate. In these ads, all the abuses were reviewed for the voter. It was off-putting to me, and I'm in the business. So, I looked at the undervote to see if perhaps voters were also disturbed by what they saw. I found that in this race—where nearly a half-million dollars was spent—the undervote was 14 percent. Given that the Democrat lost by six points (the spread plus 1 percent), one might wonder if watching this horse getting flogged repeatedly, night after night, on television contributed to the undervote and the loss.

Assigning the Undervote

In 2004, State Representative Alan Bates (D-Ashland) ran against local businessman Jim Wright (R-Medford). In Precinct 2, Representative Bates was owed 80 percent of the ballots cast, and Wright was owed 20 percent. However, Bates only received 79 percent and Wright only 17 percent. So where were the other 4 percent of the votes? If there is no third-party candidate—and there wasn't—you will find the missing votes in the undervote, that is, those who voted for neither candidate but still participated in the election.

"Our goal is progress, not perfection."
WILLIAMS & WILLIAMS

By determining a percentage of votes owed to each party candidate and then calculating the percentage received versus the percentage owed, you are able to assign both a percentage and an actual vote count of the undervote to each of the party candidates. In other words, you now know the undervote each candidate receives. So, again using our example, for Precinct 2 with a 2004 registration of 3,400 voters, Bates is attributed 1 percent of the undervote, or 34 votes, and Wright is attributed 3 percent of the undervote, or 102 votes.

Being able to assign the undervote helps diagnose potential problem areas so they may be remedied. For example, if the undervote is coming primarily from your party, your efforts must be focused on waking up and energizing your voters so they care enough to fill in the bubbles on their voter card. Typically, voters are not activated with vacuous mail that simply talks about what a wonderful person the candidate is. Similarly, negative mail may depress participation even more. Therefore, a consistent and large undervote for your party's candidates may dictate a more aggressive mail and media campaign of comparison pieces. All of this is covered more thoroughly in the appendix.

"What should be done to give power into the hands of capable and well-meaning persons has so far resisted all efforts."
ALBERT EINSTEIN

After you have completed your precinct analysis and charted your results, if some precincts consistently give more votes than are owed to your candidate's party while others consistently give more votes to the opposing party, you know where to concentrate money, canvassing, media, mail, and lawn signs as well as which areas to avoid.

Once you know neighborhoods that are swinging in your direction, use them to profile other voters outside that area. What do their homes look like? Do they have porches? What are people watching on television when a canvasser knocks on the door? Do they have children? Pets? Do they keep up their homes and property? Are they rural? Urban?

Finding Swing Voters

Although I typically determine swing based on the votes-owed model, which is covered in depth in the appendix, there are other ways to do it as well. One remarkably easy way is outlined below. Remember, it can be done only if you happen to have two very similar candidates as yours and your opponent who previously ran in different races on the same ballot. Stick with me, this is pretty cool.

In 2004 I was working for Democrat Alan Bates, a local physician who was running against a very moderate Republican from Medford—the largest city in the county. Two years before, a local physician, Dave Gilmour, also a Democrat, ran for county commissioner, and in a judicial race on the same ballot was a moderate Republican from the same neighborhood as our opponent. Although the judicial race was nonpartisan, voters knew who was the Democrat and who was the Republican.

> "80 percent of success is just showing up."
> — WOODY ALLEN

To determine swing, I matched the doctor from 2002 with the moderate Republican of 2002 just as though they were running against each other. But because voters could legitimately vote for both the moderate Republican and the doctor (remember, they were two different races on the same ballot), putting these two candidates from different races together as though they were running against each other, created an overvote. Typically, an overvote occurs when a voter votes for two candidates *in the same race on the same ballot*. However, in this instance, the overvote was artificially created by lining up two candidates from two races on the same ballot as though they opposed each other. To figure the artificial overvote, I simply added the totals of the two candidates that mirrored those in my race and subtracted their total from the total voter turnout, precinct by precinct.

> "An elected official is one who gets 51% of the vote cast by 40% of the 60% of voters who registered."
> — DAN BENNETT

The results were quite revealing. Out of the thirty precincts in the senate district, eight of them had an overvote of 2,253 votes; the remaining twenty-two precincts had a combined overvote of only 54 votes. The majority of the swing lived in eight precincts. Of those eight precincts, however, four were precincts of solid saints—that is, voters who never leave their Democratic candidate. That meant our entire campaign needed to focus only on four precincts, which is exactly what we did. We flipped a twenty-eight-year Republican hold on the senate seat while being outspent nearly two to one. It was magic.

Microtargeting is about getting those 54 votes in the remaining twenty-two precincts. Precinct analysis is about getting just the 2,253 votes in eight precincts.

Work Smart

I once worked for a candidate who did not fully believe in precinct analysis. I had conducted an in-depth analysis of a number of elections in which candidates who embraced a similar political ideology to my candidate's ran for office. I also reviewed initiatives that covered issues similar to ones with which my candidate was closely aligned. This candidate had also faced a recall attempt while in office, so I conducted an analysis of a successful recall of an elected official who also had similar political leanings. All pointed to the same precincts for sinners, saints, and savables. No exceptions. It was clear from the analysis that a handful of precincts would never support the candidate, and given that they typically turned out in lower numbers, there was a real concern that if activated they would vote for the opposition.

Notwithstanding the warning, toward the end of the campaign, after all the high- and medium-priority precincts were done, the candidate decided to burn up some restless energy by covering these low-priority precincts. His feeling was that if he personally went to the door, people would be swayed.

Not surprisingly, the low-support precincts turned out to be difficult canvasses. People were rude, and mishaps occurred. The candidate came back demoralized but decided to press on. Ultimately, he lost the election by a few hundred votes out of 30,000 cast. After the election, a postmortem analysis showed that the low-priority precincts had turned out in record numbers and voted two to one against the candidate.

Precinct analysis tells you not only where your support lives so that it can be activated, but also where the opposition's support lives so that it can be avoided. You never want to activate voters for the opposition.

Campaigns are often so strapped for money that they must be highly focused. Under these circumstances, no matter what your party, if certain areas represent solid support and solid turnout (your saints), you will need to make the assumption that they will vote for you. If they don't, you'll lose anyway, and that will be that. You must feel that you can count on them without spending too much money or time on getting their vote.

Conversely, there will also be areas that support candidates in the opposing party, election after election. With the exception of the swing or undervote alignment outlined above, these areas should be avoided so that votes for the opposition are not activated; it will save volunteer time and campaign money.

> "If you are not part of the solution, you are part of the problem."
>
> — **ELDRIDGE CLEAVER**

Not long ago, I ran into the wife of a candidate for county commissioner. She wanted to talk about her husband's loss in the November election. As a Democrat, he won Ashland, "with almost no effort," she said. In another of the county's cities, however, he had lost two to one, "and we canvassed every neighborhood there," she said. As I had never known that city to support a Democrat for a county commission seat (Republicans enjoy a seventeen-point registration advantage), I asked her why they canvassed there. She said, "Because we were such a cute couple."

It doesn't matter how swell you think you are, if you spend time, money, or energy in areas where you will lose, that means you are not spending time, money, and energy in areas where you need to win. Work smart: Write off the sinners, trust the saints, and persuade the savables.

Finally

I have received candidate calls from all over the nation, and at some point in the conversation, each person says, "I'm just going to go out and start canvassing." The single biggest challenge a campaign must face is the tendency to confuse motion with progress. Unless some study of historic voting patterns and behavior is conducted, no matter how modest the study, candidates risk contacting voters who, once activated, will support the opposition.

In the appendix, you will find the step-by-step process for conducting a precinct analysis. Do as much as you're capable of doing, but know that the more comprehensively you look at historic voting patterns and incorporate that information in decisions of message and activities, the more likely you are to win.

A precinct analysis is the first step to a winning effort.

2

The Campaign Team

For the purposes of this handbook, *campaign team* refers to all those who help organize your efforts. It is made up of the committee, the treasurer, your volunteers, and each of the individual teams that oversee a portion of the campaign. Your media team, for example, may have a liaison to the campaign committee, but the media team should be viewed as part of your overall campaign team rather than part of the committee itself (figure 2.1). Aspects of the campaign team will be covered in this chapter. Campaign efforts that involve large numbers of people and independent efforts, such as lawn sign activities, media projects, brochure development, and fund-raising, will be covered in separate chapters.

The Campaign Committee

The relatively small campaign committee serves two functions: First, it is a support group, both for itself and for the candidate or issue-based campaign; second, it is the primary source of expertise for the campaign. This small, select group will maneuver and steer a campaign while drawing on the resources

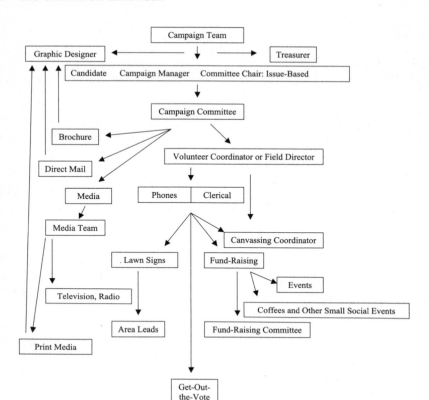

FIGURE 2.1   **Campaign Organization Chart**

of the community. The committee should consist of individuals who have different personal strengths and areas of ability.

Your campaign committee is an insiders' group. The candidate, the manager, and each of the members must feel safe in speaking candidly without fear of recrimination. Treat them like insiders and keep them informed of any campaign development. You would never want a committee member to first learn about a problem with the campaign in the newspaper or through the rumor mill. Call or e-mail your committee members often. Welcome their criticism. Encourage them and support their individual efforts in the campaign. Listen carefully to determine when they might need additional help. Be clear about their tasks, expectations, and time commitment.

> "The impersonal hand of government can never replace the helping hand of a neighbor."
> —— **HUBERT HUMPHREY**

Take time in choosing the right number of people for a campaign committee. I have worked on countywide campaigns with four committee members (including the candidate), which was too few, and citywide campaigns with twelve members, which was too many. I have found that six or seven committee members for a city with a population of up to twenty thousand is perfect. In countywide campaigns a successful committee might also include members who come from each targeted region or city and who oversee teams within their respective areas.

You want only enough committee members to cover the campaign activities that you have decided to do. Keep in mind that not all campaign activities occur at the same time, so it is often possible to have more than one task assigned to a single committee member. For example, the campaign brochure is written and printed at the beginning of the campaign, whereas the demands on the canvassing coordinator are greatest toward the end of the campaign. On the other hand, both fund-raising responsibilities and clerical team coordination are ongoing tasks and should *not* be combined with any other campaign responsibilities.

Once the campaign starts, meet with the committee each week for one hour. For citywide campaigns where people are not traveling great distances, it isn't a bad idea to meet in the evening after 8:00 p.m., when children have been taken care of and the day's work is done. Up to a point, the later you meet, the better, because people are ready for their day to be done, so they arrive on time and get right down to work. Few people function well after 10:00 p.m., so at 9:30, be ready to call it quits. Try to keep committee meetings to one hour unless it is the first meeting and you're setting up the campaign. For this first meeting, allow additional time by starting the meeting earlier, or have the meeting at a different time—for example, set up a morning retreat followed by a lunch at which the campaign becomes official. For countywide campaigns, it works well for the committee to meet in a central location at the end of the workday before dinner.

Campaign Committee Packets

Your committee may quickly break down into specialized campaign functions. Once specialized groups are formed, keep track of their progress through weekly reports. When the committee meets, meetings should be productive. Always have an agenda. It is important that all meetings begin and end on time.

A campaign committee packet is a great organizational tool for committee members (figure 2.2). (The finance committee packets, discussed in Chapter

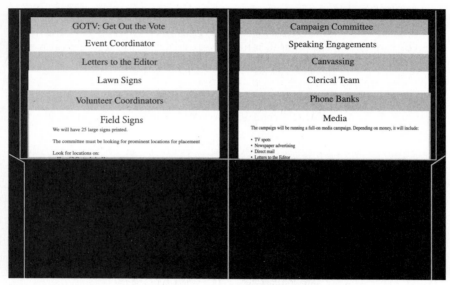

GOTV: Get Out the Vote

Event Coordinator

Letters to the Editor

Lawn Signs

Volunteer Coordinators

Field Signs
We will have 25 large signs printed.

The committee must be looking for prominent locations for placement

Look for locations on:

Campaign Committee

Speaking Engagements

Canvassing

Clerical Team

Phone Banks

Media
The campaign will be running a full-on media campaign. Depending on money, it will include:

• TV spots
• Newspaper advertising
• Direct mail
• Letters to the Editor

FIGURE 2.2   Example of a Campaign Committee Packet

5, are assembled in a similar fashion.) Each pocket folder contains tiered sheets of alternating colors organized by category for the tasks the committee will undertake in the course of the campaign, such as lawn signs, canvassing, phone banks, letters to the editor, and so on. Although one sheet should be dedicated to listing committee members and all contact information for each person, the remaining sheets clearly outline job descriptions for each campaign duty and indicate who will oversee that particular job. The folders travel with committee members to war room meetings and contain information that may be distributed there. Helping volunteers with this kind of organizational framework keeps members happy and makes your campaign a little more volunteer friendly.

> "The time to win a fight is before it starts."
> — **FREDERICK W. LEWIS**

In addition to the weekly meeting for the full committee, you should occasionally get together with the individuals who are responsible for specific campaign tasks, and bring this information back to the committee. For example, you may meet with the ad person to hammer out two or three ads and then bring these to the regular committee meeting to have them critiqued.

Other than the treasurer and the campaign manager, the makeup of the campaign committee is discretionary, based on how many people will be needed to plan and supervise the campaign. You will depend on the people you invite to join your campaign committee, so they should be capable of organizing and directing some particular aspect of the campaign. In addition to a treasurer and a campaign manager, your committee must include one or more people to oversee letters to the editor, canvassing, clerical work, brochures, the media, lawn signs, phone banks, fund-raising, getting out the vote, direct mail, the Internet, and volunteer workers.

The Treasurer

I usually ask a volunteer to serve as the campaign treasurer. I look for someone who is well respected in the community and who will lend credibility to an issue-based campaign or balance a candidate campaign. Selecting the right person for this position is one of the most important things you will do. The name of your treasurer will appear on every campaign publication. He or she may be called from time to time by the press, or even the opposition, and asked questions. Like a vice president in a presidential election, the treasurer should balance the ticket. For example, if you are a retired senior, then select a prominent, involved young person of the opposite sex. If you are a young progressive man and relatively new to your community, consider an older conservative woman who has been in town a number of years. Find a person who complements rather than merely repeats your strengths. If you're a Democrat, find a respected Republican. If you are working for more taxes for schools, get someone who is conservative and who may have sometimes spoken out against tax increases.

If possible, find someone willing to represent the campaign, discharge the official duties of treasurer, and help in other ways. For example,

> "If you want something done, ask a busy person."
> **BENJAMIN FRANKLIN**

a treasurer may take on all thank-you notes and keep donor files up-to-date in a database. In one campaign I managed, the treasurer sat in on war room meetings, canvassed, helped with lawn signs, and oversaw data input on campaign donations, but this level of involvement by the treasurer is the exception and not the rule.

The treasurer is usually responsible for obtaining and completing the registration forms required for participation in an election. The necessary forms can be obtained from the city recorder's office for city races, from the county clerk's office for county races, and from the election division under the secretary of state for elections to state offices. Don't be afraid to use these offices. The people who staff government offices are extremely helpful and accommodating.

Not all the forms and information in the election packet are necessary or applicable to every race or election. Ask exactly what you need to read, what is required, and when it is required. Ask either the clerk or the recorder for a schedule of the pertinent dates for filing your campaign contributions and expenditures. While the filing of these reports is the principal job of the treasurer, it is a good idea for both the candidate and the campaign manager to be aware of them. These tasks should be placed on your campaign flowchart, calendar, or plan as a reminder.

> "Making the simple complicated is commonplace; making the complicated simple, awesomely simple, that's creativity."
> —————— CHARLES MINGUS

I now also use a banker or retired certified public accountant (CPA) in all campaigns. If I can't find one who will volunteer to oversee the reports, I use campaign funds to hire one. Having a professional on board is actually a great comfort to the volunteer treasurer and helps reduce the overall stress of a demanding campaign cycle. The hired and volunteer treasurer should work together closely.

Note: I've found that practicing CPAs who volunteer for the treasurer position can ramp up the stress of a primary election simply because paying customers, whose taxes are due at the same time as filing periods, will get priority over a volunteer campaign position. Late filings can be a public and financial disaster for a down-ballot race.

Contributions and Expenditures

Your treasurer and the CPA or banker should be sticklers for detail. The opposition will be examining your contributions and expenditures (C&Es) filings for any mistakes to report to the state elections office. If a mistake is found, it is bound to make the local papers. That sort of damage is totally preventable.

After the C&E forms have been filed, local papers generally do a story on who spent how much on what. If you are running a modest campaign and your opposition is funded by outside money, make sure that this information makes it to the media. Running a visibly hardworking campaign with modest funds gives people the sense that you are fiscally responsible. That trait is desirable in office, and voters will make the connection.

Although it is difficult to work on a campaign whose opposition has unlimited funds, it can also work in your favor. In a small community election that involves no TV ads, there is just so much ad space to buy in the newspaper and just so much direct mail that can be sent to homes without it becoming pretty clear that the election is being bought. In one campaign I ran, we were outspent five to one by the opposition, and we publicized this spending discrepancy to our advantage. When the newspapers ran the usual C&E article, many in the community were stunned by the amount of money coming in from outside interests. Since we had a pretty good idea of how much the opposition was spending, we were ready when the press called for our reaction. Supporters wrote and sent letters to the editor for those who missed the newspaper articles when they first appeared.

In that particular race, the opposition was convinced that the accounting in our campaign was wrong and regularly sent people to the recorder's office to check our C&Es. This is where having a meticulous treasurer pays off. Finally, convinced of foul play, the opposition called the paper and suggested there must be something wrong. When the press called me, I explained that we were in fact spending a normal amount for a small-town race and it was the opposition whose expenditures were excessive. We got another great newspaper story.

Committee to Support

Given the importance of a good treasurer, what do you do if you can't find the right one for you? Not to worry. You have two options. First, you can place a short list of carefully selected supporters (six to nine) at the bottom of all your literature and ads. This "committee to support" should represent a good cross-section of the community. Although some of these people might be working on your campaign, this is not your campaign committee. The primary job of this group is to give your cause credibility by lending their

> "Putting a bunch of people to work on the same problem doesn't make them a team."
>
> **GERALD M. WEINBERG,** *The Psychology of Computer Programming*

names. Depending on the issue, the committee to support may include people in business, environmental groups, real estate, labor, and so on.

Using a committee to support works well if you have broad-based support up front, but it does not work at all if your support is marginal. I once worked on a campaign that was so controversial that I could get only three people to sign their names to the committee-to-support list. Rather than have such a short list, which didn't cover the political spectrum of the city, I dropped the notion of listing the committee. In fact, it helped the campaign to discover the level of controversy so early in the campaign. Information of this sort should not discourage, but rather help set the course.

Let me caution you here. When you are working on a very controversial campaign and have a listed committee to support at the bottom of all your literature, you run the risk that opponents to the campaign will get to one or more of those listed and will undermine your public support. The newspapers also may call these people and grill them on the cause. This can get a little dicey. I find it best to use a committee to support for relatively unknown candidates or difficult yet uncontroversial initiatives or measures such as school or public library funding.

Another option you have if the "perfect" treasurer cannot be found is to simply press on. Look for someone who is thorough, honest, easy to work with, trustworthy, and committed to your cause or candidate. Talk to your personal accountant or the person who prepares your taxes. CPAs have great community credibility, and they may be willing to provide report preparation on a pro bono basis or at a reduced rate.

The Campaign Manager

The campaign manager is the single most important position in a campaign. Where other jobs have finite responsibilities and time commitments, the job of campaign manager is open-ended. It is a lot to ask of anyone, especially on a volunteer basis. For this reason it is usually the first and sometimes the only paid position.

"Even the highest towers begin from the ground."
CHINESE SAYING

A campaign manager will interact with your volunteers more than any other person in the campaign, so good communication skills, especially phone skills, are a must. The duties of the campaign manager vary greatly, depending on the number of individuals working in the inner circle. In general, he or she will do such things as attend coffees, debates, and events with the candidate and set up sign-in sheets while lending moral support. The campaign manager also *must* give candid feedback to the candidate without being indelicate.

If you are running a countywide partisan election campaign, having a manager is critical. You need someone to oversee it all and to be a source of support for the candidate. If you're working on an issue-based campaign, you can serve as the campaign manager with the use of this handbook. Although I believe it is a mistake to run for office without a campaign manager, if you are running for office in a small city, you can probably get away with it. Whether you're serving as your own campaign manager or have hired one, you still need capable people to head up various campaign tasks such as lawn signs, canvassing, field work, the Internet, and letters to the editor. The most effective campaign teams are those with volunteer team members supervised by a strong manager.

Potential Sources for a Campaign Manager

I highly recommend teachers as campaign managers. They are generally smart, organized, articulate, and personable. They are able to speak to large groups of people and ask for things in simple, understandable ways. They tend to know computers, have a nice collection of presentable clothes, work hard, and are generally politically savvy. They are also likely to be available all summer. If you choose wisely, a teacher who is a campaign manager will force you to get everything ready during the summer so that your fall campaign will go much easier. The drawback of using a teacher is that he or she may be overwhelmed with school responsibilities in the fall and less available to the campaign.

Other potential sources for campaign managers are development directors for local charities, private schools, or nonprofit organizations. These people might consider short-term work for a candidate, and they will have a proven track record. Other leads: people who have worked on other political campaigns, for a United Way campaign, or for a Heart and Lung fund drive, and those who have organized local parades, 4-H fair shows, concerts, or county fairs.

In general, a good campaign manager is hardworking, organized, intelligent, self-confident, and loyal. And because appearance is important, this person should reflect the values and style of the candidate or campaign.

Maintaining Control

Recently I was an adviser to a campaign whose manager became problematic; he was parking illegally on city-owned land and then hassling the police with a "do-you-know-who-I'm-working-for?" attitude. To make matters worse, volunteers were complaining to the candidate about the campaign manager's unnecessary rudeness. The candidate was at the end of his rope and called me to help find a way to let this volunteer go.

> "We've run into a couple of problems, but nothing minor."
> BRENDA COLLIER

Although a candidate does not need this kind of stress, firing a volunteer manager can bring more headaches than it cures. So, short of firing the manager, what can the candidate do?

First, the candidate always has the option of reorganizing the campaign so that the manager has less involvement and responsibility. Second, the candidate could deal with the campaign manager and the situation in a clear and straightforward manner. He or she could kindly explain how others were interpreting the manager's actions and how they were reflecting negatively on the campaign and the candidate. Because campaign managers are so closely affiliated with the candidate, there is an assumption that their activities are condoned by the candidate. A problematic situation like this must get immediate attention. Campaigns not only allow the community to see how a candidate will perform both publicly and under pressure, but also allow the candidate to get some experience in dealing with awkward situations and people. Once a candidate is in office, difficult people materialize all the time. If none of this works, the volunteer must be fired.

When running for state legislative office, be prepared to pay the campaign manager handsomely. A good manager speaks truth to power, brings many skills to the table, and can mean big money to your campaign. Individuals, organizations, political action committees (PACs), and lobbyists want to contribute to a winning campaign, and your manager is a big indicator. A strong, experienced, well-organized, hardworking manager will bring an air of confidence to a candidate and campaign team. A candidate should listen to the campaign manager and follow his or her advice.

TEN TIPS FOR CAMPAIGN MANAGERS

1. Know the budget, and have control of the checkbook.
2. Allow only one person to do scheduling for the candidate. This must be someone who works well with the candidate and is highly organized.
3. Manage the team and consultants, and monitor their progress.
4. Hire professionals to develop campaign literature and television and radio spots.
5. Be positive, supporting, and encouraging to the candidate.
6. Raise money—lots and lots of money.
7. Loyalty is more important than experience.
8. Never waste donors' money.
9. Be organized.
10. Do not waste volunteers' time.

The Campaign Chair or Co-Chairs

When working on an issue-based campaign, the messenger is the message. Who heads it up is therefore directly linked to the success of the campaign. Here you have the choice of using either one person serving as a campaign chair or two people serving as co-chairs. Campaign chairs should be noncontroversial leaders in your community and may serve either in name only as a figurehead or as the actual campaign co-coordinator. Mostly they are the face of the campaign. They meet the media, they are part of the war room, and they work the endorsement circles of the community—the Rotary Club, the Chamber of

Commerce, business leaders, and more. They gain power and stature when they seemingly have nothing personally to gain by the passage of the measure. So avoid using as a campaign chair someone who has a vested interest in the outcome of a campaign, such as a county commissioner for a county tax base.

Choose your co-chairs carefully. Well-respected community leaders with a strong community network are best. Their community relationships are part of the network the campaign will lean on to raise money and activate volunteers. The co-chairs should balance each other, in gender and in interests. For a county measure, one chair may be from the rural area with ranching or farming ties, and the other from the city with business ties. Selection of your chair or co-chairs is completely dependent on the ballot measure.

> "Loyalty is more important than experience."
>
> **BILL MEULEMANS**

If the right chair or co-chairs cannot be found, don't use a campaign chair, but be sure to have top people able to respond to the press and willing to debate the opposition.

Finding Volunteers

Finding and directing volunteers is almost the same for each campaign task. Although the tasks vary considerably, only a small modification is necessary to organize your volunteer force for each specialized campaign activity.

Regardless of the activity, there are seven important things to remember about using volunteers:

1. Don't waste the volunteers' time. Have everything laid out and ready to go the moment they walk in the door. Begin and end on time. Do not encourage late arrivals by delaying the start of meetings.
2. Be prepared with anything they might need. If the task is to stuff envelopes, make sure there are enough stamps, sponges, pens, staples, and other necessities.
3. Call them ahead of time, and let them know what they need to bring, such as extra staple guns, clipboards, good walking shoes, a truck, or a hammer.
4. Be clear about their tasks, expectations, and time commitments. Give clear written instructions and deadlines. This is especially important for those on phone banks.
5. Pick the right people for the job. Don't ask out-of-shape people to canvass steep hills; don't place counterculture people as canvassers in conservative areas.

6. Keep volunteers informed, and support them. When you call, let them know how the campaign is going. Be sensitive to their schedules.
7. Treat your volunteers as you would highly paid employees.

It is a serious mistake to undervalue volunteer time simply because it is free. Disorganized campaigns lead to irritated and frustrated workers who may not return if things seem poorly run more than once. Some of the very best volunteers will not come back after even one bad encounter. To avoid such problems, the manager should assemble clerical teams to help set up other tasks, such as assembling lawn signs in preparation for the lawn sign team or looking up missing phone numbers for phone bankers. This pre-planning is vital to creating a volunteer-friendly campaign, helps ensure the success of campaign activities, and allows the campaign to place people in jobs where they will work best.

Matching Volunteers to Skills

Although a small campaign can be run without volunteers, it would be a mistake to do so. When people work for a campaign, they become invested and want to see the investment pay off. Also, involving people in the process brings more interest to government and the political system. There is, however, one caution: If potential workers indicate an unwillingness to do a particular activity, don't make the mistake of begging and pleading to get help in that task.

I once placed on the phones a woman who told me she didn't like to phone. I found it hard to believe that in this day and age anyone would have trouble talking on the phone—plus I was desperate. What a mistake. She was painfully uncomfortable calling people she didn't know and projected a poor image of the campaign. I couldn't take her off once I saw my error, because that would have called further attention to the problem, making her more uncomfortable. I left her on the phone for about a half hour and then told her that I had finished my work and asked if she would mind if we shared her phone. She gratefully gave it up. Similarly, if a volunteer reports that he doesn't like to canvass, believe him. It is better for the campaign to have people doing tasks they enjoy.

> "Nothing is particularly hard, if you divide it into small jobs."
> — **HENRY FORD**

Here is a tip for placing people who say they would rather not call or canvass: Some who do not like to work phones actually do not like to make cold calls—that is, they do not like to call people who may be opposed to the candidate or measure. Quite often, these same people may be willing to make calls to activate identified supporters, such as in a get-out-the-vote effort. Similarly with canvassers, some do not like to canvass, because they dislike knocking on doors and talking to the residents. However, these same people may be willing to do a literature drop, a door hanger, install lawn signs, or other tasks where knocking and talking are not involved.

> "In life, as in any game whose outcome depends on both skill and luck, the rational response to bad odds is to try harder."
>
> **MARVIN HARRIS**

Supervise volunteers so that workers who have difficulty with a task are not called a second time to help in the same task. For instance, if a volunteer is struggling at a phone bank because age has made hearing more difficult, simply note it in the spreadsheet you use to keep track of volunteers or on the volunteer's 3-by-5-inch contact card (see Chapter 4, "The Volunteer Organization"). In this way, campaign workers will not mistakenly call the person again for that task. Similarly, if an individual is great at a task like phoning, keep him or her away from other campaign activities to avoid campaign burnout. Use volunteers where they excel.

The same kind of supervision is necessary for each volunteer activity. For example, if a canvasser returns without notes for lawn signs, no impressions of voter attitudes, and having only partially covered the assigned area, perhaps canvassing is not the best job for that person. Note this in the volunteer data system. Be sure to make a note as to why, and move that person over to something like lawn sign placement and maintenance. If it can be avoided, do not place volunteers in jobs where they will have a bad time or may reflect poorly on the campaign. Attention to these kinds of details helps volunteers be more successful and keeps them returning to help in future elections.

Potential Volunteer Sources

Those involved in grassroots campaigning must find people willing to help. Finding volunteers can initially seem daunting, but remember, the only people you can be certain will not help you are those you do not ask. The following is a list of places to look for potential volunteers:

> "Nonpolitical issues are the most political."
>
> **BILL MEULEMANS**

- Your family, friends, and business associates
- Women's rights groups

- Former candidates, office holders, and their volunteers
- Local service groups, churches, and clubs
- Labor unions
- Teachers or school associations
- Any special-interest groups dealing, for example, with the environment, human services, hunting, and fishing

In nearly every election, there is an issue so controversial that voters will act solely on the basis of the opposing positions held by the two candidates. These issues create "ticket splitters," voters who allow an issue to influence what would otherwise be a straight-line party vote. Issues that lead to ticket splitting can motivate a voter to work or vote *against* a candidate rather than *for* a candidate.

> "Public business, my son, must always be done by somebody . . . if wise men decline it, others will not; if honest men refuse it, others will not."
>
> **JOHN ADAMS,**
> letter to his son, Thomas

In general, issues that create ticket splitters can translate into both volunteers and money for your campaign. Here is a list of some groups and issues that are more inclined than most to let a single issue influence their votes:

- Veterans
- Sportsmen, fly fishermen, and hunters
- Environmentalists
- Timber and logging advocates
- Prochoice and prolife groups
- Land-use advocates
- Seniors
- Tax and antitax groups
- Gay-rights and anti-gay-rights activists
- Public union employees
- Identifiable work groups such as teachers and firefighters
- Advocates for gun ownership

Volunteer Sign-Up Sheet

In addition to finding volunteers in the groups listed above, you can create a form for sign-ups at coffees, debates, and other gatherings once the campaign is under way (figure 2.3).

35

Name (please print)	Home Phone	Canvass Neighborhoods	Phone Banks	Clerical	Lawn Sign Location Address	Donation	Letter-to-the-Editor	Endor. ad?	E-mail

VOLUNTEER SIGN-UP SHEET

I would like to volunteer for the following (please check all that apply):

FIGURE 2.3 Example of a Volunteer Sign-Up Sheet

3

The Campaign Brochure

The campaign brochure is fundamental to a campaign. It serves as an introductory piece for candidates and should include photos, a biography, and information that identifies why the candidate would be ideal in public office. If the candidate has previously held office, the brochure underscores past accomplishments and activities and brings them to the attention of the electorate. Unless the campaign plan calls for developing different brochures for the primary and the general election, the brochure should be free of partisan politics, because it travels with the candidate to all public functions.

> "Leaders are people who step forward, who influence thinking and action. They emerge to meet the needs."
> **WILLIAM GORE**

In an issue-based campaign, the brochure may give a sense of time and history reflecting on past community goals and ideals. An issue-based brochure should clearly explain what is before the voters, delineate the potential impacts of yes and no votes, and include testimonials from important community leaders advocating the passage or defeat of the ballot item.

In either a candidate or an issue-based campaign, it is important to develop a theme and a message before writing and printing a brochure, because it is from this framework that campaign activities will develop and flow.

Campaign Theme and Message Development

Before you sit down to write a brochure, you must develop a campaign theme and message. While political strategists use the words *theme* and *message* in different ways and sometimes interchangeably, for our purposes a theme covers the overarching issues that capture the spirit of what voters want, whereas a message is a single idea used to bring that theme to the voters.

For example, if you're working on a campaign to fund cocurricular activities that were eliminated from your school district because of budget cuts, your *theme* will probably include the idea of reinstating these programs. However, your *message* will center on the idea that it is no longer enough for students to have a 4.0 GPA if they want to get into a good college or land a better job—they must also be involved in cocurricular and extracurricular school activities. Briefly, your message is "opportunity."

> "Reining in government and all of that other stuff."
>
> **BOB DOLE**, outlining his presidential campaign platform, 1995

A theme embraces what the voters want and defines the candidate or issue-based campaign in that context, whereas a message is a believable application of the theme to the voters that cuts through to the emotional level. The voters want great schools, which must have a combination of challenging coursework and cocurricular activities. You sell these programs for what they are: opportunity for our children. They help students get into competitive universities or land great jobs, they are the reason some kids stay in school, and they represent another layer of preparation that enriches the next generation's future. It all comes back to providing opportunities for youths to excel. It isn't about money; it isn't about how high your property taxes will go. If you're arguing money, you're on "their" message.

When you're selling a bond measure to expand and improve a community asset, such as a library, you are not selling what a great deal the voters are getting; you're selling much more. You know what the voters want: They want a community resource that is enhanced in some way. That's your theme, and you're going to give them what they want.

Your message, however, is about acknowledging those who gave gifts to future generations by building the first library. It's about embracing history and the rich legacy of libraries in our culture. It's about a place where old and young can gather, as they have for a hundred years, to read a book. Your message: "It's about community."

In the presidential campaign of 1992, Bill Clinton had a theme of environmental protection, lower crime rates, education, and universal health care, among other things—things that voters wanted. Each of the issues of the overall campaign theme was then conveyed to the American people through the message "It's the economy." Let me underscore that the message is never stated, but is the tool used for framing. For example, we need to protect our environment to ensure better *jobs* in the future; we need to provide our children with better education if we want a *workforce* that can compete on the world market; providing opportunities for everyone to get a college education means *keeping America competitive;* affordable health care allows a family *to get ahead;* high crime rates are destroying our communities and marginalizing *businesses;* and so on. Everything comes back to the message "It's the economy": Addressing the issues that people want will lead to a better economy.

In his 1996 campaign, Clinton's message was "It's the little issues." The theme was similar to that of the 1992 campaign, but with the U.S. economy booming, Clinton's team moved the campaign focus in and personalized it— a very effective approach that's rarely applied at the national level. In that campaign, education translated into college IRAs, computers in the classrooms, and a million volunteers to ensure that every American child could read by the third grade. Environment

> "Leaders can conceive and articulate goals that lift people out of their petty preoccupations and carry them above the conflicts that tear a society apart."
> **JOHN W. GARDNER**

became gifts to our grandchildren and ways to recreate with our kids in the summer. Combating crime became distributing fifty thousand cell phones to neighborhood crime watch groups. Health care became welfare reform and allowing new mothers to stay longer than forty-eight hours in the hospital. The Clinton campaign assumed that while people care about world peace, worry about the global economy, and dislike political repression in foreign lands, it was personal issues that connected directly with Americans and their lives. By delivering seemingly simple solutions to community and family issues, Clinton presented a clear message of hope in the context of home and community, making the issues tangible.

A campaign message is how a theme is communicated to the public. It's a story you tell over and over, a story you can tell in a few seconds: "It's the economy"; "This is about opportunity"; "It's the small issues"; "It's hope"; "It's about community." A well-crafted message moves the debate away from which candidate can be trusted to whom the voters trust to do the job. A theme and message articulate the point that the candidate knows *what* job needs to be done. Voters will naturally make the connection that the candidate who knows what needs to be done will be the one more likely to do it.

In an issue-based campaign, a message should tell the voters *why* a task needs to be done. The message should reach them on an emotional level: hope, opportunity, safety, service, preserving our past, planning for the inevitable.

To create a theme and message, your campaign committee must assess the strengths and weaknesses of your candidate or ballot measure. Ask, and answer, the questions of who will vote for your candidate or proposition over your opposition, and why. You must also look for any fatal flaws in your candidate or issue. The campaign message and theme will develop from this process and will become the foundation for your slogan, ads, and media efforts. Once you have a message, do not get off it, and don't let your opponents pull you off.

> "What are you planning to do Mr. Bell . . . wire up every house in the country?"
>
> Ridicule leveled at Alexander Bell as he presented plans for wire telephony to bankers and investors in Philadelphia

By taking a critical look at your candidate or issue and listing the strengths and weaknesses, your campaign team is better able to shape and communicate the theme of a campaign through the message. For example, a woman who is energetic, feisty, and steadfast translates into pluses and minuses. The pluses are that she's a fighter, has integrity, is honest, and will fight for the community. The minuses may be that she is pushy, shrill, dogmatic, or overbearing (a word reserved in American society almost exclusively for women).

The charge of the campaign committee is to frame the negative into a positive: Pushy becomes persistent or steadfast; dogmatic becomes directness, which goes with honesty and integrity. All this is communicated through the message that flows from what the candidate represents. For instance, if a community is being overrun by developers and the quality of life is compromised by the inherent impacts of growth, couple a message of thoughtful, planned growth with a candidate's strengths of honesty, integrity, persistence, and willingness to fight for the community. Again, the message is planned, thoughtful growth, and every question answered comes back to this message—all under the umbrella of the theme "quality of life."

Through this process, campaigns identify issues that create relationships with the voters and that translates into money and volunteers. For example, people in a particular neighborhood are concerned about development, so the campaign underscores the creation of a park near the neighborhood. It is not about stopping growth but rather about mitigating the negative effects of growth. The campaign looks at the impacts growth has on the community and presents approaches that allow growth without compromising quality of life. This in turn will create relationships within the community. For parents and teachers, growth affects class size; for others, it's about traffic, open space, or availability of resources, such as water. If you present yourself as antigrowth, you risk being tagged as a single-issue candidate. Instead, lead people to where two worlds can coexist or even enhance one another rather than prophesying what will happen if these two worlds are allowed to collide. In short, planning for growth is good for business, education, resources, neighborhood integrity, and so on.

> "I use not only all the brains I have, but all I can borrow."
> **WOODROW WILSON**

This concept is important in direct mail, ads, brochure development, speaking engagements, debates, and campaign endorsements, and it will be given further attention in later sections and chapters. Establishing a strong, succinct, and believable theme and message creates relationships, which in turn creates voters interested in helping and giving.

Very simply, you want a majority to see your side as a better choice than the other side. This is the time to assess the strengths and weakness of your opponent. If your opponent has not defined himself or herself, you can work this process in reverse and define that person for the voters: "My opponent is progrowth."

The brochure is basic to your campaign. You will walk it door-to-door, mail it to households, and hand it out at debates. The message

> "Leaders have a significant role in creating the state of mind that is society."
> **JOHN W. GARDNER**

must resonate with voters who receive the brochure, which will state in subtle and not-so-subtle ways why people should vote as you want them to. It should also imply why they should *not* vote for your opponent.

Polling

Polling provides a campaign with a snapshot of public opinion. While a benchmark poll looks at where the candidate or a ballot issue is ranked among voters before any campaigning or distribution of information has been done, tracking polls provide ongoing feedback on the impact a campaign has in swaying public opinion.

> "Public sentiment is everything. With public sentiment, nothing can fail. Without it, nothing can succeed."
> **ABRAHAM LINCOLN**

Benchmark Polls

Conducting a benchmark poll may be the most efficient and accurate way to determine voter concerns before you develop your message. As First Lady Rosalynn Carter remarked, "It is difficult to lead people where they do not want to go." While it is important to have elected officials with strong core values, it is even more important that officials listen to and embrace "where people want to go." Having a clear reading of voter concerns will help your campaign develop and direct a message that will be heard. It can also inform you about when to keep quiet and which issues to avoid. Generally, a benchmark poll is done in advance of a campaign, and it can be invaluable in developing a campaign strategy, theme, and message.

A good benchmark poll can take as long as thirty minutes per call. It will include questions that lead to information about the following:

- The name recognition of the major candidates
- The favorability of that name recognition
- The voter's knowledge of state and local politics
- The degree of partisanship of the voter
- The issues most important to the voter, by gender, age, and party affiliation
- The education, age, and gender of those who support you and of those who support your opposition
- The income level of those who support you
- Whom the voter will support if the election were held tomorrow (or which direction the voter is leaning)
- Whether the voter intends to vote, is likely to vote, or is unlikely to vote
- What form of message works best, both for your candidate and for the opposition
- What attacks will hurt the most, for both you and your opposition

Polling Message with Push Questions

Push questions, not to be mistaken with push polling, "are recognized by all the major associations and leading political consultants as a valid and legitimate research tool for the purposes of testing ad messages and examining the collective viewpoints of electorate subgroups."[1]

> "I've got to follow them; I am their leader."
> — ALEXANDRE LEDRU-ROLLIN

Push *questioning* will ask whether a statement is very, somewhat, or not at all convincing and will do so for both the candidate paying for the poll and the candidate's opponent. The questions will test both positives and negatives on each of the candidates—and will do so equally.

In one section of a benchmark poll for a state legislative race between our candidate, Democrat Alan Bates, and his opponent, Republican Jane Hunts, we were looking for what the opposition might use against our candidate as well as how negatives might play against his opponent. Of the questions testing the negatives of Alan Bates, this question came out on top:

Is this a very convincing, somewhat convincing, not very convincing, or not at all convincing reason to vote *against* Alan Bates?

"Alan Bates is opposed to every antitax measure on the ballot this fall. He opposes cutting the state income tax, opposes increasing the deductibility of federal tax, opposes allowing voters the right to decide on all new or increased taxes, and opposes amending the state constitution to require government to return the tax kicker."

This question had a "very convincing" rating of sixteen points and a total "convincing" score (the total of "very" and "somewhat convincing") of fifty-two points. The "not convincing" side weighed in at thirty-seven points.

Of the six anti-Hunts push questions, this one came out at the bottom:

Is this a very convincing, somewhat convincing, not very convincing, or not at all convincing reason to vote *against* Jane Hunts?

"Jane Hunts has absolutely no government experience. She has never been elected or appointed to any office. In order to effectively represent southern Oregon in Salem, our representative needs the experience Jane Hunts just doesn't have."

This question came in with a total "convincing" score of forty-one (of which only nineteen points were for "very convincing") and with forty-eight points for "not convincing." Hmmm. Better think twice about going after Hunts on experience.

Our benchmark poll gave us information about what would or would not work for both Bates and Hunts as positive messaging as well as what would and would not work on attacks.

Getting Data Without a Poll

If your campaign has no money or, more to the point, does not want to spend thousands on a benchmark poll, you can get much of the information a benchmark would give you, for free. Using recent voting history of issue-based campaigns can provide candidates with a clear road map of voter opinion—precinct by precinct. For example, in the 2000 general election,

Oregon had twenty-five ballot measures before the voters. Among other things, the measures covered issues involving school funding, gay and lesbian rights, mandatory sentencing, campaign finance reform, drug-related property forfeiture, land use, taxes, powers of the state legislature, tobacco settlement funds, baiting traps, background checks for firearm purchases, and linking teacher pay to student performance. Although some of these measures passed (or failed) in every county, that does not mean they passed or failed equally in every precinct within the county.

If you're running a campaign in a state that is not as measure-happy as Oregon, potential campaign issues in your voting area can be ferreted out in other ways: letters to the editor, minutes of city council or county commissioner meetings, editorials, general news stories, blogs following local articles, and county and city elections. Given that issues pop up in candidate elections, reviewing which issues were at the center of those campaigns can be very helpful.

> "When two people agree all the time, one of them is unnecessary."
> — **WILLIAM WRIGLEY**

In 2002, I worked on a county commissioner campaign in which the candidate had been elected to his conservative city council post on a no-growth platform. Knowing that growth was an issue in my city as well and that the two cities represent opposite ends of the political spectrum, we knew we had an issue that would transcend the county's political schism: growth and the effects it has on our region. Using a tone of "keeping a little of what makes this area special" in our candidate's last television ad before the election, we were able to take an issue that everyone cared about and couple it with a pro-environment undertone. This allowed us to go back and lock his drifting base without losing swing voters. The approach proved to be an important move in this close election.

Be Creative

Many small communities conduct citizen surveys as a way to track residents' concerns and to assess the job performance of city employees. This is part of the public record and is available for the asking. You can get similar information, minus the job performance of the governing body, at the local chamber of commerce. The census also has a wealth of information, and although it doesn't go to the precinct level, it does have helpful information broken down by cities, counties, regions, and states.

Special-interest groups that support your candidate or issue may have recently conducted a poll to track voter support of a particular issue, especially if that issue has been or soon will be placed before the voters. Such polls typically assess support according to voter profile within a region, county, or city.

Benchmark Polls on a Shoestring

If you have no money and are determined to run a benchmark poll, you can do so using volunteers and a professional pollster or a college professor who knows or teaches polling. Depending on the length of the questionnaire, each caller can complete three to five calls per hour.

To pull this off, you must have three things in order. First, draft the questions for the professional who is overseeing the project. I don't care how impartial you think your questions are—they're biased. If you do not have a seasoned pollster reviewing the questions, you will spend a lot of volunteer-hours on a poll that may or may not give you accurate results and, in a worse-case-scenario, could lead your campaign in the wrong direction.

Second, have plenty of volunteers who excel on the phone. Let's say you want to conduct a benchmark poll with three hundred randomly selected voters. If each caller can poll three people per hour, you need a hundred volunteer hours. Should you be lucky enough to land a phone bank location with ten lines and each worker puts in a one-hour shift, that means you need two shifts of ten phone bankers (twenty volunteers) per night for five nights. That's a lot of volunteers.

> "Imagination is more important than knowledge."
> **ALBERT EINSTEIN**

Third, obtain (or generate) a random voter list from your county clerk or election office. The clerk's office will sell you a printout with the number of voters you need to reach to achieve a 3 to 5 percent margin of error. In my county, 25 to 30 percent of the lists provided by the clerk's office include phone numbers. No matter how many phone numbers are on your lists, do not expect your callers to look up numbers in addition to polling. To fill in all the phone numbers on your lists, do one of three things: Set up a clerical team to look up phone numbers; turn the list of registered voters over to data-entry volunteers, and have them drop in phone numbers from the Web; or buy phone lists.

It has been a decade since I've needed a clerical team to look up phone numbers. Although it's difficult for nonpartisan, down-ballot races and issue-based campaigns to acquire voters' phone numbers, most partisan races have access to voter activation networks (VANs) and therefore voter phone numbers. So, calling a friend who works within another campaign and who may have access to a voter database is a great option. If that is not a choice, voter databases are often available to down-ballot, nonpartisan races for a price. Call your local or state parties to determine what data systems may be available.

Another alternative is to ask groups endorsing your campaign if they have access to phone numbers of registered voters for your area. Many endorsing organizations make this sort of information available to all candidates or issue-based campaigns they support. Often these lists include more information than the county lists, including voting frequency and phone numbers. This should be listed as an in-kind contribution to your campaign.

If getting phone numbers from Web-based phone books or through party voter databases is not a choice, let me emphasize one caution on having a clerical team look up phone numbers from the phone book: It is not a task for everyone. Be sure to ask your volunteers when signing them up if this is something they like to do. Some people are quite good at it, while others are painfully slow. For the work party, make sure everyone has a comfortable chair and table, good lighting, a phone book, and a straight-edge—such as a ruler or a strip of card stock. This is a two-hour shift. Avoid gregarious and chatty volunteers in this task.

Creating a Random Voter List for Polling

To generate your own calling list of randomly selected voters, either use the list of registered voters acquired by an endorsing organization, or obtain a list from your clerk's office or elections department. For campaign polling purposes, you really don't need to call nonvoters. So if you are able to obtain a list that indicates whether those listed have voted in recent elections, all the better. Clearly, if someone registered fifteen years ago and hasn't voted since, there is no reason to believe that he or she will suddenly start with your race. Our state is authorized to strike from the rolls anyone who has not voted in the last five years. Check with the county or the secretary of state's office to determine how often (if ever) the voter rolls are purged in your area.

However you acquire your list, be sure to ask for it in Excel format. (Remember that Excel has only so many cells per page, so if you have more registered voters than Excel can handle, break it down into smaller files.) Also make sure there is a heading identifier for each column. If the county uses codes for the column headings, ask for a legend so you can figure out what's what when you begin working with the data.

In our county, every registered voter is identified by an assigned number. Similarly, statewide organizations assign their own numbers. Make life easy on yourself: Whether you're working from county or state lists, never separate this number from the assigned voter. An Excel document created for polling needs only a first and last name, a phone number, and the voter ID number.

The next two things you must do are important, so pay attention. First, you must use a process for random selection of voters from the database. Second, you need to make sure that the number of voters selected is proportional to the total number of voters in your election area.

For the first step, insert a column in your Excel spreadsheet, assign a random number within that column for each of the voters, and then sort these numbers numerically. If you don't know how to do this and have no friends with this skill, go to the help menu and type in "random sampling" or something similar until you find what you need. If all else fails, read the Excel manual.

Once you have a random sample of voters, sort it again for phone numbers. You do this for three reasons. First, you only want to call people whose numbers you have: If you have names with no phone numbers, volunteers get confused. Second, you want to be able to organize lists to delete duplicates for your volunteers. Believe me, you do not want to call a home and ask for Mary and then, ten minutes later, call the same number and ask for George while a volunteer down the hall is calling the same number asking for one of George and Mary's voting-age children. This, my friend, drives voters crazy. The third reason to sort your random list by phone number is so you can check for balance within the list itself.

Balancing Your Random List

If you are generating your own randomized voter list using Excel, take the time to calculate the percentages of phone numbers within each prefix to be sure that your list reflects the percentages of voters registered within those areas. For example, if voters living in the 488, 482, and 552 prefix area represent 10 percent of the county vote, then make sure those numbers are close to 10 percent of all the voters called.

In the 2002 general election in Oregon, a local television station hired a polling firm from Maryland to conduct a tracking poll about a week before Election Day. The poll included a community college bond measure, a local school measure, the governor's race, and the voters' opinion on the war in Iraq. After the survey was conducted, I was called and told that the poll indicated voter approval of the community college measure by five points, with 11 percent undecided. After the two money measures went down by fifteen points, I checked around and found that the poll not only indicated that the community college bond measure would pass but that the other money measure would, too, and that our very conservative county supported the democratic candidate for governor and opposed the war in Iraq. All suspect.

We contacted the polling firm and were told, "Those interviewed were selected by the random variation of the last *four* digits of telephone numbers.
A cross-section of exchanges was utilized in order to ensure an accurate reflection of the *state* [emphasis added]. Quotas were assigned to reflect the
voter registration of distribution by county."

While southern Oregon may be an anomaly, voters within this area vote
very differently according to where they live. Some areas are the most progressive in the state while others are the most conservative. By using the *last
four digits* of the phone number without taking into account prefixes, which
delineate different areas of the county, one might conclude that a dispro-
portionate number of voters in the more progressive prefixes were polled,
skewing the results. The clearest evidence that this had happened was in the
results of the question about the war in Iraq. That question alone could be
a litmus test of the validity of the poll. It is simply not possible that the majority of residents in Jackson County, Oregon, would be opposed to U.S. involvement in Iraq at the start of the war. While some areas in the county
would register overwhelming opposition, that would not be true of the majority of the county.

One last step in creating a polling list: Be sure your final list reflects countywide gender and party registration. For example, if your area registration is
52 percent women and 48 percent men, keep those percentages; similarly, if
Republicans outnumber Democrats by 10 percent, be sure your poll list has
the same breakdown.

Bear in mind that benchmark polling can be an enormous undertaking.
However, because it can and should be done before your campaign kickoff,
it is often possible to do one without adding stress to a volunteer force or
your campaign budget.

Finally, remember to break your area into zones and only poll party registrants.

Polling for Dollars

If you're working on a state legislative race, a professionally conducted poll
can mean money for your campaign. Lobbyists and PACs are reluctant to
give money to campaigns that "think" they will win. However, show that
you're close to your opponent in a legitimate poll, and checkbooks will open.
To spend thousands on a poll in hopes of attracting PAC money is risky and
works against common sense. Still, it happens, and if the numbers are good,
it can pay off. Polls run by volunteers don't count here.

Professionally conducted polling tends to be expensive. To cut costs, you
might consider offering to include other candidates in the poll if their cam-

paigns will contribute to the cost or ask a PAC or state party to financially help by paying the polling firm directly.

Polls can also cost a campaign support and money. Although this will be covered in subsequent chapters on targeting, a professional poll indicating a losing effort will shut all sorts of doors. So if your registration is wildly skewed, resist doing a poll; save your money.

Push Polling

Push polling is a form of negative campaigning. Rather than using print media, television, YouTube, direct mail, or radio, push polls come to the voter through telemarketing disguised as a legitimate poll. The objective of push polling is to *persuade* voters, not to gain information. And since they are only about persuasion, push polls typically do not collect data.

Because many confuse push questions with push polling, it is important to again underscore the difference: As indicated above, benchmark polls ask push questions that reveal the dark side of *both* candidates. Campaigns do this so they know the effectiveness of hitting an opponent (or receiving hits from the opposition) with little-known but truthful information. All campaigns want to know what will work for and against both their campaign and the opposition.

> "[Push polls] breed cynicism about politics, and we believe they contribute to declining response rates for polls."
> **MICHAEL TRAUGOTT**

Benchmarks take twenty to thirty minutes, whereas tracking polls are relatively quick, grabbing a snapshot of a moment. Only a very specific voter will invest twenty or thirty minutes in a benchmark; many more will jump in on a tracking poll.

Push polls use the goodwill of tracking polls, which are based on brevity ("If the election were held tomorrow, would you vote for Candidate A or Candidate B?") to persuade unwitting voters. Push polls typically take under five minutes, but unlike their tracking-poll sister, they add a little "something, something" at the end to close the deal.

Here is how Rachel, a blogger on the *Huffington Post,* described a push poll regarding the Obama and McCain 2008 presidential campaign in Ohio:

> When I said that I was voting for Obama, they asked if I would be more or less likely to vote for Obama if I knew that he voted to let convicted child sex offenders out early, voted to allow convicted child sex offenders to live near schools, is for sex education in Kindergarten, voted for some offensive

and incredibly graphic abortion procedure, and so on and so on for 5 min-utes. This was a really offensive push-poll. They also brought up the state-ments of Rev. Wright and Michelle Obama.[2]

That is a push poll: It typically shares with the voter something inflam-matory and wildly skewed about the opposition. The polls call as many vot-ers as humanly possible before getting busted by the media. Because there must be some tangential thread between the question and truth, push polls can tip leaning voters. Both ways.

Push polling is condemned by everyone and yet is seemingly done all the time—or so some think.

In 2004, I worked on a state senate campaign where Alan Bates, a Demo-cratic state representative and doctor, ran against Jim Wright, a local Repub-lican businessman and beloved philanthropist. Wright was the embodiment of a McCall Oregonian: that is, fiscally conservative and socially liberal. Bates and Wright were identical on every single issue, from sales tax to education. However, Wright enjoyed a 6 percent registration advantage and was so well known and well liked that he could routinely turn out four hundred people for a 6 a.m. breakfast or three hundred for a Tuesday lunch. Yikes.

Then a friend called and read me the riot act.

Apparently, her husband had received (ostensibly) from our campaign a call that was obviously "push polling," she said. After assuring her that it was not us, I asked her on what she had based her allegation. She said her hus-band was asked if he would be more or less likely to vote for Jim Wright if he knew he was blind.

The truth is, Jim Wright, who had suffered from macular degeneration for most of his life, *was* legally blind. However, I do not believe you can poll for prejudice, because when you try, voters lie.

There are many examples of campaigns in which polling for prejudice re-sulted in unreliable data. The so-called Bradley effect in the 1982 guberna-torial race in California is one such example, and the appeal to people's prejudice through their love of the Confederate flag in Georgia and South Carolina in the 2000 gubernatorial races is another.[3] Similarly, there was a reason FDR kept his wheelchair from public view.

Further, I argued against a question in our benchmark regarding our op-ponent's vision problems. Besides being shallow, it seemed disingenuous if we allowed a doctor to attack an opponent on a disability; some might even see it as cruel. So, my contention was, if we would *never* use it, why ask? In-deed, polling this question could actually inflame the narrow swing vote needed to win.

Some on our team argued that "to ask" was not "to use."

Don't be fooled: If you have a handgun in your pocket while committing a robbery, the jury doesn't care if you never intended to use it. Voters are no different. In small communities, friends share information about telephone polls.

On the bright side, our opponents revealed important information:

1. They wondered about their candidate's disability.
2. They did not know polling for prejudice often leads to unreliable information.

Knowing the opposition was worried or at least curious about voter response to our opponent's macular degeneration was gold. Indeed, service in government is largely about being able to quickly move through unbelievable volumes of material and grasp information for effective communication. How to convey and remind voters of this without hitting them over the head became an important component of the campaign (figure 3.1).

Brochure Development

While the campaign committee will help in developing the campaign message and theme, you should have only one or two people work with you or the candidate in writing the brochure. Obviously, you want a good writer who has a couple of free days. The initial writing takes only a few hours, but it is almost always followed by many rewrites. These rewrites should return to the committee to check message and theme, and before the brochure is sent to the printer, the committee must have the final say over the content, theme, message, and "look." Give yourself enough time. If the committee does not like what it sees, you need time to make the necessary corrections before delivering the material to the printer.

If you write your own campaign brochure, have someone read it critically when you've finished. The emphasis here is on *critically*. We all love our own words, and our friends are often loath to condemn them. You need someone you can trust, someone who has the political savvy to read your work, correct any errors, and make appropriate suggestions.

Pictures

Before you lay out a brochure, the candidate should visit a professional photographer. Well-meaning friends with above-average equipment may not get what you want—and, really, nothing compares with professional work.

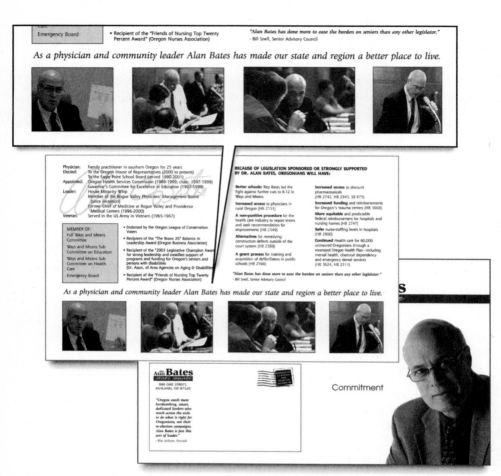

FIGURE 3.1 Example of a Full-Color Brochure That Subtly Addresses Voters' Concerns with the Opponent

In 2004, Democrat Alan Bates ran for a state senate seat recently vacated by a twenty-eight-year Republican veteran; the seat had a six-point Republican registration advantage. His opponent, a highly respected, fabulously wealthy, and generous philanthropist, was legally blind. Once we discovered that the opposing campaign polled for, and was concerned about, his disability, the challenge became how to subtly remind voters of the importance of sight in dealing with the sheer volume of material coming across a legislator's desk. (Design by Brian Freeman, Crystal Castle Graphics)

Amateurish photos will hurt your campaign. I have never understood how candidates will spend thousands of dollars to get elected but cut the corner on professional photography. Take a moment and look through any voters' pamphlet; it is simply mind-boggling what people will put out there. If a professional will not volunteer his or her time, this is a good place to spend money. If the first sitting does not produce the right photo, invest in a second shoot. Also provide the local papers with a photo (usually different shots but from the same sitting) so they will use your photo rather than one generated by their news team. If you e-mail a good-quality photo, it will be particularly easy for the newspapers to use. After your candidate is elected, continue this practice.

> "The aim of marketing is to make selling superfluous."
> **PETER DRUCKER**

When you are campaigning for an issue-based campaign, photos are often easier to come by, although more time-consuming to gather. For example, if you're working on a school tax base measure, visit the yearbook class at the middle and high school. They save photographs of all age groups and in many activities. For a park program, try the YMCA or the parks department; even city and county offices may have photos, so check there as well. For historic photos of your city or county, try a local historian or historical society. Show what will be accomplished with the passage of your measure through pictures as well as text. Many photographers will let you use their photos in issue-based campaigns as long as their name appears with the photo in a credit line.

Use pictures as a way to break up the text and give the brochure a substantive feel. Most brochures for candidates contain at least one picture of the candidate. This is important to increase name and face recognition. With that recognition comes familiarity, which is psychologically important for the voter. The candidate begins to feel like a friend and a celebrity all at once. You may also carefully select other photos to create an image of who this person is. There may be pictures of the candidate at work, with the family, at play (e.g., batting in a softball game or fly-fishing), with seniors, or at a preschool, a public school, a hospital, or a park. Include whatever might both positively connect the candidate with his or her lifestyle and characterize what is important in the community.

Depending on your budget and the size of your brochure, you may just stop with the picture of the candidate. But if you have more resources, be sure the pictures add to or underscore the story the campaign wants to tell. Put thought into the selection of pictures. Try to show the diversity of your community in the photos: people of all ages and ethnic groups, working class and professionals, men and women. Whether the campaign is doing a studio shot or one of the candidate on the stump, be sure to bring extra clothes for different settings. Brochures that show a candidate at a school, at a senior center, in a park, with family, or whatever, are ostensibly intended to show the individual in his or her everyday life over a period. But if the candidate is wearing the same clothes in each shot, the result looks contrived and you miss an opportunity to create the feel you want.

One caution here: Avoid photos that picture the candidate standing or sitting coincidentally near a celebrity. Novice campaigners are anxious to show they hobnob with the elite and will select pictures that show themselves in the general proximity of a celebrity. If you want to use a photo of your candidate with the governor, be sure it is a photo of your candidate with the governor. One brochure I saw had the candidate looking around a plant that was situated behind the governor, who was being photographed with other people. This is interpreted for just what it is by the voters.

Some candidates when being photographed with a "name" lean toward or tilt their head toward the celebrity ("I'm with him"). This pose suggests weakness on the part of your candidate and may have a subtle but negative influence on the voters.

Urge the photographer to take some pictures of the candidate outside. Change the background, walk toward the camera, sit on a bike and lean on the handlebars. (This particular pose, with or without the bike in it, makes a great shot.) Arrange for people to meet you and the photographer for a few shots that can be taken outside, in front of businesses, backdropped with trees or historic buildings (figures 3.2A and 3.2B).

Anxious to show a candidate with all the typical campaign requisites, campaigns will typically use pictures of their candidate at a senior center, in front of a police car, shaking hands with a business leader in front of a factory, reading to children, and on the front lawn with the family. But when a majority of campaign brochures include the same array, your literature will fade into the wallpaper. Make an effort to use the medium effectively, and bring spontaneity and motion into your brochure photos. Capture your candidate in a quiet moment reading over papers, through a window at night burning the midnight oil, conferring with a colleague while leaning over a desk, and playing with the family from last summer's vacation. This might be where your friend with above-average camera skills can help.

When selecting pictures for either a candidate or issue-based campaign, be sure to look at the whole picture, not just the subject of the picture. In the Campaign for the Carnegie, a local library campaign for capital improvements, I selected an interior library photo with a young patron reading in a crowded, cluttered room to demonstrate the dismal state of our library. However, I did not notice that directly behind the subject was a display rack with *Mad* magazines. Luckily, the librarians on the committee caught my error.

Photo by Christopher Briscoe

Photo by Cathy Shaw

Photo by Christopher Briscoe

Photo by Christopher Briscoe

Photo by Marietta Gilmour

FIGURE 3.2A
Examples of Candidate
Photos That Work
Well in Brochures

Photo by Cathy Shaw

Photo by Marla Cates

Photo by Cathy Shaw

FIGURE 3.2B
Examples of Photos
That Work Well in an
Issue-Based Brochure

When selecting photos for
issue-based campaigns, look
for ones with movement and
that elicit emotion. The photos
above were used for funding
youth sports programs, water
conservation, and state
funding for seniors and
public schools. The bottom
right had the caption "What
future do we offer them?"

Campaign Slogans

Years ago, slogans were printed next to a candidate's name on the ballot. At that time, with media playing a lesser role in politics, having a catchy slogan was critical for a win on Election Day. Slogans can still be very effective, but they require a great deal of thought by the campaign committee. Do not invent a slogan just to have one. Use your campaign message and design a slogan that underscores and reinforces it. Sit with your committee, list the strengths of your candidate or measure, and brainstorm possibilities. Once you think you have one, brainstorm on all the ways it could be used against you or hurt your cause. Work through this process until you come up with the right combination.

> "Out of intense complexities, intense simplicities emerge."
> — WINSTON CHURCHILL

The slogan is a simple statement about why you should be elected or why the voters should vote for your measure. It should also imply why *not* to vote for your opponent or what a no vote may lead to in an issue-based campaign. Your slogan must not depart from your campaign message, and it should evoke a gut emotion. One very effective slogan used in an issue-based campaign in California simply said, "Share the Water." Who can argue with the idea of sharing? It is a friendly thought that is encouraged throughout our lives. It also implies that the water is not being shared.

I was on a campaign that used the slogan "Now Let's Choose Leadership." I was concerned that this slogan would sound patronizing. I was also concerned that those who previously voted for the incumbent, who enjoyed a six-point registration advantage, would feel they were being scolded. Furthermore, this slogan tended to reinforce the perception that our candidate was arrogant.

A Democrat running against an incumbent for the Second Congressional District in Oregon used another problematic slogan. Since the district was formed three decades ago, only Republicans have been elected—four to be exact—and by overwhelming numbers. However, in this particular election, the incumbent had committed so many campaign violations and was misbehaving both in public and in Congress in such a way that it looked as though this Democrat might win the seat.

The Democrat called on me and some other local people to talk strategy in our part of the district, and he also took that opportunity to show us his brochure. Although it was a handsome brochure, it featured a poorly conceived slogan: "It's time we had a Congressman we can be proud of." While I understood that the brochure referred to the incumbent, who was in core meltdown, it overlooked the fact that for more than ten years, Second District Oregonians had voted in huge numbers for a congressman they were very proud of. You can't hope to attract voters to your side of the street by insulting them.

Most important, the slogans in both of these examples imply that the campaign is about the candidate. Effective slogans stem from messages that are about the voters and their communities, not the candidate or, as in these two examples, the incumbent.

In 2008, a police officer of a neighboring community living in Ashland wanted to run for city council and asked for my help. He had run and narrowly lost in 2006 after the Green Party attacked his occupation and Republican registration. (In Ashland, there's a pronounced anti-law-enforcement sentiment, and better than eight in ten voters cast a Democratic ballot.)

His opponent in the nonpartisan race was both a green Democrat and an incumbent with loyal supporters. However, she also had detractors. Publicly, she was accused of micromanaging city departments and grinding council action to a crawl. Some believed that she was responsible for elevating the dysfunctional city government to national attention when a therapist was hired and paid $37,000 in tax dollars to help the council work together more productively.[4] With nearly every Ashland voter supporting Obama, we looked for a way to piggyback on those coattails without being obvious. To do so, we used the same font as Obama (Gothic), took an Obama lawn sign to the graphic designer to match the colors exactly, and used the slogan "Change starts here." Our council candidate won by eighteen points.

For a local restaurant tax to fund wastewater treatment plant upgrades and open-space land acquisition, our opposition used the slogan "Don't Swallow the Meals Tax." This is a clever slogan because it works on different levels: People who swallow something are duped, and then, of course, the tax was on food.

In one open-space campaign, we used the slogan "Parks, Now and Forever." People who opposed the measure saw our slogan and used their own modification: "Parks: *Pay* Now and Forever." A very clever counter slogan. We should have chosen ours more carefully.

In 1997, a group of Oregonians put together an initiative to overturn a previously voter-approved ballot measure allowing physician-assisted suicide. The new initiative was well financed, with billboards and lawn signs everywhere. In the upper right-hand corner of the signs, they had the previous measure's number (16) in a circle with a line through it. Next to that was the slogan "Fatally Flawed" and below the slogan was "Yes on 51."

While this was clearly a professional campaign, they mistakenly used a very ambiguous slogan. Basically, it meant to state that the previously passed ballot

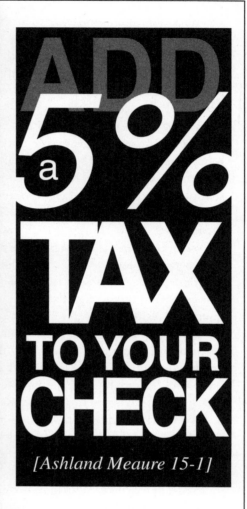

DON'T
SWALLOW
THE MEALS
TAX

[VOTE N⊙ 15-1]

Measure 15-1, Ashland's proposed meals tax,
is a regressive tax because:

15-1 IS NOT A TOURIST TAX. THE BURDEN OF THE TAX
WILL BE PAID BY YOU, THE ASHLAND CONSUMER.

FOOD IS A BASIC NECESSITY. THIS TAX WILL SE-
VERELY IMPACT STUDENTS, THE ELDERLY, THE POOR,
AND OTHERS ON A FIXED INCOME.

IT IS NOT A LUXURY TAX. BECAUSE OF TODAY'S BUSY
SCHEDULES, AN AVERAGE OF 48c OF EVERY FOOD
DOLLAR IS SPENT ON PREPARED MEALS OUTSIDE THE
HOME.

IT WILL AUTHORIZE INCREASES UP TO 5% WITHOUT
FURTHER VOTE FROM THE PUBLIC.

IT IS CONFUSING, DIFFICULT TO MANAGE, AND COSTLY
TO IMPLEMENT.

IT IS SHORTSIGHTED. IF THE STATE LEGISLATURE
IMPOSES A STATEWIDE SALES TAX IT COULD NEGATE
ANY LOCAL SALES TAXES.

IT WILL PUT ASHLAND ON THE MAP AS THE ONLY CITY
IN AMERICA TO IMPOSE A MEALS TAX WITHOUT FIRST
HAVING AN OVERALL SALES TAX IN PLACE.

BROCHURE DESIGN BY ERIC BRADFORD WARREN

ADD a 5% TAX TO YOUR CHECK

[Ashland Meaure 15-1]

Back **Front**

FIGURE 3.3 "Don't Swallow the Meals Tax" Brochure

Brochure layout: two-panel, front and back pictured above. Note that the front and top back of the brochure are visually striking, but the lower, dense, reversed type is hard to read. Also note that this brochure went to press with a typo on the front panel. This is not the responsibility of the graphic designer but rather the campaign team. Avoid errors like this by having a number of people proofread the text. (Design by Eric Bradford Warren) initiative (Measure 16, for physician-assisted suicide) was "fatally flawed" and that a yes vote on *this* measure (51) would overturn that one. However, the way the sign was laid out, it appeared that Measure 51, not 16, was "fatally flawed."

During the campaign, I was called by a local organizer to help defeat the referendum. I suggested that the campaign did not need any help; it only needed to adopt the same slogan that the opposition had used: "Fatally Flawed." Because voters naturally associate a negative slogan with a negative vote, every "Yes on 51" lawn sign, billboard, and commercial would become a "No on 51" pitch. Whether the team members took my advice or came to it themselves, the "No on 51" campaign co-opted the same slogan of the "Yes on 51" campaign, and with very little money, the referendum was defeated at the polls—only this time instead of losing by one point, the referendum lost by twenty. Further, because the "no" campaign co-opted the slogan of the "yes" campaign, those supporting the referendum had to create a new slogan, reprint field and lawn signs, and replace all installed billboards and field signs with the new look. Changing the look of a campaign in the middle of a cycle is a death knell.

As a general rule, you don't want a negative slogan or idea associated with a yes vote ("Fatally Flawed"). It's preferable to have a negative slogan, such as in the meals tax example given above, associated with a no vote and a positive slogan ("Share the Water") associated with a yes vote on a ballot measure or proposition. In the campaign to overturn the measure allowing physician-assisted suicide, the slogan "Yes on 51" campaign expected too much of the voter.

During my first run for mayor, I used the slogan "Building a Better Community." I chose this slogan because of citywide concerns about growth and development. I wanted a positive slogan that suggested to the voters that more was not necessarily better and that it was "community" that needed to be built, not indiscriminate construction.

People love to throw exclamation points into campaign literature and especially slogans. Avoid this. In 2008, a candidate committee and I came to the slogan "It's about integrity." We landed on this because her opponent, a local Realtor, was using his position in the legislature to pass legislation to protect his industry and because of reversals of his votes once industries got to him. For example, he changed his mind on a vote to impose a cigarette tax to fund children's health insurance, after which his campaign was rewarded with contributions from the tobacco industry. At some point, the period in the slogan turned into an exclamation point: "It's about integrity!" The first version implies, in a matter-of-fact way, that the opponent is bought and sold; the phrase reinforces the need to have leaders of integrity in government doing the people's business. Once the exclamation point was added, the slogan became a statement about the candidate herself and not the unseemly practice of using government position to feather the beds of family and friends.

And while we're here, if you love to use exclamation points, remove them from every single little thing you do in a campaign; once the campaign is over, you can go back to using them as you please.

The following are examples I have pulled from brochures in my files. Using a slogan is optional. Better to omit it than have a bad one.

"It's about people, not politics."
"Experience * Leadership * Commitment"
"The best . . . for the best"
"A voice that will be heard"
"A Strong Voice for [Place]"
"With his experience . . . It makes sense."
"Unbought and unbossed"
"Because nothing counts like results"
"Straightforward, Fair, Effective"
"Tough, committed, fighting for us"
"It's time to rotate the crops."
"A leader who makes a difference"
"At a time when experience and dedication are needed most"
"Taking care of [Place]"
"Experience money can't buy"
"This is about governing . . . and I've done it."
"People over politics"
"The Change Will Do Us Good."
"It's Time for a Change."
"Change We Can Believe In."
"Change starts here."

For more ideas, go to www.presidentsusa.net/campaignslogans.html or http://en.wikipedia.org/wiki/Political_slogan.

Logo

I regularly use the lawn sign image as the logo on my brochures and ads. I think it adds continuity to a campaign, conveying a subtle message that it is well organized and connected. If your race is a difficult one, such as a write-in, a logo can be more important. Write-ins for candidates are covered in Chapter 9.

A logo is like a trademark. It can simply be how the candidate's name is written, or for an issue-based campaign, it can be an image. Figures 3.4, 3.5, and 3.6 present some very effective logos. Obviously, if you have a name like that of Shayne Maxwell, a candidate for the Oregon legislature, you want to take advantage of it in your logo: "Maxwell for the House." In the Maxwell for the House race, we continually had people say "good to the last drop" after hearing her name. It did not hurt that she ran in an area whose residents were predominantly seniors—and undoubtedly still bought their coffee in a can. Spend some time thinking about the name of the candidate, and come up with creative ways to link the name with the office being sought, like Audie Bock, who used a play on her name in a reelection campaign: "Bock By Popular Demand."

Layout

The layout of a brochure depends on its size, how much you want to say, and the quality and quantity of photos. Unless you know the business professionally, you will need the help of a layout artist or graphic designer. Do not make the mistake of trying to save a hundred bucks by doing this yourself or by using someone just because he or she has a desktop publishing program.

A good way to get ideas on layout is to go over past political campaign brochures. Often, you can find the look you want and then emulate that look. Some examples of different types of brochures are presented later in this section, but your best resource will be the politically experienced graphic designer or layout artist.

Although many experienced campaigners believe that brochure copy should be kept to a minimum, there is the possibility of offending the astute voter with an empty brochure. The challenge is to include enough information without overwhelming the voter with a sea of words. Consider minimizing the impact of the text by placing it in boxes and using bullet points for a candidate's qualifications and experience.

Avoid long narratives. In an effort to establish credibility, candidates will drag out every accomplishment since high school and argue vociferously that it's all essential. In my first run for mayor, my opponent had his picture taken in front of the local high school with the caption "When he graduated, he never dreamed he would one day be mayor of Ashland." Candidates love to underscore their longevity in a city, county, state, or region: "born and raised." Voters put very little into presumptive entitlement to an office based on birthright.

FIGURE 3.4 "Maxwell for the House" Walking Piece

Example of a logo using the candidate's name to piggyback onto a positive corporate slogan. We used this walking piece to get newspaper endorsements to homes in the district; the back had photos, a bio, and individual endorsements. (Design by Crystal Castle Graphics)

Similarly, voters care little about experience. At some point, a candidate and the team must decide between including everything, with nothing read by the voter, and including a partial list of accomplishments—a list that is read by most. Remember, if George Donner had left either the organ or wood cook-stove behind, his family might have made it over the Sierra Nevada.

COMMITTEE FOR THE CARNEGIE

FIGURE 3.5 Example of a Logo for a Campaign to Restore and Expand Ashland's Carnegie Library

The logo builds one idea on top of another. (Design by Crystal Castle Graphics)

FIGURE 3.6 Example of a Logo Using Lettering That Appeals to the American Love of Baseball

(Design by Eric Bradford Warren)

If you want people to read your literature, don't waste their time. A good rule of thumb is that your pictures and graphics should consume as much space as, or slightly more than, the text. No one, not even the most sophisticated voter, will read unappealing brochures. Brochures are advertisements, so they must catch the eye and create a feeling or positive reaction in seconds.

In 2006, I began a practice that completely works: I ask the candidate or team to first do the voters' pamphlet statement. In Oregon, the voters' pamphlet is limited to 325 words, which, as it turns out, is the exact number of words that works in a brochure. The voters' pamphlet form also requests and lists all the necessary information appropriate for a brochure. Further, this practice gets the pamphlet out of the way early—always a plus. If you live in a state that does not publish a voters' pamphlet, you can still use the voters' pamphlet form as a guideline for your brochure; it can be found on the Oregon Secretary of State Web page. Voters' pamphlets are discussed in more detail in a later section in this chapter.

Use testimonials to get the candidate's message out. To obtain testimonials, I first identify people who support the candidate and might participate in the brochure, and then I try to balance age, gender, party registration, and big names. Once I have a list of people willing to participate, I guide them to cover a specific area I want covered. I then edit or rewrite their missives as needed to fit space, message, and appeal.

> "When I am getting ready to reason with a man, I spend one-third of my time thinking about myself and what I am going to say, and two-thirds thinking about him and what he is going to say."
> — **ABRAHAM LINCOLN**

Brochures can easily be created on a tight budget. A brochure may be laid out three up on a single sheet of paper so that each sheet yields three brochures. Although each sheet of paper must be cut into thirds, the cost of cutting is less than the cost of folding. Consider using card stock for a three-up brochure. By using card stock, you have the advantage of being able to shove the brochure into doorjambs. Go to a print shop, and check out colors and sizes. Clearly, in this small format, text will dominate. However, pictures add very little to the cost and provide an effective visual relief, so they remain important, no matter what the final brochure size is.

Consider using an 8½-by-14-inch paper for a bifold or single-fold brochure. This size lends itself to easy layout and visual impact, and it breathes. As paper size increases, layout becomes easier, but paper costs increase. Obviously, the size of paper you use determines the number of pictures and the amount of text in your brochure, so decide how much you need to say and how much you can afford to say. When the content and layout of

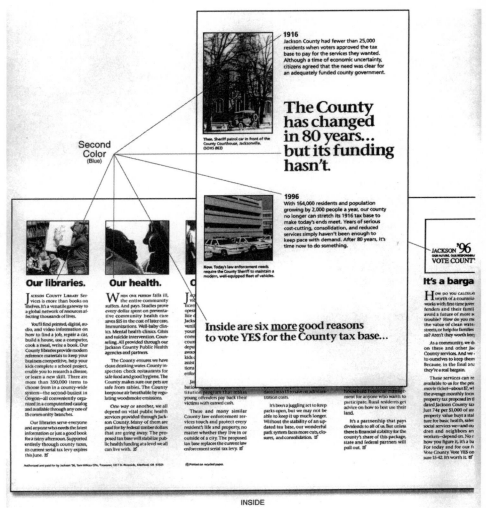

FIGURE 3.7 "The County Has Changed" Brochure

Example of a bifold brochure on 8½-by-14-inch paper. Larger pictures with less text would make a better presentation. Also, the front images work against each other here.

the campaign brochure are mocked up, be sure to run it by your campaign committee for final approval.

Figures 3.7 and 3.8 are examples of bifold brochures that were used for local money measures: one for a new county tax base and the other for extracurricular programs for Ashland schools; both are also examples of what to avoid in a brochure. The county tax base brochure had a couple of fundamental problems that should have been corrected (figure 3.7). First, the

Questions & Answers

WHAT IS THE CHILDREN'S CULTURAL & RECREATIONAL TAX LEVY –15-3?
The city charter allows the Parks & Recreation Department to propose a two year serial levy that would fund recreational and cultural activities usually provided by the school district. If approved by the voters, the city would collect the money and contract with the school district to provide the activities. The two year levy will restore funds to the Ashland School District budget to accomplish the return of some of the programs now designated for cuts. This is designed to provide interim financing only.

IF THE LEVY PASSES, WILL MY PROPERTY TAXES GO UP?
No. They will still continue downward, as mandated by Measure 5, but just not as much. Each of the next two years, they will drop by $1.53 per thousand, instead of $2.50 per thousand.

WHY HASN'T THE SCHOOL DISTRICT PLANNED AHEAD AND SET ASIDE FUNDS IN ANTICIPATION OF THESE CUTS?
The school district made the decision to use all monies available to continue the very programs we are now wanting to fund with the tax levy.

WILL THE LEVY SOLVE ALL OF OUR FUNDING PROBLEMS FOR THE SCHOOLS?
No. With a 2.9 million dollar shortfall this $800,000 is truly a temporary measure to bring back or keep in place a portion of the essentials, until the state comes up with replacement revenue that would make up the lost funding for the school district.

WHY ARE WE DOING THIS? ISN'T THE STATE SUPPOSED TO HANDLE IT?
The state failed to resolve the school funding crisis brought on by Measure 5. Ashlanders said, "Let's raise our own money and keep it in Ashland so we can save these programs and also regain some local control."

FUNNELING MONEY FOR EDUCATION THROUGH CITY GOVERNMENT SOUNDS UNUSUAL — IS THIS LEGAL?
Yes. Legislative Counsel has researched and confirmed it.

Questions & Answers

HOW WERE THE PROGRAMS TO BE REINSTATED SELECTED?
The list represents the best ideas of the whole community. It was developed by parents of Ashland students, the school board, the city Parks and Recreation Commission, the Booster Club, Ashland Community Coalition, city government officials and the Ashland Schools Foundation. The list was endorsed by school principals.

YOU HEAR A LOT ABOUT "GETTING BACK TO BASICS" AND "CUTTING FRILLS" IN EDUCATION — ISN'T THIS FUNDING DROP A GOOD STEP IN THAT DIRECTION?
No. We are trying to keep the basics: this levy directly protects co-curricular activities that public schools throughout the United States have offered for most of the 20th century: just check your own high school yearbook.

WILL CITY RESIDENTS END UP FOOTING THE BILL FOR THE 20% OF ASHLAND STUDENTS WHO LIVE IN THE COUNTY?
County students will have to pay to participate in these "co-curricular" programs.

WHY DOES IT SEEM LIKE SO MUCH IS GOING TO THE HIGH SCHOOL AND NOT MIDDLE OR ELEMENTARY SCHOOLS?
Remember this is a stop gap measure. If the students now attending high school do not have these programs, we jeopardize their opportunities for college entrance or securing skilled labor jobs. Hopefully, as funding becomes available, many of our excellent elementary and middle school programs will be reinstated.

WHAT HAPPENS IF THE PROPOSED STATE SALES TAX FOR SCHOOLS DOES PASS THIS FALL?
It will not be in time to save the cut programs for the 1993/94, 1994/95 school years. If broader funding sources become adequate again to fund the programs, this levy can be eliminated.

Authorized by United Ashland Committee, Linda and Chuck Butler, Treasurers, P.O. Box 1145, Ashland, OR 97520.

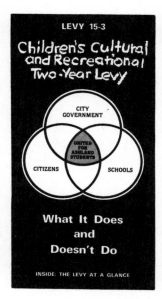

RECREATIONAL AND CULTURAL PROGRAMS AFFECTED BY LEVY	WHAT LEVY DIRECTLY PAYS FOR	PROGRAMS BROUGHT BACK BECAUSE OF MONEY FREED UP BY LEVY	PROGRAMS CUT IF LEVY FAILS	PROGRAMS PARTIALLY FUNDED IF LEVY FAILS	NON SCHOOL RELATED PROGRAMS NEEDED TO COMPLY WITH STATE LAW	AFFECTS HIGH SCHOOL	AFFECTS MIDDLE SCHOOL	AFFECTS ELEMENTARY SCHOOLS	NUMBER OF STUDENTS AFFECTED
RESIDENT OUTDOOR SCHOOL (ROS)	•		•				•	•	280
LIBRARIES (½ of Budgeted Amount)	•			•		•	•	•	3,431
CO-CURRICULUM:									
SPEECH & DEBATE	•		•			•			
DECA (Marketing)	•		•			•			
FBLA (Business)	•		•			•			
VICA (Industrial)	•		•			•			
YEARBOOK	•			•		•			400
NEWSPAPER	•			•		•			
DRAMA	•		•			•	•		
K-12 MUSIC PERFORMANCES						•	•	•	
ORCHESTRA						•	•	•	
BANDS						•	•	•	700
CHOIR						•	•	•	
ATHLETICS:									
SOCCER	•		•			•			
CROSS-COUNTRY	•		•			•			
FOOTBALL	•			•		•			
VOLLEYBALL	•			•		•	•		
SWIMMING	•		•			•			
WRESTLING	•					•			
BASKETBALL	•			•		•	•		
GOLF	•		•			•			650
TRACK	•			•		•			
SOFTBALL	•			•		•			
BASEBALL	•			•		•			
TENNIS	•			•		•			
INTRAMURALS	•		•					•	
STUDENT AT RISK PROGRAMS:									
SUBSTANCE ABUSE COUNSELOR		•	•			•	•	•	
CHILD DEVELOPMENT SPECIALIST		•	•					•	860
YOUTH AT RISK SERVICES		•	•				•	•	
FOREIGN LANGUAGE		•				•			670
TEEN CENTER	N/A	N/A	N/A	N/A	•				
COMMUNITY CENTER ACTIVITIES	N/A	N/A	N/A	N/A	•				

FIGURE 3.8 "Youth Activities Levy" Brochure

Example of a bifold brochure. Although this was a very complicated serial levy presented to the Ashland voters, we made matters worse with this brochure. The levy was intended to bring back extracurricular and co-curricular activities that had been cut by a statewide property tax limitation measure. Our idea was to let people know exactly what it would bring back. It was too much information, presented too sterilely. (Design by Brian Freeman, Crystal Castle Graphics) pictures were too small in relation to the text inside the brochure. A greater effort to reduce the amount of text and tell the story more through pictures would have strengthened the piece. Second, the front of the brochure features two photos (also too small) that should have been selected more carefully. While they were intended to show that government has dramatically changed since the approval of the last tax base, they actually tell another story. The historical photo evokes more emotion and reflects back to a simpler, less chaotic time. The current photo, of an ugly, new building, suggests that we would be better off not encouraging that kind of architecture with our tax dollars.

> "It's about the right message to the right people at the right time."
> **ELAINE FRANKLIN**

The other example of a bifold 8½-by-14-inch brochure was one we used for the Children's Cultural and Recreational Two-Year Levy (figure 3.8). This may be the worst brochure I have ever been associated with and breaks just about every rule I outline in this chapter. In our defense, it was a complicated proposal that I had thought up just weeks before it was placed in front of the voters. It didn't help that only two members of the campaign committee had any campaign experience or that the group had a fundamental breakdown about which voters the campaign should talk to and which ones should be ignored. The measure failed by just a few hundred votes.

Less than a year later, we came back to the voters with the Youth Activity Levy, but used a single-fold 8½-by-14-inch brochure (figure 3.9). In both brochures, we asked for the same amount of money and sold the same thing: hope and opportunity. But the way the message was delivered in the single-fold brochure is more compelling. Ironically, the second brochure is less clear about *where* the money would be spent. This is great information to have. Most voters don't want to be a curriculum committee for a school district at the ballot box. Their preference is to know where the money would be spent (bricks versus programs), with technical decisions made through the elected school board, school administration, and a citizens budget committee.

Brochures designed for mailing can be reconfigured for a walking piece. One will reinforce the other, and the two can be done at the same time by your graphic designer (figures 3.10 and 3.11).

Voters' Pamphlet

If your campaign has an opportunity to be included in the voters' pamphlet, do it. Many voters pay little attention to campaign propaganda and instead rely on the information passed through the county or state elections office in

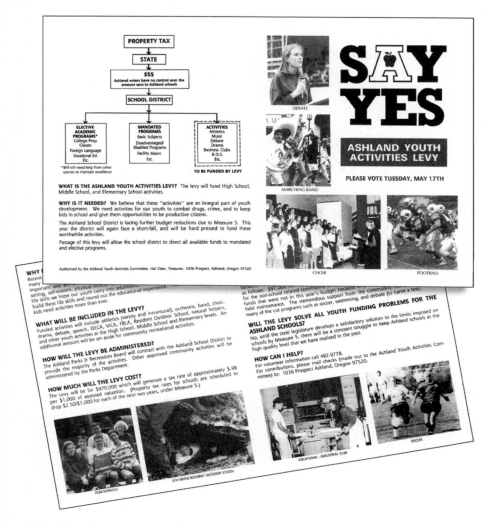

FIGURE 3.9 "Youth Activities Levy" Brochure, Take 2

Example of a single-fold brochure on 8½-by-14-inch paper. After the failure of the first Youth Activities Levy, this brochure was designed to speak more to emotion and less to nuts and bolts. It makes great use of pictures and clearly relays the message: opportunity. (Design by Brian Freeman, Crystal Castle Graphics)

a voters' pamphlet. Although there is a fee, whatever it is, it's worth it. Candidates and campaigns love to whine about a $300 or $500 charge for being in the voters' pamphlet, but don't think twice about spending $10,000 on a direct-mail piece. Although the value of direct mail is debatable, the value of being in a voters' pamphlet is not.

FIGURE 3.10 Front of Full-Color Brochure to Elect Dr. Alan Bates, State Representative

Because the candidate was an unknown, we wanted to push people to open the brochure, so the front is intentionally ambiguous. People did just as we hoped. Voters tested on the layout said, "Who's the candidate?" while flipping it open. (Design by Crystal Castle Graphics)

Getting your candidate or measure into the voters' pamphlet comes with very specific admission criteria, which should be available online from the county, state elections office, or the secretary of state's office. Do not beef up your résumé in a voters' pamphlet with false information. You might get away with that in direct mail or in advertising, but listing false information in a voters' pamphlet is a felony. Nevertheless, there are ways to get the most out of what you have. For example, you attended Harvard as an

FIGURE 3.11 Full-Color Walking Piece for Alan Bates

We wanted this piece to reinforce the brochure (figure 3.10), which was mailed during the primary campaign. (Design by Crystal Castle Graphics)

undergraduate but dropped out before receiving a degree. Later you were accepted into graduate school at Stanford University, solely on the basis of your Graduate Record Examination scores, and there, you received a master's degree in communications. Under "education," you would list "Harvard, undergraduate; Stanford, Masters in Communication." While voters may assume you received an undergraduate degree at Harvard, you never actually say one way or another. If you completed only a couple of years of undergraduate work at a college or university before heading out into the real world, you would simply list the institution without reference to any degree or year of graduation.

In Oregon, the criteria are the same for a primary and a general election voters' pamphlet. Candidates have the option of including a photo, which has to be a certain size. In Oregon, the photo cannot be any more than four years old—although election authorities would be hard-pressed to determine whether a picture is more than four years old unless you used the same one in a previous voters' pamphlet. Photos cannot have any identifying props, such as a stethoscope around a physician's neck or a union bug on your lapel. This is where you will use your best mug shot. Photos of poor quality get worse when put in the voters' pamphlet, so pay attention to this detail.

> "Little things can make as much difference as big things."
> **MALCOLM GLADWELL**

Candidates are given a certain number of words under required and optional categories. Required categories may include occupation, occupational background, educational background, government experience, and community service. Under optional information, you may include a statement from the candidate or testimonials from community leaders that say what you need to have said. If you include testimonials, check to see if the elections department requires a signed form from those you wish to quote in the pamphlet. If so, keep in mind that this takes time and must be handled before the voters' pamphlet deadline. Also, it is important to work with those who are drafting testimonials to include in the pamphlet. Even if you list names, they must each have a signed form. Given word count restrictions and the campaign's need to stay on message, the campaign may need to draft the testimonials and run them by the potential signatory. Keeping control over what goes into the voters' pamphlet is extremely important.

> "First they ignore you; then they laugh at you; then they fight you; then you win."
> **GANDHI**

Primary Voters' Pamphlet

Remember, your objective in the primary is to lock your base. Given that the voters' pamphlet goes to every registered voter and is referred to by most, you need to be in it, whether you have an opponent or not. While your text should keep partisan material to a minimum, those whose names are included in testimonials may be closely aligned with your party. Each testimonial should bring voters on board, from both the name and the text. Here, less is more. On one issue-based campaign in 2006, there was a vote to change the Ashland city charter to a weak-mayor form of government. Initially, I thought about filling the voters' pamphlet just with names in opposition, but ultimately decided that six names were better than a long list of hundreds of names especially since the six were a former congressman; a sitting state senator; a sitting state representative; a current county commissioner; a former, well-known, and well-liked radio personality who was also a former county commissioner; and, finally, a former mayor of Ashland. The voters' pamphlet was the entirety of my campaign in opposition of this shift of power. We turned it away by 28 percent.

General Election Voters' Pamphlet

A statement for the general election voters' pamphlet will look a lot like that for the primary, except for the candidate statement or testimonial section. For the general election, you are looking for names and statements that will give voters in the other party permission to jump ship on party and split their ticket. However, you must also speak to those within your party, so look for balance in the big names you use.

In 2006, Arizona placed on the ballot an initiative that would have awarded $1 million to a random voter each general election as a way to increase voter turnout.

Figure 3.12 is an example of a candidate statement used in the 2002 Oregon voters' pamphlet.

Layout of Voters' Pamphlet

Although much of the voters' pamphlet statement may be dictated by election offices, portions that are not dictated allow for highlighting, italicizing, underlining, and such. So here are a ten dos and don'ts to consider when accenting your portion of the voters' pamphlet.

1. Use a professional photo of the candidate and face it toward his or her admission to the pamphlet.
2. Let others do your bidding through testimonials, and put their names in boldface. When using testimonials and names for an endorsement, always boldface the name, not the testimonial. A common practice is to make boldface what someone says about a candidate rather than the

Occupation: Family physician for 24 years in the Rogue Valley; Oregon State Representative 2001 to present.

Occupational Background: Former Chief of Medicine at Rogue Valley and Providence Medical Centers; Director of Valley Family Practice.

Educational Background: D.O., 1977; College of Osteopathic Medicine, Kansas City, Missouri. B.A., 1969; Central Washington State University.

Prior Government Experience: Eagle Point School Board, 1990 – 2001; Governor's Committee for Excellence in Education, Member (1997 – 1999); Oregon Health Services Commission (1989 – 1999, chair: 1997 – 1999).

Military Service: US Army (1965 – 1967); Served in Vietnam.

What others say:

The **Oregon Business Association** ranked Representative Alan Bates among the top ten legislators in Oregon: courageous, smart, thoughtful.

The **Oregon League of Conservation Voters** gave Rep. Bates an 82% pro-environment rating.

The **Oregon Education Association** rated Dr. Bates in the 90th percentile for his advocacy of public education.

"As a freshman legislator, he shined as he forged consensus legislation ensuring a healthy and competitive workers' compensation market in Oregon. It was Dr. Bates who kept the interests of the insured and the small businesses first."
Coalition for Economic Security for Oregon (Small Business Alert, August 2001)

Because of legislation sponsored or strongly supported by Dr. Alan Bates Oregonians will have:

- increased access to higher education (HB 2521)
- a patient bill of rights (HB 3040)
- reduced prescriptions costs for seniors (HB 3300 & SB 819)
- improved roads and highways (comprehensive transportation package)
- government made more accountable through annual audits (HB 3980)
- a cleaner and safer environment (mercury reduction legislation)

"Representative Alan Bates was one of the most effective and respected freshman legislators in Salem this last session. His success was due to hard work, determination, and his ability and willingness to work with both sides of the aisle.
"Alan consistently placed consensus over conflict, compromise over partisanship, and communities over special interest.

"He deserves our support."
Governor John Kitzhaber, MD

FIGURE 3.12 Example of Voters' Pamphlet Candidate Statement

endorser's name. Do not make this mistake. When entire lines are boldface in a small area, they will make anything in between the bold-face area actually recede and seemingly disappear into the page. You do not want the endorser's names to disappear. If voters do not know a candidate, they will look for prominent names; make these names easy to find.

3. Boldface headings. Voters will often skim a pamphlet, so boldface what you want them to see. The ten-second rule of direct mail applies here as well. Do not randomly make words boldface in the middle of a sentence or a bullet point.

4. Avoid using all caps. An exception may be headings. It looks FRAN-TIC and unsophisticated when words are capped in the middle of sen-

tences. Similarly, do not use exclamation points. Frankly, exclamation points should be removed from all campaign literature, but especially the voters' pamphlet.

5. Do not use narratives. No one cares where you were born and raised or what you were thinking when you moved to your community. Keep the pamphlet crisp with bullet points and breathing space between lines. Break things up.

6. Cite accomplishments. If your candidate has held office and the community is a better place because of legislation he or she designed, be sure to place bill numbers next to the claim.

7. Place your Web page address at the bottom, and place your voter-pamphlet statement on your Web page.

8. Use the available space wisely. Do not bunch everything at the top, leaving white space at the bottom. Lay out your submission so it fits comfortably in the available space.

9. Don't use the voters' pamphlet to attack your opponent. Stay on the sunny side.

10. Don't exaggerate; don't lie.

4

The Volunteer Organization

IN THIS CHAPTER
- Methodology
- Phone Banks
- Phone Bank Locations
- Clerical Workers
- Time Allotments for Volunteer Tasks

No matter where you find your volunteers, a campaign must have a system to organize, direct, and assign responsibilities. The system I describe here can be used either with index cards or with a spreadsheet program such as Excel. The methodology as presented in each of these activities works. If you use it as outlined, you will be able to utilize your volunteers better and run a more effective campaign.

Methodology

Here is how to keep track of campaign volunteers: Using volunteer sign-up sheets, remittance envelopes (the return envelopes sent out for fund-raising and described in more detail in Chapter 5), and lists from other campaigns and support groups, you can begin to amass names of people willing to work, contribute, host a lawn sign, and write letters to the editor. If your campaign is beginning cold, the first thing to do is to contact other campaigns of like-minded people or similar efforts to de-

> "These things are good in little measure and evil in large: yeast, salt and hesitation."
>
> **THE TALMUD**

termine whether those campaigns will give you their list of supporters. Contact all of your friends, local family members, people on committees or organizations in which you participate, business associates, members of your

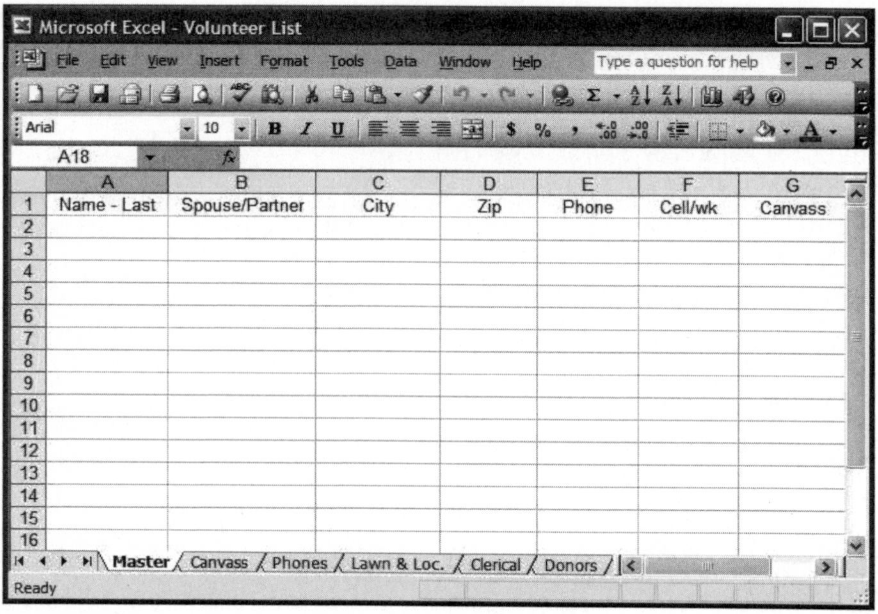

FIGURE 4.1 Example of an Excel Spreadsheet for Keeping Track of Volunteer Workers

church and of any clubs you belong to, and members of organizations with similar political leanings. You can also use names and workers from issue-based campaigns that reflect your campaign's philosophy. Build a database as quickly as possible.

If you are using a spreadsheet program, list all of your contacts, from your initial cold calls as well as from cards, remits, and sign-up sheets generated by yours or other campaigns. This will be your master list. Here are examples of column labels that could run along the top of your master list: last name, first, spouse/partner, street number, street, city, zip, phone. Volunteer work and services categories (which can be filled in with yes or no) include phone work, canvass, clerical, lawn sign, lawn sign install, LTEs (letters to the editor), data input, Web page design/upkeep, and endorsement ad. Finally, a column labeled "$" indicates whether a volunteer has also contributed funds, and a column labeled "notes" may contain brief comments (figure 4.1).

Although you usually include a column for donations ($), remember, this sheet is for *volunteer* activities. The $ column simply tracks which of your

> "To get the most from the people you manage, you must put them in the right spot at the right time."
>
> **JOE TORRE**

volunteers have also contributed money. Since states have specific filing requirements for campaign donors, it is important to keep track of donor information apart from your volunteer spreadsheet. Check with the elections office or secretary of state to determine the required information on each of your contributors. For example, in Oregon a campaign must list the person who signed the check, the contributor's occupation, the address

"It is one of the beautiful compensations of life that no one can sincerely try to help another without helping himself."

RALPH WALDO EMERSON

of the contributor, and the name and address of the contributor's workplace. Specific ways to keep track of your donors and an example of a donation spreadsheet are presented in Chapter 5.

If you are using index cards, place all information for each volunteer on a single card (figure 4.2). Because index cards cannot be sorted by category as easily as spreadsheet entries, you need a system that will give you the volunteer information at a glance. Before I moved all my systems to Excel, I color-coded my cards with colored stickers. Working from the upper right-hand corner toward the left, fold the stickers over the card's top edge so that they look like half circles on each side of your card; this way the color coding can be seen in a glance. For each person contacted, an index card will be generated. Keep all cards together in one box.

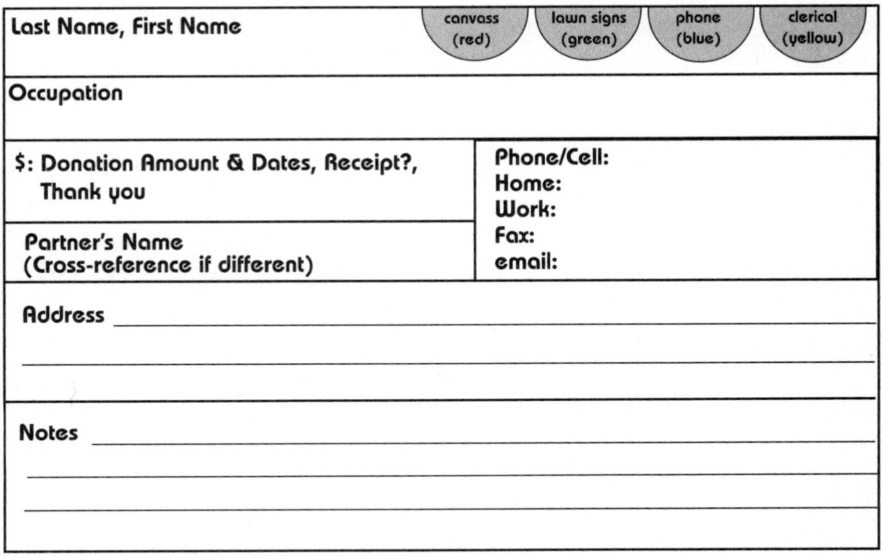

Last Name, First Name	canvass (red)	lawn signs (green)	phone (blue)	clerical (yellow)
Occupation				

$: Donation Amount & Dates, Receipt?, Thank you	Phone/Cell: Home: Work:
Partner's Name (Cross-reference if different)	Fax: email:

Address _____

_____

Notes _____

_____

_____

FIGURE 4.2 Example of a 3-by-5-Inch Contact Card

The color coding indicates which campaign activities the volunteer will work on, such as lawn sign placement, phone banks, canvassing, or clerical work. Use a color scheme that works for you and your campaign, but keep in mind that using more than four colors can easily crowd a 3-by-5-inch card.

The "notes" section of your spreadsheet or card is important. This is where you note such information as "Won't canvass hills"; "Don't call early a.m."; "Don't call after 8:00 p.m."; "Horrible on phones"; and "Has three staple guns." Also use this section to make a note when someone has been rude ("Do not contact again"), so that other campaign volunteers needn't be subjected to verbal abuse. After hundreds of phone calls, it is impossible to remember such details if a record is not kept somewhere.

Organize Volunteer Activities

Once information is in your spreadsheet or on the index cards, you're ready to set up volunteer activities. If you are using Excel, follow these directions carefully: The spreadsheet containing the information about the volunteers will say "Sheet 1" in the tab at the bottom of the Excel document. Right-click the "Sheet 1" tab and rename it "Master" or "Raw Data." It is important that one sheet remain intact in case subsequent sorting goes awry and the original information has to be retrieved for the list to be rebuilt. Using Access, instead of Excel, eliminates this sort of problem. Naturally, as your pool of volunteers grows, you will add names to the Master sheet, and over time you will add notes and make address changes, but you never want to actually "sort" this list for any activity.

> "You can't have divided authority around a campaign headquarters."
>
> **JAMES FARLEY,** campaign manager for Franklin D. Roosevelt

Once you have renamed Sheet 1 as "Master" (or whatever name you choose), go to the top and click on the empty corner in the upper left-hand corner of the sheet, between the row beginning with A and the column beginning with 1. This will highlight your entire master list; now click Edit, click Copy, click the tab for Sheet 2, click the same empty square in the upper left (now this sheet will be highlighted), click Edit, and click Paste. You now have a duplicate of your master list that you can sort and play with all you want.

If you want to set up a phone bank, highlight all the data that you have entered (you need to do this manually—not by clicking the upper right-hand corner this time—because Excel will only sort a defined area). Click Data, click Sort, and under "Sort by," select the letter of the phone bank column. Then highlight the cells only of those who are willing to phone, and copy them to a third sheet, which you can label "Phones." Go through this list and delete all but the name and phone number(s), and add a column labeled "CB?" (call back?). Obviously, if I am just contacting people to see if they will help in a phone bank, I don't need the information in all the other categories listed on my master list. Before printing this page, be sure to insert gridlines (on the page setup menu), as they make the list a lot easier to read. Also, increase the width of the columns, so that you can easily write information as needed. Repeat this process for whatever activity you wish to undertake.

> "With their budgets warped towards media spending, candidates and their organizations are led to measure the progress of their campaigns only in terms of dollars raised and tracking polls. Many [candidates] lose due to their failure to organize large numbers of people in their campaigns."
> **MORTON BLACKWELL,**
> the Leadership Institute

When using the index-card system to organize campaign volunteers, create campaign activity cards with 5-by-8-inch lined index cards set up as shown in figure 4.3. The following process works for activities such as phone banks, clerical work, canvassing, and lawn sign placement or maintenance. Once you have the 5-by-8-inch cards prepared, copy the names and phone numbers from the appropriate 3-by-5-inch cards onto them or a sheet of paper. (The 3-by-5-inch cards should never get far from their box.)

The following recommendations apply to both spreadsheet and index card systems. Whatever the activity, have a number of dates lined up for it so that

Activity: Canvass 10/14				
NAME	PHONE #	CB?	9:30 AM–12:00	2:30–5:00 PM

FIGURE 4.3 Example of a 5-by-8-Inch Canvass Activity Card

each volunteer is called only once for scheduling. When calling for an ongoing activity such as canvassing, have four or five dates and times, so if one date doesn't work, another may. If a volunteer can do none of the times offered, it is important to determine why and to note this on the card or spreadsheet. If it is a temporary scheduling conflict, note when the conflict will be resolved. However, if it sounds as though the volunteer will never do the activity, offer another campaign job. Keep this person on the phone until it can be determined what is going on. If it is clear that he or she will never volunteer, that person's name should be removed from the volunteer list. For now, however, the name remains on your working list with a line through it so that you will remember that you called. If you do not do this, you will forget and call again. If you are working directly from a list on a computer rather than a printout, you can distinguish those who have been called and who will never volunteer by highlighting the cell and changing the color of the font.

A couple of days before the activity, call back every volunteer who agreed to work and place a check in the "CB?" column. It is best to actually talk to the worker on the call-back, so leave a message only as a last resort. On the call-back, do not ask workers if they still intend to help. Do not even call to remind them directly of the upcoming volunteer activity. They said they would do it, and the tone of your conversation should reflect that verbal contract. Plus, if they are very organized, they will resent the call. Instead, think of this call as a small rattling of the cage and make it about something else: Remind them to bring a clipboard, or ask if they mind doing hills, or check to make sure that they were given the correct meeting place or the correct time. Whatever it is, it's your fault or it's about a small detail that wasn't addressed in the first conversation. You're just checking to make sure the information given previously was correct. If the volunteer has forgotten, the call serves as a reminder. If the person inadvertently made other plans, this is your opportunity to reschedule. Potential no-shows, discovered by a phone call, are incredibly easy to reschedule.

Applying the Methodology

Every campaign consists of basic campaign activities, such as these:

- Running phone banks
- Canvassing the voters
- Developing campaign events
- Designing ads or other media
- Organizing clerical support (including thank-you notes)
- Preparing, installing, and maintaining lawn signs

- Raising money
- Data input
- Web page upkeep

Each of these activities is volunteer intensive. You can apply the techniques described above to find and keep track of volunteers, but each activity requires specific techniques. The method described above will be applied throughout this handbook to organize each activity.

Phone Banks

Phone banks can be used throughout a campaign and are the most efficient way to retrieve information in a short time. They can be used to get a head count for a fund-raiser, to get lawn sign locations, to raise money, and to get the campaign more volunteers. If you plan to do a get-out-the-vote (GOTV) effort on Election Day, you will have to identify voters who intend to vote for your candidate or cause. This can be done while canvassing, but it is easier and far more efficient to do it by phone. The GOTV effort itself is primarily done by phone. When signing up volunteers, assure them that they will receive training before actually working on the phones.

> "Let us endeavor so to live that when we come to die even the undertaker will be sorry."
> **MARK TWAIN**

Generally, I schedule a phone banker to work for one hour and fifteen minutes (fifteen minutes for training and then one hour on the phone). Almost anyone will give up an hour or so for a campaign they believe in, and if it turns out that the volunteer is bad on the phone, an hour is plenty. However, if I am desperate or conducting fast, important calls, as in a GOTV effort, I will put seasoned callers on the phone for up to two hours. A caller who has worked for me in the past will let me know if the full two hours is too long. I then have others scheduled in to replace a caller coming off the phones early.

Have two to three shifts each evening. Volunteers must arrive fifteen minutes before their shift for training. No one likes to go on the phone cold, so people rarely miss training when it's offered and expected. Should time allow, consider doing a role-play with your volunteers—having one volunteer pretend to call another.

Each phone bank should have a "lead." This is the person responsible for unlocking the doors of the phone bank location, training volunteers, picking up after the volunteers leave, calling the next evening's callers, answering questions for phone bankers, and, finally, closing up the phone bank. Training begins by handing a phone banker a brochure and an instruction sheet, which should include prepared scripts. If the campaign is using volunteers to conduct a poll, a prepared script must be followed to the letter; in all other phone bank activities, however, a caller who ad-libs will generally do best.

Once the volunteers have read the instructions, do a walk-through of what is expected on the phones, and explain any peculiarities the phone system may have (such as dialing 9 first). Tell volunteers where the bathroom is, and let them know that you will be providing water. For the lead person, have a list of all the details that need to be shared with a new volunteer before he or she starts working the phone.

After a fifteen-minute training session, volunteers begin calling. The first twenty to thirty minutes that volunteers are on the phone, the lead should circulate, answer questions, and take water to people rather than making calls. The lead will have only ten or fifteen minutes between shifts, as the second crew will arrive for training fifteen minutes early, or forty-five minutes into the hour of the previous shift's calls. This way, exactly one hour after the first shift starts, volunteers get a tap on the shoulder from someone on the next shift, and they are off the phones.

> "It does not require a majority to prevail, but rather an irate, tireless minority keen to set brush fires in people's minds."
> —— **SAMUEL ADAMS** (1722–1803)

Never tell people that you want them for a specific amount of time, then push them to stay longer. This is how a campaign can lose volunteers. When you ask someone to work for you, you have made a verbal contract with him or her for a specific job and a specific amount of time. Don't nudge.

Once the second shift is in place, happily making calls, and supplied with water, and all campaign questions asked and answered, the lead must then call all those listed to volunteer on phone banks for the following evening. Giving a quick reminder of place and scheduled time for work avoids no-shows.

Note: Do not expect your phone bank people to look up phone numbers. Use a clerical team or a voter database to do that ahead of time.

Phone Bank Training

The following is an example of what you might prepare for your volunteers who are phoning for the campaign:

Thank you for your help. Tonight we are calling people who live on arterial streets in hopes of beefing up our lawn sign list. While the lists you're calling have the same party registration as our candidate, they have not been previously identified as a supporter. Just so you know, that may make some

"Hello, this is (your name). Tonight I am volunteering to help the Alan Bates campaign. As you may know, Alan is running for reelection to the House, and I was hoping you would consider having one of his lawn signs in front of your home."

If no, thank the caller and ask if Alan can count on his or her support in the upcoming election.

If yes, verify address and ask if there are any special instructions for where and how the homeowner would like the sign placed. Then say:

"Someone will be coming by to place the sign about six weeks before the election. We will also have some maintenance crews checking signs from time to time. However, if you would occasionally check the sign and set it up if it falls over, that would be very helpful. When the sign is placed, there will be a note left on your door so you can contact the campaign should it disappear or be vandalized. Thanks for helping us out."

BOX 4.1 Example of Phone Instructions and Script for Lawn Sign Locations

Before You Pick Up the Phone—

1. *Be proud of what you are doing.* You are working for a cause you believe in. You are on the front line of a campaign.

2. *Think about what has motivated you to give up your time to work for the candidate (or ballot measure).* People will ask how a candidate stands on a particular issue. While you cannot speak directly to that, you can share why *you* are working for this individual (or cause).

3. *Identify yourself only as a volunteer working for the campaign.* In general, you want the candidate's name to make it into the consciousness of the voter, not yours, unless, of course, you know the person.

4. *No matter what else happens, get something from the individual before you get off the phone.* "You can't canvass, ever? How about a lawn sign?" "You have a bad lawn-sign location? Do you have a friend who might want one?" "Can we use your name on the endorsement ad?" "Would you make a contribution?" Whatever. You want them in on the campaign with that single call, or to know how they will be voting. (This is helpful information for the campaign.)

5. And thank you for taking the time to help in this important cause.

BOX 4.2 Example of Phone Bank Instructions

of the calls a little harder. Please make a note on your list next to the name of the voter whether he or she will take a lawn sign, and if not, whether that person will be supporting our candidate.

Boxes 4.1 and 4.2 are examples of materials given to phone bankers.

What you ask for will vary according to the phone bank. You could be calling for lawn sign locations, money, volunteer workers, a head count for an event, or voter ID (that is, finding out whether or not a voter supports your campaign). Think about your mission, and prepare a short introduction for the caller.

Phone Bank Locations

It can be difficult to locate enough phones for an effective phone session. I have found that real estate offices work best because people love to have company when calling, and real estate offices usually have five or more lines in the same room. Law offices also may be an option, but in the typical office, callers wouldn't be able to see each other. Also, many law offices will be off-limits because of confidentiality concerns. Sometimes campaign headquarters for a bigger race (such as a presidential or gubernatorial contest) will let you use an office. You might also try labor unions and physicians' or insurance offices. In the past, many businesses that supported a cause or a candidate would open their doors for phone banks after hours. However, the advent of caller ID has made it tougher and tougher to find such locations. Still, it never hurts to ask; on one campaign I was running, a Realtor who was working for the opposition let us use his phones because we were friends.

> "Make no little plans; they have no magic to stir men's blood. . . . Make big plans, aim high in hope and work."
> — **DANIEL H. BURNHAM**

A word of caution on real estate offices: In the last campaign cycle, while we were working phones at a real estate office we had used for years, one of the agents dropped in to pick something up. The next day, I received a call from the broker, who said that the agents in his office were apoplectic because one of our callers was from another real estate office, and they worried that this "competitor" could avail herself of secret documents.

In 2004, I installed two additional phone lines in my home (I already had three) because I got tired of getting bumped around on phone bank locations. By 2006, with so many cell phone users and plans with unlimited minutes, I reduced my house lines to two and people brought their own phone. By 2008, we bought prepaid cell phones by the box and used those. When you think about it, a phone bank location can be anywhere if the phones are portable.

> "There is as much greatness of mind in acknowledging a good turn, as in doing it."
> — **SENECA**

Scripts

Wherever your phone bank is located, the important part of campaign phoning is to have an effective message. You should have scripts made up in advance for each campaign activity. While it is preferable to have callers ad-lib, they generally need a prepared script for the first few calls. It gets much easier after that. I also don't have the volunteers ask the person, "How are you doing tonight?" The reality is that the volunteer doesn't care, and the person on the other end knows it. When I am calling for money, the calls will be a bit longer and more involved, so I usually start by asking the person who answers if they have a moment to talk. However, with volunteer recruitment, the calls are so short that I just cut to the chase. The following paragraphs suggest some sample scripts for typical campaign phone sessions.

> "The whole is greater than the sum of its parts."
> **BUCKMINSTER FULLER**

Lawn Sign Location. "Hello, I'm a volunteer working for the Kate Newhall campaign for state senate. Tonight we're looking for locations for lawn signs. Will you be supporting Kate in the general election? Great, could we place a lawn sign? Let me verify your address. Someone will be coming by about six weeks before the election to place it. We also have a crew who will be maintaining these signs; however, if it needs some attention, maybe you could help with it. Great. Thanks."

Special Activity. "Hello, I'm a volunteer working for the Alan Bates campaign for state senate. Did you receive the invitation for the campaign dinner this Saturday? The restaurant needs a pretty accurate head count, so we're trying to get an idea of the number of supporters who will be attending the dinner for Alan. Will you be joining us?"

> "It is better to wear out than to rust out."
> **RICHARD CUMBERLAND**
> (seventeenth century)

Canvassing. "Hello, I'm a volunteer helping in the Peter Buckley campaign. We are hoping to canvass the city this Saturday with a last-minute door hanger and need about eighty-five volunteers. There will be no door-knocking, just great exercise. Can you help?"

Another. "Hello, I'm a volunteer working for the 'JoAnne Verger for Senate' campaign. Our notes indicate that you might be willing to canvass. Is that correct?" [Answer] "Great. I have a number of dates for some upcoming canvasses. Do you have your calendar handy?"

GOTV for Absentee and Mail-in Ballots. "Hello, I'm a volunteer from the Jeff Barker campaign. We're down here working on phone banks tonight to turn out as many of Jeff's supporters as possible. As of a couple of days ago, your ballot had not yet been received at county elections; is it possible you still have it at home?"

Voter ID. "Hello, I'm a volunteer working for the Amy Amrhein campaign. As you may know, Amy is a candidate for school board. Do you know if you'll be supporting her this November?" [Yes, No, Need more info]

Undecided: With any of these scripts, if I call and discover that someone is undecided or leaning, I ask whether the person would like more information from the candidate or campaign committee to help in deciding. Finally, whatever a potential supporter might say, I ask my volunteers to make a note so that the campaign can follow up if need be.

Negative Response: Get off the phone as quickly as possible, and make a note for the campaign.

Clerical Workers

The clerical team is an extremely important part of your campaign. Normally, you think of people sitting around, addressing, stamping, and stuffing envelopes. While these tasks might make up the bulk of your clerical team's work, you should think of this group in broader terms.

Wherever I can break activities down into more manageable units, I do so. For example, on the day that lawn signs go up, you *cannot* expect your lawn sign team to arrive early in the morning, staple lawn signs, organize lists, and then head out for two hours of stake pounding. Each of these functions is very different and should be treated differently.

> "It's not very difficult to persuade people to do what they already long to do."
> — **ALDOUS HUXLEY**

Your clerical team can come in days ahead of time to staple lawn signs or bolt them to the stakes, depending on the type of sign you use. They can come in on still another day to help organize the lists, maps, and locations of where those signs are going.

Your clerical team is crucial in keeping your campaign tight and organized. Use them creatively wherever they can help with your workload or with the organization of an upcoming activity. Here are some examples of how the clerical team can be used:

- Staple lawn signs at the corners (if using poly tag)
- Attach lawn signs to stakes (if using corrugated)
- Look up phone numbers for an upcoming phone bank
- Assemble maps for a canvass
- Attach inserts in the brochures for a canvass
- Write thank-you notes for money, lawn sign locations, or volunteers' time
- Stuff, stamp, and address a mailing
- Prepare items for a fund-raiser, such as a yard sale or an auction
- Set up for a campaign gathering—decorate, print name tags, etc.

To set up a campaign activity requiring clerical workers, contact people who have indicated they will help with clerical work. If you need additional volunteers, try the League of Women Voters, your friends and neighbors, and senior groups that support you. Given how much fun a clerical work party can be, it is usually pretty easy to turn out a crowd.

A clerical work party is a social time in campaigns; it's a time to chat with friends while helping with a cause everyone supports. It's a time to share war stories about canvassing, to talk news, to gossip, or to do whatever else while having coffee and cookies and doing a mindless task. These meetings are enjoyable and highly productive for the small effort involved.

It is important for people to be comfortable while working and sitting for two or more hours, so be sure to

> "We are here to add to what we can to life, not to get what we can from it."
> **WILLIAM OSLER**

have enough table space for each volunteer. Do not do clerical work in an already cluttered house. Because no one's back is getting younger—and many of the clerical volunteers are older—I take the time to put together a comfortable work area. Avoid having people work on their laps in soft, overstuffed couches and chairs; they will not be as productive. This is akin to cleaning house or doing yard work in flip-flops—you can do it, just not as efficiently.

Have some snacks around—coffee, tea, cookies, and the like—but not on the table where work is being conducted.

Have everything set up. Do not waste your volunteers' time.

Do one activity at a time. If the task is to get out a mailing or to staple lawn signs, do just that. When the task is done—and usually they're done ahead of schedule—don't bring out one more thing for people to do. Remember, as with any other task in a campaign, you have made a verbal contract with your workers. Once they are captive workers in your home, to ask them to work past the designated time or beyond the designated task creates hard feelings. Workers who complete a task early and then go home feel good about their participation and feel that they are helping in a well-organized effort.

Make sure that you have all the necessary materials at each station, so that people are not idle. Have extras of everything you need—staplers, sponges, stamps, envelopes, telephone books, rubber bands, electric screwdrivers, drywall screws, washers, or whatever else the task might require.

Time Allotments for Volunteer Tasks

Below are some general guidelines for what volunteers can do in a designated amount of time. From here, you can calculate how many people you'll need to accomplish a task in the time available. For the task to be completed by a certain date, work your way backward from that date so that you have enough time to complete the task, given your resources and task goal—number of calls to make, signs to put up, homes to canvass, and so on.

> "Luck is the crossroads where preparation and opportunity meet."
> — ANONYMOUS

Phone Banks

In general, each volunteer can complete twenty to thirty calls per hour, depending on the nature of the calls. In a GOTV effort, people can make fifty calls during a ninety-minute shift. So, for example, if you want to make four thousand calls by Election Day and have only one phone bank location with six phones, you will need people on all six phones, for two ninety-minute shifts, for seven nights. Naturally, if you have more phones or another phone bank location, the number of calling nights goes down and the number of volunteers per shift goes up.

> "The feeble tremble before opinion, the foolish defy it, the wise judge it, the skillful direct it."
> — JEANNE ROLAND

Canvassing

Some precincts are huge, either by population or geography, and can have anywhere from three hundred to three thousand voters per precinct, or 120 to 1,500 homes. You can use voter lists to get an accurate number of houses in each precinct.

Two types of canvassing are used for our purposes here: a knock, and a simple drop without talking.

Knock. Depending on how hilly, rural, or compact a neighborhood is, canvassers can cover 10 to 15 houses per hour. That means that a precinct with 120 to 200 houses would require six canvassers working two to three hours each to cover the distance.

> "The success of any kind of social epidemic is heavily dependent on the involvement of people with a particular and rare set of social gifts."
> **MALCOLM GLADWELL**

Drop. A literature drop can be done quite a bit faster than a knock canvass. With a drop, again depending on street grade and the density of homes, a canvasser can cover thirty to forty-five homes in an hour.

Clerical (Direct Mail)

A mailing of five hundred requires a fifteen-person clerical team working one hour to stuff, stamp, seal, and address envelopes.

Lawn Signs

One lawn sign team—a driver and a pounder—can put up about twelve lawn signs an hour. So, for example, if you have two hundred lawn signs to place, you will need sixteen people (eight teams) working two hours each.

5

Fund-Raising

Although this handbook suggests a number of ways to stretch your campaign dollars, no matter how many volunteers or friends with special talents you may have, eventually you will have to spend money to get your message out. Production and media buys require up-front, cash-in-hand transactions. The U.S. Postal Service will not send direct mail on a promise, and most places that print anything for campaigns require payment when you pick up the product. Although volunteers can cut your debt load, the larger the campaign, the more these volunteers become a valuable resource not to be squandered.

> "Apart from the ballot box, philanthropy presents the one opportunity the individual has to express his meaningful choice over the direction in which our society will progress."
> **GEORGE KIRSTEIN**

The bottom line is that if you want to get your message and your candidate's face into the public view, you must raise and spend a certain threshold of money to be competitive. What that threshold is depends on your race, the voting population, and which campaign activities you intend to implement.

I have worked on campaigns where money was no object and others where every decision was a financial trade-off, and, yes, it's more fun to work on campaigns with ample funds. Most important, money can buy you the opportunity, ability, and freedom to respond immediately to anything coming at the campaign.

While there are always stories of winners being grossly outspent, history indicates that the inverse is more often true, especially as you move up the food chain. According to the Center for Responsive Politics, in the 2002 midterm elections, "just under 95 percent of U.S. House races and 76 percent of Senate races were won by the candidate who spent the most money."[1] Subsequent election cycles reveal little variation in the ratio of winners to losers based on money spent, according to OpenSecrets.com and the Center for Responsive Politics.[2]

In the eleven close Oregon House races in the 2002 general election, only four who were outspent survived. Of those races, two of the losers had extenuating circumstances under which no amount of money would have delivered the votes.

Both the message and the quality of candidates (or issues) matter when it comes to raising money. However, campaign organization is a major factor in determining whether contributors are willing to "invest" in your campaign throughout the campaign cycle. Relationships that develop as a result of the candidate, the campaign team, your message, and your organization will bring in early money and early endorsements from individuals, companies, political action committees, and formal organizations. Indeed, a well-run, well-organized, professionally executed campaign does not go unnoticed by the electorate. The voters correctly assess the job a candidate will do once in office by the campaign he or she runs to achieve that office. That is true from president of the United States to the county tax assessor. Further, when voters determine that a campaign is disciplined, they equate that with winning and contribute.

Early Endorsements = Early Money = Early Media Buys

Early money is a way to communicate to the public that a cause or candidate has the necessary support to pull off a win. Also, throughout the campaign, major donors can serve as another type of communication tool with the electorate. For example, in Oregon, individuals who give more than $100 must be listed separately on the contributions and expenditures forms (C&Es) filed with the secretary of state. If this is true in your state, look for well-respected people whose names can draw votes, and ask them to give an amount that will get them listed in a prominent way in the local paper, which in turn may bring in money from their friends and business associates. Obviously, this amount varies with the type of race. A $250 contribution may be news for a city councilor or alderman in a small town, but not in a large city mayoral race or congressional district race.

> "Too often leaders are soft on issues and hard on people. We need to be hard on issues and soft on people."
> **CHARLES MACLEAN,**
> Philanthropy Now Consulting

Unfortunately, contributions from individual donors tend to arrive late in a campaign, as things begin to heat up. When supporters see the campaign in the paper and on television or hear it on the radio, they know that this takes money. What they may not realize is that media time must be bought weeks in advance. *Early money is critical to a successful media campaign.* That is why many candidates take out personal loans to get their campaign rolling.

The urgency to raise money for media buys changes with each election cycle and is influenced by other races on the ballot that may be competing for media time. For example, in the presidential cycle, all down-ballot races in our area have to buy television by August to secure time for the general election. In 2008, one of my clients decided not to buy TV, and when he changed his mind in October, basically Saturday cartoons were left. Talk about testing the "trickle up" theory.

Know the law: In some states, you may not legally begin collecting money until you have filed with the county clerk, city recorder, or secretary of state. However, from the moment you decide to run or work on a ballot measure, you can begin calling and lining up pledges that will come in as soon as you file.

Campaign Budget

It is pretty easy to put together a cursory budget sheet based on the activities you intend to conduct throughout the campaign; all it takes is a few phone calls.

Figure 5.1 is an actual budget sheet from a 1998 city council race, which I updated by calling around. While the original brochure was black-and-white, I have listed costs for a full-color brochure. If your budget is tight, using black-and-white instead of color will cut the printing costs. This race

Campaign Activity	Cost in Dollars
Brochure	
Layout and design	110.00
Printing (8,000 full-color brochures)	2,936.00
Ads (three)	
Layout and design	225.00
Newspaper: three ads, run three times each	1,500.00
Lawn signs	
Design	100.00
Printing (250 at $2.52 each, two-colors, two sides)	630.00
Stakes (250 at $20 per bundle of fifty)	100.00
Hardware	30.00
Voter lists from county for absentee, GOTV	50.00
Direct mail: one piece (postcard)	
Postage, layout, mail charge	1,240.00
Photocopying misc. office supplies	60.00
Candidate photo session	500.00
Voters' pamphlet	100.00
TOTAL	7,746.00

FIGURE 5.1 Example of a Campaign Budget for a Candidate in Small-City Race

covered a city of 19,000 people and 8,000 homes. There was no TV or radio advertising.

Figure 5.2 is the budget from a countywide, issue-based campaign. The county covers about 2,000 square miles and has about 180,000 residents and some 100,000 registered voters. Because of the size of the county and limited volunteer help, lawn signs gave way to 4-by-4-foot and 4-by-8-foot field signs placed along highways.

In 2002, hotly contested Oregon House races came in around $225,000 each for the general election. By 2008, this doubled. On the high end, a Portland metro-area campaign bumped up against a half million in 2002, and on the low end, a couple of races in the outlying areas spent less than $150,000. Figures 5.3, 5.4, and 5.5 are examples of budget components for a 2004 state senate race. Figure 5.3 is the expense portion, Figure 5.4 income portion, and Figure 5.5 the media detail. In this particular race, we came in on budget and overcame a 4 percent registration advantage, winning by 2 percent. Media was bought in August.

> "It's difficulties that show what men are."
> ————— **EPICTETUS**, Greek philosopher

Campaign Activity	Cost in Dollars
Direct Mail	
Fundraiser letter: 1,000 pieces, three times	
Design	300.00
Printing and postage, plus remit envelope	1,500.00
General mailer: full color, 50,000 pieces	
Design	300.00
Printing and mailing	10,000.00
General mailer: black-and-white, 50,000 pieces	
Design	300.00
Printing and mailing	9,000.00
Targeted mailer: black-and-white, 25,000 pieces	
Design	300.00
Printing and mailing	4,000.00
Walking/info piece: 5-by-11, color, 30,000 pieces	
Design	300.00
Printing	2,000.00
Precinct Analysis	900.00
Voters' Pamphlet	300.00
Big Signs (200)	5,000.00
GOTV	
Voter registration database from county	100.00
GOTV inactive reports (four reports)	400.00
Data consultant	3,000.00
Media Advertising	
TV ad development: four ads at $1,000 each	4,000.00
Cable buys	6,000.00
Network buys	12,000.00
Radio development: five spots at $250 each	1,250.00
Buys	4,000.00
Newspaper	
Ashland	3,500.00
Medford	9,000.00
Other Advertising	
Insert in chamber newsletter	75.00
Car/business signs, 500 pieces	200.00
Campaign Management	10,500.00
Office Supplies	200.00
Celebration Party	200.00
	TOTAL 88,625.00

FIGURE 5.2 Example of a Countywide, Issue-Based Campaign Budget

Campaign Activity Expense	Amount in Dollars
Direct mail: 11 pieces 125,000	50,000.00
Design	5,500.00
Direct-mail fund-raising	3,950.00
Polling	6,000.00
Voter ID (18,000)	7,000.00
Printing cartridges	1,000.00
Letterhead envelopes	704.00
Headquarters	1,500.00
Data services	—
Volunteer support	
Food, refreshments (war room)	600.00
Field signs	
Design and layout	100.00
Printing	2,500.00
Staff	
CPA	1,000.00
Campaign manager	30,000.00
Field coordinator	7,500.00
Activities coordinator	3,000.00
Media (see media budget, figure 5.5)	102,478.00
Office supplies	
Postage, pens, software	500.00
Telephone, fax	1,500.00
Staples, envelopes, etc.	2,500.00
Paper	400.00
TOTAL	227,732.00
Anticipated and available income	158,915.09
Difference (must raise)	68,816.91

FIGURE 5.3 Example of an Expense Budget for a State Senate Campaign

To get an estimate of how much money your campaign will need, consider talking with people who have previously run a similar race. Some will have budgets with predicted and actual money spent. The county clerk or state election office should have C&E forms on file, and a little time with these records provides an opportunity to reconstruct what was spent, and where. The following sections show how you might go about determining a budget for specific campaign activities.

Fund-Raising Activity	Cost in Dollars	Anticipated Income in Dollars (and Amt. in Bank)
Donor/volunteer mailing (600 pieces)	600.00	6,000.00
Physician mailing (500 pieces)	500.00	6,000.00
DO mailing (200 pieces)	200.00	4,000.00
State/nation physician mailing (1,000 pieces)	500.00	1,000.00
Pharmacists	150.00	1,000.00
Medford Education Association		3,000.00
Oregon Nurses Association		20,000.00
Oregon League of Environmental Voters		
Oregon Education Association		
Pledges		14,600.00
Money in the bank		90,840.09
Deposit 8/27		3,475.00
Events		
Chiropractors		2,000.00
Portland physician event		3,000.00
Ashland physician event		1,000.00
Optometrists (20 pieces)		1,000.00
Owed for Medford fund-raiser	1,000.00	
Misc. gatherings	1,000.00	2,000.00
TOTAL	3,950.00	158,915.09

FIGURE 5.4 Example of a Fund-Raising Budget for a State Senate Campaign

Media Component	Buys in Dollars
Charter	6,600.00
AFN	4,000.00
FOX	23,400.00
KTVL	25,228.00
Radio	20,000.00
TV production (3 @ $1500 each)	4,500.00
Radio production (3 @ $250 each)	750.00
Print media	
Ashland Daily Tidings	5,000.00
Medford Mail Tribune	10,000.00
Layout and design	1,000.00
Inserts	1,000.00
GOTV Post-it notes	1,000.00
TOTAL	102,478.00

FIGURE 5.5 Example of a Media Budget Detail for a State Senate Campaign

Brochure

1. Find another brochure with a design and layout you like.
2. Get a price quote from a graphic designer for something comparable that's camera ready.
3. Determine which precincts you will target (you will determine this from your precinct analysis, as described in Chapter 1); using voter registration lists for those precincts, calculate how many brochures you'll need to print. Call a printer and get a price quotation; you can always have more done later, so don't get carried away. Remember that the number of registered voters and that of actual homes are two different things. You need enough brochures so that one will go to each home, regardless of how many registered voters live there. To get the actual number of unduplicated households, try calling an electric utility company, the county clerk, or a mail house.
4. Call a photographer, and ask how much a photo shoot will cost.

Things that affect the cost of a brochure:

- Color costs; the choices, in descending order of cost, are full-color, spot color, and black-and-white.
- Paper can have a dramatic impact on cost as well as printed quality. Be careful not to use paper that will absorb the ink too much. I think the feel of the paper is very important, and I tend to spend a little more for a more professional feel. You're looking for something along the lines of 80# Vellum Bristol.
- Does it need to be folded or cut? Each of these brings additional charges. Cutting is cheaper than folding. Die cuts for a door hanger also come at a cost.

In 2008 a candidate for mayor of Ashland had his graphic designer create a brochure that he could e-mail to friends and supporters. The idea was that they would print as many as necessary for their own canvassing in support of the candidate. The brochure (obviously, black-and-white) dictated the lawn signs, which were also black-and-white paper, as were the newspaper inserts.

Lawn Signs

Use steps similar to those listed above for the brochure. First, determine the total number of signs you will need. I have worked on campaigns with as many as one lawn sign for every thirty homes and others where we had as few as one for every sixty homes. It really depends on whether you can get the locations for signs and whether you're in an urban race or one with an urban/rural mix. Does the race warrant a large number of signs? Again, one way to determine the number of signs you need is to call someone who conducted a similar campaign covering the same geographical area and ask how many signs were put up. While you're on the phone, ask for their list of lawn sign locations.

Once you know the number of signs, get the same number of stakes plus a few more. Signs run around $4.00 to $5.00 each with stakes and the miscellaneous stuff you will need for them. Unlike brochures, short runs for signs may take as long as two weeks to print, and they can be costly. For example, in southern Oregon, a run of twenty-five signs costs $13 per sign, whereas the cost for a run of five hundred is $2.45 per sign. So get enough printed the first time.

If you need hardware or staple guns and staples to attach the signs to the stakes, price these items and list the cost. If you end up using staples and staple guns, be sure to call any friends you have in construction and ask if you can borrow their staple guns. Better yet, ask them if they will help to put up the signs and bring the staple gun to use. *Label all borrowed tools.*

If you have no locations for signs, you can buy lists of registered voters

> "It's not how much money you raise. It's how you spend your money."
>
> **JEFFREY GILDENHORN,** former candidate for mayor of Washington, D.C.

from the county and call those living on arterials for possible locations. Ideally you would get locations from other campaigns, but in my first race for mayor, that wasn't an option. Volunteers went down the voter registration list, cold-calling those on arterials—a brutal but very effective technique.

In general, try to think of every little thing you will need to do to complete a specific activity. After you have done these tasks, take an hour or two and call around for some prices.

In a small community, a fairly reliable ballpark figure of the amount of money you will need to raise is $1 per household in the voting district. If you have strong opposition, especially in a bigger field, such as a state senate race or state representative race, you will need up to $50 per household. Remember, this figure is for households, not voters. The type and number of media buys you plan to make will greatly influence the amount you need. Similarly, the number of direct-mail pieces you send will influence the final budget figures. If a mail house is to handle all of your mail pieces, it will cost more than if volunteers at your local party headquarters label and mail campaign pieces. As your target population increases, you may find an economy of scale. For example, an Oregon House race with 40,000 voters will cost anywhere from $3 to $20 per registered voter. A county race of 100,000 registered voters may come in around $80,000, or $0.80 per registered voter. Budgets are more a function of the race than anything else.

Everything you do in a political campaign requires money. While many of the people who work for you will also give you money, the bulk of it will come from people who are not directly involved as volunteers.

I never apologize or feel as if I am begging when I ask for money for a candidate or ballot measure. I assume that the potential contributor wants my candidate in office (or wants the benefits of the ballot measure) and is willing to back up that desire with money. When I ask for money, I think of it as providing an opportunity for the voter to get involved at a level other than the voting booth. I also look at a request for money as less demanding than a request for an individual's time. The reality is this: If you can find excellent candidates to serve in office implementing programs that you support, more power to them; do all you can to help get them there. And money is a lot easier to give than time.

> "The highest use of capital is not to make more money, but to make money do more for the betterment of life."
> — HENRY FORD

In Oregon, anyone who contributes to a political campaign may file for a state income tax refund of up to $50. If a husband and wife file a joint tax return, they can get a refund of $100. Sadly, only about 16 percent of citizens take advantage of this. The refund tends to level the playing field for grassroots campaigns. If your state has a similar opportunity, find out about it and get this information to your potential donors.

Figure 5.6 is a template of a budget sheet you can use or modify for your purposes. Many local campaigns are too small and underfunded to have a campaign headquarters (other than in your home) or even staff. However, I included a staff section just in case you need it. Feel free to photocopy this page and modify it to fit your budget needs.

Direct Mail for Money

While direct mail can help create a relationship between your campaign and the voter, it is also an opportunity to raise money where those relationships are established. Given that efficient direct mail requires a mailing list of an already identifiable group of voters, I prefer to see which lists I can get and then formulate a letter or piece that will appeal to those voters. Remember,

BUDGET FORM

CAMPAIGN ACTIVITY	AMOUNT	CAMPAIGN ACTIVITY	AMOUNT
Brochure		Billboards or field signs	
Layout & design		Rental space	
Photography		Design & layout	
Printing		Printing	
		Lumber	
Advertising		Staff	
Ad layout		CPA or bookkeeping (contract)	
Photography		Attorney (contract)	
(I would run a separate		Campaign manager & other staff	
print advertising		Salaries	
budget sheet and include		Insurance, taxes	
the number of ads, the			
size of ads and the cost		Television	
of each for the		Production	
number of runs. Put		Buys	
the total for all here.)		(Again, use the ad rep of	
		each station to set up a	
Research		schedule and budget	
		according to exposure you	
Direct mail		want. Put total here.)	
(Do this for each piece)			
Layout and design		Radio	
Printing		Production	
Postage		Buys	
Lists and labels (or)			
Mailing house (they handle		Office supplies	
labels & postage)		Postage, pens, software	
		Telephone, fax	
Polling		Staples, envelopes, etc.	
Benchmark poll			
Tracking poll		Headquarters	
GOTV		Volunteer support	
Voter ID lists		Food, refreshments	
Absentee lists		Staples, envelopes, etc.	
(list it all)			
		Fund-raising expenses	
Lawn signs		Invitations, layout, printing	
Design & Layout		Postage	
Printing		Decorations	
		Prizes	
Misc. printing			
Bumper stickers			
Flyers			
Body badges			
(canvassers & volunteers)			
Letterhead, envelopes			

FIGURE 5.6 Sample Budget Form

Enclosed:

_____ $1000
_____ $500
_____ $250
_____ $100
_____ $50
_____ $25
_____ Other

I/we volunteer to:

_____ Canvass
_____ Host event
_____ Phone bank
_____ Stuff Mail
_____ Display lawn signs
_____ Put up lawn signs
_____ Sign Maintenance

❏ Use name(s) as supporter
_____

❏ email address:
_____

Alan Dr. **Bates**
State Senate

The following information is required in order to comply with Oregon Campaign Law:

Name _____ Phone _____
Address _____
City, State, Zip _____
Occupation _____
Employer _____
Employer's Address _____
City, State, Zip _____

Please make checks payable to Committee to Elect Alan Bates. Contributions may qualify for an Oregon tax credit of $50 per person filing a single return, or $100 per couple filing a joint return.

Authorized by the Committee to Elect Dr. Alan Bates, Salley Jones, Treasurer,

FIGURE 5.7 Example of a Remittance Envelope

Don't forget to include a line for an e-mail address.

your direct mail is only as good as the list to which it is sent. Carefully match your appeal to the people you are targeting.

In a direct-mail piece, you might include a targeted letter, a campaign brochure, and a remittance envelope (figure 5.7). Direct mail can be used simply to align your candidate with an issue such as a concern for jobs where

"My practice is to go first to those who may be counted upon to be favorable, who know the cause and believe in it, and ask them to give as generously as possible. When they have done so, I go next to those who may be presumed to have a favorable opinion and to be disposed to listening, and secure their adherence. Lastly, I go to those who know little of the matter or have no known predilection for it and influence them by presentation of the names of those who have already given."

—— **BENJAMIN FRANKLIN**

unemployment is high, parks and playgrounds where there are none, or anti-growth in a neighborhood where a big development is planned. Be sure to color-code your remittance envelopes with your direct-mail pieces so that you know who is responding to what. That way, you get some feedback on which letters are the most effective. By running a marking pen along the edges of a stack of remittance envelopes, a campaign can cheaply, quickly, and easily color-code envelopes.

Direct-Mail Tips for Success

There are all kinds of opinions on the length, the type of paper, and the look of a direct-mail piece. While direct mail is used widely to move voters toward a candidate or an issue, it can also be an inexpensive and effective way to raise money. Here are some things I've found in soliciting with direct mail.

> "I have only made this letter rather long because I have not had time to make it short."
> **PASCAL, 1656**

1. Use quality paper stock and printing. Keep graphics and fonts simple and clean.
2. People in lower economic groups and those with less education respond in greater numbers to a longer "the house is on fire" solicitation. This group gives less money and votes less, so be sure you have targeted correctly before spending lots of money on a multipage solicitation.
3. Wealthy, well-educated Republicans respond to letters that are no longer than two pages with lots of "this is what I've done, this is what I will do." A single page will work fine for them.
4. Well-educated, affluent Democrats respond in greatest numbers to short, single-page letters explaining the community needs that you will address and how their contribution will make a difference.
5. Only solicit targeted lists. Most people using direct mail to raise money will send to prospect lists (sometimes thousands of voters) in order to generate a "house list" from those who respond. The first mailing loses money, and subsequent mailings to the house list make money. This works well for big campaigns, but local campaigns often cannot send to enough people to generate a large enough house list to make money on subsequent mailings.
6. If you have no targeted lists, spend the money and mail to as big a class of voters as possible to make money on subsequent mailings. For example, mail to everyone in your political party in your targeted precincts.

7. Once people respond to the first mailing, solicit them again. For those responding the second time, solicit them again. After three letters, go back to your house list.

8. A direct-mail piece followed up by a phone call from the campaign substantively increases your response rate.

9. Always include a remittance envelope and a P.S. The P.S. should not be a throwaway. This is often the only thing that is read in a fund-raising letter, so make it count.

10. Personalize the letter and envelope if at all possible. And I don't mean by putting your picture on the outside of the envelope, as one of my candidates did in 2008. Use a size and color of envelope that does not scream junk mail; 6½ by 5 inches works well. Have volunteers hand-address and use a stamp, even if it's a bulk stamp. If you do not have the volunteers to hand-address, then select a script font when printing your list directly onto the envelope.

11. I have stopped using bulk-mail stamps on direct-mail solicitation. It is simply too big of a reveal and too much work. First-class stamps get a far better response rate; for all other direct mail, I use a bulk-mail permit number that gets printed in the upper right-hand corner when everything else gets printed. Have the graphic designer create a sort of canceled-stamp look with the bulk-rate number. Check out the stamp that I use in figure 3.1.

Finding Targeted Mailing Lists

Throughout this handbook are tips and suggestions for establishing relationships with special-interest groups in your community or region. Such alliances can really pay off in mailing-list dividends. Think about who would be most interested in seeing you get elected or seeing your measure passed. Will other candidates or office holders turn over their house lists to your campaign? Consider asking someone who previously ran for the office you are seeking, especially if an incumbent is leaving. Think about other organizations, too: Which ones would sell you their mailing lists? Here are some possibilities of lists that could generate money:

- Teachers, especially if you're working for a school or library bond measure or running for school board
- Environmental organizations such as the Sierra Club, fly fishermen, League of Conservation Voters, Friends of the River, clean-water groups,

greenway organizations, Critical Mass, or any organization that sends a newsletter to a specific group of supporters
- Women's organizations such as Planned Parenthood, National Organization for Women, or Women's Political Caucus
- Your church
- Civic clubs, firefighters, law enforcement groups
- Historic preservation groups

Determining the Amount of Money You Will Need for Direct Mail

1. Decide how many mail pieces you intend to send throughout the campaign.
2. Look at some other direct-mail pieces you like, and get a cost estimate for layout and design.
3. Decide which groups you are mailing to, and then determine the number of households that will receive the piece. For example, if you want to send a direct-mail piece to your top five priority precincts but want to send it only to members of the Green Party, members of the Peace and Freedom Party, Independents, and Democrats who voted in at least two out of the last four elections, you can calculate this number from a voter activation network or from your disk of registered voters from the county. Alternatively, you can call the county clerk to get a count for each of these group members in those precincts. Because you want a household count, be sure to ask for unduplicated households. Often, the clerk's office will download all the necessary information onto a disk for a nominal charge, and you can deliver it to a mailing house where the merge-sort can be done. With that said, find the local mail house that sends all of the voters' pamphlets or absentee ballots and they will already have these data.
4. Use this number to figure your printing and mailing costs for each piece; $0.50 to $0.65 each is a good ballpark figure. However, economies of scale do count here.
5. Multiply the per-piece cost by the number of direct-mail pieces you want to send, and add a bit more. That will make up your direct-mail budget line item.

Special Events

Special events are campaign-sponsored activities intended to raise money and support for the campaign. Examples are a coffee at a supporter's house or a campaign-organized luncheon, dinner, or picnic. Although I have had many successful special events for campaigns, compared with the candidate calling supporters directly, special events raise very little money and take untold amounts of campaign time. The people who attend are usually supporters who have already given and have every intention of voting for the candidate or cause.

> "Every experienced campaigner knows that money follows hard work. It is not the other way around."
> — MARGARET SANGER

Nevertheless, it is important to stress that fund-raisers are not just about raising money. Special events are also for public visibility and education, for involving volunteers so they are more committed to the campaign and candidate, and for promoting "friend-raising" by strengthening the bonds volunteers and guests have with the candidate.

When approached as an opportunity to advertise the candidate and cement relationships, special events can be worth the necessary resources. But don't underestimate the commitment involved. You need to be cautious about the strain special events put on the campaign committee, the volunteers, and the candidate. If someone other than the campaign committee is sponsoring the event, as is often the case with a coffee, you need to be ready to help ensure that the event will be a success.

> "It's nice to have some money, but it's pressing the flesh that's going to win this election."
> JEFFREY GILDENHORN, former candidate for mayor of Washington, D.C.

Ensure a Good Turnout

The one thing you must avoid if you schedule a special event is a poor turnout. If it looks as if a fund-raising event will have marginal attendance, I invite all my volunteers to attend for free. Numbers are more important than money when holding a special event in political circles. Whatever the attendance, you need to be certain that the people who do attend don't have a bad experience. If people can't find the location, can't find parking, or were inadvertently left off the reservation list, they are likely to blame the campaign. You never want to lose a supporter over an avoidable organizational error at a fund-raising event. Take care of your supporters by taking care of details.

Holding a Special Event

A good rule of thumb for planning special events for fund-raising is that it takes one week of preparation for every ten people you expect to attend. Obviously, this time frame becomes tight in a three-month campaign, but the rule underscores the importance of ample preparation time for a successful event. The preparation takes place in four stages:

1. You must *define* the purpose or purposes the event is to accomplish and what type of event you want.
2. You must *plan* the event.
3. You must *promote* the event.
4. You must *conduct* the event.

Tips for handling each of these stages are discussed below.

1. Determine the Purpose and Type of Event

Be clear about the purpose of the event. Is it to attract donors, raise money, raise support, thank volunteers and supporters, or just get the word out on the measure or the candidate? Special events can, of course, have more than one purpose, but you need to focus on one purpose before you can pick the event. Focus on the main purpose when choosing the type of event; then see whether other purposes might be accomplished as well.

> "Where there is no vision, the people perish."
> **PROVERBS 29:18**

Dinners. I have had great results hosting dinners as fund-raising events. I contact a supportive restaurant and ask whether the owner will donate the dinner at cost in the restaurant. I then sell it to the guests at retail. Generally, the restaurant can't afford the whole affair, so I go to another eatery and ask whether that owner will donate the dessert, another for a donation of the coffee, a local vintner for the wine, and so on. You can ask a local musician or band to volunteer talent to make the occasion special (consider looking at the high school music department for great talent). Restaurants are often closed on Mondays, making it a perfect night for your fund-raiser.

I have also had great success with intimate affairs at people's homes. In this approach, the host produces the invitations and provides the food. If the person hosting the event is new to this sort of thing, it's important to check in frequently and help as needed. These events usually involve having a well-known person provide a lavishly catered meal for a well-known candidate at a fairly hefty price. I try, in this scenario, to be selective about whom I invite, although the price will usually select who will attend, and the invitees know that. We have brought in as much as $6,000 in our small area at this type of dinner.

If I am working for a relatively unknown candidate, I do not have a cover charge or a "suggested" donation, for two reasons: First, because the candidate is new to the political circuit, people will stay home rather than give money to a candidate they do not know. Second, I want people to give more than I could possibly charge for such an event. For example, if you charge $25 for a meet-the-candidate event at someone's home and yet many attendees can give more, the campaign will get only the $25 cover. To lend credibility to my political newcomer, I will bring in a well-known political figure, such as the governor, and will schedule two events back-to-back in two cities. The first event can run from 6:00 to 7:30 in one city, and the second from 8:00 to 9:30 in another. To make sure there will be plenty of money flowing, I arrange for one or two people at each gathering to announce that they have just written a check for $1,000 and would encourage all to give as generously as possible. In one campaign, we raised $10,000 in three and a half hours with this approach; there was no suggested contribution on the invitation, no cover charge to get in.

> "Never think you need to apologize for asking someone to give to a worthy object, any more than as though you were giving him an opportunity to participate in a high-grade investment."
> — **JOHN D. ROCKEFELLER, JR.**

Coffees. Coffees sponsored by a supporter can be easy and quite successful. However, they can also be a miserable failure. To be successful, coffees must be closely supervised. Since the campaign is not the sponsor, the critical factor is who hosts the coffee for you. If the sponsor is a local leader, such as a county commissioner, state representative, mayor, president of a college or university, business leader, philanthropist, or anyone else with a following, there will be a good turnout.

Most people do not like attending political fund-raisers such as coffees, so the drawing card should be the combination of the candidate and the host of the coffee. Regardless of who hosts the event, the campaign should oversee the invitations and be ready to help with follow-up phone calls to ensure good attendance. A host who invites sixty people, only to have three show up may feel humiliated because he or she let you down. Or the host may feel the candidate is responsible for the poor turnout. Either way, the candidate and the campaign manager have been deprived of one more night at home or of time that could have been spent raising money by phone, preparing for a debate, or getting volunteers for a canvass.

A few years ago, I started the practice of having one person whose sole campaign job was to oversee coffees. This person should work closely with the campaign scheduler and serves as the campaign's liaison to any host who wishes to sponsor a coffee but does not need to attend war room meetings. The coffee coordinator should be well connected in the community and, ideally, have ready access to lists that may help the hosts in beefing up the invitation list. The coffee coordinator helps with sending invitations, call-backs, and any other tasks that can help the coffee be as successful as possible.

If at all possible, have the candidate call the people invited to the coffee, or at least some of them. This will ensure a donation if they are going, and if they can't make it, it is an opportunity to ask for money or support.

The candidate's call would go something like this:

"Hello, Sam? This is Al Bates. Say, I just got a list of all the people invited to Shirley's coffee, and when I saw your name, I had to take a moment to call and tell you how much I'm looking forward to you being there. It should be a lot of fun. Bring some tough questions for me, will you? Great, see you there."

Using coffees effectively will bring in money, but what's more important, they are a great resource for finding campaign workers and lawn sign locations. So if you are going to have coffees, pay attention to the details and make each one as successful as possible.

Auctions and Yard Sales. Another good fund-raiser is an auction. You and your campaign team can go to businesses and supporters and get a wide variety of donations. For example, ask four different video stores to donate one children's movie, and then put the DVDs all together for one auction item. Your campaign volunteers can donate baked goods for the auction. It may work well to have the candidate or the spouse serve as the auctioneer. For this task, I have used a popular high school teacher who is funny and can really work the crowd. Be creative, and you can have a fun event that actually brings in money. A good auction can bring in as much as $6,000 in a small community.

A yard sale is another option. If you're going to plan one, make it an event. Get a huge yard and lots of donations, old and new. Advertise the great stuff well in advance. Yard sales can be very good fund-raising events because almost no money is needed to set one up. However, they require plenty of time. An effective yard sale will take days to set up, two days to run, and two days to put away. Because a big yard sale can be grueling work, be sure not to schedule one during other labor-intensive activities such as canvassing. A good yard sale can bring in $2,000. Since most of the money comes in on the first day, I strongly recommend you advertise

> "I've learned to use the word *impossible* with the greatest caution."
> **WERNHER VON BRAUN**

it as one day only. Should you decide to do two days, cut the second day so it ends by noon or 1:00 p.m. Be sure to buy pizza for your volunteers for lunch from some of the proceeds.

Involve Attendees. One event I held in a small community was a dessert bake-off. I called specific supporters in that area and asked them to bring their very best dessert. I charged an entry fee for all but the bakers. The campaign provided the coffee (donated), and I recruited other locals to serve as the judges. I made up ribbons for different awards, such as "Dessert Most Likely to Keep a Marriage Together," and each entry won a prize. Because it was held in a small community, all who attended knew each other. Everyone had a great time, and the only cost to the campaign was the rental of the building.

General Considerations. Whatever the type of event, the location is a big consideration. Is it big enough? Too big? How about the atmosphere? For indoor events, *never* use a huge hall or room, unless you are expecting a huge crowd. When selecting locations, I look for places where rooms can be closed off in case of poor attendance. No matter how many people come, I want the event to look well attended and successful, leaving attendees with the impression that just the number expected came. In selecting a restaurant for a dinner, try to find one that has a medium-sized room with another adjoining it that can be used or closed off as needed.

> "One of the symptoms of an approaching nervous breakdown is the belief that one's work is terribly important."
> — **BERTRAND RUSSELL**

Consider your budget when deciding what type of event to have. Then figure roughly what it will cost the campaign and what income it is likely to generate. You also need to estimate the commitment necessary from the candidate, the campaign committee, and your volunteers. Don't forget to consider the economic climate in the community. A $50-a-plate dinner in a town where the last factory just closed might not be a very good idea even if it would make you money. When considering an event, always ask, Does this make sense? Does it fit? Does it feel right?

2. Plan the Event

Planning an event is an extension of choosing the event. All the considerations that informed your choice of the event must now be put into an action plan. In other words, it is time to sort out the details. For instance, some events will require licenses or permits from local government. Such requirements can be a factor in the decision to hold an event, but once the decision is made, someone has to make sure the license or permit is obtained. Similarly, the location, which helped you decide on the type of event, must now be

"Fatigue makes cowards of us all."
VINCE LOMBARDI

secured. The theme of the event, whether it is a human services luncheon, an environmentalist dinner, or a school auction, now influences the details of the event.

To run a successful special event, it is critical that you know who your audience is and how to reach it. For example, are you planning a dinner to support your library? If so, you need to get a mailing list from the Friends of the Library.

Once you know whom you want to reach, you must decide how to reach them. Printed invitations with a telephone follow-up might work well for a formal dinner. However, if the event is a yard sale, just advertise it in the paper or place flyers around town. Whatever the means, people must be assigned to accomplish it. Invitations must be printed; flyers must be designed, printed, and distributed; ads have to be written and delivered. All this takes time and people, and you will need to plan accordingly.

A good way to make sure the details are taken care of is to put the event on a timeline, just like the one for the whole campaign, only smaller. Scheduling in all the tasks and placing the event on a timeline requires someone who is in charge. That person needs to have volunteers assigned to all aspects of the event. Like the campaign itself, successful special events are the product of organization. If you assign the leadership of a special event to one person, provide ample volunteer help, develop a timeline, and plan a budget, you will have a successful event.

While budgets are an extra step, making one will not only help you get a handle on expenses, but also remind you of things that need to be done. For example, listing the cost of the room expense may remind you to check the date of the event to see what else is going on in the community at that time. If you're hosting that dinner to support your town library, you don't want to find out right after you printed the invitations and rented the hall that it is on the same night as the American Association of University Women annual dinner at the college. Paying for the ads for your auction may remind you to check whether the hospital auction is on the same weekend. Here is a list of the things that could be included in a budget:

- Site rental
- Food
- Drinks
- Rental (sound system, tables, chairs)
- Printing
- Supplies
- Mailings
- Entertainment
- Professionals

- Parking
- Advertisements
- Decorations
- Insurance
- Other fees
- Use permits
- Liquor licenses
- Cleanup
- Awards, door prizes
- Thank-you mailing

Although someone in your organization is in charge of planning the event, when it comes time to implement the plan, provide additional help in the training and staffing of volunteers. Training and staffing requirements must be met before the actual setup begins.

In addition to having trained helpers available, you must plan for the supplies you will need. Often, supplies must be ordered well ahead of the event—decorations, for instance—and these should go on your special-event timeline. Also, things that will cost you money—here again, decorations are a good example—are listed in your special-event budget. If you keep going back to the budget and to your expense list, you will be reminded of things you might have forgotten.

Keep in mind that in the planning of an event, some things that do not appear in your budget or timeline may nonetheless be critical. For instance, legal issues such as prohibitions against holding political fund-raisers in public buildings must be considered. On a more mundane but no less critical level, be sure to have duplicates of essential items. If a slide projector is needed for an event, it is wise to have two projectors on hand, or at least two bulbs. How about extension cords and an extra microphone? Also have duplicate lists of all the important phone numbers of the people you are depending on, such as the vendors, caterers, entertainers, staff, and volunteers. These lists will also help you remember all who need to be acknowledged at the end of the event.

It is helpful, too, to know the earliest possible time you can get into the building where the event will be held. Early access provides an opportunity to set things up and test all systems before people arrive.

3. Promote the Event

To promote a special event properly, you must have a target audience in mind. Consider the income level and age of your target audience. Once these details have been established, consider how best to reach them. Your first task is to determine where to get lists of the people in your target audience. If you have a narrow group in mind, such as teachers, doctors, or human-service advocates, you can often get mailing lists from the special-interest groups these people belong to or support. If your audience is broader, as it would be for a neighborhood bake sale, you can take the list from a general source such as your voter activation network (VAN). Re-cently, a friend was holding a coffee for a candidate for state representative and asked if I could come up with a list of his neighbors and provide phone numbers as well. Using the VAN and street names near his home, I generated and e-mailed a list in less than ten minutes.

"Action is eloquence."
WILLIAM SHAKESPEARE

Once you know whom you are trying to contact, you must decide how best to do it. Some possibilities are:

- Invitations
- Flyers
- Radio and television ads
- Press releases
- Posters

- Newsletters
- Handbills or flyers
- Calendars
- E-mail
- Phone call

The content and design of any such announcements must be attractive, professional, and clear. Include the date, place, time (beginning and end), and cost, and provide a map or clear directions for getting there. Note whether any of the cover charge is tax deductible or refundable. For instance, if the event costs $25 for the attendee but your cost per attendee is $10, then the difference, $15, is a straight campaign contribution. Instead of including the math in the ad, simply put a footnote at the bottom stating what amount of the price is deductible.

4. Conduct the Event

When it is time to conduct a well-planned and well-promoted special event, the most important thing you can do to ensure success is to set up early. Everything should be ready forty-five minutes to an hour ahead of time. As the organizer, you need to keep focused and calm. Your volunteers will take their cue from you, and the message you convey must be calm efficiency. It is a nice touch to have a packet for volunteer organizers with their names on it. Include the overall plan as well as the names of the individuals responsible for each of the volunteer activities. I set up packets similar to the campaign committee packets described in Chapter 1. Although the packets take a while to write and assemble, volunteers love this format as it keeps materials well organized.

Once people start to arrive, your focus is on hospitality. How you greet people and work with them will set the tone of the event. Allow adequate time for the candidate to circulate. Do not schedule or allow the candidate to "help" with the operation of the event. The candidate should not be doing things other than meeting the supporters. Name tags will help the candidate when greeting the guests. Be sure to have attendees place the name tag below their right shoulder so that the tag can be read discreetly as it moves closer to the candidate's line of sight when he or she is shaking hands.

Remember to thank everyone, even the people who sold you things. Everyone involved—volunteers, guests, and vendors—is forming an impression of the candidate and the campaign, and you need to do everything you can to make a positive impression. That includes a good cleanup, even if you have rented the facility, so make sure there are volunteers who will stay to clean up. As an organizer, never leave an individual to clean up alone. Stay until everything is done.

Candidate Calls to Raise Money

Direct contact by the candidate remains the quickest, cheapest, and most effective way to raise money. It is critical to the success of a campaign. Remember, as the candidate, you are willing to do a job and volunteer your time at a task that few want to do. If people support your core values and ideas, they must show that support by contributing to your campaign, thereby helping you get your name out. Do not sound apologetic. You are doing the community a favor.

While the campaign manager can call for moderate amounts of money, the calls to major donors should be conducted by the candidate or a close family member, such as a spouse, a sibling, or a parent. It is very difficult for people to turn the candidate down on a direct "ask."

Set up some time each day to make the calls. It is important that calls be made from a prepared list that includes phone numbers, addresses, party registration, giving history, personal notes about the prospective donor, and a suggested amount for the ask. Be sure to have accurate information on what name the candidate should use when speaking with the donor: Is it Katherine, Kathy, Katy, Kate, or Kay?

Because it is so difficult to get a candidate to actually sit down every day and dial for dollars, I assign a person to assist with the task. First put together a three-ring binder that has a list of all those who will be called. Within the binder, also have an individual sheet for each contributor. The individual sheets will list name, phone number, work, giving history, and notes of previous attempts to call. My campaign worker stays with the candidate throughout call time and makes notes on the call sheet for the candidate.

Calling for Money for Ballot Measures

When fund-raising for ballot measures, it is sometimes easier to set up a goal for a specific item, such as a full-page newspaper ad. Let people know what you are trying to buy and how much it will cost so they can contribute accordingly. For example, I might tell people that I am trying to raise $1,500 for a last-minute ad campaign and ask what they can give toward it. If you are going to use a phone

> "A great leader is seen as servant first, and that simply is the key to his greatness."
> **ROBERT K. GREENLEAF**

bank for fund-raising, use just a few people who are committed and are identified with the measure in the community. Provide each caller with a list of the people you want to call; the list should include their giving history along with their phone numbers.

Since people prefer to sign on to something that's going to fly, I tell potential donors that we are X dollars away from our goal. Keep track as pledged dollars roll in, and if the campaign hasn't received the check within a week, make a quick reminder call.

Voters do not look favorably on campaigns who cannot live within their fund-raising abilities, so while waiting for fund-raising to catch up with spending, consider setting up business accounts with as many of your vendors as possible. Although TV and newspapers require that campaign advertisements be paid in full before the ad runs, printers, typesetters, and other vendors may allow you to run an account and pay monthly or at the

> "The palest ink is better than the most retentive memory."
> **CHINESE PROVERB**

end of the campaign. Although the money is technically spent, it does not show up on your financial reports until the campaign has received an invoice.

Raising Money on the Web

Given the online fund-raising success of the McCain campaign in 2000, the Dean campaign in 2004, Obama in 2008, and online giving during national crises, Web-based fund-raising must look like the answer for easy, cheap money. After all, it doesn't involve stamps, printing, folding, stuffing, or any of the items listed on the budget sheet. No clerical team necessary.

Indeed, according to Blue State Digital (BSD), retained by Obama "to manage the online fundraising, constituency-building, issue advocacy, and peer-to-peer online networking aspects of his 2008 Presidential primary campaign," by October 2008 better than half of Obama's eventual $750 million raised came through the Obama Web site using the BSD online tools suite.[3] However, before you opt out of the inefficient and costly means of raising campaign dollars through direct mail and events, consider this: Although there will always be exceptions, online contributions for down-ballot races are a relatively small part of a campaign's overall income stream.

In 2008, former Speaker of the Oregon House, Jeff Merkley (D), challenged incumbent and moderate Republican, Gordon Smith, for a seat on the U.S. Senate. In that race, Merkley raised and spent a little better than $6 million to Smith's $13 million.[4] In a recent interview, Jon Issaacs, Jeff Merkley's campaign manager, explained that Merkley received less than 16 percent from online donations (compared with Dean's 2004 and Obama's 2008 online contribution percentages of 53 percent) and that this amount was only after the campaign received national attention that Smith was vulnerable. For now, down-ballot campaigns should add the Internet to the fund-raising tool box while continuing to employ more traditional fund-raising methods such as events, direct mail, and dialing for dollars.

The following are ten tips to help your online fund-raising efforts. These tips are based on observations of the Obama Web site by David Erickson of eStrategy Internet Marketing Blog.[5]

1. Make it easy to contribute by allowing supporters to donate small amounts of money, $20 or less. "By lowering the barrier to entry, Obama attracted 100,000 more donors than all of the 2004 candidates *combined*."
2. Create multichannel marketing: Place Donate buttons everywhere— within Internet ads, social networking profiles, or in blog posts. This provides as many opportunities as possible for people to contribute.
3. Use spot color to make the donate buttons pop on the Web site. "The red Donate button was ever present on the upper right-hand side of nearly every page of the [Obama] site."
4. The Web site should be able to reload the donation form with information the donor gave previously (name, employment, address, zip code, and phone number). Small contributors often give repeatedly and

do so at times impetuously following an irritating comment by the opposing candidate or in support of something your team has said or done. Make it easy.

5. Include next to the donation form a short video of the candidate underscoring the importance of the donor's support.

6. The design of the donation form is important. Place labels so the donor does not have to look back and forth to fill in data, and include only the information necessary to complete the donation. The submit button should be obvious.

7. This is not the time to gather unrelated information about your contributor. You want the donor doing only one task: giving money. Remove all distractions, and omit from the donation page any links that will take the donor away from it.

8. Give donors opportunities to give incrementally, $20 per month or whatever amount they choose, so multiple donations continue to come in with little or no campaign effort.

9. People are more likely to give to a candidate or a cause that their friends endorse, so build in incentives to encourage supporters to "bundle" their friends for giving. Besides bringing in money, it also expands a campaign's money network. Obama personally called contributors who exceeded personal fund-raising goals and in one case called the father of a volunteer to tell him what a great job his daughter did in fund-raising for his campaign.

10. Your Web site is integral to the success of fund-raising. People will not give to a cheesy Web site. It must look professional; colors, font, layout—all this matters. Spend some money on the design of your Web site if you hope to attract money with it. For more ideas, check out "The Political Consultants' Online Fundraising Primer," from the Institute for Politics, Democracy and the Internet.[6]

The Campaign Finance Committee

A campaign finance committee can assist the overall effort by focusing a small, committed group to some or all of the activities described above. One efficient use of a committee is to follow up on direct-mail solicitations. Depending on who is serving on the committee, it can also be responsible for developing and soliciting major donors. If you are running for an office that covers a fairly large geographic area, you may want more than one finance committee, but within a city, county, or state house and senate district, one will do.

Selecting Finance Committee Members

A great fund-raising committee begins with a strong chair. Your chair should be energetic, charismatic, aggressive, and outgoing and someone who likes asking for money. The chair should have no other campaign tasks during the time of this fund-raising effort. He or she must have great follow-through abilities and a reputation for getting things done. You do not want your campaign to have to use precious time to clean up after a mess has been made, so choose this person carefully and work closely with him or her to make sure things are going according to plan.

> "Lives based on having are less free than lives based either on doing or being."
> — WILLIAM JAMES

The chair, like all members of the committee, should have experience in raising money or in sales. People who have been involved in fund-raising efforts for other political campaigns, charities, nonprofits, churches, civic organizations, academic institutions, foundations, or clubs make excellent committee members. Look also for people who are involved in politics, because they feel passionately about an issue, such as school funding, environmental causes, prolife or prochoice, labor unions, gun ownership, health care, land use, and housing. Those who have a history with a specific interest group will be able to raise money from others with similar interests.

Look for members who have personal resources, who have a name that means something to your constituency, and who work hard. Too often, campaigns and organizations make the mistake of bringing someone on board simply because the person has a big name. When there are people serving on the finance committee in name only, other members who are working hard may feel resentment, which can cause the committee to break down. While big names work well on the "committee to support" outlined in Chapter 1, they should serve elsewhere in a campaign only if they're willing to roll up their sleeves and work in the trenches like everyone else.

Using the Finance Committee for Direct Mail Follow-Up

If you are using a finance committee to increase returns on a direct-mail solicitation, begin by sending a letter of solicitation to people who have previously supported the candidate, supported similar candidates, or supported issues embraced by the candidate—especially if they are different from those of the opponent. For an issue-based campaign, send the letter to people who have given to causes or organizations that best reflect the ideals of the ballot measure or proposition.

For local campaigns, which are often strapped for time, money, and human resources, I like to keep the work and scope of the fund-raising effort at a low enough level that it can be managed by a small group of dedicated volunteers and completed within a short time frame. This committee works independently of the candidate's efforts to raise money and, depending on the composition of the committee, may or may not include major donors. It is always preferable to have major donors approached by the candidate or someone close to the candidate. However, if members of the finance committee personally know a major donor, use that connection.

When I chair finance committees, I evenly divide the members into groups of three or four and have each team select a name for itself. For example, one could be called the Animals, another the Vegetables, and the third the Minerals. These teams compete with each other for prizes that depend on how many dollars each team brings in. The prizes are usually nothing big but tend to make things more fun—such as coffee from a local coffee house ("thanks a latte"). At the end of fund-raising efforts, I have bigger prizes, such as donated pottery or artwork, for the team that raises the most money. Each of the teams should have a team captain who calls team members on a regular basis and keeps everyone competitive and happy in a friendly way. The team captains report back to the chair.

> "The first thing you naturally do is teach the person to feel that the undertaking is manifestly important and nearly impossible. . . . That draws out the kind of drives that make people strong, that puts you in pursuit intellectually."
>
> **EDWIN H. LAND,**
> founder, Polaroid Corporation

Campaign Finance Committee Packets

Providing an effective organizational structure for the campaign finance committee not only results in a more successful effort by committee members but also keeps people coming back to work on other campaigns and efforts. Campaign finance is really a tough job for people, and while some are better than others, an organized effort on your part helps both the seasoned and the novice fund-raiser to be successful. Creating a packet as shown in figure 5.8 keeps the members organized and the campaign contained. Clearly, these are not scraps of paper to leave lying about. They often contain a donor's giving history and personal information.

Details must be attended to in creating these packets just as they must be in preparing packets for the war room. Both the campaign committee and the finance committee are the most important in the campaign. Their members

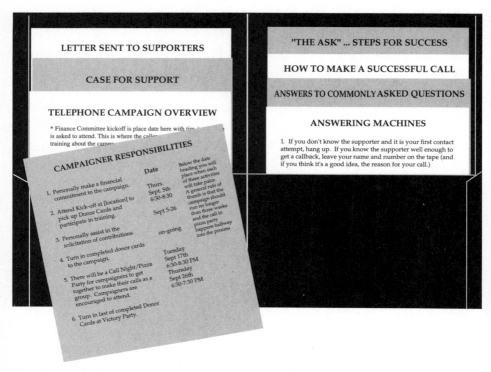

FIGURE 5.8 Example of a Campaign Finance Committee Packet

contribute time, resources, energy, and sometimes prestige to your campaign. While the campaign committee provides the organization and legwork, the finance committee helps raise the funds to make everything possible.

In preparing campaign finance committee packets for each member of the committee, include each of the tiered sheets shown in figure 5.8 and detailed in figures 5.9A–H, modified to fit your needs. To give these sheets substance for presentation and durability during the campaign, print them on a heavy paper (no lighter than 80-pound vellum Bristol), and alternate in a two-color scheme—avoid loud or garish colors. Each packet includes eight pieces of paper, in different lengths to create a tiered effect, as well as campaigner cards (figure 5.10), donor cards (figure 5.11), and a "Friends I Will Call" sheet (figure 5.12).

Each of your finance committee members is given a campaigner card (figure 5.10), which will be used to enlist two additional people to assist in the fund-raising effort. This method of recruitment increases the finance committee threefold and often brings new faces to a campaign. Campaigner cards can be printed on regular-weight paper.

CAMPAIGNER RESPONSIBILITIES

(Below the date heading place when each of these activities will take place. A rule of thumb is that the campaign should run no longer than three weeks, and the call-in pizza party happens halfway into the campaign).

Date

1. Personally make a financial commitment to the campaign.

2. Attend Kickoff at *(location)* to pick up Donor Cards and participate in training.

   Thurs.
   Sept 15
   6:30-8:30

3. Personally assist in the solicitation of contributions.

   Sept 5-Oct. 6

4. Turn in completed Donor Cards to the campaign.

   ongoing

5. There will be a Call Night/Pizza Party for campaigners to get together to make their calls as a group. Campaigners are encouraged to attend.

   Tuesday
   Sept 27th
   6:30-8:30 PM

6. Turn in last of completed Donor Cards at Victory Party.

   Thursday
   Oct. 6
   6:30-7:30 PM

Cut to create a tiered look in the packets.

FIGURE 5.9A Sample "Campaigner Responsibilities" Sheet

TELEPHONE CAMPAIGN OVERVIEW

- The finance committee kickoff is (*place and date here with time*). EVERYONE is asked to attend. This is where you will pick up your Donor Cards (approximately 35), get more detailed information and training about the campaign, and meet your team members.
- The Donor Cards will have names of those individuals who have a history of giving to this campaign or similar causes. During the three-week fund drive, campaigners will call these supporters at their convenience.
- There will be three teams consisting of approximately six campaigners and one team captain.
- Teams compete with one another for a variety of awards and prizes.
- Cards are turned in to the captains or the campaign as they are completed. This is done either directly to your team captain or to the campaign office.
- There will be a Call Night/Pizza Party on (*day and date*) for the finance committee to get together to make their calls as a group. Callers are encouraged to attend.
- A party is scheduled for (*day and date*). All remaining cards must be turned in on this evening. The winning teams will be announced and honored. We will all be winners at this point, and so will the campaign.
- Fun **is** a requirement for this campaign, so plan on having a good time for a very good cause.

IMPORTANT INFORMATION
All Donor Cards **must** be returned (even if they haven't been called).
Please do not give Donor Cards to supporters.

THANKS FOR YOUR TIME AND SUPPORT

FIGURE 5.9B Sample "Telephone Campaign Overview" Sheet

CASE FOR SUPPORT

This page is where you most clearly outline what your candidate (or issue-based campaign) stands for. It may be an opportunity to outline the differences between the candidates or to simply make your case without regard to the opposition.

Depending on whom you are soliciting, this sheet may change to accommodate a different focus or emphasis. For example, if you are targeting a Sierra Club mailing list with a letter and follow-up phone call, you may want these notes to include the candidate's stands on environmental issues or past votes if the candidate previously held an office. If you are calling members of a teachers union, you may want to include the candidate's stands on school issues and libraries. For the Chamber of Commerce membership or Rotary Club list, you might focus on the candidate's strengths around business issues. And so on.

It will keep your caller more focused if you match this white paper with the potential donor's interests. You can best determine those interests by knowing the origin of the mailing list.

If you are simply calling a list of general supporters, have a number of important community issues itemized here and your candidate's stands on them. If you're working for an incumbent, list accomplishments while in office.

FIGURE 5.9C "Case for Support" Sheet

LETTER SENT TO SUPPORTERS

(This page should include the complete solicitation letter sent to potential donors. Reduce it so it will fit on a single page and still allow room for the above heading.)

ELLE DANIELS FOR MAYOR
BUILDING A BETTER COMMUNITY

COMMITTEE TO SUPPORT ELLE DANIELS FOR MAYOR

Your logo, message should be part of your letterhead.

It is sometimes effective to list your big-name people on your letterhead. If you are working in a county, you may choose to list support by city. Remember, these are not necessarily the same names that form the campaign committee.

Work with your committee to draft the body of your letter.
You may include:

1. Who you are and your background/roots
2. Why you want the office you seek
3. Ways to impress upon your supporters that the undertaking is manifestly important and nearly impossible (this brings out the best in people)
4. No more than two or three issues that will *really* matter to your readers
5. Include a "Donation Card"

Remember:
- Campaigns are about emotion.
- The letter should be kept to one page if possible.
- Include a remittance envelope.

P. S.   A "P.S." is sometimes the only thing that gets read. It is *very* important.

KNOW THE LAW: Don't forget your disclaimer: Paid for by or Authorized by... committee name and treasurer, whatever wording is required by election law. Make it microscopic.

FIGURE 5.9D Sample Letter Sent to Supporters

ANSWERING MACHINES

1. If you don't know the supporter and it is your first contact attempt, hang up. If you know the supporter well enough to get a call-back, leave your name and number (and if you think it's a good idea, the reason for your call).

2. If you don't know the supporter well and it's your second or third taped greeting, rather than give up, leave your name, volunteer status, reason for the call, and phone number:

   Example:

Hi, this is _____ calling at _____ o'clock on (day of the week). *I'm volunteering for* (name of campaign) *in hopes that you would consider a gift to help support...* (place short message here—it could be the candidate's name and office or it could be something that the candidate stands for that will resonate with this particular donor. For example: management of forest land or fly fishing or choice issues or libraries. This must be worked out ahead of time with your volunteer caller and/or noted on the donor card).

I've tried to reach you a number of times by phone and although I <u>am</u> giving up reaching you in person, I'm <u>not</u> giving up on the idea that you'll support (name of candidate and office sought). **I'll ask** (name of candidate) **to send you another return envelope. We would be <u>so</u> grateful if you would use it to support** (again, place an issue here that will resonate—appeal to interests over intellect. For example, you might say, "to support better management of our forest resources through [candidate's name]").

This is an extraordinarily close race with a lot at stake, and we can win only with help from people like you. If you have any questions, please give me a call at _____.

3. On the donor card write that another blank return envelope needs to be sent to the supporter and get it back to the campaign as soon as possible. A nice touch is to include a short handwritten, signed note, such as: "Sorry, I missed you."

4. If leaving a message does not fit your style, perhaps you could send the potential supporter a note and enclose it with an envelope from your folder. Please note on the donor card that you have done so.

FIGURE 5.9E Sample "Answering Machines" Sheet

ANSWERS TO FREQUENTLY ASKED QUESTIONS

Sample questions:

Didn't I already give to this candidate (campaign)?

   Previous gift information, when available, should be on the donor card or printouts, depending on which you are using. It's OK to give the information to the donor, but volunteer it only when you have a purpose. For example, donors gave $50 to a similar candidate or cause and you want them to increase their gift.

I give money to my PAC at work, and they're already supporting this candidate.

   "That's great. However, if we can show that the bulk of our money comes from individuals, such as you, rather than PACs, it encourages others to contribute also. While PAC money will help, we depend on direct support from individuals to pull off a win in November."

I don't know much about either of these candidates. How are they different?

   Have two or three key issues that clearly show the difference between your candidate and the opponent and place that here. These key issues should be appropriate for the donor list you are soliciting.

How does this candidate stand on _____?

   Think of two or three issues that might come up in a phone solicitation. This is the place to touch on a couple of key issues that might be of concern to the community. However, volunteers should use caution in discussing campaign issues in too much detail. However, for the caller to have more background, your *"Case for Support"* sheet should cover the issues in greater depth.

Who else supports this candidate?

   Include a short endorsement list here of organizations and well-known citizens that support the candidate.   Prepare here! For example, if you're calling Realtors, don't list an antigrowth group to the potential supporter. Instead it might include members of the chamber of commerce, the Rotary Club, or your downtown association. Again, fit the endorsements with the people being called.

FIGURE 5.9F Sample "Answers to Frequently Asked Questions" Sheet

HOW TO MAKE A SUCCESSFUL CALL

BEFORE YOU PICK UP THE PHONE:

1. Be proud of yourself for working on the front lines of a campaign. Many talk a good game, but you act.
2. Feel camaraderie with the person you're calling. In nearly every case, the person has previously given to an organization supporting our efforts, directly to our candidate, or to another candidate who embraces ideals similar to our candidate's.
3. Remember what motivates you about *(the candidate or ballot measure)* and why you agreed to pitch in with the campaign.
4. Decide how much you will ask for. If you know the person and their giving capabilities, don't be afraid to be bold. Otherwise you might say that people are giving $50 on average but that any amount would be welcome and put to good use. I often just let the people tell me what they want to give. ("What should I put you down for?" Offering increments of $25, $50, $100 works well.) It is important to get an amount.

MAKING CONTACT WITH THE DONOR:

5. Identify yourself by name and as a volunteer, and ask for the donor by her or his first name.
6. If a couple is identified on the donor card and you don't know which one cares about the campaign, an effective approach is to give your name and say you're a volunteer working for *(name of campaign)* as part of a fund-raising effort to get *(name)* elected. Then ask whether it is X or Y or both who support the candidate. Then ask to speak with that person. Say you'll call back if the person is not then available.
7. Show the donor that you are sensitive to the possibility that your call might come as an intrusion. For instance: ***Do you have a minute to talk now?*** If the answer is "no," ask when it would be convenient to call back. Note the call-back time on the donor card, and then follow through. If the answer is "yes," you're on your way!
8. Refer to the letter sent out by our campaign. Included in your packet is a "Case for Support" paper that will help guide you.

FIGURE 5.9G Sample "How to Make a Successful Call" Sheet

"THE ASK" . . . STEPS FOR SUCCESS

1. Strategies for The Ask:

   The campaign should have some issues that are important to the donor. For example, if the donor's name came from a NOW list and choice is an important component in the campaign, use this information. Use the information about where the donor's name came from to build a relationship. Whether the source is the chamber of commerce, a school union, an environmental group, a women's activist organization, or even the town you live in, use this information.

   Find ways to connect with the potential donor. For example: In a countywide race you may live in the same town as the prospective donor and recognize the last name as a parent with children going to school with your children. *"Hi, I'm a volunteer out working for [name] tonight. As a parent of the Jacksonville School District, I'm supporting [name] because of her leadership within our community schools. Tonight we're raising money to send [name] to the Board of Commissioners, and we're hoping you will join our effort. Would you consider a pledge of $50 toward the campaign?"*

   A very effective technique is to tell the donors how much you are trying to raise for a specific campaign function. For example: *"Hi, I'm a volunteer helping [name of campaign]. We're trying to raise $12,000 for some TV spots that have to be bought now for the November election. Would you be willing to make a pledge or send a gift to support our efforts?"* If they say yes, ask what you can put them down for. If they say no or are curt with you, ask if they would rather be removed from the mailing list.

2. Once you have made the request for money, let the donor respond. Do not distract the donor with nervous small talk. Just be silent. Remember: after the ask, the first one to speak, loses. If the donor declines the ambitious amount you've suggested, ask if he or she would prefer to break the gift down by half and give twice. If that doesn't work, fall back to a more modest amount.

3. If the donor indicates that he or she will probably make a pledge but hasn't decided how much, suggest that the campaign can send another envelope as a reminder, and the donor can send whatever amount he or she feels comfortable with.

4. Finally, verify the address on the donor card, and ask if the donor has any objection to being acknowledged in an endorsement ad. Please note the response on the donor card, and use the card to record any other information that has even the slightest chance of being useful, such as issues that the voter cares about, if he or she wants to work for the campaign or would like a lawn sign.

5. Thank everyone, including turndowns, for their time.

FIGURE 5.9H Sample "'The Ask' . . . Steps for Success" Sheet

```
          ELLE DANIELS FOR MAYOR
              BUILDING A BETTER COMMUNITY

                  CAMPAIGNER CARD


  Finance Committee Member  _____

  1st Campaigner's Name _____  Phone _____

  Address _____ City _____ Zip _____

  2nd Campaigner's Name _____  Phone _____

  Address _____ City _____ Zip _____
```

FIGURE 5.10 Sample Campaigner Card

Print three to a sheet of paper, and cut to size.

FRONT:

```
Daniels for Mayor                    Place donor label here.  Include:
PO Box 1                        Name (include partner or spouse)
Ashland, Oregon 97520           Address
555-2003                        Phone number
                                Email
Amount Pledged_____       Giving history

Payable:   Send envelope and information sheet        Turn Down

           Pay half now, half later              Contact/Attempts:_____

           Other Arrangements                         _____


     Visa        Mastercard #_____Expiration Date _____
```

BACK:

```
Campaigner:  Please fill out card, front and back, and return with your weekly reports.
Email address_____
New address (street or box, city, zip)


New Phone number (cell phone?) _____
Out of town; expected return date
Contact later; date to contact
Wrong phone number; present number unknown
If turndown, reason given
Comments
```

FIGURE 5.11 Sample Donor Card (Front and Back)

These are printed on card stock.

FRIENDS I WILL CALL
(Business-Social)

Caller's Name_____

Name		Phone	
Address			
City	Zip	Pledge	

Name		Phone	
Address			
City	Zip	Pledge	

Name		Phone	
Address			
City	Zip	Pledge	

Name		Phone	
Address			
City	Zip	Pledge	

Name		Phone	
Address			
City	Zip	Pledge	

Name		Phone	
Address			
City	Zip	Pledge	

Name		Phone	
Address			
City	Zip	Pledge	

Name		Phone	
Address			
City	Zip	Pledge	

IMPORTANT: **PLEASE BRING THIS LIST TO THE CAMPAIGN KICK-OFF SO WE CAN CHECK FOR DUPLICATIONS.**

FIGURE 5.12 Sample "Friends I Will Call" Sheet

The donor cards are for potential contributors who were mailed a letter of solicitation but have not yet responded by mail. You or the chair will prepare these cards for committee members. To do so, make as many donor cards as there are people who have been solicited by mail, minus the number who already responded, and place a name label in the corner with as much information as you have about the potential donor (figure 5.11). Donor cards must be printed on card stock, because once they are divvied up, committee members handle them a lot while attempting to call from home, the office, or a cell phone at the gym after work.

Once my original finance committee members have enlisted their additional workers, the candidate should mail a letter to the full committee welcoming them on board, thanking them in advance for their commitment to work on the campaign, and reminding them of the first meeting (figure 5.13). Include with this letter the "Friends I Will Call" sheet and a copy of the "Telephone Campaign Overview" (figure 5.9B).

Dear Bonnie,

Thank you for volunteering as a campaigner for the Daniels for Mayor campaign. This fundraising effort promises to reach an all-time high in dollars raised and fun to be had.

Please pull out your calendar and write the following dates and times down.

ALL EVENTS ARE LOCATED AT CAMPAIGN HEADQUARTERS
LOCATED AT 525 BEACH STREET

CAMPAIGN KICK-OFF	THURSDAY	SEPT. 15 6:30–8:30PM
CALL NIGHT PIZZA PARTY	MONDAY	SEPT. 27 6:30–8:30PM
TURN IN PLEDGE SHEETS	ON GOING THROUGHOUT MONTH	
VICTORY PARTY…LAST OF		
PLEDGE CARDS TURNED IN	THURSDAY	OCT. 6 6:30–7:30PM

Now that you have these important dates written down, take a second to look over the enclosed information. I have included a campaign overview to let you know just where we are going with all of this and a "Friends I Will Call" sheet.

Please pay special attention to the "Friends I Will Call" sheet. This important list will accomplish two things. It will help you think of friends and acquaintances you could call who may be interested in supporting Elle Daniels for Mayor. It will also allow us to cross-reference those individuals with the list being called to eliminate the chance of call duplications. Please send it to me as quickly as possible or bring it to the campaign kick-off.

If you have any questions please feel free to contact me at work (number) or home (number).

Thank you again,

FIGURE 5.13 Sample Letter Welcoming Finance Committee Member to the Campaign

Dear Peter,

Just a quick note to let you know how great it was to talk to you tonight and to thank you in advance for your generous pledge.

Without support from people like you we would not be able to pull off a win this November.

Oh, I hope your son did well on his Spanish test.

Thanks again,
Joan

FIGURE 5.14 Sample Thank-You Note from Campaign Finance Committee Member to Campaign Donor

The "Friends I Will Call" sheet is important because finance committee members list *their* friends or co-workers who they believe are supportive of the cause. Obviously this does two things: It increases your donor base, and it gets friends to call friends. This form should be filled out and returned to the campaign before the kickoff party to give the campaign an opportunity to remove any duplicates of names that are already in the mix for a call from the committee. Because many sheets end up arriving on the night of the kickoff (no matter how much you plead to have them back earlier), have a couple of campaign workers on hand to check these lists against your existing donor cards and the other names on the "Friends I Will Call" sheets. Remove duplicates before members begin their calling. This is important because people who hate being called once for a solicitation can get downright nasty on the second or third call in a single evening, plus it makes your campaign look disorganized and committee members go ballistic. Once donor card duplications have been removed and duplications within each of the lists eliminated, return each "Friends I Will Call" sheet to the volunteer who generated it so that he or she can make contact with those on their list during the fund-raising campaign.

Include in each finance committee packet some paper and envelopes so that callers can jot a quick thank-you note to the donor after the phone contact (figure 5.14). This provides the added benefit of allowing for a personalized

> "I am deeply touched—not as deeply touched as you have been coming to this dinner, but nonetheless it is a sentimental occasion."
>
> **JOHN F. KENNEDY,** at a political fund-raiser

message while the conversation is still fresh in everyone's mind. It is most effective if done between calls; if left to the end, it usually does not happen.

This personal and efficient touch works. Use nice paper cut in half and a small envelope (4½ by 5¾ inches). Prepare and include a few thank-you notes generated by the campaign for the committee, and word them in such a way that they will not need a salutation—only a signature. Whether personal or prepared, completed thank-you notes are paper-clipped to the donor card for mail preparation—don't forget to include a remittance envelope (figure 5.7).

Because callers are more successful when they have plenty of information, finance committee packets should include a lot of detail about the candidate or issue-based campaign. Obviously, callers do not have to read everything in the packet, but those who do are often more at ease in the task. Here, as with canvassing, discourage volunteers from answering specific questions about a candidate's stands on issues. Although a caller can share his or her motivation for volunteering in the effort, specific questions can best be answered by directing the donor to call the candidate directly.

It's a nice touch to personalize each of the finance committee packets by putting the member's name on the front, even if it's in the form of a printed label; it tells the volunteer that he or she is important and is being counted upon.

On kickoff night, when each committee member is to receive a packet and a stack of donor cards, the candidate and the campaign manager should be present. The candidate says a few words of thanks and inspiration, and the manager gives an overview of the fund-raising effort.

> "You may never know what results from your action. But if you do nothing, there will be no results."
> GANDHI

Callers are to make the calls within a three-week period, usually from home. However, it is a good idea to set up a phone-bank party midway. This really gives callers a shot in the arm, and most will complete their calls at this time. In general, people prefer to call in the company of others, and many save their calls for this night—so make it a fun evening with great food and drink (donated, of course).

It is important to remember that the people being solicited in this manner are not major donors. Major donors are contacted by the candidate, his or her spouse, or someone else close to the candidate.

Potential Sources for Names

The following individuals and organizations may be able to provide names or generate lists of names:

- The candidate
- The candidate's spouse and relatives
- Contributors to other campaigns
- Members of the finance committee, including the chair
- Friends of the campaign
- Campaign staff

- Business associates
- Clubs
- Professional organizations
- College classmates
- Churches
- Issue groups
- The party
- Unions

Tips for Successful Fund-Raising

1. Campaigns are about emotion, not intellect.
2. Be visionary, present a vision, address opportunity. People need to feel that investing in a campaign will make life better, both now and in the future. They should feel that your winning will strengthen the community. Make your case larger than the office you seek or the program you hope to fund.
3. Invite donors to invest in leadership, solutions, and vision. Through a candidate or a campaign, people are making an investment in their community. Generally, people contribute to a campaign or candidate because they believe that they will get something in return. Describe to the donor, the voter, or the citizen what he or she will get with a victorious election. Use issues that are in front of voters.
4. Look for early money. "He who gives early gives twice" (Cervantes). Do not look at fund-raising as though there is just so much money and no more. Money flows like a river; don't think of it like a well or a pond. There's plenty of money if you can show that the gifts will be used wisely. This applies to money for candidates and campaigns as well as money for schools, libraries, parks, and other issue-based campaigns.
5. Sell ideas and hope, not the candidate. You're offering something that the voter wants: opportunity, vision, solutions, parks, better schools, less traffic, lower crime rates, cleaner air, whatever. Look at your campaign as the vehicle for the voters to get what they want. Charles Revson, founder of Revlon, said, "In the factory, we make cosmetics. In the stores, we sell hope." Sell hope.

> "It does not matter so much where we are . . . as the direction which we are moving."
> — GOETHE

6. Never think of fund-raising as begging. If you're a candidate, you're putting yourself out there, at no small sacrifice, to do a job that peo-

ple want done. If you're working for a ballot measure, you're creating opportunities for a community to realize a vision.

7. There's a difference between an underdog and a losing effort. People want to help an underdog but usually will not help finance an effort they believe will lose. Presenting your campaign as an underdog suggests that people are investing in the American Dream.

> "Men take only their needs into consideration, never their abilities."
> **NAPOLEON**

8. Stay on your message. Your message should always be at the center of every appeal. Incorporate it into the "ask" while keeping the targeted donor's profile and interests as the focus.

9. Be organized. Because people equate organization with winning, by showing a strong organizational core you are more likely to get people to give.

10. Think community. Community campaigns are the most successful. Such a campaign presents issues that people understand. It presents solutions, involves volunteers, and encourages investment in the future. Do not talk about the mechanics of the campaign. A campaign and a candidate don't have needs; the community and the people in it have needs and challenges. The candidate or campaign should represent opportunity, solutions, answers, and the ability to meet those needs.

> "A person is known by his charity."
> **IRISH PROVERB**

11. Don't be afraid to ask for money. Asking for money is how you fund a campaign.

Fund-Raising Ideas That Take Less Than One Month of Preparation

1. Personal solicitation.
2. The "Friends I Will Call" sheet.
3. Dinner at a restaurant as outlined above.
4. "Sponsored by . . . " dinner or brunch at the house of someone well known. This is a variation on a theme of a coffee, but whereas coffees are usually free, a dinner has an admission fee.
5. Theme dinner. These are great fun. First, and most important, you need an incredible friend who is willing to open his or her home and do the preparation of food with other friends. A theme dinner usually will focus on a period in history (such as the turn of the century), an author

or a set of authors, an important leader, and so forth. For example, you might have an evening focusing on Jane Austen. One friend would research her life and prepare some text that may be read throughout (or between) courses of the meal. Others would prepare the meal that features the types of foods eaten at that period. A theme dinner can also center on many authors. In this case, your really great friend might prepare favorite dishes of certain authors or dishes featured in books—such as *Like Water for Chocolate*. We have done this with high school girls and boys acting as the servants (dressed in black and white). You will also need different people to read appropriate passages from books that pertain to the courses being served. As these dinners are a real treat—almost like time travel—and lots of work, charge plenty. Make sure you sell enough tickets to make it worth your while before you head out to shop for groceries and spend days cooking.

6. Small auctions. They are surprisingly easy to conduct. You need volunteers who are willing to approach businesses and friends to get donations for a candidate. Combine donations to make more attractive prizes. Auction a pair of shoes from a local shoe store or a backpack from a mountaineering supply store; find someone willing to give tennis lessons or golf lessons; ask a historian to donate a tour of your town's historic district; ask a pilot to donate a ride in a private plane; and so on.

7. Softball tournament. This requires lots of work and makes very little money, but is great fun and a perfect project for that guy who wants to help, but doesn't quite fit in anywhere else. The admission fees go to the campaign.

8. Birthday party for the candidate. The price of admission in dollars should be the candidate's age in years.

9. Raffle. This requires someone to be completely on top of the event, someone who can really track where the tickets are. You need a big prize and some lesser prizes plus a bunch of people to sell tickets. Again, you can combine things to create a big prize, such as dinner for two, plus two theater tickets, after-theater dessert, and nightcap at a popular spot.

10. A donated weekend in a cabin, at the lake, in the woods, or near a ski resort. Do you know anyone with a condo in Hawaii? If a supporter has lots of frequent-flyer miles, he or she could donate the required miles to get your winner to the final destination. Be creative.

11. An afternoon with . . . Have a local celebrity or author put together entertainment or a reading. How about asking the governor to pop in

as he or she is moving through town? Have some great donated pastries and assorted hot beverages on hand.

12. Tasting and toasting. This is a theme coffee with an admission. It is just what it sounds like: wine tasting with finger food and a couple of big names present.

"Hey, Big Spender"

If you've read this far, chances are you don't have millions of dollars to throw at your campaign—maybe not even thousands. So what happens when you head up a ballot measure or pull a petition against big money? Don't worry, there's hope. Big spenders may get a lot of press, but they don't always win. In fact, the Center for Responsive Politics reported that in the 1996 congressional races, only 19 of the 149 candidates who spent more than $100,000 of their own money won—that's less than 13 percent. Similarly, in the 2002 midterm elections, 19 of the 20 U.S. House and Senate candidates who spent $1 million or more of their own funds on their campaigns lost. Of the 23 candidates who spent $1 million or more of their own money in the 2004 cycle, only Michael McCaul (R-Texas) was elected. In 2008, 49 congressional candidates spent more than $500,000 of their own money, and just 6 House candidates and 1 Senate candidate won.

> "We make a living by what we get, but we make a life by what we give."
> **WINSTON CHURCHILL**

While deep pockets can't always buy a win on Election Day, they can buy name recognition. So, if you're running a campaign against someone with unlimited resources, you'd better have a tight message, a lot of volunteers, a well-organized campaign, and an edge. In this handbook you'll find a number of tips to help you compete with big money. However, if you know you will be outspent, pay close attention to developing a powerful message and communicating it in effective ways that resonate with the voters.

> "Big money brings big problems."
> **BILL MEULEMANS**

With the complexities of government more in focus for the voter in recent years, experience is playing a larger role in electing and reelecting candidates. While "I don't know" can initially sound romantic and even charming, it wears thin with the voters as time goes on. Although there are exceptions, candidates who are vague about issues eventually will come across as lacking substance, whether they have lots of personal wealth or not.

In a special election in 1999, Audie Bock won a seat in the California State Assembly with $40,000, one direct-mail piece, a few lawn signs, and one hundred volunteers. Her opponent spent $600,000, including $100,000 in the last two weeks on twelve direct-mail pieces.

In Nebraska's 1998 gubernatorial primary, Mike Johanns, who was hugely outspent by his two opponents, won using the slogan "This is about governing . . . and I've done it." This slogan focused on the candidate's experience—something money cannot buy.

> "Nobody roots for Goliath."
> _____ **WILT CHAMBERLAIN**

By contrast, an underfinanced Republican, Bill Redmond, of New Mexico, was elected to Congress in 1996 in a district heavily populated by registered Democrats. He did so by focusing not on his experience but rather on questionable ethical activities of his opponent. And his campaign used another very effective trick. With a strong Green Party candidate, Carol Miller, in the running, the Redmond campaign sent a direct-mail piece to Democrats, urging them to vote for her, thereby splitting the Democratic vote.

In all these campaigns, the focus on message, a disciplined organization, volunteers, strategy, and communication pulled out not just difficult races, but, in the Redmond and Bock examples, seemingly impossible races, all while the candidate was being outspent. While Redmond and Bock incorporated negative campaigning, in the Nebraska election Johanns never went negative.

> "A man's real worth is determined by what he does when he has nothing to do."
> _____ **_MEGIDDO MESSAGE_**

In my town, we effectively fought and won a campaign for a prepared-food and beverage tax to pay for an open-space program and wastewater treatment plant upgrades. We prevailed against restaurateurs, realtors, editorial boards, the chamber of commerce, and the Oregon food and beverage industry. Although we were outspent five to one, we had an effective message that resonated with the voters and hundreds of volunteers to deliver that message.

Five Reasons Why Personal Wealth Doesn't Necessarily Translate into Winning Campaigns

1. Many voters feel that money is not an entitlement to hold a public office. Candidates must have substance, a clear stand on issues, and related experience.

2. A candidate who appears to be working hard to get into office will be perceived as someone who will work hard once in office. A candidate who buys everything for support does not always appear to be working as hard as the candidate who can't buy so much.

3. Clear communication will beat money every time. The voter knows that if a candidate can clearly communicate during an election, there's a good chance that he or she will be a good communicator in office.
4. Because there is a perception that candidates with great personal wealth do not need financial support, they have a more difficult time raising money. Money raised is itself a way to communicate with the voters: It tells them who supports a candidate and, in essence, why.
5. Similarly, there is a perception that candidates with great personal wealth do not need as much volunteer help—that they can buy strategists, pollsters, campaign managers, phone bank callers, canvassers, and envelope stuffers. Fewer volunteers on the campaign also means a smaller number of potential supporters from among the friends and family of existing volunteers.

Outside money can also be a liability. There is fundamental suspicion among voters when outside money tries to buy an election. This is most apparent in small communities that take on money measures that poke at large political action groups with unlimited resources to influence the outcome of an election. However, I have also seen allegations that outside money was used to influence statewide ballot measures.

So what if you have plenty of money and want to get elected or pass your ballot measure? Here are some tips:

1. If you're working to pass or defeat a ballot measure, remember, the messenger is the message. Carefully choose who will deliver the message to the voters. In the 1998 California general election, the Indian gambling proposition had the out-of-state Las Vegas casinos fighting it while the proponents used Native Americans to promote it. The casinos lost. During a recent tort reform ballot measure, lawyers used victims of drunk drivers rather than themselves in ads. Carefully consider your messenger, and use one who evokes an emotion or a positive feeling with the voters.
2. Hit the campaign trail. Don't spend all your time with the high end of society. Get out and meet the public, kiss babies, shake hands, get your face or issue out there. Do the walking and talking. If you're independently wealthy and financing your own campaign, you get to spend time with the voters rather than on the phone dialing for dollars, so do just that.
3. Distance yourself from any legislation or policies that look as though they will benefit your business, either directly or indirectly. A good

politician will embrace issues that are good for the community, especially the community in the long run. While that may not be good for
your business in the immediate future, it will be good for you as a candidate and an office holder.

4. Being rich doesn't mean you shouldn't be informed on the issues, have
a tight message, and be able to communicate it well to the public. Get
your campaign organized, and don't apologize for your money.

5. Spend your resources as though you don't have a lot. Use lawn signs,
newspaper ads, radio ads, and direct mail. Even though you can afford
it and it's easier, you should avoid communicating with the voters exclusively through TV ads.

6. Don't run as a businessperson; run as a leader in your community. Talking about your business success can be misconstrued by the voter. Instead, relate your business experience to serving in office. While people
love to say government should be run like a business, that's not exactly
true; streets make no money, sewer and water services make no money.
Government is not about making a profit; it's about service to the
community—it's business with a heart. Characterize the differences so
voters know that you understand what they are.

7. Don't parade your wealth to the voters by saying how much you will
spend to win. You never want to appear as though you're buying votes.
To the voters, it's far more important that you earn the votes.

8. Most important, always appear to be one with the average person. Inte-
grate this idea as part of your core. Too often, those who are very wealthy
project an image of being out of touch with the common person.

The World's Smallest Brochure: Direct Mail That Works

Most direct mailings have a rate of return of 3 to 6 percent without call-backs.
Because a campaign does not want to send a direct-mail piece to raise funds
that costs more money than it brings in, the challenge lies in designing a piece
that has a higher rate of return and is inexpensive to produce.

> "Time is the most valuable thing
> one can spend."
> —— THEOPHRASTUS, 300 B.C.

People have become very sophisticated at
detecting junk mail. To increase the rate of
return, the piece must first get opened; second, it must be read (at least in part); and finally, it must be compelling enough to
motivate the reader to give. Anything in a business-size envelope (a number
9) with an address label, a bulk stamp, or a meter mark is suspect and apt to

be thrown away without being opened. So the first task is choosing an envelope size that will make it more likely that the piece will be opened.

In 1999, the Reform Party created a direct-mail piece that went out nationwide to seventy thousand recipients. By using an oversized (5 by 7 inches) courier envelope and an easy-to-read three-page note, the mailing drew a return rate of 4 percent. This return rate was double the national average, and the piece realized a two-to-one profit.[7]

A mailing this large enjoys an economy of scale that few local elections can attain; in this case, it cost only $0.67 per piece, including postage. The cost of a mailing like this for a short run in a local election could easily be more than twice as much; in fact, postage alone (if using first class) would have come in at $0.57 per piece in 1999.

While oversized pieces work well with some voters, they do not work at my home. The size that I most consistently open looks like an invitation or a greeting card from a friend; that is, 6½ by 4¾ inches. This size is large enough to hold a remittance envelope (without folding) and will comfortably hold a half-sheet of paper folded in half. Given that a shorter letter is more likely to be read, do not make the mistake of folding an 8½-by-11-inch sheet in four.

Once the envelope is open, it is important that the piece offer plenty of information, be pleasing to the eye, and have a weight and feel that says the recipient is important, without looking lavish or expensive. The challenge, then, is how to make it all fit in a small format.

To accomplish such a package, my graphic designer and I put together what we call the world's smallest brochure: a half sheet of 8½-by-11-inch 80-pound vellum Bristol, folded in half. The front of the piece featured a photo of the candidate and a list of his accomplishments and ratings during his first term in the Oregon House (figure 5.15). The inside had another photo of the candidate and a letter with a P.S. on the state's tax refund policy on political contributions; each piece was personally signed by the candidate in either blue or green ink (never use black) (figure 5.16). The back had an endorsement from the governor. Given the space constraints, we skipped the usual business-letter practice of including the donor's address in the upper left-hand corner. Some letters had a "Dear Friends" salutation, and on others, we used no other identifier than the recipient's first name to make it a personalized letter; this created more work, but was worth it. To keep everything looking sharp, the letter, envelope, and remittance envelope were all printed on white. To encourage the recipient to turn the envelope over (one step closer to opening it), we had the representative's name and address printed on the envelope flap rather than on the front in the upper left-hand corner.

REPRESENTATIVE BATES' 2001 REPORT CARD

The Oregon Business Association ranked Representative Alan Bates among the top ten legislators in Oregon: *"courageous, smart, thoughtful."*

The Oregon League of Conservation Voters gave Rep. Bates an 82% pro-environment rating.

The Oregon Education Association rated Dr. Bates in the 90th percentile for his advocacy of public education.

"As a freshman legislator, he shined as he forged consensus legislation ensuring a healthy and competitive workers' compensation market in Oregon. It was Dr. Bates who kept the interests of the insured and the small businesses first."
- **Coalition for Economic Security for Oregon**

Because of legislation sponsored or strongly supported by Dr. Alan Bates Oregonians will have:

- *Increased access to higher education (HB 2521)*
- *A patient bill of rights (HB 3040)*
- *Reduced prescriptions costs for seniors (HB 3300 & SB 819)*
- *Improved roads and highways (comprehensive transportation package)*
- *Government made more accountable through annual audits (HB 3980)*
- *A cleaner and safer environment (mercury reduction legislation)*

FIGURE 5.15 Front of the "World's Smallest Brochure"

To test a "Dear Friends" salutation versus a personalized one, I divided the mailing into two parts. The first was sent to five hundred people who had canvassed, had a lawn sign, or volunteered time to the campaign in some way. Although some had also given to the campaign, I did not have the donor list at the time of the mailing. This group had a letter that began "Dear Friends," which allowed me to have the whole thing printed, cut, and folded at a local print shop. Using a clerical team of sixteen seniors, we hand-addressed, stuffed, sealed, and stamped the envelopes (using bulk, not first-class postage) in one hour and fifteen minutes. The mailing cost was $425 ($0.85 apiece)—for printing, postage, paper stock, layout, and remittance envelopes.

Because the candidate was a physician, I sent the second mailing to one hundred local physicians whom he knew, either personally or peripherally, using a letter designed to address their interests. This mailing was identical to the "Dear Friends" mailing except for four things: the text of the letter, the personalized salutation, a first-class stamp rather than a bulk stamp, and a computer-generated "handwriting" font on the envelope. A volunteer printed and stamped the envelopes. One side of the letter was printed at a local print shop, and I used my printer to add the personalized salutation and letter on the other side; I cut and stuffed the letters as they came out of the printer. Increasing the postage from bulk to first class increased the price by $0.14 per piece, but saved an enormous amount of time going to the post

Dr. Alan Bates
State Representative
Oak Street
Ashland, Oregon 97520

Phone and fax: (541) 482-1427
Email: repbates@internetcds.com

Dear Friends,

I wanted to take a moment to thank you for the opportunity to serve southern Oregon in the legislature. When I first ran for State Representative I never realized how much I would love this work.

Although veteran legislators told me I accomplished more than most freshmen—especially of a minority party—I sometimes felt frustrated watching excellent bills (such as campaign finance reform) die in committee. Still, there were many successes of which I am quite proud. I have included a few in this mailing.

I believe my success was due not only to the support of so many in southern Oregon who helped me get to Salem, but also those who continued to help throughout the session with emails, phone calls, and letters alerting my office to problem legislation. With 5,000 bills to read we relied on those back home to help. We were not disappointed.

Now, I need your help again. I've been told this area will be targeted in the next election and that I must expect a tough and expensive race. While I am willing to put in the time needed to win the next election, I know that hard work alone is no guarantee. To win, I need your support of both time and money.

Please, take a moment to return the enclosed envelope and, please, consider a contribution today.

Thank you,

PS. Political contributions (up to $50 per person, $100 per couple) are *refundable* on your Oregon tax return. That applies whether you file the short or long form.

FIGURE 5.16 Sample Fund-Raising Letter Inside the "World's Smallest Brochure"

All were personally signed by the candidate.

office and dealing with the bulk-mail process. The cost of the second piece was $1 each, for a total of $100.

For the five hundred "Dear Friends" letters, the rate of return was 19 percent, with an average donation of $61. This $400 mailing brought in $5,745. The mailing with the personalized salutation and first-class postage stamp had a 53 percent rate of return, with an average donation of $97. This $100 mailing brought in $5,125. The two mailings combined realized a twenty-to-one profit. We did not make follow-up phone calls for either mailing.

Keeping Track of Donations

One enormously helpful contribution a volunteer can make to a campaign is to keep the records of donations as they come in. By having these records complete and in one place, your campaign will save money in accounting fees and will have at hand the information needed for filing with the secretary of state or the elections department. Figure 5.17 is an example of headings you can use in a spreadsheet for keeping track.

Name, last	First: (signer name)	Spouse/ partner	Address/PO box	City	Zip	Occupation (signer)	Donation amount	Date received	T.Y.	Phone #

FIGURE 5.17 Example of Headings for the Donor Spreadsheet

For filing purposes, your campaign must have the occupation of the person who signed the check and the date the check was received.

6

Lawn Signs

To Be or Not to Be

Lawn signs are a unique animal, so consider the following before making a decision to use them:

- Lawn signs work in nonpartisan races; partisan, uncontested primaries; areas of homogeneous populations; and contested primaries.
- Lawn signs are *not* about voter persuasion; they're about voter activation.
- Placed in enemy territory, lawn signs can do more harm than good.
- The number of lawn signs placed for a candidate or issue does not necessarily coincide with a win.
- Lawn signs are a great way to increase name or issue recognition in an area that will support the candidate or issue anyway.
- Lawn signs are a high-maintenance relationship.

Because lawn signs are almost entirely about voter activation, they should be used primarily where a candidate or an issue already enjoys support or registration advantage. As outlined in Chapters 1 and 7, Americans are relocating to communities where political and cultural ideology is shared. In partisan races, if you are not among the majority of the party faithful in a community or an area of your candidacy, you risk—by incessantly reminding people of your candidacy with lawn signs—activating voters who will vote against you.

Since the late 1990s, I have tracked registration and cautioned campaigns that voters were (and are) moving to "their" side of the room by flipping registration or relocating to communities with like-minded residents. It makes sense: People want to live next door to those who are similar to them; it's a self-selecting process. Further, even in areas where eight out of ten voters will vote with one party or the other, neighbors in the minority, as well as majority party, look to see whose lawn sign is where to help them "categorize" a candidate as left or right.

Oddly, lawn signs help most in areas where candidates or issue-based campaigns need them the least, that is, where they will win anyway, thereby reducing the undervote. They remind voters of pending elections (especially helpful for special elections) and are a public endorsement for a candidate or an issue. These kinds of endorsements hold the most sway among small communities and neighborhoods where people know each other. Most important, because lawn signs are mostly about activation, when placed in areas of overwhelming support, they can increase the margin of win and push down an undervote.

Lawn sign placement and maintenance is a great opportunity to involve people who want to volunteer in a campaign but are not interested in working directly with the public. It is also an ideal activity for campaign workers who you feel might somehow make an unfavorable impression. Although it's a huge time and money commitment, with enough volunteers a well-run lawn sign campaign is an excellent way for a voter to feel involved in a campaign while elevating

> "Few things are harder to put up with than the annoyance of a good example."
> — **MARK TWAIN**

candidate name recognition or increasing awareness of a ballot issue. And, as indicated above, lawn signs also demonstrate support for a candidate or an issue within a community. However, that is really all they do. Given the expense and hassle of lawn signs plus the demands on your volunteer base, your campaign committee should consider carefully whether to use them. Nevertheless, if your opponent is using them, you should, too.

In my town, lawn signs cannot be placed more than forty-five days before an election. In anticipation of the big day when all the signs suddenly appear,

I ask one person from the committee to be in charge of overseeing the activity. If I am working on a campaign that involves more than one city, I have captains in each town who will oversee placement and maintenance in their area.

There are two schools of thought on lawn sign placement. One is not to worry if you don't have a lot of locations at first, since it is what you end up with that counts. In this view, what is important is the appearance of building momentum. The other school of thought is: *Boom!* Here comes the candidate! Suddenly the name is out, and everyone supports that person. I am an adherent of the latter school. I work like crazy to get as many locations as possible for the big day. I do this to make a big visual impact, of course, but also because this way, I only have to organize sign placement once. I know that there will always be additional requests as the campaign progresses, but not so many that a few people can't handle them easily. I always have volunteers whose sole job throughout the campaign is to put up lawn signs as requests come in.

> "To a large degree reality is whatever the people who are around at the time agree to."
> **MILTON H. MILLER**

As in all campaign-related activities, have everything ready and organized for the teams. Also note that it is especially important that people work in pairs in this activity: one to drive the car or truck and the other to hop out and install the sign.

Logo and General Information

For our purposes, a logo is your name or ballot measure and a slogan written in a memorable way. Sometimes the name will be written with a star and streamers behind it, or a waving American flag, or stars and stripes. In my first run for mayor, I had one that was quite blocky with the name written in different-colored bars. In my second bid, I did another one that was fairly complicated with a backdrop of the city, trees, and clouds. Because I have no imagination and even less talent in these areas, I leave this task to a professional. The going rate for developing a logo in my area is $200 to $600. Because you will be looking at your logo for months, it's well worth investing time and money into it.

I recently worked on a campaign in which we were asked to develop a logo, a walking piece (i.e., a piece used for canvassing), and a brochure. My graphic designer put together an excellent logo, but the campaign committee rejected it. Instead, the committee developed a similar design using a desktop publishing program. Although the alternative logo looked fine on a small mockup, it had a fatal flaw that did not materialize until the logo was printed on lawn sign stock and field signs. As this logo increased in size, its readability decreased. As a result, the lawn signs were difficult to read, and the field signs (4 by 4 feet, and 8 by 4 feet) impossible. When I asked my graphic designer about it, he told me it was because the new logo included an additional line. This experience is one more reminder to follow the advice of professionals you hire.

Lawn signs, like trademarks, must easily identify your cause or candidate. You need to develop a "look" that distinguishes your campaign from all others on the landscape. Once you have a logo, try to use it in all campaign literature and advertising.

Regardless of who does your signs and logo, it is a good idea to visit local vendors who print lawn signs. They usually save at least one of each sign they have ever printed. This way, you can shop for ideas in style and color combinations without any out-of-pocket expenses. When you're designing your sign, keep in mind that using two colors costs a lot more than one but is well worth it (figures 6.1 and 6.2). To save some money, you can get a two-color (or even a three-color) look by having almost a solid color printed over the white stock while leaving the lettering with no color. This produces white lettering on what looks like colored stock. Then use halftones (a mix of the white sign and the solid color showing through) in the design or part of the lettering for the "third" color. The result is very classy.

Your lawn signs can provide help in subtle ways. For example, in 2008, Obama had formidable support in my town, where I was also helping out in a city council race for an outsider who was attempting to unseat an incumbent. Since the Obama signs might reinforce the city council race I was helping, I took an Obama lawn sign to a graphic designer and had him match font and colors and then selected a slogan that piggybacked onto Obama's theme: "Change Starts Here."

Weatherproof Stock

Even if money is a big problem, do not cut costs on your stock. Get good paper stock that is weatherproof; poly tag or corrugated works well. The corrugated stock is nice because it is printed on both sides of the same sign, thus eliminating the need to staple signs back-to-back. Stapled signs often come apart and need repair. Also, corrugated can be attached to the stake before pounding it into the ground, which speeds up the work of the crews putting them up. Be sure to use screws and washers to attach the sign to the stake. Corrugated signs with wooden stakes must be printed so that the tubes inside the sign run horizontal. If you do not do this, the sign will bend with

FIGURE 6.1 Example of a Lawn Sign Using Logo and Theme: Campaign for the Carnegie

In an issue-based campaign it is advantageous to connect a positive image with the ballot item. This logo was in red, black, and white and was so well liked that voters who had never had a lawn sign before called and requested one for their yard. (Design by Crystal Castle Graphics)

FIGURE 6.2 "Maxwell for the House" Lawn Sign

In the first post–September 11, 2001, general election, we correctly guessed that all political signs would incorporate images of the American flag. To stand apart, we used magenta for the name and slogan and a deep teal for the bar under the candidate's name and the border. As with the Carnegie lawn sign, we received numerous requests for this sign simply because people loved the look.

the first wind. Should your printer mess up and print them with the corrugated tubing running perpendicular, you can save the sign by using H wickets that slide up inside the sign and hold it.

If you are using poly tag, remember to bring in your clerical team to staple the signs back-to-back. This needs to be done before the signs are put in place. Do not staple poly tag signs to the stakes before pounding the stakes in the ground. The sign will fall off.

Have the signs and the stakes in piles of twenty-five when crews arrive. If you have the signs and stakes already counted, you need only assign the area and direct the team to take the appropriate number of bundles of stakes and signs.

Remember, any sign material that is not weatherproof will curl with the first heavy dew or light rain, and your campaign "look" will be one of litter. Political lawn signs are a touchy subject in some communities. Keep lawn signs neat and complete at all times. If you're sloppy about quality, placement, or maintenance, lawn signs may do your campaign more harm than good. But if you do it right, they make your campaign look well organized and well staffed.

Stakes for lawn signs are expensive. To save money, I ask other campaigns to give me their stakes after elections. I then bundle the stakes in sets of twenty-five and lend them to campaigns I support. Call around to those who have run and lost or are not running again, and collect stakes. This works especially well if you are running a single campaign in the fall and someone you know lost in the primary election.

> "Taxation with representation ain't so hot, either."
> — **GERALD BARZAN**

If you have no luck, try to get a secondary wood products company or nursery to donate them. Still no luck? Ask supporters in the construction industry to make you some. Still no luck? Just buy them. Four-foot stakes work best.

You can count on your lawn signs plus stakes costing four to five dollars each, depending on the size and number of colors. Budget accordingly, and place them carefully.

Obviously, the size of your lawn sign can affect the cost of printing as well as the cost of stock. Lawn signs come in all sizes, so while you're visiting the printer to look at past political signs, check out their sizes as well. A typical sign is 18 by 24 inches, although I've seen some very effective signs that were 9 by 24 inches. This longer, narrower size works quite well if your candidate has a long name that fits comfortably in that space.

In the 1992 presidential campaign, the local Clinton-Gore team used 20-by-30-inch signs in my area. The stock was so heavy that it continually fell off the stake. The teams eventually had to go back and place each sign on two stakes. It still looked bad. Finally, the teams went back again and added a stick across the top of the stakes and then attached the sign on three sides. I would not recommend something that large.

If firefighters or other well-organized groups endorse you, they may have the ability to print lawn signs, with some limitations, such as number of colors or size. It's worth checking; such groups could save your campaign a lot of money. Keep in mind, however, that you would have to post such a contribution under "in-kind" on your contributions and expenditures form.

Another style of lawn sign uses a U-shaped metal rod, like a large croquet wicket, that holds a printed plastic sleeve. This type of sign costs as much

> "Eliminate risk and you eliminate innovation . . . don't eliminate risk; knowingly take it on."
> **VAUGHN KELLER**

as, or more than, the conventional lawn sign, but the plastic signs and metal rods are easy to transport, the wickets are practically indestructible, and the sign stock itself does not need to be stapled or attached with hardware to stakes. All the advance work to prepare the signs for placement is eliminated, and the wickets are easy to push in and pull out of the ground; there is no need to carry mallets and staple guns or to look for soft ground. The downside of these signs is that they are not particularly attractive.

More and more campaigns are using these wicket and baggie (plastic sleeve) signs. Since it is the wickets that drive up the cost—especially shipping costs, we now save the metal hoops. To store wickets, we made a two-bar, modified sawhorse that the wickets simply straddle. Wickets thrown into a pile until the next campaign are a nightmare, and wickets stored outside become rusty immediately, later covering your workers' hands and the inside of their cars with rust.

> "He who gets a name for rising early can stay in bed until noon."
> **IRISH PROVERB**

Lawn signs should be a work of art. You want the homeowner hosting the sign to be pleased with its look. You know you have a winner when people call and ask for a lawn sign simply because they like how it looks.

Halloween

If you're running a fall campaign, you should be prepared to send your entire lawn sign workforce back out the day after Halloween, which falls just a few days before the general election. You want your campaign to look great right up to the end. Extra effort and foresight are not lost on the electorate, nor are the opposite traits.

I know this may sound obvious, but be sure the signs are put up perpendicular to the street. The point of lawn signs is for people to see them from a distance as they drive by. To get any benefit from lawn signs, you need to attract the attention of voters.

Your "look" and how you present it will determine the success of lawn signs. In a Portland, Oregon mayoral race some years ago, an outsider ran a really great lawn sign campaign. One of the most distinguishing marks of his campaign was small, undersized lawn signs that he used in place of the normal-sized signs. Neighborhoods began having competitions to see who had the most signs up. Some houses would have ten of these signs on the front lawn. In some areas, neighbors would try to get their entire block covered with the "cute" little lawn signs. Meanwhile, the opponent ran a very traditional campaign using only billboards and, needless to say, lost. Don't hesitate to be creative and bold. You never know what will work. Bold, however, does not mean elaborate. Simple signs with a simple theme are the least offensive and the easiest to read, especially when observers pass by at high speeds.

Location, Location, Location

Getting good locations to display your signs is the second half of using lawn signs effectively. Often people who have run for office in previous elections will have a record of where their lawn signs were placed. Try to get such lists, and call those people first. This works best when you share a political ideology with a former candidate.

In 2004, I ran a campaign for Representative Alan Bates, who announced his candidacy for the Oregon Senate. We had no opposition in the primary, but because our opponent for the general election was someone who was enormously popular across the district, we wanted to mount an aggressive lawn-sign campaign for the primary.

I had run dozens of campaigns in various parts of the county, but had not worked a campaign that covered the additional area of the senate race for fifteen years. Suddenly, we needed lawn sign locations—lots of them. Because I had worked on a countywide effort that focused primarily on identifying supporters for a state money measure for schools the year before, I took the list of IDs and set up phone banks to call through these voters. One night became two, two became a week, and we were still woefully short of locations. I called other candidates I'd helped in the past and got their lists. Another week of calling—six to ten people per shift per night called. Most voters were not home or did not answer. We added on arterials and cold-called people in the candidate's party. It was brutal. We finally had about six hundred locations of our thousand-location goal and called it quits; we'd run out of time and now needed to get teams together to put up the signs and organize the installation activity.

Meanwhile, I organized an assembly party. We bought out all the washers and short drywall screws from the local hardware store, dragged five hundred stakes out of my barn, and purchased five hundred more. To put the signs together, we set up tables in the back yard. Thirty people arrived, half with electric screwdrivers, to help assemble and load seven hundred signs into trucks to be delivered to team leaders in each of the cities. Of the one thousand assembled signs, three hundred would remain with me for volunteers who would launch from my home in my city.

Next we needed to do the mapping—that is, organize the locations so they coincided with an attached map. It would be easy; I'd done it a million times, and indeed, Ashland and other smaller cities *were* easy. But when it came to do the packets for the paltry three hundred signs in the county's largest city, Medford, I realized I had no idea where streets were—no idea if a location was at one end of an eight-mile-long street or the other end. I knew only that each area had to be organized so that volunteers were not driving from one corner of the city to another to put up two signs. When that happens, you never see that volunteer again.

One of the committee members and I began our work of assembling map packets the afternoon before the signs were to be installed. We did the small cities first and then, laying a huge map of Medford across the dining room table, began the laborious process of laying three-by-five-inch cards with names, locations, phone numbers, and instructions for the installer on top of the map in the general location of the address. Still, there were more than two hundred locations we could not find easily. I hit the computer looking for them; my helper hit the map in the phone book looking up location after location. Afternoon turned into evening, which turned into night; 3 a.m. rolled around to 4 a.m. and then 5 a.m., and we were still working. I panicked because volunteers would be showing up from each of the cities at 6:30 a.m. to take packets back with them to meet their installation teams at 7 a.m. This felt pretty much like a pending disaster, and I literally "wrote the book" on how to avoid this sort of thing.

One hundred people, or fifty teams, were to help us at 7 a.m. My friend and I worked fourteen hours straight and still did not have the task done. Partial lists were sent off to Medford with me hoping above hope that not everyone would show up. No such luck. Everyone showed up, and then some:

As requested, volunteers had brought friends. There were not enough completed packets to give to all the teams, and the candidate drove back to Ashland to pick up what were now partially finished packets. It was ugly.

I thought: Never again.

The next day, I contacted a friend who knew geographic information system (GIS) mapping, and he said if I got a list of locations to him in Excel, he could map all the locations for me in under an hour. He handled the general election for us.

Yes, it was a nightmare, but it was a nightmare that happened in an uncontested primary and better there than in the general. *This* is why you run a primary.

This chapter includes instructions on how to do lawn sign organization without a computer, because the procedure is still pretty straightforward for a small city or district. But keep in mind that there's a whole new world out there. I have worked on at least fifteen campaigns since the 2004 debacle and have always had someone do the locations using a mapping program for lawn sign installation. The way the little red dots are dropped onto the map directly from the address on the Excel sheet is completely civilized.

If you are working with a voter activation network, trust me, the network has a mapping program—there has to be one, as it's what campaigns use to cut turf for canvassing. It's there for lawn sign installation as well. I even had one volunteer download some obscure mapping program, and with only longitude and latitude of the city, she was able to drop all the locations from my Excel sheets onto maps for Obama's signs in the primary.

Guilt by Association

In 2008, I worked on a nonpartisan campaign of a former Republican. Needless to say, of the remaining 13 percent of Republicans in my city, every one of them wanted my candidate's lawn sign. But when these same Republicans put up signs for McCain and Palin, my candidate had to pull his signs out or suffer backlash-by-association at the ballot box.

In my neighborhood, which is still relatively mixed politically, I had a lawn sign of the above candidate in my yard, as did a very conservative neighbor of mine down the street. When I canvassed my neighborhood, a half dozen neighbors commented that it was the first time in twenty years that they had seen the same lawn sign in front of my home as my Republican neighbor. People are always looking for clues to contextualize a candidate, and lawn signs are the easiest way to do that. It can be a good or a bad thing.

Requests

You will find that supporters will call the campaign and request lawn signs throughout the campaign. It is important to accommodate them. However, this means that your campaign must be discerning about initial lawn sign placement. Hold some back to replace lost or vandalized signs and to accommodate requests. Avoid placing signs on culs-de-sac or overloading some streets while others go bare. Let supporters know from the beginning that the number of signs is limited and that the campaign needs to place them in areas of high visibility.

Finally, avoid placing your sign in yards already teeming with political signs, and keep away from coupling yours in hundreds of locations with the same signs from other campaigns. Keep in mind that voters are highly sensitive to visual cues. They know their neighbors and look to those they respect for help in making decisions about candidates and measures. They are also likely to spot patterns, and although lawn sign patterning is bound to happen, make it a priority to mix things up. By occasionally coupling your signs with those of candidates running in the opposing party, you give voters "permission" to split their ticket.

Preparing for the First Day

Setup for lawn sign installation follows the same process as the other campaign activities. After getting locations and making sure that the signs and stakes are ready to go, you need to organize the teams that will put up the signs.

Although I maintain lists of all donors, volunteers, and lawn sign locations on a spreadsheet, I find three-by-five-inch index cards to be very useful for my lawn sign teams. This is true even though I use mapping programs to place the locations on maps.

One reason is that an average team can place twenty-five signs in a two-hour block of time and index cards make it easy to move locations from one group to another. That is, if a logical area for one team to work has thirty-five locations, index cards allow quick shifting of signs to other teams working in adjacent sections.

Another reason to include index cards is that installation instructions can be written for each location at the bottom of the card. For example, some people want to put up their own sign or want the sign stapled to their fence or placed in the hedge or left on the porch. Directives, jotted on the bottom of the card, help the teams be more efficient and keep the homeowner happy.

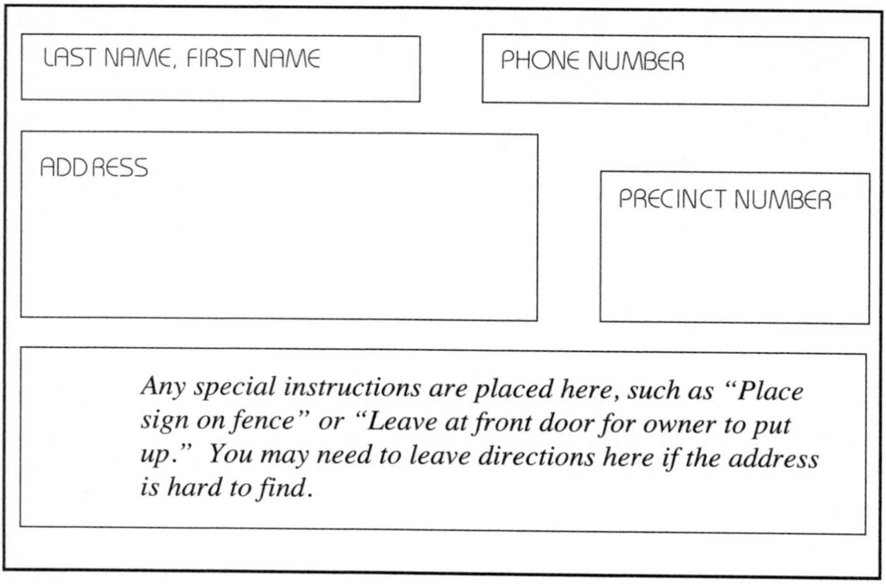

LAST NAME, FIRST NAME	PHONE NUMBER
ADDRESS	PRECINCT NUMBER

Any special instructions are placed here, such as "Place sign on fence" or "Leave at front door for owner to put up." You may need to leave directions here if the address is hard to find.

FIGURE 6.3 Example of a 3-by-5-Inch Lawn-Sign Card

Plus, although I typically organized the cards for the most efficient installation route, drivers and installers sometimes want to organize their own course and it's pretty easy if they have cards that can be shuffled.

Installers can also use the card to record information to get back to the campaign, should there be a problem. For example, "couldn't find this address" or "bad location—pick up sign if we run short." That sort of thing. Further, using index cards and map packets means that lawn sign removal after the election is already organized and ready to go.

Begin by printing out, from your spreadsheet, a list of those who have agreed to host a lawn sign. For each location, create a index card that includes the address, name, and phone number of the homeowner (figure 6.3). This can also be done on the computer using card stock printed eight to a page— like labels—and then cut into individual cards. Once the cards are filled out, organize them by addresses that are close to each other. What you are after in grouping the cards is some kind of logical walking or driving pattern that will allow your placement team to work efficiently. I use groupings of no more than twenty to thirty locations, each of which will take about two hours.

After you have the location cards organized, place them for each grouping in a ziplock bag along with a map with the target area highlighted. Number each packet, and when crews arrive, ask them to sign in and indicate the number of the packet they took. Take a few minutes the night before to record the lawn sign packet numbers in your spreadsheet containing the lawn sign locations. This is helpful if a packet gets lost; it also allows you to print out a list for your maintenance people during the campaign.

Placement crews work in pairs. If you are using poly tag signs, the crew needs a staple gun (to attach the sign to the stake), a stapler (in case the sign comes apart at the corners), and a mallet (to pound the stake into the ground). If they are placing corrugated signs, they will need only a mallet and maybe a metal pole for making a pilot hole. In either case, it is a good idea to bring along extra signs or repair kits and tools (washers, screws, electric screwdrivers, staple guns, staples, stakes) in case a sign breaks. If you are using something other than these two types of signs, just remember: Send extras of everything.

> "Sometimes you can observe a lot just by watching."
> YOGI BERRA

Assigning crews is then simply a matter of handing them a ziplock bag with the location index cards, a map with their area highlighted, and the appropriate number of signs and stakes. Ask as many volunteers as possible to bring tools, or borrow enough ahead of time from friends. Be sure everything borrowed by the campaign is labeled and returned promptly.

It is also critical that the volunteers bring back the plastic bag with the index cards. You will need the cards for the maintenance crews to repair signs after Halloween and for sign pickup after the election.

In 2008, I organized the lawn signs for the Obama campaign in my corner of the world. After they went up, so did gas prices, and as gas reached four dollars a gallon, I was disinclined to send volunteers back out to pick up the signs after the primary just to reinstall them in October. So I mailed a postcard to each house that hosted a sign and asked that the owner bring in the sign after the primary. I also indicated on the postcard when it was legal to put them back up before the general. I included my phone number on the postcard in case a sign went missing. It completely worked. Supporters pulled in their signs and put them all back out before the general election on the designated day.

I firmly believe that poorly designed, poorly constructed lawn signs hurt your campaign more than they help it. If you are going to use lawn signs, they are way too expensive and too labor-intensive to cut corners on design and production. If you can't raise the money to do them right, don't do them.

Even so, sometimes you must deviate from this rule for strategic reasons. In one campaign, because of a lack of funds, we printed only one-third the normal number of lawn signs. Although they were carefully placed to maximize visibility, they soon began to disappear (it was a very controversial money measure). People who wanted signs were calling, and others were calling to

Dear Alan Bates Supporter,

Thank you for displaying a lawn sign. Your public support for Alan will help raise visibility of his candidacy.

Although we try to contact each and every homeowner where a sign is placed, there is still room for error—especially given that our campaign is largely staffed by volunteers.

If we have installed this lawn sign incorrectly or if there is any problem with your sign (either maintenance or if it disappears) please call us at 555–1427 and we will repair, replace, or remove the sign as needed.

We will return within two days of the general election (November 2nd) to remove your sign.

Thank you,
Committee to Elect Dr. Alan Bates

FIGURE 6.4
Example of
an Instruction
Door Hanger for
Lawn-Sign Hosts

request replacements. We knew it was a close race, and our diminishing number of signs looked as though our support was waning.

So, using the same color of ink as our signs, I hand-painted more signs in my barn on the back of old poly tag lawn signs. In the middle of the night, I placed them throughout the city. I did not want them to be next to each other; rather, I wanted to create the impression that homeowners had taken the initiative to paint their own signs and put them up. I wanted the look to be one of individual, rebellious support for our side and angry opposition to the money fighting our effort. We won the election by fewer than three hundred votes out of five thousand cast.

Finally, no matter how careful you and your team are, mistakes happen: Addresses get inverted, people hear yes when no is really spoken, signs get vandalized or stolen. Further, if you have an incorrect address and do not know it and the homeowner pulls in the sign, your campaign may assume it disappeared for completely different reasons and continue to replace it.

In short, the host of your lawn sign must be able to reach the campaign in case something goes wrong. To make this easy, the campaign should include a door-hanger for each of the locations where a lawn sign is installed. These notes are printed four-up on brightly colored paper, usually shocking orange or yellow (you want them to be seen), and then they're cut so that each sheet of paper makes four.

Hole-punch an upper corner, and include enough rubber bands within the packets for the instruction cards. These are hung by your teams on a door knob of each address where a sign is placed (figure 6.4).

Field Signs

Field signs placed along highways are very effective in raising name recognition for campaigns. I have worked on campaigns where field signs have been professionally painted by hand and others where they were commercially printed. Naturally, such signs are not cheap. My preference would be to have volunteers paint them for free, but we must be realistic about these things. Not only is this task a lot to ask of anyone, but you also risk wasting time and losing volunteers if the signs end up looking amateurish and you feel placement would be problematic for the campaign. Regardless of how the signs are produced, location is the primary concern when using field signs. Figure 6.5 is an example of a field sign.

Field-sign locations can sometimes be found by calling real-estate agents who have parcels listed along highways or in cities. Ranchers, farmers, and owners of large, vacant lots will occasionally allow signs to be placed on the corners of their land. If you're running a local campaign during a general election, talk to other campaigns about locations that they have landed. Also, some counties now have property and their owners online, so if you find a location you like, consider looking for the owner through the county assessor's office.

The volunteer crew putting up field signs must be carefully selected. These people should have some construction experience so that the structure can withstand wind and the weight of the sign. The crews will need more than a hammer and nails to put up a field sign. Supply them with, or ask them to bring, post-hole diggers, shovels, screws, electric screwdrivers, and additional lumber for supports or bracing. This is a big production. With that said, some field signs can be attached just to metal fence posts with wire. This would require only a hand sledge for installation.

Know the law: Be sure to contact city and county authorities to find out size requirements and any other regulations on field signs. In one election, it suddenly came to light that our county had a size limit on large political signs.

FIGURE 6.5 Example of a Field Sign Used in an Issue-Based Campaign

This campaign used only field signs. The sign was a deep red with white lettering and silhouetted people in black. The sign was incorporated into the television spots so that the field signs and TV spots could reinforce each other.

Although I'd worked for nearly twenty years in campaigning in southern Oregon, I had somehow missed this, and of the five races I was working on, four were out of compliance in this regard. There was some discussion about making candidates and issue-based campaigns remove all signs that were too big, which would have been financially difficult for many of the races. Luckily, two of the three county commissioners were up for reelection, and they had illegal signs themselves. They temporarily changed the law to allow the larger signs.

Another area in which field signs create problems for campaigns is along state highways. Sometimes, a state highway right-of-way is as much as fifty feet on either side of the road. Although cities and counties may look the other way when a campaign encroaches on a right-of-way, the state generally does not. To have field signs installed (which can take crews up to an hour per sign) only to have them ripped down by state workers is maddening and wasteful. (When I say ripped down, I mean ripped down. State workers do not take the time to carefully unscrew each of the sides, nor to be careful in setting your $300 sign in the back of the pickup.) Also, locating your removed sign among state yards is more difficult than you might think. Save the campaign time and money: Call the local office of the state department of transportation, and ask about any locations where you are uncertain of the right-of-way.

Maintenance of Signs

Large or small, campaign signs must be maintained once they are up. Depending on the circumstances, you may use the same crew that placed the signs to maintain them throughout the campaign, or you may use a completely different crew. The maintenance crew must travel with a mallet, staple gun, extra signs, stakes, stapler, and so forth, in their cars at all times.

"Whatever is worth doing at all, is worth doing well."
EARL OF CHESTERFIELD

Ostensibly, maintenance crews are ready to repair any ailing sign they see in their normal daily travels. From time to time, however, there may be a need for the crews to travel their assigned placement routes for a more systematic check of the signs.

As noted earlier, you will need to keep your maps and plastic bags of lawn sign location index cards for your maintenance crews for post-Halloween repairs and for sign removal after the election. But for ongoing maintenance, use the packet number that you recorded in the spreadsheet, and sort the list according to that number. This way, you can print lists or e-mail them to your maintenance workers.

Besides maintenance, there will be the chore of putting up new signs as people call in requesting them or as canvassers return with requests for lawn signs. If there aren't too many requests, you can assign new locations to the appropriate maintenance crew or have special volunteers to do this chore on an ongoing basis. Believe it or not, having the candidate help with new location installations is great PR. As the campaign progresses, voters increasingly recognize the candidate and will often honk and wave as they drive by. Such a simple thing makes the candidate ap-

"A problem adequately stated is a problem well on its way to being solved."
BUCKMINSTER FULLER

pear more accessible and "like one of us." In one campaign I worked on, the candidate, a local physician, went out and helped put up field signs on the weekend. He reported that lots of people honked and waved and that some even stopped to help or say hello. A couple of days later, when the signs that the candidate himself had helped erect fell down, I got a number of calls from people I did not know asking if they could help get the signs back up for "Doc." We all laughed about how quickly the candidate-erected signs had fallen down, including the candidate, who is a very likable, self-effacing guy. Deficient carpentry skills aside, his initial efforts got him a lot of mileage and brought us some great workers.

In another campaign, there was a street where all the lawn signs disappeared every night. The man who put the signs in that area was also in charge of maintenance and just happened to drive along this street to and from work each day. After the signs disappeared and he had replaced them a couple of times, he decided to take them down on his way home from work and put them back up each morning on the way to work. You can't buy that kind of loyalty.

It is best to get requested signs up as soon as possible. However, if there are too many requests, it may be necessary to organize another day for placement. If you do this, be sure to include all of your current locations so that signs can be repaired or replaced if missing.

Lawn Sign Removal

Most localities have regulations requiring that campaign signs be removed within a certain period after the election. Whatever the regulations, your crews should be ready to remove all your lawn signs the day after the election. If the signs are left up longer, homeowners begin to take the signs inside or throw them away, making it difficult or impossible for your crews to retrieve them. Although corrugated signs begin to break down after a few years, poly tag and plastic-bag signs seem to last indefinitely, which is money in your pocket for the next election. At a minimum, you will want to retrieve the stakes or wickets for future campaigns. Since you have to get the signs down eventually, you might as well look organized and responsible by retrieving them as quickly as possible.

I like to get the crews set up beforehand for the day after the election. Here again, volunteers work in pairs with maps and the index cards containing the addresses. And again, have volunteers sign in and note which numbered packet they took. When they return, you must remember to get your cards and maps back for the next election. This is also a great time to get together a volunteer thank-you party to disassemble your lawn signs, put them away for the next election, and bundle your stakes in sets of twenty-five with duct tape or twine.

Finally, crews removing signs can pull in twice as many as they put up in the same period. That means that a team of two can generally bring in up to fifty lawn signs in a two-hour shift, depending upon how spread out the signs are.

Summary of Lawn Sign Tasks

1. Mail literature to potential hosts.
2. Use a phone bank to obtain locations.
3. Secure locations where your swing and base votes live.
4. Design the sign, print it, and obtain secure stakes and hardware.
5. Assemble the signs.
6. Use a phone bank to assemble installation teams.
7. Prepare packets for installation.
8. Install the signs.
9. Maintain them.
10. After the election, remove them.

Bumper Stickers and Buttons

Bumper stickers are an inexpensive way to familiarize the community with your name or ballot measure. Although bumper stickers are used predominantly in large city, county, state, and federal races, they can also be quite effective in the small election simply because they continue to be a novelty there.

This is one application for which I would relax my strong recommendation to place your campaign logo on all your materials. Bumper stickers are small and hard to read, so clarity is what is important. On a bumper sticker, ideally you want your candidate or measure before the voters, nothing more. In one campaign for which we used bumper stickers, we placed the logo along with the name. Despite being modified, it was still difficult to read.

> "In life and business, there are two cardinal sins. The first is to act precipitously without thought and the second is not to act at all."
>
> **CARL ICAHN,** investor and entrepreneur

A bonus with bumper stickers is that they are occasionally left on cars if a candidate wins, giving the community the impression that the individual is well liked in office. People who like to display bumper stickers are often willing to kick in a dollar or two to buy them.

Three points of caution on bumper stickers: First, should you decide to print bumper stickers, be sure to print them on removable stock. If people know the stickers will easily come off after the election, they'll be more inclined to place one on their car. Second, urge people to drive courteously while displaying your name on their cars. If they are rude on the road, the only thing the other driver will remember is the name on the bumper sticker.

Finally, keep in mind that the use of bumper stickers, like lawn signs, is an untargeted campaign activity.

Buttons are walking testimonials or endorsements. If supporters actually wear them, this tool further serves the goal of getting your name in front of the voting public. My experience is that very few people put candidate buttons on each day, and these items tend to add clutter and expense for the campaign.

However, since all canvassers should have some sort of official identification with the campaign, this is what I recommend: At a stationery store, buy a box of the type of plastic name holders used at conventions and meetings. Ask the graphic design artist who put together the lawn sign logo to make a miniature version of it, sized to fit the plastic badges. Also ask the designer to lay out as many of these as will fit on a sheet of paper. Reproduce on brightly colored card stock as many as you think you will need, keeping the original to make more throughout the campaign. Cut out your miniature "lawn signs," and slide them into the plastic holders. After the campaign, you can reuse the plastic name badges.

7

Targeting Voters

IN THIS CHAPTER
- Finding the Likely Voter
- Partisan Gaps
- Canvassing
- Direct Mail
- Tracking Polls

After using a precinct analysis to determine the best zones or precincts on which to focus your attention, the next challenge is to determine, within that context, which voters are most likely to vote and how to persuade them. Incorporating individual traits such as turnout history, education, income, gender, or race within the social context outlined in Chapter 1 offers a winning strategy for finding and persuading voters at affordable prices.

Finding the Likely Voter

Here are the top five indicators for predicting voter participation:

- Voting history
- Education
- Income
- Absentee voting
- Age

Voting History: The Most Reliable Method of Determining Future Participation

Accessing past voter participation is as easy as contacting the local clerk or election office, your political party, a voter contact service, or even a PAC that routinely helps partisan races. Any campaign vendor specializing in direct mail will have access to voting history. Who voted, not how one voted, is a matter of public record and remains the most reliable predictor of future voter participation; indeed, it "exceeds the effects of age and education."[1] And those who vote in a primary are 42 percent more likely than nonprimary voters to vote in the general election.[2]

> "Campaigns are preparation, organization, execution, and luck."
> **ELAINE FRANKLIN,** Republican strategist

A voter is typically referred to as a four, three, two, or one, that is, someone who voted in four out of four of the last elections, three out of four, and so on. Fours will vote. The others can be a little trickier to pin down. However, with a little prodding, threes and, often, twos can be activated to do their civic duty. Unless your race is during a presidential cycle, people who went to the polls only once in the last four elections may be a waste of time and money.

Education

According to a 1993 Simmons Market Research Bureau study, college graduates were 33 percent more likely to vote than the average adult, and those with a graduate degree were 41 percent more likely to vote. In November 2002, the Field Institute in California released a study of expected turnout in which it compared the characteristics of the state's voting-age population, its registered voters, and its likely voters. The study revealed that those who have no more than a high school education constitute 42 percent of the state's adults but only 24 percent of registered voters (and likely voters), and those with a college degree constitute just 28 percent of the adult population but 42 percent of likely voters.

Further, college entrance increases voter participation by between twenty-one and thirty points.[3] Similarly, the Center for Information on Civic Learning and Engagement reports that 70 percent of all voters eighteen to twenty-nine years old come from the subset of the same age group who have ever attended college (57 percent).[4]

Income

Turnout can also be predicted by income level (figure 7.1), which correlates with education. According to a 1999 report by the U.S. Census Bureau, people in the workforce with a college degree in 1976 had, on average, an in-

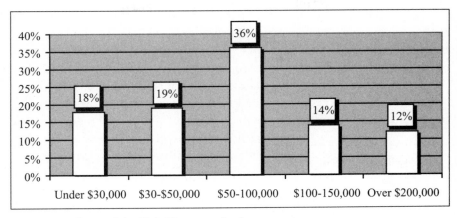

FIGURE 7.1 Share of the U.S. Electorate by Income

come 57 percent higher than those with only a high school diploma. By 1999, the proportion had increased to 76 percent, and by 2006, people with advanced degrees were earning four times what one could earn with a high school diploma alone.

Identifying these voters early and persuading them to support your candidate or measure is one more component of a win, because they will vote or are likely to vote.

> "The Ministry have caught the colonies as I have often caught a horse, by holding an empty hat, as if it was full of corn."
>
> **JOHN ADAMS**

Absentee Voting, Early Voting, and Voting by Mail

Voters who request an absentee ballot have long been among the most likely of likely voters. While the percentage of people requesting an absentee ballot may vary among states and regions, their turnout doesn't. Absentee voters can represent a substantial proportion of the overall turnout. In Oregon, before people could register absentee permanently, those requesting absentee ballots typically ran about 25 percent of all the registered voters. In the 1998 primary election, after voters were given the option to register absentee permanently, 41 percent of the voters did so. In that election, absentee ballots accounted for nearly two-thirds of all ballots cast. Absentee voter turnout was 53 percent, whereas turnout

> "Get your facts first and then you can distort them as much as you please."
>
> **MARK TWAIN**

among those casting their votes at the polls was only 22 percent. In the 1998 general election, 73 percent of those requesting an absentee ballot returned their ballot.[5]

In 2008, the Field Research Corporation of California (www.field.com) reported a record 13.7 million Californians voting. Of those, nearly 42 percent (5.7 million) voted by mail, an increase of 1.6 million over those voting by mail in 2004 and more than twice the 2.7 million who did so in the 2000 presidential election.[6] Currently, permanent mail ballot registrants represent better than 32 percent of the state's total registered voters—more than twice the permanent mail ballot registrants in the 2004 presidential election. In 2008, 84.9 percent of the 6.7 million registered voters issued a mail ballot returned their ballots, compared with a 75.9 percent turnout of all other registered voters.

> "A great many people think they are thinking when they are merely rearranging their prejudices."
> — WILLIAM JAMES

Absentee voters can have a regional context that should be examined by a campaign. For example, 29 percent of California's mail ballot registrants are from the San Francisco Bay Area, whereas only 13 percent of them are from Los Angeles.

And party demographics are typically different. Again in California, 46 percent of precinct voters are Democrats, compared with 30 percent Republicans, whereas Democrats hold only a 4 percent margin over the GOP for mail ballots.

Other demographic characteristics should also be studied. The Field Institute of California reports that mail-ballot voters have these characteristics:

- Older, although this margin has narrowed over past elections
- White non-Hispanic (70 percent, versus 23 percent Latino)
- Female (54 percent, versus 46 percent male)
- More conservative (32 percent, versus 24 percent liberal)

Given the potentially high percentage of overall voter turnout that absentee ballots can represent, your campaign should work them long before the get-out-the-vote (GOTV) effort, with a separate, focused campaign. Methods for both timing and reaching these voters will be covered extensively in Chapter 11.

The following states permit no-excuse, in-person early voting at election offices and, in some states, other satellite locations (voter registration and early voting are allowed at the same time in Ohio and North Carolina):

Alaska
Arizona
Arkansas
California
Colorado
Florida
Georgia
Hawaii
Idaho
Illinois
Indiana

Iowa
Kansas
Louisiana
Maine
Montana
Nebraska
Nevada
New Mexico
North Carolina
North Dakota
Ohio

Oklahoma
South Dakota
Tennessee
Texas
Utah
Vermont
West Virginia
Wisconsin
Wyoming

The following states permit any registered voter to vote by absentee ballot. Voters are not required to state their reason or excuse for voting by absentee ballot:

Alaska
Arizona
Arkansas
California
Colorado
Florida
Georgia
Hawaii
Idaho
Iowa

Kansas
Maine
Montana
Nebraska
Nevada
New Jersey
New Mexico
North Carolina
North Dakota
Ohio

Oklahoma
Oregon (all mail)
South Dakota
Utah
Vermont
Washington
Wisconsin
Wyoming

For information on when absentee ballots are counted and by whom, visit the National Conference of State Legislatures at www.ncsl.org. For additional detail of voting history from 1988 through 2008, by age, gender, ethnicity, political party, and more, go to nationaljournal.com.

The following states have some form of Election Day registration (EDR):

Connecticut (only for presidential elections)
Idaho
Iowa (since 2008)
Maine
Minnesota
Montana (since 2006)
New Hampshire

North Carolina (since 2007; EDR occurs 3–19 days before an election)
Wisconsin
Wyoming
North Dakota (no voter registration requirement at all)

In 2006 and again in 2008, states with EDR reported 10–12 percent higher turnout than states without EDR. People most affected by EDR are middle- and low-income voters, youth voters, and recent transplants (en.wikipedia.org).

Age

Voters aged 18 to 24 essentially abdicate their voting power to older Americans, who both register and turn out to vote in greater numbers. For example, those 18–24 outnumbered those 65–74 by 7 million, yet represented 1 million fewer voters at the ballot box in 2004 and 6 million fewer in 2006 (tables 7.1 and 7.2; figures 7.2 and 7.3).

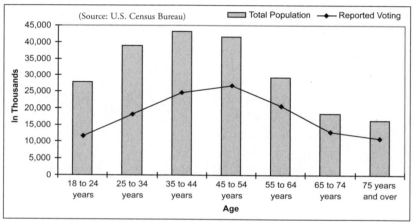

FIGURE 7.2 U.S. Voter Turnout by Age, 2004

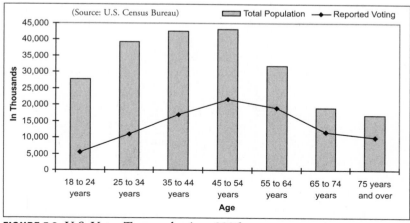

FIGURE 7.3 U.S. Voter Turnout by Age, 2006

TABLE 7.1 U.S. Voter Registration Versus Voter Performance, 2004

			Total Population November 2004								U.S. Citizen	
		Total	Reported Registered		Not Registered		Reported Voted		Did Not Vote		Reported Registered	Not Registered
Age	Total	Citizen Population	Number	Percent	Number	Percent	Number	Percent	Number	Percent	Number	Number
18–24	27,808	24,898	14,334	51.5	13,474	48.5	11,639	41.9	16,169	58.1	14,334	10,564
25–34	39,003	32,842	21,690	55.6	17,313	44.4	18,285	46.9	20,718	53.1	21,690	11,152
35–44	43,130	38,389	27,681	64.2	15,450	35.8	24,560	56.9	18,570	43.1	27,681	10,709
45–54	41,589	39,011	29,448	70.8	12,141	29.2	26,813	64.5	14,775	35.5	29,448	9,563
55–64	29,426	28,173	22,212	75.5	7,214	24.5	20,513	69.7	8,913	30.3	22,212	5,961
65–74	18,363	17,759	14,125	76.9	4,239	23.1	13,010	70.8	5,354	29.2	14,125	3,635
75+	16,375	15,933	12,581	76.8	3,794	23.2	10,915	66.7	5,459	33.3	12,581	3,352

Numbers are reported in thousands. (Source: U.S. Census Bureau)

TABLE 7.2 U.S. Voter Registration Versus Voter Performance, 2006

			U.S. Citizen November 2006								Total Population	
		Total	Reported Registered		Not Registered		Reported Voted		Did Not Vote		Reported Registered	Not Registered
Age	Total	Citizen Population	Number	Percent	Number	Percent	Number	Percent	Number	Percent	Percent	Percent
18–24	27,774	24,954	11,554	46.3	13,400	53.7	5,524	22.1	19,431	77.9	41.6	19.9
25–34	39,370	33,215	19,822	59.7	13,393	40.3	11,137	33.5	22,079	66.5	50.3	28.3
35–44	42,633	37,520	25,277	67.4	12,244	32.6	17,079	45.5	20,441	54.5	59.3	40.1
45–54	43,183	40,322	29,054	72.1	11,267	27.9	21,708	53.8	18,614	46.2	67.3	50.3
55–64	31,823	30,433	23,117	76.0	7,316	24.0	19,017	62.5	11,416	37.5	72.6	59.8
65–74	18,954	18,208	14,283	78.4	3,925	21.6	11,700	64.3	6,508	35.7	75.4	61.7
75+	16,867	16,420	12,740	77.6	3,680	22.4	9,954	60.6	6,466	39.4	75.5	59.0

Numbers are reported in thousands. (Source: U.S. Census Bureau)

In Oregon, final activity reports list every voter who participated in the election and include the date the ballots were received by local election officials. To determine who was voting when, we began tracking ballots by age in 2004. While voter turnout among age groups varies between presidential and nonpresidential cycles, the voting behavior of age groups does not. Essentially, the older the voter, the sooner the ballot is returned.

For example, in 2008, 35 percent of those 65 and older returned their ballots during the first week of voting and then continued to vote at an even rate up until Election Day. This compares with 76 percent of those 18–24 and 24–34 who voted in the final week and 76 percent of those 35–49. The 65-and-older group outpaced the other age groups' turnout up until Election Day and at times was outperforming the other groups by as much as 30 percent.

That older voters consistently vote earlier would indicate that their minds are made up long before Election Day and should be the first voters courted by a campaign.

Partisan Gaps

Youth Voters and the Growing Age Gap

Millennials, as 18- to 29-year-olds are called, represented a dramatic change in youth voting and involvement in the 2008 presidential election, with 53 percent reporting for civic duty and adding more than 2.2 million voters to the overall turnout. More remarkable is that the turnout in 2004 represented a 9 percent increase over 2000, when only 42 percent weighed in on the presidential election.[7] One in ten youth voters contributed to the Obama campaign, and many more volunteered. While their overwhelming support of Obama (66 percent) did not make or break the race for him, it certainly helped.[8] In 2000, registration among the 18–29 group was almost evenly split between the Democrats and Republicans. By 2008, the gap widened to nineteen points (table 7.3).

> "Once the game is over, the king and the pawn go back into the same box."
>
> **ITALIAN SAYING**

According to Pew Research, "the divergence between the candidate preferences of the youngest and oldest voters was the widest in decades, perhaps ever."[9] Indeed, of those 65 and older, 45 percent supported Obama, compared with 53 percent for John McCain, as revealed in exit polls by both CNN and the New York Times.

Youth voters now comprise 22 percent of the population and 18 percent of the 2008 voter turnout. Those 65 and older are slightly more than 12 percent of the adult population and 16 percent of the electorate.[10]

TABLE 7.3 Party Trends by Age

	Republicans (%)	Democrats (%)	NAVs and Others (%)
2008			
Total voters	32	39	29
18–29	26	45	29
30–44	32	38	30
45–64	33	37	29
65+	36	39	26
2004			
Total voters	37	37	26
18–29	35	37	29
30–44	40	34	26
45–64	36	37	27
65+	39	38	23
2000			
Total voters	35	39	27
18–29	35	36	29
30–44	36	38	27
45–64	33	39	28
65+	37	43	21

(Source: NBC Exit Polls)

Scott Keeter, Juliana Horowitz, and Alec Tyson, all from Pew Research, have studied the demographics of the young electorate: "Young voters are more diverse racially and ethnically than older voters and more secular in their religious orientation. These characteristics, as well as the climate in which they have come of age politically, incline them not only toward Democratic Party affiliation but also toward greater support of activist government, greater opposition to the war in Iraq, less social conservatism, and a greater willingness to describe themselves as liberal politically."[11]

> "The art of persuasion depends mainly on a marshaling of facts, clarity, conviction, and the ability to think on one's feet. True eloquence consists of truth and rapid reason."
>
> **JOHN ADAMS**

The researchers also described the overarching political result of their findings: "This pattern of votes, along with other evidence about the political leanings of young voters, suggests that a significant generational shift in political allegiance is occurring."

But before Democrats cheer and Republicans hang their heads, consider this: In Jackson County, Oregon, where I've tracked voter patterns for thirty years, a troubling pattern emerged in the 2008 presidential cycle. For months, the Obama campaign had been registering new voters and re-registering nonaffiliated voters to the Democratic Party. All in all, voter registration disparity narrowed from an eleven-point Republican advantage to a modest two-point advantage. However, after the votes were counted, Obama had received 8,000 (8 percent) more votes than any of the down-ballot Democratic candidates and 7,000 more than the Democratic candidate for U.S. Senate. The difference was found in the under-vote, which leaves a distinct impression that many voters simply voted top of the ticket and then did not go further down the ballot. (Roll off.) Compare this with the Republican ticket, where down-ballot candidates received vote totals nearly identical to those of John McCain (within 100 votes).

This level of down-ballot disengagement may indicate that first-time vot-ers lag behind when it comes to other campaigns within communities. Fur-ther, it suggests that reaching new registers with campaign resources should be a top priority for down-ballot campaigns.

Mobilizing Young Voters

A number of studies have been conducted on how to mobilize the 18- to 25-year-olds on Election Day. The 2002 Michigan Democratic Party's Youth Co-ordinated Campaign and two studies conducted by Alan Gerber and Donald Green in 2001 reported similar findings: This young group of voters responds best to canvassing or personal contact from the candidate or campaign (table 7.4). Also of interest is that while phone canvassing was found to increase young voter participation, multiple calls generated no increase beyond single calls.[12]

> "This country will not be a good place for any of us to live in unless we make it a good place for all of us to live in."
> — THEODORE ROOSEVELT.

So if you're going to contact these voters by phone, it is better to do more of them than to make repeat calls to the same voter. Also worth noting in these studies was the lack of impact that direct mail had on young voters. Given the cost of direct mail and the annoyance to the voter created by the sheer volume of campaign mail, this is good news for financially limited un-derdogs struggling to get their message out.

Two excellent resources for targeting youth voters are George Washington University's *Young Voter Mobilization Tactics* booklet and Tuft University's Center for Information and Research on Civic Learning and Engagement (CIRCLE).[13] The following tips originate from these two sources as well as the above-referenced studies:

- *Personalized and interactive contact counts.* The most effective way of get-ting a new voter is the in-person door knock by a peer; the least effec-

TABLE 7.4 Mobilizing Young Voters: What Works and What Doesn't

Nonpartisan tactic	Mobilizing effect	Dollars/vote	Notes
Door-to-door	8–10%	$12–20	Tested on young voters
Volunteer phone bank	3–5%	$12–20	Tested on young voters
Professional phone bank	0–2%	$140 and up	
Multiple calls	0–1%	n/a	Tested on young voters
Leafleting	0% (party affiliated voters)	$40 and up	7% effect on unaffiliated
Direct mail	0–1%	$40 and up	

Summary of Alan Gerber and Donald Green's 2001 findings. (Source: Alan Gerber and Donald Green, "Getting Out the Youth Vote," December 2001, summarized by Ryan Friedrichs, "Mobilizing 18–35-Year-Old Voters," John F. Kennedy School of Government, Harvard University, April 2002)

tive is an automated phone call. Canvassing costs $11 to $14 per new vote, followed closely by phone banks at $10 to $25 per new vote. Robocalls mobilize so few voters that they cost $275 per new vote. (These costs are figured per vote that would not be cast without the mobilizing effort.)

- *Begin with the basics.* Telling a new voter where to vote, when to vote, and how to use the voting machines increases turnout.
- *The medium is more important than the message.* Partisan and nonpartisan, and negative and positive messages seem to work about the same. The important factor is the degree to which the contact is personalized.
- *In ethnic and immigrant communities, start young.* Young voters in these communities are easier to reach, are more likely to speak English (cutting down translation costs), and are the most effective messengers within their communities.
- *Initial mobilization produces repeat voters.* If an individual has been motivated to get to the polls once, he or she is more likely to return. So, getting young people to vote early could be key to raising a new generation of voters.
- *Leaving young voters off contact lists is a costly mistake.* Some campaigns still bypass young voters, but research shows they respond cost-effectively when contacted.

By largely overlooking 18- to 25-year-olds, candidates and campaigns are perpetuating a vicious cycle: Young people don't vote, so no funds are spent informing them, so they do not become invested, and therefore do not vote. Campaigns spend so much time and money focusing on seniors—who would turn out to vote with little or no campaign effort—but spend almost none targeting the youth vote. Neglection 2000, a project funded by the Pew Charitable Trusts and sponsored by Third Millennium looked at TV ad placement in four media markets in the 2000 presidential primary. They found that 58 percent of the ads were placed in markets for the 50-and-over crowd, while only 17 percent were placed with younger voters in mind.[14]

> "To have doubted one's own first principles is the mark of a civilized man."
> — OLIVER WENDELL HOLMES

There are important similarities between what activates the young voter and what activates the sporadic adult voter.

1. Both groups respond best to canvassing, and when younger voters are canvassed by a campaign, they activate adults living in the same house, creating a "trickle up" effect.[15]
2. Young voters identify the voting process itself as part of the problem for low voter turnout, saying it is designed to discriminate against people who move, are overwhelmed with day-to-day concerns, are poorer, or are living on the edge. Priscilla Southwell's 1996 report to the state of Oregon's Vote-by-Mail Citizen Commission, "Survey of Vote-by-Mail Senate Election," showed that those who were younger, worked hourly-wage jobs, were students, were single parents, were minorities, and were registered as independents all turned out in greater numbers in vote-by-mail elections than in polling elections.

> "A candidate or party that can gain the trust and loyalty of young adults now, before their opinions and beliefs are set, can build a generational voting base that will remain for years."
> — CAMPAIGN FOR YOUNG VOTERS

3. Young voters respond best to candidates who are genuine, speak frankly and directly, and are involved in community activities. These traits are valued by all age groups.
4. Young voters respond best to GOTV phone calls that inform—such as identifying the polling place location.[16] GOTV work I've conducted in southern Oregon with older voters mirrors this pattern. As a result, the script of our GOTV calls changes almost daily, and all include some bit of information the voter may not know. "Did you know the county still has not received your ballot?" "This is the last day that ballots can be safely mailed and still make it to the clerk's office by Election Day." "There isn't enough time to mail your ballot, you will now need to hand-carry it to . . . "

Ethnic and Gender Gaps

Although, for many years, more women than men have been eligible to vote, it wasn't until 1976 that women actually registered nationally in greater numbers, and not until 1984 that they began to turn out in greater numbers. By 1996, over 7 million more women voted in the presidential election than men. For our purposes, however, it's important to look not only at who votes but also at how they vote when they do.

In a 2006 survey, Public Opinion Strategies found that white men were more inclined to support Republican candidates over Democratic candidates— 53 percent compared with 45 percent. Although this gap has closed considerably since the 28 percent spread in 2002 and the 24 percent spread in 2004, it remains an important predictor of voting behavior.[17]

> "Ninety percent of the politicians give the other ten percent a bad reputation."
> **HENRY KISSINGER**

Similarly, the *National Journal* presented an overview of voting demographics by age, religion, marital status, and race in October 2008; some categories were updated after the 2008 presidential election. Each year shows little or no movement toward the Democratic Party by white men, who consistently have given just 36 percent to the Democratic nominee.[18]

In 2008, white voters accounted for 74 percent of the electorate and 43 percent reported supporting Obama in exit polls vs. 55 percent voting McCain. This is in stark contrast to blacks who represented 13 percent of the electorate yet overwhelmingly supported Obama (95 percent), Hispanic represented 9 percent of the electorate with 67 percent voting Democrat which mirrored Asians (2 percent of the electorate) that voted Democrat 62 percent vs. 35 percent Republican.[19]

Figure 7.4 provides details about the electorate in 2008. CNN and the *New York Times* have excellent presentations of all the political trends from 2008's major media exit poll on their Web sites.

The Ethnic Gap

African American, Hispanic, and Asian voters can have an impact on the outcome of an election. For example, in 1997, the Asian vote in San Francisco had a large impact in a freeway retrofit measure. In the same year, San Francisco approved funding for a football stadium, largely as a result of the number of minorities voting in predominantly ethnic areas. Whites living in the

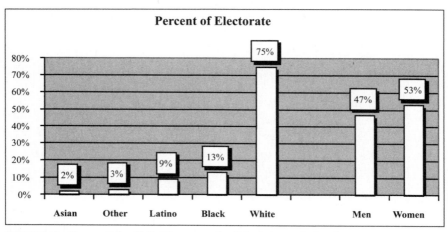

FIGURE 7.4 Share of the U.S. Electorate by Ethnicity and Gender

(Source: www.nonprofitvote.org)

upper-income sections of the city opposed the measure, but ultimately were overwhelmed by minorities hoping for improvements in a marginal neighborhood. Minorities living outside the affected neighborhood indicated that they had supported the stadium in hopes that their neighborhood would be next. Ironically, the very people who supported and voted for the stadium bill are among those least able to afford tickets to see the games.

In 2008, the black vote was ascribed the blame for the passage of Amendment 2 in Florida and Prop 8 in California. And indeed, the math works: In 2004, blacks in California were 6 percent of the California electorate; in 2006, the U.S. Census placed them at 6.7 percent. But in 2008, they jumped to 10 percent of the electorate and voted for the ban on same-sex marriage by 70 percent. If they had turned out closer to historical percentages, the amendment would have failed with a 49.3 percent approval vote (figure 7.5).[20]

> "How few aim at the good of the whole, without aiming too much at the prosperity of parts!"
> — **JOHN ADAMS**

The Hispanic vote has become the most sought-after, for both parties, both in national politics and in states with Hispanic populations large enough to influence the outcome of a close race. However, for the down-ballot race, there are a few things to consider with any minority vote (figure 7.6):

1. Always consider social context first: Minorities, like white voters, Republicans and Democrats tend to self-segregate, moving to states, cities, communities, and neighborhoods where people of similar cultural, social,

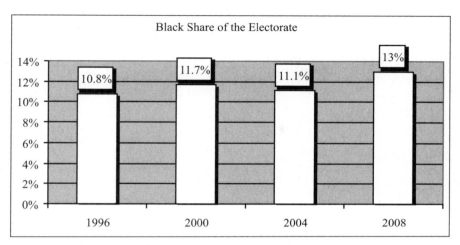

FIGURE 7.5 Black Share of the U.S. Electorate over Four Presidential Cycles

(Source: CNN, National Exit Poll for 1996, 2000, 2004, and 2008, for general elections, at
www.cnn.com/ALLPOLITICS/1996/elections/natl.exit.poll/index1.html,
www.cnn.com/ELECTION/2004/pages/results/states/US/P/00/epolls.0.html, and
www.cnn.com/ELECTION/2008/results/polls.main/; Pew Hispanic Center, at
http://pewhispanic.org/topics/?NewsTopicID=1; Dave Leip, "Atlas of U.S. Presidential Elections," at
www.uselectionatlas.org/; Secretaries of State)

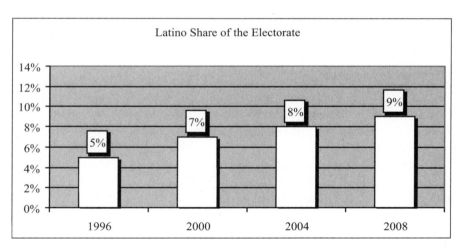

FIGURE 7.6 Latino Share of the U.S. Electorate over Four Presidential Cycles

(Source: CNN, National Exit Poll for 1996, 2000, 2004, and 2008, for general elections, at
www.cnn.com/ALLPOLITICS/1996/elections/natl.exit.poll/index1.html,
www.cnn.com/ELECTION/2004/pages/results/states/US/P/00/epolls.0.html, and
www.cnn.com/ELECTION/2008/results/polls.main/; Pew Hispanic Center, at
http://pewhispanic.org/topics/?NewsTopicID=1; Dave Leip, "Atlas of U.S. Presidential Elections," at
www.uselectionatlas.org/; Secretaries of State)

ethnic, political, educational, and economic similarities live. Large, segregated populations, whether white, Latino, black, Native American, Asian, or religious, are best studied and targeted using precinct analysis.

2. Fully integrated minorities tend to be more invisible and therefore ignored by campaigns. This results in lower voter performance than targeted minorities living in large homogeneous neighborhoods.[21]

The Marriage Gap

Although white men have shown little deviation from their support of the Republican Party candidates, white women have been less predictable. Once marital status is broken apart, however, a more reliable predictor than education, gender, or age emerges for determining voter patterns.[22]

Currently, there are as many unmarried women in America as there are married. Although unmarried women constitute 26 percent of the electorate, they did not flex their voting potential until 2004, when they moved from 19 percent of the electorate to 22.4 percent, an increase of about 7 million voters. In 2004, unmarried women voted for John Kerry by a twenty-five-point margin, while married women voted for George W. Bush by an eleven-point margin. These numbers are mirrored by all age groups, including 18- to 29-year-olds. Although white voters supported President Bush in 2004 by seventeen points, Kerry did well among white unmarried women, who gave him an eleven-point advantage.

In 2008, young married women (18–29 years old) supported John McCain by twelve points, while young unmarried women dwarfed those numbers, giving Obama 77 percent of their vote. Similarly, among white college-educated women, Obama enjoyed a sixteen-point plurality over McCain, but married non-college-educated white women weighed in for McCain with a twenty-seven-point margin.[23]

In the final days of the 2008 election, Democracy Corps conducted a tracking survey of battleground states. The results indicated a forty-one-point marriage gap compared with a seventeen-point gender gap. Of those, unmarried women gave Obama a forty-point lead, compared with married women, who gave McCain a one-point advantage. Following the election, these numbers held, with Obama receiving a dramatic 70 percent of the vote cast by unmarried women. This is the highest margin recorded since marital status has been tracked and a sixteen-point net gain over Kerry in 2004. Of men, Obama split the vote with McCain (49–48 percent), but lost married women by 3 percent.

Overall, the 2008 election saw a forty-four-point marriage gap, while the gender gap remained constant at twelve points. A full 20 percent of un-

TABLE 7.5 Television Programs Typically Viewed by American Women

Type of Programming	Unmarried Women (%)	Married Women (%)
Local News	61	67
Movies	59	57
Comedies	53	53
Dramas	53	48
National News	44	49

(Source: Women's Voices, Women Vote)

married women voted for the first time in 2008, compared with 4 percent first-time voters among married women and 11 percent overall first-time voters. Of all unmarried women, 41 percent registered to vote in the last four years.

Access to, and Use of, Media
When targeting women voters, the following should be kept in mind: Married versus unmarried women

- watch television at different times,
- watch different shows,
- read different news sources,
- respond to different strategies,
- watch different amounts of TV (3.43 hours per day for unmarried women, versus 2.76 for married women).[24]

Of unmarried women:

- 79 percent of those registered to vote got campaign information from television news
- 74 percent saw political ads on TV
- Of those who voted in 2004, 83 percent of unmarried women reported watching programs about campaigns, versus 50 percent from radio.

Among married women, 89 percent have watched programs about campaigns on TV, versus 43 percent on the radio.[25]

Clearly, television is the best way to reach both unmarried and married women (table 7.5).

According to 2008 Nielsen data, of unmarried women, the most-watched network is ABC (76 percent). Their most-watched cable channels are as follows:

TABLE 7.6 Internet Usage by Unmarried American Women

Sites Visited in the Last 30 Days, 2004	
Unmarried Women	
Voters (%)	*Non-Voters (%)*
News—73	News—69
Travel—60	Travel—69
Work—54	Health–69
Political—53	Hobby–56
Financial Info—51	Work–56
Education—50	School–51

(Source: Women's Voices, Women Vote)

Business or news network (64 percent)
Cable news (51 percent)
Discovery Channel (36 percent)
A&E (36 percent)
Weather Channel (33 percent)
CNN (31 percent)
Lifetime (31 percent)
USA (30 percent)

Access to, and Use of, the Internet

Only half of unmarried women have access to the Internet at home, compared with three-quarters of married women.[26] Of those who are not married, non-voting women and voting women have different Internet habits (table 7.6)

Economics of Unmarried Versus Married Women

Married women and unmarried women differ in many economic and political aspects:

- Unmarried women are less likely to have a college education (19 percent) than their married counterparts (29 percent).[27]
- Nearly one in five (19 percent) unmarried women are raising children.[28]
- Children being raised by unmarried mothers account for nearly half of the children living below the poverty line.[29]
- Unmarried women make fifty-six cents for every dollar that married men make.[30]
- All in all, unmarried women live on the edge financially, especially compared with married women and men (table 7.7).

TABLE 7.7 U.S. Household Incomes by Gender and Marital Status, 2006

| | Women | | Men | |
	Unmarried	Married	Unmarried	Married
Less than $30,000 (%)	42	14	30	13
$30,000–$50,000 (%)	21	18	22	18
$50,000–$75,000 (%)	16	23	20	23
$75,000 or More (%)	21	46	29	46
Average	$50,768.50	$87,948.50	$62,703.60	$88,269.80
% Committed to Basic Household Costs	37	32	31	31

(Source: U.S. Census Bureau, American Community Survey, 2006)

Because unmarried women tend to be less engaged in politics, they are consequently targeted less by campaigns and therefore participate less in politics. In this way, they are just like the youth vote and integrated minorities. However, if reaching unmarried women is one of your campaign's goals, then keep in mind that unmarried women are more inclined to vote early and vote by mail.[31]

Canvassing

Typically to get a vote, you must ask for it anywhere from three to eight times. Newspaper, television, and radio advertising, direct mail, special events, phone banks, and canvassing are the most common ways to ask for a vote. However, canvassing remains the most effective tool in a campaigner's bag of tricks. In small communities, canvassing is an ideal way to check in with the voting public and can be elevating and gratifying for the candidate. While TV, newspaper, and radio ads target groups, canvassing (like phoning and direct mail) is about targeting individuals—specifically, voters who are inclined to support your efforts.

Canvassing is not primarily about changing minds but rather about voter turnout in areas that historically have supported candidates and ballot initiatives similar to the one you are promoting. By going door-to-door in areas of high support but of low to medium turnout, you activate your voters for Election Day.

An example of the effectiveness of canvassing supportive precincts while ignoring precincts inclined to vote against your efforts is provided in figure 7.7. Identical ballot measures were placed before Ashland voters in 1993 and

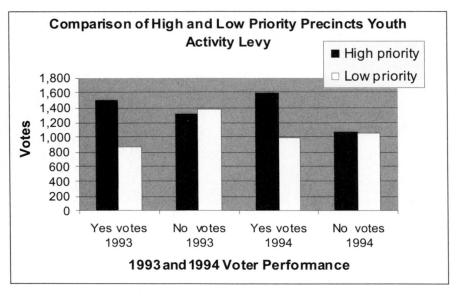

FIGURE 7.7 Voter Performance on a Youth Activity Levy in Ashland, Oregon: A Case for Activating the Right Voters

The difference in the election outcome between 1993 and 1994 is mostly played out in the low-priority precincts, where the biggest shifts occur.

then again in 1994. Our supporting campaigns were the same, with two exceptions. First, in 1993 both high- and low-priority precincts were canvassed, whereas in 1994, only high-priority precincts were targeted. Second, in 1994 we conducted a voter identification and GOTV effort. The combination of activating only high-support precincts with a GOTV effort worked. The same measure that lost in 1993 by 326 votes passed in 1994 by 447 votes.

In February 2004, we used this same model after the failure of a January 2003 statewide initiative to backfill state-supported programs with additional income tax revenues. In 2004, we effectively increased support of the second attempt on the revenue measure by decreasing the no vote. To do this, the campaign focused only on precincts where the previous revenue measure narrowly passed or where it failed up to 10 percent. Any precincts where it passed handily or was defeated in large numbers were ignored. Voter identification was implemented in the targeted precincts as well as canvassing. There were no lawn signs and almost no media (outside unions came in and advertised on radio, of all things, before we got hold of them and asked that it stop). A killer GOTV was conducted leading up to the election. In the end, the county vote came in 2 percent higher in 2004 than in 2003, but the yes vote was virtually unchanged between the two elections. The improvement came almost entirely out of a decrease in the no vote in the precincts that were ignored. While this may not seem like an overwhelming endorsement, you must consider that statewide, the second measure failed by a 15 percent higher margin than the vote in 2003.

When low-priority precincts are activated by canvassing or untargeted activities, nonsupport increases. However, when supporting voters are identified in low-priority precincts, and when only they are activated in a GOTV effort, two important things happen: First, the overall number of no votes decreases, because nonsupporting voters are ignored, and second, the number of yes votes increases because of GOTV activation. While yes votes increased slightly and no votes decreased in high-priority precincts between 1993 and 1994 and again in the 2002 and 2003 elections, the lower turnout combined with the decline of no votes in the low-priority precincts is what made the difference.

Canvassing Leaning Voters

In areas of medium support with low to medium turnout, canvassing can actually pull votes over to your side. All things being equal, the candidate or cause that gets to a leaning voter first and with the best message has a better shot at winning support. Should these voters already be moved by your ads, brochure, debating prowess, command of the issues, and good looks, then, as with the first group of high-support precincts, canvassing will serve to activate that support—that is, to remind the voter to vote.

Canvassing is a time-consuming, resource-intensive way to activate sympathetic voters and bring your message to the people. It can also be a great way to get a feel for your chances of winning. In my second bid for mayor, lawn signs for the opposition lined the main street through town, making my prospects seem bleak. However, after I started canvassing, I realized how handily I would win, and I therefore felt much more relaxed in all my campaign activities. Canvassing will give you information about voter intentions. It can also help you get additional lawn sign locations in key spots.

If canvassing is done right, you will also get valuable feedback on voter concerns. This information can help you adjust your ads, direct mail, and debate emphases to meet those concerns. For example, in Ashland's prepared-food and beverage tax campaign, a canvasser stopped at a home that already hosted a lawn sign in support of the tax measure. The homeowner told the canvasser that it was fine for the lawn sign to stay, but that she was rethinking her decision to support the tax measure because of all the controversy and seemingly overwhelming support for the opposition citywide. In another campaign, a canvasser reported that the base party voters did not know who was

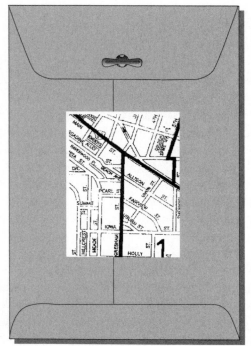

FIGURE 7.8
Example of a
Canvassing
Map Packet

running for the office. In both of these examples, thanks to the canvassers, we were able to address the problem, fix it, and win the elections.

Although there are few, if any, campaign activities that have a greater return on investment than canvassing, it is important to keep in mind that canvassing is not for everyone. Also, some places are too risky for the traditional canvass. Be careful, and know the areas you are going into. Never send someone to canvass alone or go alone yourself, and never enter a house, if for no other reason than that your partner will not be able to find you.

Map Packets

Before volunteers or the candidate can canvass, you must first do a precinct analysis to determine where you're targeting your efforts. Then you must prepare maps of those areas for your canvassers. After these tasks have been completed, the canvassing activity itself begins.

Setting up canvass map packets is an important detail to a successful canvass (figure 7.8). Do not wait to do this with the canvassers when they first arrive, or even the night before. Map packets should be organized in advance, and a generous amount of time should be allotted for the task.

Setting up map packets for canvassing begins with great maps. You can get them from the clerk's office or online from your voter activation network, which, by the way, should also have a program to help you cut turf. *Cutting turf* is simply assigning areas on your map that can be canvassed by two people in a two-hour canvassing session. When possible, use maps from the county clerk's office or the county geographic information system (GIS) department so that precinct lines are identified. In fact, GIS mapping programs (such as ESRI's Arcview and ArcGIS software) are a great option for canvass maps. With GIS programs, you can list which doors to knock on according to income, the number of voters living there, how many of the past four elections the occupants have voted in, marital status, registration, and more.

If your canvass is a *knock* (actual knocking on doors to speak with people), you can count on canvassers covering anywhere from fifteen to twenty-five homes in an hour. If it's a *lit drop* (leaving literature at the door without knocking), you can figure thirty to fifty homes an hour for the canvassers. The time it takes depends on the density of housing and the steepness of the terrain. If it's your campaign, you should know your precincts better than anyone. If you don't, hop in the car, take a little drive around, and get to know them.

When dividing precincts for canvassing teams, it is best to use one team to cover both sides of a normal city street. Doing so

> "You just can't buy your way out of a bad impression."
>
> **PAUL NEWMAN** in *Cool Hand Luke*

may require that portions of two or more precincts be included on the same map. However, efficiency is more important than precinct lines. This rule applies inversely, too: If a precinct jumps a major thoroughfare, do not expect your canvassers to hop across four-lane highways while canvassing.

For each of your teams, make two identical map packets, with the assigned area for canvassing highlighted (figure 7.8). It is sometimes helpful to line up your team maps on a window, or at least side-by-side, to check that streets haven't been missed or highlighted on two packets of adjoining canvass areas. Canvassing houses twice wastes both the volunteers' and voters' time and is annoying to both. It's bound to happen, but do your best to minimize it.

No matter how well someone claims to know an area, every canvasser needs to work with a map. No exceptions. That is why two identically highlighted maps must be created for each pair of canvassers. Have canvassers mark off the blocks they complete on their map. This information helps you keep track of both the canvass and canvassers.

Once the maps have been prepared, tape each one to a manila envelope, which will then be used to keep brochures protected in bad weather and looking fresh by the time they reach the doorstep. Manila envelopes are fairly cheap, but they are also easy to find used. If you tell friends and co-workers that you need manila envelopes from their mail trash, you'll have more than you can use in a very short time.

Remember, you have two identical packets. People work in pairs, so the two packets must stay together. To make sure the duplicate packets are not separated from each other, fold and place one inside the other, or staple the two together. If they get separated, you are bound to have two different teams pick up the same packet and canvass the same area twice, so pay attention to this detail. Also, be sure to number your packets so that you can quickly see if any are missing.

Place the materials necessary for the type of canvass you are conducting into each envelope. If you are doing a GOTV canvass or using walking lists to contact particular people, this is the packet in which you place those materials. Just put the voter lists and the matching envelope inside one envelope. The canvassers will separate out the walking lists when they divide up how they want to work. You may either place a bunch of brochures into the packet or leave them

> "Only a life in the service of others is worth living."
> **ALBERT EINSTEIN**

loose in a box by the door for the volunteers to pick up on their way out. Either way, volunteers should take additional brochures to avoid running out before they have finished their areas.

I tape an index card to the back of the manila envelope. That way, if someone canvasses the home of a strong supporter, he or she can write the information on the card so it can get to the campaign. For example, supporters may tell a canvasser that they want a lawn sign or would like to be in an endorsement ad or to contribute money if the candidate calls. If you do not have time to tape a card to each envelope, canvassers can write on the envelope itself, although in that case, you must get the information before the envelope goes out again.

Each canvasser will need a pen, so have plenty on hand. I remind people to bring pens during the call-back before the canvass, but there will be those who forget. It's a nice touch to have your canvassers write on the front of the brochure "Sorry we missed you" for people not at home. Have them do it in a color that stands out, like red or green.

Consider posting a large map of your city or county on a wall where you can mark off areas as they get canvassed. Color-code the wall map according to high, medium, or low canvass priority. As volunteers complete streets, mark off the streets in different-colored inks. That way, volunteers get to see their collective work and know they are part of a bigger effort.

As mentioned before, number the map packets to make sure they all come home. It's also a good idea to have one master map for each city, color coded with each of the canvassing areas marked. This allows easier replacement of a missing map.

In 2004, the Oregon Bus Project (busproject.org) came to help us canvass. One of the agreements with the organization is that the campaign matches every canvasser the Bus Project brings on the bus with one from the campaign. On its first visit, the organization brought fifty canvassers. This meant that we needed to provide fifty volunteers and assemble one hundred canvassing map packets and attach them with the walking lists to a clipboard. However, clipboards for that many people would not only be too expensive, but also difficult to store after their departure. So I called Ashland Lumber up the street, and it offered to cut three pieces of four-by-eight-foot, quarter-inch Masonite into ninety-six clipboard-sized pieces. To this we added metal clips to hold papers secure. The whole thing ran the campaign just over a dollar per clipboard. And after removing the oversized metal clips, the Masonite stores neatly in a box because nothing protrudes.

Finally, make and keep a complete duplicate set of maps that you can quickly copy should one go missing or for the next canvass or campaign. Don't give in and use your backups when you're in a hurry, or you'll be sorry the next time you need them.

Organizing the Volunteer Force

Have your volunteers arrive fifteen minutes early if they have not canvassed for you before. The moment they walk in, ask them to read the brochure to familiarize themselves with the contents. Generally, I have a plate of cookies, brownies, or some little thing to eat, plus juice and water. For morning canvasses, I have coffee on hand if someone asks for it, but I do not set it out; after coffee, people will have to go to the bathroom the minute they get out the door and usually go back home to do it. Coffee or not, urge people to use the bathroom before they head out to canvass.

In training canvassers, I tell them never to talk issues. That's for the candidate or the campaign committee to do. However close a canvasser is to the candidate, none can possibly know how a candidate stands on all the issues. When asked a question at the door, canvassers can say, "Why don't you give [the candidate] a call and ask her [or him]?"

Canvassers should tell people why they are out working for the candidate. It might be because of the candidate's stand on the environment, development, timber, air quality, transportation, education, taxes, jobs, libraries, public safety, or human resources. Every person who works for you will have a reason for volunteering. Urge your volunteers to think what that reason is before they head out to canvass. This directive should be part of your pre-canvassing spiel. Be sure to include things like "What would motivate you to get out and canvass on a beautiful Saturday, when you would probably rather be home with your family?" This is a nice way to let volunteers know you understand what they are giving up to work for you and that you appreciate it. I also include in my pep talks or training how difficult the odds are of winning the campaign, and how important it is that we, not the opposition, win. This brings out the best in your workers.

Unless otherwise directed by the candidate, the canvassers should not offer to have the candidate call to answer a question. Instead, leave the candidate's phone number, and urge the voter to contact him or her. Too often, when a phone call from the candidate is offered, the message doesn't get through or the voter can't be reached, which makes the candidate the bad guy. If a voter truly wants an answer to a question, he or she will take a moment to pick up the phone. And for those who prefer not to call, include in all of your material a Web address that will get a voter to an e-mail contact for the candidate or campaign.

Scheduling the Volunteers

More than anywhere else in the campaign, I try to accommodate volunteers' schedules for canvassing. Generally, I set up four time slots for people on a given weekend. If none of those times work, however, I will send volunteers out whenever they can go. Nine times out of ten, there will be someone else who can or must fit into the same time slot, so I can usually provide a partner. If no other volunteer is available at that time, I'll send the candidate or will go along myself. I do this because it's safer for canvassers to work in pairs and because it's good for the candidate or campaign manager to canvass from time to time. Personally, I love canvassing. I think it's the best job in a campaign. Not only is it a great stress reducer, but you also become more empathetic about the efforts of your canvassers and get out to hear about voter concerns. But most of all, it demonstrates your willingness to work as hard as the volunteers. Volunteers love to canvass with the candidate or campaign manager.

It is important to accommodate your canvassers in other ways, too. If someone tells me she does not like to walk hills or that she wants to work in her neighborhood, I tell her that I'll set aside a packet for her, and then I make sure I follow through. This further reduces the possibility of no-shows. Box 7.1 summarizes some good rules of thumb for your canvassers to follow.

Canvassing Directions

1. Split the street with a partner (Opposite sides of the street; or wraparound method).
2. Walk fast; talk slow.
3. Respect property and lawns.
4. Look for clues, and look at the list for information.
5. Smile; be friendly.
6. "I'm a volunteer." Say it and wear it.
7. Say their name, say their name.
8. Sincerity counts—deliver the message sincerely.
9. Say the candidate's name.
10. Ask, listen, and write things down.
11. Get a commitment: e-mail addresses, lawn sign location, bumper sticker, endorsement ad.
12. "Pitch and lit"—after listening.
13. Get IDs.
14. Take good notes.
15. Move on—don't drag it out.
16. Use good literature placement— *no* mailboxes.
17. Be aware of stranger danger—be careful; never go inside a house.

BOX 7.1 Canvassing Directions

These guidelines will help your volunteers have a successful canvass.

A big part of a good canvassing effort is placing the right volunteer in the right precinct. For example, if you have an area with a senior population, place your oldest canvassers in that area or other elected officials or well-known local personalities. Canvassing works best if it is about community talking to community.

If you have canvassers whose manner of dress is new age or in some way inappropriate for a given neighborhood, put him or her in a more progressive area or have the person work lawn signs. People should canvass their peers. Whomever you assign, remember that when they knock at the door, they represent the campaign. Let people know before they canvass that they must present themselves well to the public and look nice, because for that moment, they are the face of the campaign. Also, keep in mind that canvassing young voters will often activate adults in their home.

> "You can't hold a man down without staying down with him."
> **BOOKER T. WASHINGTON**

Sometimes, you will have volunteers in areas of swing voters who are overwhelmingly registered with one party over another. (Remember, swing voters are those who do not always vote along party lines.) In such cases, try to place a canvasser who has the same party affiliation as the voters being canvassed. For example, if you want to swing Democrats, use a Democrat; Republicans, use a Republican. That way, when you hit a voter who says he or she always votes party, the canvasser can confess to being registered like the voter while explaining that this candidate is different and deserves attention.

> "There are very few people who don't become more interesting when they stop talking."
> — MARY LOWRY

Bad Weather

There are bound to be days of bad weather when volunteers are scheduled for a canvass. When I am working on a campaign, I pray for a rainy drizzle and tell my canvassers to do the same and dress accordingly. When it rains, more people are home, and your campaign gets bonus points for getting out in bad weather. When people open the door, they feel empathy for you and admire your dedication. I have also noticed that volunteers don't mind canvassing in bad weather, which makes sense: If it is a sunny, glorious spring or fall day, wouldn't you rather be in the yard working? Up to a point, if the weather is lousy, canvassing is a good thing to do with your time while getting some exercise. However, canvassing in really bad weather doesn't help your cause: Canvassers will hate it, and voters will wonder about the campaign's judgment.

> "The reasonable man adapts himself to the world; the unreasonable one persists in trying to adapt the world to himself. Therefore all progress depends on the unreasonable man."
> — GEORGE BERNARD SHAW

A very effective technique for getting more people to canvass is to ask every person who has agreed to walk to bring a friend. This makes it more fun for those who do, increases your volunteer numbers, and helps reduce the possibility of no-shows. Since canvassing is conducted in pairs, it is an ideal activity for friends or couples.

Canvassers often ask if they can bring their children to help. If the kids are old enough, it should be fine. I started canvassing for my mom when I was in middle school, which is probably too young. I believe in children having a hand in campaigns, not least so that they celebrate the win with their parents. I especially like to have kids along with canvassers when I'm working for a library or school funding measure. After all, they have a stake in the outcome, and it doesn't hurt for the voters to have a stakeholder at their door. Young children, however, can be a distraction and can really slow a canvasser down. If you are the candidate, you should not tow your kids along, unless, of course, you're a man with a baby.

Remember, don't put any campaign literature in or on mailboxes, and be sure your campaign material does not become litter. When residents are not home, volunteers should wedge the brochure or walking piece into doorjambs, screen doors, and trim boards so that it cannot escape into the wind. If it appears that the residents are out of town and campaign literature and newspapers are already littering the doorstep, consider skipping that home.

Candidates should always get out and canvass along with the volunteers. Because it is much more effective for the candidate to knock on the door, cover as much ground as possible. Start early in the campaign in order to canvass as many homes as possible. The personal touch really works. Lots of voters have told me and the candidates I work with that they will vote for any candidate who knocks on their door. It's shocking, really. The only drawback of a candidate's knocking is that he or she often gets hung up talking with voters, so be sure a partner goes along to help cover the area and prod candidates out of doorways. Candidates who canvass lose a lot of weight. On a recent campaign, one candidate I was working with lost forty pounds; another lost thirty; and another, twenty-two. By the end of the 2004 campaign season, I had one candidate who was swimming in his clothes, he had lost so much weight.

> "You work three jobs? . . . Uniquely American, isn't it? I mean, that is fantastic that you're doing that."
>
> **GEORGE W. BUSH**
> to a divorced mother of three,
> Omaha, Nebraska, February 4, 2005

Get to Know Your Voters by Where and How They Live

When you canvass, you are moving about in neighborhoods that have supported candidates or causes like yours in previous elections. You can learn a lot by studying the neighborhoods that have popped out as your top- and medium-priority areas. Are the homes historic or modern ranch? Are they well cared for? Is the neighborhood made up largely of working-class or retired people? Minorities, single parents, college students, mill workers? Look for clues as to why these voters may have trouble getting out to vote. Are they simply overwhelmed with life, children, work, school, poverty? As Jim Gimpel, a professor of political science at the University of Maryland, has remarked, neighborhoods tell us about the voters who live there. They "reveal housing preferences, spending habits, racial and ethnic composition, lifestyles, levels of geographic mobility, voting habits and other traits relevant to predicting political participation and attitudes."[32]

Direct Mail

Vendors who specialize in direct mail often serve as campaign strategists, so it is in their best interest to send as much direct mail as your bank account will afford. This section is not only about what works, but also about re-thinking the idea that more is better when it comes to direct mail.

If you have a high-turnout and high-support voter, that is, one who always votes and lives in an area that votes for your party or issue by overwhelming percentages, why would you send him or her twenty pieces of mail? It's a waste of money and resources.

Similarly, if a voter is registered in the opposing party, always votes, and lives in an area that overwhelmingly rejects issues or overwhelmingly supports candidates in the opposing party, why would you want to spend money there? Even worse is to communicate with someone who is low-support and medium or low turnout. Why activate a voter who will cast a vote against your cause if summoned to vote? The best you might get out of these voters is an undervote. To facilitate an undervote, you want to minimize communication so they will hopefully leave the decision up to others—like your saints.

> "Public officials are not a group apart. They inevitably reflect the moral tone of the society in which they live."
> — JOHN F. KENNEDY

A few years back, I worked with a vendor from another part of the state. He presented to me a mail plan that appeared to be a little thin on strategy. Based entirely on issues that polled well in the benchmark, it exclusively targeted voters on individual traits, with no consideration of social context. Although the benchmark had been broken into zones, there was no acknowledgement or awareness of the unique voting patterns of the small local cities within the district.

For example, Ashland, polled favorably on any question dealing with schools or education, while thirty miles away, another city, similar to Ashland in income, tourism-based economy, education levels, and support of historic preservation, polled poorly on schools. But not just poorly; this city liked its school—just not the larger district the school was a part of. Nor did the city like the state system that oversees the entire system. Further, it didn't like higher education, back-to-work vocational problems, or Head Start. Understandably, the Oregon Education Association had a negative net-favorable in this community. And yet the mail plan of the campaign I was working on included several education pieces that were to go to all Democrats, nonaffiliated voters, and women Republicans throughout the district. I knew better. Indeed, all in all, the vendor's plan had twenty-one pieces of mail to be sent—

that is, eight hundred thousand printed—to every Democrat, nearly every nonaffiliated voter (irrespective of where he or she lived), and nearly every Republican woman. It was a recipe for disaster.

Included in the mail plan were twenty-one pieces to be sent to Ashland, a city with a Democratic registration advantage of fifty points (seventy points in one precinct) that never deviated from party. At the time, I explained that two mail pieces would be adequate for Ashland plus a brochure; just enough to remind the base what a great guy their candidate was. Any more, I explained, would result in angry phone calls slamming the campaign for wasting money and resources. But when I said this in a conference call, the vendor bellowed over the phone, "You send only two pieces, you'll *lose*; you'll *lose!*"

They never say, "Send twenty-one, you'll win; you'll win."

As outlined in Chapter 1, small communities in this great land are fiercely independent; people somehow find other like-minded people and relocate to live closer to them. As Bill Bishop says in *The Big Sort*, "They can smell them." You can only hope that your mail vendor, who may live in a large, homogeneous city, understands this.

Direct mail typically falls into three categories: advocacy, comparison, and attack. Advocacy is just that: It states what a terrific person the candidate is; comparison draws distinctions between the two candidates. Attack goes after a candidate on a personal or public level.

Advocacy ads are the weakest in terms of voter activation and work best for an incumbent. Challengers really cannot use advocacy, as their mission is to explain why the incumbent should be relieved of duty.

Comparison works the best on mobilizing voters in part because voters see comparison as the most truthful.[33]

The most credible studies on the influence of attack advertising on performance (turnout) and persuasion found the following:

1. Strong attack advertising can demobilize the electorate.
2. Pure attack advertising reduces turnout and harms the *sponsoring* candidate's share.
3. Attack is weakly and negatively related to turnout (advocacy is weakly and positively related to turnout).[34]

Whereas canvassing is about activating voters who, according to past precinct voting patterns, are inclined to vote for your candidate, direct mail is about activating voters around specific issues that transcend voting tendencies.

Direct mail can cultivate a relationship between your campaign and the voters on the basis of issues. These issues should resonate with your base vote and the swing vote. Again, the goal is to lock in your base vote and move swing voters your way—regardless of party affiliation or prior voting tendencies.

The strategy you use here is the same one you use in an issue-based campaign. With an issue-based campaign, you are looking for ways to package a single issue (such as building a new library) so that voters will identify with it. With candidates, you use direct mail to package issues as a way to move voters both away from the opposition and toward your candidate. Although there will be specifics on which you and your opposition disagree from the outset, such as taxes, choice, or gun control, the issues that you will use in direct mail are often the result of things said or done by the opposition during the election process. These things may not be readily apparent at the beginning of the campaign, so pay attention. Once the game begins, you are looking for anything that will pry support away from the other side. By offering voters simple, additional information, you're providing a shortcut that will help them make a decision. Direct mail is a way to get a specialized message to individual voters, regardless of where they live or how their precincts tend to vote. Although campaigns are relying on direct mail to do more of the communications with the electorate, remember that it is just one part of a campaign. Direct mail is most useful when it augments the more comprehensive campaign.

Direct mail is more than a letter or brochure stuffed into an envelope. It is the most selective of all media forms, and because of its selectivity, it offers distinct advantages over TV, newspaper, or radio ads. Using direct mail, a campaign can align an exact issue with an exact voter in a specific house. To do this effectively requires research on the part of the campaign. You must know your opponent's stands on specific issues as well as specific issues that will influence specific voters. It requires a well-constructed and well-organized database. Besides party registration, it is helpful to know the person's voting frequency, age, gender, neighborhood, marital status, general economic category, and educational level and whether there are children at home. It can also be helpful to have access to information about whether a hunting or fishing license was issued; if the voter belongs to the National Rifle Association; is a veteran, a union member, a teacher, a police officer, or a firefighter; or works in a medical facility. Basically, you want any information that will help categorize likely voters on the basis of demographics (individual traits) and areas of interest—that is, "universes." For direct mail to be truly effective, you must look for specific universes of people who can be moved or activated by new information that is related to an area of personal interest to them.

Direct Mail to Persuade Voters

Through direct mail, you aim to move the leaning voter or to create "ticket splitters." Remember, these voters will split the ballot between parties, voting Democratic for one office and Republican for another on the same ballot. Ticket splitters are moved by emotion and issues rather than loyalty to party. Any of the items listed in "The Cardinal Sins of Campaigning" at the beginning of this book will create ticket splitters.

The following are examples of issues that could be used to move voters to cross party lines. Each of these examples actually happened in local campaigns.

Military Votes. You are running against an incumbent who was one of two no votes in the state senate on a bill designed to protect the job security of National Guard volunteers after a military rotation. This is information veterans should have.

Libraries. Your opponent voted to close the public library during tight budget years while voting to increase his salary. Friends of the Library, district school-teachers, volunteers associated with the libraries, and faculty and students at a local college should know this.

Women's Right to Choose. Your opponent voted against sexuality education in the high school curriculum while serving on the school board, and the number of teen pregnancies increased. Supporters of NARAL, the Women's Political Caucus, the American Association of University Women, Planned Parenthood, and the Presbyterian and Unitarian Churches should know this.

Environmental Issues (timber, rivers, deserts, parks, and wildlife areas). You are running for county commissioner against an incumbent Democrat who worked outside her office purview to reduce the acreage of a federally designated monument. The federal designation was the result of nearly two decades of work by local environmentalists. The city representing the incumbent's base polled five to one in favor of the monument as designated. Furthermore, in an effort to reverse the federal designation, your opponent, along with her two fellow county commissioners, skewed numbers on public testimony to make it look as though fewer people supported the designation than opposed it. Getting this information to people in the city of the incumbent's base support and to environmentalists countywide could induce voters to vote against their party or to undervote in the election. Unseating an incumbent generally requires capitalizing on key constituencies that have been alienated.

Lying to the Voters. In the above example the incumbent is also vulnerable because of the role she played in misrepresenting data in public testimony. It is not a huge leap to suggest to the voters—whether they are environmentalists or not and whether they support the monument or not—that if she lied to get her way on one issue, she might lie elsewhere to do the same.

State- or Area-Specific Issues. There may be area-specific issues that are not openly addressed in a campaign. For example, in the 2002 Georgia gubernatorial race between incumbent Democrat Roy Barnes and his GOP opponent Sonny Perdue, an underlying issue appeared to be Barnes's replacement of the state flag with one that did not have a confederate emblem dominating it. In Oregon, the mere suggestion that a candidate supports a sales tax is akin to touching the third rail. Voted down by Oregonians in nine elections by overwhelming numbers, a sales tax polled only 35 percent, even as Oregon was in economic freefall in 2002 and again in 2008.

> "The world is moving so fast these days that the man who says it can't be done is generally interrupted by someone doing it."
> —————— **ELBERT HUBBARD**, 1856–1915

Flip-Flopping. Your opponent tells a school group that she will support a sales tax after emphatically saying she would not in debates. Voters look for consistency in candidates. If candidates express support for an issue while speaking to one group and opposition to the same issue while speaking to another, it will catch up with them. If your candidate genuinely changes his or her mind on an issue, hang a lantern on it. Make it clear why, and turn this potential liability into an asset. ("I am committed to studying issues and basing decisions on sound information. If new information should come to light after I've made a decision, I will weigh it carefully, and if it is in the best interest of my constituency, I may change my mind.")

Other Issues That Create Ticket Splitters. A wide variety of other issues can engender enough concern among voters that people may be willing to split their ticket:

- Air quality
- Traffic (congestion, bikes, pedestrian walkways, mass transit, and so forth)
- Airports, especially general aviation
- Seniors, especially health-care issues

- School funding, teacher salaries, and school infrastructure
- Unions
- Small businesses
- Land use, development, and parks
- Taxes
- Gun control
- Party switching (candidates who have recently switched party registration)

Although you may intend to use these issues to differentiate yourself from your opponent, your opposition can do the same to you. Your team must carefully examine where you may be vulnerable to losing your base or leaning voters. For example, if the campaign committee counsels a candidate to avoid an issue—say, sales tax—when the candidate is open to the idea, or even supportive of it, there is potential trouble. It is not enough for the committee members to tell the candidate to "avoid" an issue, especially if it is bound to be brought up in a campaign; it is their job to help the candidate resolve this internal conflict and to prepare him or her with answers for any questions on the subject.

Effectiveness of Direct Mail

Direct mail basically has two forms. The first is a letter mailed in an envelope, designed to move the voter by the way an issue is presented in the copy or by the effect of the person who sent the letter (or both). Long ago, such letters capitalized on the personal relationships the author of the letter had with the recipients. However, they now include mass-mail letters sent from movie stars and current or past office holders from larger or different arenas, including former presidents. The former personal solicitation from one business colleague to another has morphed into something that casts a huge net in hopes of capturing many small contributions. Although direct mail for fund-raising purposes is covered more thoroughly in Chapter 5, it bears repeating here that your piece is only as effective as your mailing list. For smaller, local campaigns that work within tight budgets, each direct-mail piece designed to make money must do just that. And the best way to raise funds is to use lists of individuals who have a history of giving to your kind of candidate or issue-based campaign.

The other type of direct mail generally comes as a glossy, full-color, flat or folded, oversized piece of paper that is issue- and voter-specific. This type of direct mail is not about raising money but is similar to fund-raising direct mail in that it goes to targeted voters. This can be a sophisticated medium and should be treated as such.

Let me give you an example. Some years ago, I received a direct-mail piece from Gordon Smith, a Republican state senator running for the U.S. Senate. The piece was intended to hit his opponent, Democrat Ron Wyden. Apparently, in an interview with a Portland newspaper, it emerged that Wyden did not know the cost of a loaf of bread, a gallon of gas, or Oregon's unemployment rate, among other things. Personally, I didn't know these things, either, and couldn't care less that Wyden didn't know. However, there were some who thought he should. The direct-mail piece I received from Smith painted Wyden as an out-of-touch Washington politician and connected his inability to answer these questions with related votes in the House and general trends in Washington.

Two days later, I received another direct-mail piece from the Smith campaign. On the front was a photo of Smith walking through grassland with someone else. Both men were looking down at where they were walking, and the picture was slightly out of focus, making it seem like early-morning light. It was very evocative. On the bottom it said: "One U.S. Senate candidate shares the values of rural Oregon."

Inside were four photos. The first was of Smith with his family and their horse; the caption read: "A Senator who's one of us." The second was a panoramic view, with the caption: "Defending our property rights." The third was of farmers, with the caption: "A Senator who shares our values." The fourth was a picture of Smith with his son and their bird dog. Both Smith and his son held a gun. The caption on the final picture read: "Standing up for Oregonians."

On the back was a picture and a quotation from the executive director of the Oregon Farm Bureau and a list of endorsing groups. It was an effective piece, but I noticed there were no women in it.

The next day, I received yet another piece of direct mail from Smith. The outside was solid blue with white lettering that read: "Have you heard what women say about Gordon Smith?" Inside were pictures and quotes from four women: the president of Crime Victims United in Portland, a mother of two from Salem, a teacher from Silverton (a very cute, small rural town), and a small-business owner from an affluent city outside Portland. Each woman had appropriate quotations for her special interests: crime, families, education, and a balanced budget. And three of the four talked about how Smith was not like other Republicans within the context of their subject. This piece, by using validators (other women like me), was designed to give me permission to jump party.

I live in a rural part of the state, on two acres, in a conservative county with deep roots in the orchard industry. Many of my neighbors have horses and live on similar-sized lots. My precinct has a high Democratic registration and a mix of people that reflect the full political spectrum in America; voters here will ticket-split. Through direct mail, Gordon Smith took his campaign to a home of a single mother in the rural part of the state, hit his opponent with an issue that should resonate with those of us who have to budget our money, and established himself as part of my geographic world and then part of my personal world.

What's important is that these pieces were designed to go after potential swing voters within a well-defined universe to deliver a very specific message, and they did so with specific cues (validators) intended to give the recipients permission to split their ticket. This is really important. When your campaign is wooing swing voters, you must provide validators to give that particular part of the universe permission to stray from party voting. It is really no different than looking for lawn sign locations that couple your candidate with lawn signs of candidates in the other party or using validators for canvassing. All well-run campaigns look for an issue or a cue to present to potential swing voters that will enable them to shift their allegiance from their party.

For example, when the GOP held its convention in 2000, on the stage were people of many ethnicities, more so than at any Republican convention in history. Although many assumed that it was about wooing the black and Hispanic vote, it was actually about giving swing Democrats permission to jump party. In fact, "despite a display of diversity at the party's national convention and the support of prominent blacks like retired Gen. Colin Powell, Bush drew less than 10 percent of the African-American vote."[35]

People who tend to be swing voters have specific issues that will move them. Knowing who these voters are and where they live is often enough to bring before them an issue that will make them split their ballots.

> "A word once let out of the cage cannot be whistled back again."
> **HORACE** (first century b.c.)

For direct mail to be effective, you need to work an angle with the voter. In the November 2002 election, an Oregon House candidate mentioned that he would raise taxes on SUVs because of the impact they have on the roads and air quality. The opposition used that opportunity to send a mailing to all soccer moms—women over age thirty-five with school-age children—who voted in two of the last four elections. In another campaign, one candidate made a damaging remark about health care. The opposition sent a direct-mail piece to alert people over the age of fifty-five who voted in two of the last four elections.

A few years back, a governor from one of the northeastern states suggested banning disposable diapers because they were adding tons to landfills each year and were considered a health hazard as they contain untreated human waste and could potentially contain live viruses from vaccines. Understandably, people with small children were not pleased. However, the diaper manufacturers, seeing trouble, immediately introduced biodegradable disposable diapers, which satisfied the governor.

When I told this story to a friend of mine who had very young children and who was a well-educated progressive and a strong environmentalist, she leaned forward, looked me in the eye, and, her voice dropping, slowly said, "No one is taking my disposable diapers from me." Truly effective direct mail aims to touch a nerve that elicits that kind of emotion in a voter. You're hoping for a swing vote or at least an undervote on the opposition.

Direct Mail to Hit Your Opponent:
It Takes Research, Opportunity, and Timing

Direct mail is often based on your research of the opposition. Many candidates hype their background in community service and draw inferences from that experience. So if a candidate claims to be in tune with and committed to education because she served on the school board, your job is to see how well she served. Did she miss a lot of meetings? Was she effective? Likewise, does your opponent claim to be a rancher but keeps only a mobile home on a small piece of dirt while traveling extensively throughout the year? Does your opponent claim that you are out of touch, yet he or she spends more than half the year at a second home in another state?

A few years back, a direct-mail hit piece went out on a state senate candidate, Phil Warren, who claimed to be a farmer. The full-color piece had minimal copy that appeared below each of six simple pictures: a garage door, labeled "A barn"; a push mower, labeled "A harvester"; a square of grass, labeled "A crop"; a poodle, labeled "Animals." The last two pictures were one of the candidate and one of a dollar bill.

Below the candidate, the copy read: "Phil Warren grows no crops, milks no cows and sells no cattle. So why does he call himself a farmer?"

Then, below the dollar bill, it said: "So he can get a $42,000 break on his property-tax appraisal. Phil Warren in the State Senate? All fertilizer. No farm."[36]

Still, there are some pretty despicable direct-mail pieces that come out each cycle. In 2004, a Republican strategist from Portland area hit Democrat Rob Brading with a direct-mail piece suggesting that Brading defended the right to pornography over the rights of children because Brading served on the library board when computers were brought in for public use. The disclaimer at the bottom of the piece was a Web site (probably generated for that piece alone) called Friends for Safer Libraries. It worked.

Pointing out how your opponent has voted while serving in office does not constitute negative campaigning, and juxtaposing actual votes with campaign claims in direct mail can be very effective. To do it well, however, your team must do its homework. Did your opponent claim to support education and yet vote down the school funding package? Did she claim to support people with mental illnesses but vote no on the health and human services budget? Did she vote no on contraceptive parity? Did he receive obscene amounts of money from right-to-life organizations and then vote against a bill that would cover a morning-after pill for rape victims? Is your opponent bought and owned? Show the voters the bread-crumb path.

Know where the opposing campaign's money comes from. For issue-based and candidate campaigns alike, follow the money and follow the endorsements. Look at the principles on which the opposition is basing its campaign—that is, the campaign message. If the voting record directly contradicts the message, you can raise the question of integrity. Campaign themes, like voting records, are fair game.

A voting record is not only a verifiable set of facts, but one that goes to the very essence of why we have elections. Have at least one volunteer dedicated to researching your opponent's voting record. What the research turns up may be useful not only for direct mail but also for debates.

Direct mail should be both clever and simple. Democrat Jeff Barker, a candidate for the Oregon House, faced Republican Keith Parker in the general election and found that the voters were having trouble differentiating the two because of their similar surnames. To help voters, Barker incorporated into the mail pieces a barking dog that strongly resembled his family dog, which was in campaign photos. Barker won by 44 votes out of 15,720 votes cast.

Being clever can also backfire. In January 2003, a special election was held in Oregon to backfill falling revenues in the state budget. Opponents of the tax measure said that government, like everyone else, needed to tighten its belt. In response, proponents of the tax measure sent a direct-mail piece featuring the gut of an overweight man with a belt cinched about as tight as possible (figure 7.9). The message was to underscore the difficulty schools were having with budget cutbacks as Oregon faced monumental budget deficits in the 2003–2005 biennium. However, in the context of the criticism that had been leveled against the measure, one look at the photo brought to mind the opponents' real message: Cut the fat.

FIGURE 7.9 Example of Direct Mail That Can Reinforce the Opponent's Argument

Be sure the image you present to the voters is the image you want to communicate.

Reference Your Comparison Pieces

I usually mail or walk a comparison or persuasion piece to voters the week before the election. During my last run for mayor, I did so, as I had in previous elections for other candidates and issues. Each point I listed about my opponent had been said during one of the five debates we had or was part of the public record of his voting history. However, I made a fundamental mistake: I did not reference any of these items. When the piece came out, voters felt it was unfair to bring these quotes up at the last minute when they "did not come up during the campaign." At that late date, no

> "Washington is a city of Southern efficiency and Northern charm."
> **JOHN F. KENNEDY**

amount of my saying when and where they were said really mattered. I could have avoided this simply by putting dates and events next to each item.

Direct Mail on a Budget

If you are campaigning in a relatively small area, combining direct mail with canvassing can save a campaign a lot of money and is far more effective than mailing a piece to the voter. Some years back, I ran a campaign in which we canvassed direct mail attached to the brochures. In that campaign, we were trying to get approval for an open-space park program designating where future parks and walking paths would be in our city. Each neighborhood of the city was slated for a park in the plan. So we drafted a specialized campaign piece pointing out what kind of park each specific neighborhood would get and asked four to six supporters from that neighborhood to allow their names to be printed on the specialized piece. Volunteers hand-carried it into the appropriate

> "Words that come from the heart enter the heart."
> **ANONYMOUS**

neighborhood as part of our canvassing effort. With this approach, the campaign piece became both a personal letter and an endorsement. We also had neighbors canvassing neighbors, an extremely effective canvassing technique.

In most small towns and counties, specific issues will be important in certain neighborhoods. If you can connect the issues with the neighborhoods, hand-delivering direct mail can be very effective and far cheaper than mailing it or printing up three or four different campaign brochures.

Walking direct mail to the door is also a good way to time your mailing. For example, in the above-mentioned campaign for the open-space program, the voters approved the open-space program but turned down the funding proposal. The city council immediately sent another proposal out to the voters, and it went down as well. At this point, the entire voter-approved park component would be threatened without a funding package. In a narrow vote, the city council presented the public with a proposal for a prepared-food and beverage tax to fund both parkland acquisition and Department of Environmental Quality–mandated upgrades to our wastewater treatment plant.

However, no city in Oregon had a tax on prepared food and beverages, and the industry did not want a domino effect starting in southern Oregon. As a result, our opposition included all but one eating establishment in Ashland, the Oregon food and beverage industry lobby, local businesses, and Realtors who did not want land taken out of the inventory for parks. Again, our campaign had little or no money for lawn signs or advertising, and because of the controversy, people told us they were reluctant to write letters to the editor.

> "A test of a man's or woman's breeding is how they behave in a quarrel."
> — GEORGE BERNARD SHAW

The weekend before Election Day, we hand-delivered a direct-mail piece to every home in the city. In the piece, we pointed out nothing more than who was financing the opposition. This tactic worked, probably for two reasons. First, it clearly showed that our side was rich with volunteers: Close to one hundred people walked the streets for that canvass. Second, we canvassed the city on the same day that the opposition coincidentally took out a half-page ad that actually reinforced what our flyer said.

> "The first and great commandment is, Don't let them scare you."
> — ELMER DAVIS

Given that our measure passed by 150 votes out of 5,000 votes cast, I'm convinced the flyer was the single biggest reason why we won that campaign. This program—both the parks component and the funding mechanism—won state recognition in the Cities Awards for Excellence Program.

To save money, you might also consider a mailing of postcards. One sheet of card stock can make four postcards, saving your campaign money in paper stock, printing, and postage.

Another option for saving money is to change the size of the universe you are mailing to. If money is short, rather than mailing to voters who voted in at least two of the last four elections, just mail to those who voted in three of the last four elections. This approach is most effective in nonpresidential elections. Still too costly? Select only those precincts with the most swing voters, or mail to the difficult-to-walk rural precincts and then canvass the incorporated areas with volunteers.

The Urban Versus Rural Divide

As you have undoubtedly discovered from your precinct analysis, voters have very different attitudes within an incorporated city as opposed to rural areas outside the cities. Small cities provide great opportunities for the campaign.

1. There exists far more area-specific information available through the U.S. Census for small cities than for their rural neighbors in the same county.
2. Many small cities are a single postal route, so a saturated mailing to a city is more affordable than mail sent to rural voters.
3. Small cities are easier to canvass and easier to get volunteers to canvass.
4. Small cities often have many citywide elections covering issue-based and candidate elections that provide additional information to your targeting model.

Remember, too, that as the campaign progresses and your issue or candidate looks like a winner, more money will come in to support your efforts. Even if you have a very limited direct-mail budget, chances are that there will be additional opportunities before Election Day, especially if you target small, distinct universes.

Mail Preparation

A lot of money can be saved by having a group of dedicated volunteers willing to repeatedly prepare and send your direct mail. If this is a possibility, be sure to have the bulk mail stamp printed on your piece to save time and effort. If you have no bulk permit number, which generally runs about a hundred dollars, and plan to do a lot of mailings, that initial outlay will quickly pay for itself. If not, your party or even an organization you're working with for an issue-based campaign may well have a bulk permit number you can use. Return address should always be part of the printing to save time.

> "Americans will put up with anything provided it doesn't block traffic."
>
> **DAN RATHER**

Once you have decided what you are going to do and the direct-mail piece has been written and printed and is back at your home or headquarters in boxes, here's what you do:

1. Organize a clerical work team to assemble or label your direct-mail piece; have everything lined up and ready to go when people arrive.
2. If the mailing is not a flat or postcard, it must be stuffed and addressed. Hand-addressing and first-class stamps really do increase the number of people who will open the piece and look inside. However, if you are mailing to specific precincts, you may prefer labels. If you do, the label should be either clear or the same color as the envelope or mail piece so as not to draw attention to it.

3. Visit the post office to get all the particulars for bundling and preparing your bulk mailing.
4. Once everything is together according to their standards, take your bundles to the post office to fill out the paperwork and place the appropriate post office stickers on the front of each bundle. The post office will provide stickers and forms. Be prepared to stand in line three times. If this is a year-end mailing with Christmas lines, consider sending your mailing first class.

Often at the end of a campaign, when the committee suddenly decides to create and send another direct-mail piece, the grassroots campaign does not have the ability to pull together the people to get the piece out on time. This is a great time to consider a mail house. Again, if you're activating your base and the swing voters to vote, go to the county and ask for the full registration list for the targeted precincts.

> "The only thing that saves us from the bureaucracy is its inefficiency."
> —— EUGENE MCCARTHY

The mailing house can download which parties you want, eliminate household duplicates, and print the name and address directly on the piece. Be aware, however, that mail houses are often flooded by last-minute requests from political candidates, which can affect timing.

Direct mail is different from targeting neighborhoods for canvassing in that you are directing your pitch for voter interest rather than voting patterns. Also keep in mind that by using direct mail, you can address subjects that, if put in a more public forum, might activate a lot of heated letters to the editor. Well-targeted direct mail reaches potential friends of the campaign and lets them know where you (or your opponent) stand and where to send money. Used properly, direct mail can be very effective.

Tracking Polls

Tracking polls are used to fine-tune direct mail and radio and television spots as well as to monitor candidate or issue support. They are generally brief, with only a handful of questions, and they are most helpful when conducted regularly throughout the campaign. However, if you are running a small campaign on a low budget with an overextended volunteer base, a tracking poll may be out of the question.

> "For purposes of action nothing is more useful than narrowness of thought combined with energy of will."
> —— HENRI FREDERIC AMIEL

An alternative would be to piggyback on a tracking poll being conducted for another candidate. This might cost your campaign a little money, but it would be far cheaper than if you were to go it alone. Often, when someone is running for state office, where partisan politics plays a more significant role than in local elections, political parties will conduct tracking polls for their candidates. Also, PACs might be willing to conduct tracking polls for a candidate or issue their organization has endorsed. Be sure to report this to your treasurer and include it on your contributions and expenditures forms as an in-kind contribution.

> "If it is a blessing, it is certainly very well disguised."
> **WINSTON CHURCHILL,**
> after losing the 1945 elections

A tracking poll can be especially helpful in fine-tuning a campaign in a close election and shaping the spin either to increase your support or to erode that of your opposition. Say, for example, that in the final days of a campaign, you find that the support among women is shifting away from your candidate. You may then go back to your benchmark poll and, using a high-priority issue for women, generate direct mail to draw back and lock in this support.

A tracking poll may be used to do several things:

- Track candidate or issue support.
- Fine-tune a campaign message.
- Tell you if a particular campaign event or ad has left you or your opponent vulnerable.
- Determine whether negative campaigning, on either your part or that of your opponent, is helping or hurting (this is generally tracked in a quick response poll following an ad).
- Indicate what groups are still undecided.

Tracking Polls Without the Poll

If you cannot afford a tracking poll, even as a tag-along, there are some telltale signs that will give you an idea about the progress of your campaign and that of your opponent. Here are just a few examples:

Attendance at debates. At the beginning of a campaign, while voters are still undecided, attendance at debates is often high. Once voters have decided how they will vote, they tend to stay home. This phenomenon will vary from city to city. If it

> "As people do better, they start voting like Republicans—unless they have too much education and vote Democratic, which proves there can be too much of a good thing."
> **KARL ROVE,**
> February 19, 2001

> "Candidates have to fight back hard, or else voters don't believe they'll fight for them."
> —— **SID BLUMENTHAL**, former Clinton aide

happens in a city in which you enjoy support, that's great. If voters are still coming out in droves to hear you and your opponent in an area that does not belong to you, that's bad news for your opponent.

Your opponent, who had been straddling the fence, suddenly moves to the extreme of his or her base. Chances are, when a candidate moves toward the base, it's because information has come in that the opponent's base is not secure. Remember, just because you are not polling, that does not mean your opposition is not polling. Trying to lock your base late in a campaign is difficult and can be a sign that a campaign is in trouble.

A week before the general election, canvassers report that people still do not know your candidate. In general, astute canvassers bring back valuable information about your candidate or issue-based campaign. If they report

> "When I hear another express an opinion which is not mine, I say to myself, he has a right to his opinion, as I to mine. Why should I question it? His error does me no injury, and shall I become a Don Quixote, to bring all men by force of argument to one opinion?"
> —— **THOMAS JEFFERSON**

that many people still don't know your candidate, you must find a way to go back and grab your base without losing swing voters. Not ideal, but it can be done. Suggestions for how to do this are covered in Chapter 8.

8

Media

Campaigns are about selling a product. That product is a candidate, library, school, parkland, civic building, water system, or whatever. But just as the local skateboard shop would not waste money sending direct mail to the senior center for an upcoming sale, you should not waste campaign money trying to solicit individuals who will never buy your product. If you have not conducted a precinct analysis, stop what you're doing and get it done. You're about to spend a lot of money, and you want every penny to count.

Remember, your precinct analysis will give you a road map as to which neighborhoods, precincts, and communities will support—or not support—your candidate or issue-based campaign. If you do not know the social context of your voters, individual traits such as gender, ethnicity, voting history, education, income, and age have less relevance. While many strategists and vendors rely exclusively on individual traits for targeting voters, that can be a perilous prospect when a voting area consists of many small towns and both rural and urban voters. Targeting voters on the basis of individual traits works fine if your campaign covers a single, homogeneous city or a county where registration plurality substantially works in your favor, but for anything outside of that, you need to know who you're talking to.

Precinct analysis will tell you where your base lives, what your base supports, where your swing voters live, and what they support. The analysis will also tell you where your opposition's support lives and what these voters do or do not support. From this information, you can generate a message to target swing voters. Message discipline is the foundation of your media campaign.

As with other campaign activities, your theme and message must be at the center of all media efforts. No matter what comes at the candidate or the spokesperson for an issue-based campaign, they must be disciplined about staying on message.

Print Media: Paid and Unpaid

Americans have become as divided over their opinions of the credibility of news sources, as people have become isolated by partisan leanings in their neighborhoods and cities. Democrats watch their networks and listen to their radio programs, Republicans watch other networks and listen to other radio programs, and each group believes that the other's news sources are biased and lack credibility. Further, the programs that people listen to and watch break down by age as well. For example, nearly six in ten young voters get their news online, while older Americans receive news from more traditional venues—such as newspapers and network television news.[1]

> "The charm of politics is that dull as it may be in action, it is endlessly fascinating as a rehash."
> — EUGENE MCCARTHY

Newspaper readership, which has been in steady decline for over a decade, now hovers around 34 percent.[2] More problematic, however is the relationship of newspaper credibility and partisanship (figure 8.1). This relationship plays out when it comes to newspaper endorsements for candidates and issue-based campaigns. In my conservative corner of the world, newspaper endorsements of Democratic candidates seemingly do little to boost these candidates, even though not receiving an endorsement seemingly still hurts. This trend began nearly a decade ago, and it now appears that a newspaper endorsement does little more than to affirm the Democratic base of what it will do anyway; further, it has only a little sway with the swing vote and virtually no impact on Republicans. Newspaper endorsements do, however, continue to influence voters in primaries and city-wide races of communities with overwhelming Democratic registration.

> "Make ads that get viewers to look up and down."
> — MALCOLM GLADWELL

As populations become more segregated by political ideology, it follows that Democrats believe and are swayed by some media just as Republicans believe and are swayed by other media. Knowing your audience will lead to smarter media buys that target both your base vote and the potential swing vote while avoiding media that may activate your opposition.

Partisanship and Credibility

	Rep %	Dem %	Gap
Believe all or most of what organization says			
BBC	9	28	-19
NPR	18	37	-19
NewsHour	16	34	-18
NBC News	16	31	-15
C-SPAN	17	31	-14
New York Times	10	24	-14
Time	12	26	-14
CNN	22	35	-13
60 Minutes	24	37	-13
MSNBC	18	29	-11
Newsweek	10	21	-11
Your daily newspaper	19	29	-10
ABC News	19	28	-9
Associated Press	14	22	-8
CBS News	18	26	-8
Local TV news	27	32	-5
U.S. News	19	19	0
USA Today	16	15	+1
Wall Street Journal	29	24	+5
Fox News Channel	34	19	+15

Percentages based on those who could rate each organization.

Figure 8.1   Partisanship and Credibility

(Source: The Pew Research Center for the People & the Press, "Key News Audiences Now Blend Online and Traditional Sources," August 17, 2008)

Still, no matter what presence your daily newspaper holds where you live, issue-based campaigns and candidates on either side of the aisle should never squander opportunities with local papers. Thoroughly prepare for interviews, editorial boards, and any campaign events that will be covered by the media.

Unpaid Print Media

I recently had a candidate announce his intentions to move from the state house to the state senate during an interview regarding the incumbent who was resigning midterm. Naturally, the announcement was buried in the article that covered the real story—a thirty-year veteran leaving office. If the candidate had waited even one day, his announcement would have received front-page coverage. As a campaign manager, you must be ready for the candidate who is so excited about running that the person gets ahead of himself or herself. In general, a candidate who wishes to seek an office that is being vacated by an incumbent who has either resigned or died must give an appropriate amount of time and space to the exiting office holder. It's just polite. If this is not done, at best it will cost the campaign money to come back in and fabricate an announcement event, and at worst it leaves the public with the impression that the candidate wishing to seek the office is lying in wait politically, is ambitious, or is arrogant.

The announcement of your candidacy or your issue-based campaign is the first piece in your free media tool kit. Announcements should be timed to have the biggest impact and the best news coverage. The following tips should help make this exciting day more successful.

Have your campaign team gather as many supporters (cheering throngs) as possible for your announcement: Make your announcement in a public place that is both well known and well liked by your community. Just as candidates seeking state office go back to their hometown, and presidential candidates to their home state to announce, you should choose a place that is significant to you and your community.

Know the law. Avoid announcing on publicly owned property such as a school or a civic building, and do not involve people who are on taxpayer-funded payrolls (such as school or government officials) during the workday, even during the lunch hour. While an announcement may be legal on publicly owned property, collecting money for a political cause may not be, and it is typical for people attending an announcement to hand the candidate a check.

> "Did you ever get to wondering if taxation without representation might have been cheaper?"
> — ROBERT ORBEN

Know the schedules of the press. An announcement should be held at a time and place that is convenient for the press, even if they are not convenient for your supporters. Call the local papers, and ask what time would work best for them, given their deadlines. If you know that some of the media cannot attend, have printed news releases delivered to those who will miss the announcement. Be sure to include a photo.

Schedule the announcement at the convenience of television crews rather than newspapers. Getting your face in front of the camera is important, and the print media can be covered with a press packet. Keep in mind that television news crews typically work late at night and are not available until late morning.

If your announcement is too late for the newspaper reporters to attend, provide them with the needed information before their deadlines. You want your announcement to be covered everywhere on the same day. If you are putting together a press packet, include a photo of the candidate and another of the candidate with his or her family, a list of supporters and their phone numbers that the press can call for quotes (don't forget to give these supporters a heads-up), your announcement speech, a bio, and a brochure if you have one.

Find a good date and time to announce a candidacy or to kick off an issue-based campaign. You have to know what else is going on in the community. Avoid major holidays, as people don't watch the news or read the papers as much on those days. For the same reason, don't announce on a three-day weekend or on a Friday, as fewer people read Saturday's paper or watch Friday evening news. If it is a nonpartisan race with only a general election, announcing in June gives you the opportunity to participate in Fourth of July parades and to let people know before summer vacations. The objective is to do whatever you can to get your name out in an inexpensive and effective way.

> "Word of mouth appeals have become the only kind of persuasion that most of us respond to anymore."
> **MALCOLM GLADWELL**

Line up supporters to write letters to the editor immediately after your announcement. Letters should be short and simply say how glad the letter writer is to see that you decided to join the race. The letter writer should also mention one or two things that are central to your theme.

Letters to the Editor

If you don't have the funds for a sustained paid advertising campaign, letters to the editor can carry a campaign until paid advertising begins. Depending on your area, using the letters-to-the-editor section of the local paper can be a very effective media tool. Letters show that a voter cares enough about a candidate or ballot measure to take the time to write a letter and get it to the paper. E-letters are limited in length, which is good, because short letters tend to get read more. Also, papers tend to run them more quickly than more traditional letters to the editor, and they are often the lead letters, which gives them prominence.

Once letters are published, they are in the public domain, so the campaign can pull great nuggets from them to use in paid endorsement ads as the campaign progresses. Plus, referenced quotes tend to have more credibility.

Assign one of the campaign committee members to oversee letters to the editor. The letters-to-the-editor coordinator should be prepared to write

FIGURE 8.2

Example of a Letter
to the Editor

Letters to the editor are
most effective if they are
short and appear early in
the campaign cycle.

Vote for Daniels

Elle Daniels would be an excellent school board member. Elle has devoted her life to education as a volunteer in the classroom.

We need people in decision-making positions who know first-hand what is going on with our children. Elle Daniels has my vote.

C. Golden,
Ashland, OR

several sample letters as well as some general instructions and tips to give people guidance, and he or she must be able to constantly remind supporters about getting letters to the papers. It is the most difficult job of a campaign, so choose this person carefully, and do not assign any other campaign tasks to him or her until after the deadline for letter submissions.

Early letters get read. Later in the campaign season, readers become numb and rarely read the last-minute opinions of their neighbors. Also, because long letters are not read as much as shorter letters, remind all who may write on your behalf to be brief. A good rule is for a letter to cover one subject and to be no longer than one or two short paragraphs. As important as a letter may be, the heading placed above it is more important. Shorter letters mean more boldfaced titles, which will be read, even by those just scanning the page. Finally, short letters, like e-letters, are often printed more quickly, and sometimes they are printed after the paper has said, "No more letters." Figure 8.2 is an example of a letter to the editor. Remind supporters to send copies of letters to all the local papers, as you never know who reads what.

Many papers will not print letters received a certain number of days before the election. Get this information for each local paper, and include it in the letters-to-the-editor sheet you prepared for your committee (in the campaign committee packet). Most people procrastinate, so keep supporters apprised of the deadline as it approaches. If letters to the editor are a critical component of your media package, their being too late for publication could be fatal to

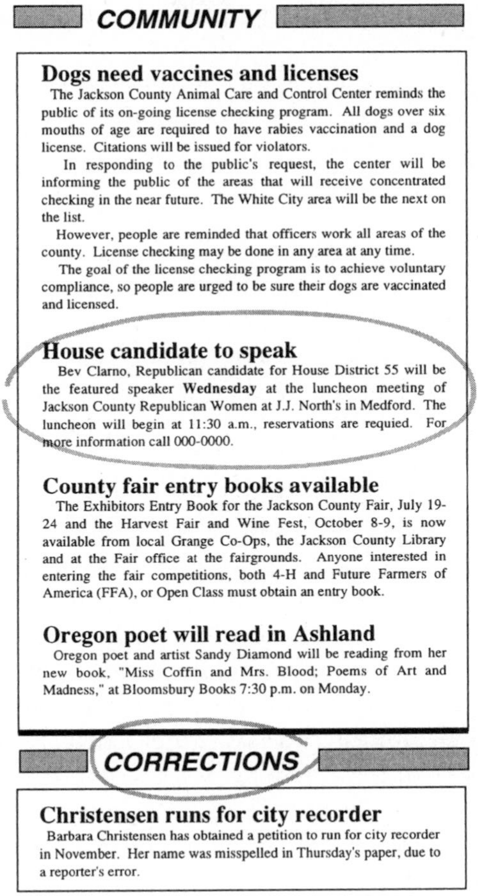

COMMUNITY

Dogs need vaccines and licenses

The Jackson County Animal Care and Control Center reminds the public of its on-going license checking program. All dogs over six mouths of age are required to have rabies vaccination and a dog license. Citations will be issued for violators.

In responding to the public's request, the center will be informing the public of the areas that will receive concentrated checking in the near future. The White City area will be the next on the list.

However, people are reminded that officers work all areas of the county. License checking may be done in any area at any time.

The goal of the license checking program is to achieve voluntary compliance, so people are urged to be sure their dogs are vaccinated and licensed.

House candidate to speak

Bev Clarno, Republican candidate for House District 55 will be the featured speaker **Wednesday** at the luncheon meeting of Jackson County Republican Women at J.J. North's in Medford. The luncheon will begin at 11:30 a.m., reservations are requied. For more information call 000-0000.

County fair entry books available

The Exhibitors Entry Book for the Jackson County Fair, July 19-24 and the Harvest Fair and Wine Fest, October 8-9, is now available from local Grange Co-Ops, the Jackson County Library and at the Fair office at the fairgrounds. Anyone interested in entering the fair competitions, both 4-H and Future Farmers of America (FFA), or Open Class must obtain an entry book.

Oregon poet will read in Ashland

Oregon poet and artist Sandy Diamond will be reading from her new book, "Miss Coffin and Mrs. Blood; Poems of Art and Madness," at Bloomsbury Books 7:30 p.m. on Monday.

CORRECTIONS

Christensen runs for city recorder

Barbara Christensen has obtained a petition to run for city recorder in November. Her name was misspelled in Thursday's paper, due to a reporter's error.

FIGURE 8.3
Example of the "Community" Section from a Local Paper

On this day, two candidates got some free ink.

your cause. Because many papers must verify authenticity of mailed letters before they will print them, hand-carrying a letter usually results in an earlier publication. Letters that are typed, e-mailed, and faxed also get printed faster.

Other Free Media Coverage

Many newspapers have a public interest section that serves as a community chalkboard. Find out how often it runs and what the deadlines for submissions are. If your candidate is speaking at the Rotary Club or the League of Women Voters, or if one of your committee members is giving a presentation on your ballot measure, be sure it gets into the community activity section of the paper. Figure 8.3 is an example from a local paper in my town.

I once saw a notice in a community activity section that a particular candidate would be canvassing that week in a neighboring town. It really got my attention. To the average person, something like this highlights the hard work of a candidate who is walking the neighborhood and available to the voters.

Press Conference

If there is an opportunity to call a press conference, do it. When I was working on our food and beverage tax campaign, members of the opposition called a press conference to announce a funding scheme for open space that they said would make our tax measure unnecessary. They gathered together a broad range of local and prominent people to show support for their argument. To counter, we called a press conference as well.

> "What we are voting on is far more important than buying cereal. The last thing we should be doing is advertising that dumbs us down."
>
> **CINDY WILSON**, public relations and marketing specialist

We also had a broad range of local leaders represented at our press conference. We took advantage of the occasion to point out why the funding proposed by the opposition would fall short of the community's needs. We also went one step further and used the press conference as an opportunity to promote our campaign. We were thus able to prevent any damage the opposition's proposal might have caused and to use the opportunity to advance our own campaign goals. We kept our campaign message out front. Politics is motion: Take energy that is coming at you, and redirect it at your opposition.

In general, don't invite the media to coffees or fund-raisers. If for some reason an event is poorly attended, media coverage could work against your cause. Furthermore, supporters need time with the candidate without the press around. If the media are there, many will have the sense that everything is staged and that those attending are merely props. Do not, however, hesitate to include the media if a big-name politician or movie star is willing to endorse you or your measure on your home turf. I once worked for a candidate who chose to turn down an endorsement and visit from the governor because he felt that the governor was not that popular in our end of the state. That was a mistake. A big political figure can get you the only page of the paper that is not for sale—the front page—not to mention all of the leads on the evening news.

> "I do not take a single newspaper, nor read one a month, and I feel myself infinitely the happier for it."
>
> **THOMAS JEFFERSON**

A number of other tricks can be used to get your campaign on the front page of the papers. Challenging your opponent to a series of debates is a time-honored way to get local coverage. Another is to announce that you are challenging your opponent to campaign on a limited budget. If you issue the challenge, you get to come up with the amount; set it at a level you can live with but doubt that your opponent can. If you're an incumbent, this can really work to your advantage. In small-city elections, incumbents are better known and don't need to spend as much as outsiders do to get their names out. Because the public tends to think incumbents are compromised, this has the effect of making them seem more pure. However, one caution here: If you propose a spending limit and your opponent is unwilling to go along with it, you have a problem and should be prepared to drop the idea. Campaigns require an enormous commitment of time and energy by many people, so do not needlessly hobble your campaign with a tight budget when no one else is doing so.

> "Never argue with people who buy ink by the gallon."
> **TOMMY LASORDA**

Press Events

Whenever possible, create press events. This is where your research can really pay off. Examine what the opposition is claiming, and then look for inconsistencies in past actions, voting records, and money trails. Dribble this information to the press so that it comes out in increments. Look for where your opposition is getting money and support, and if their sources are inconsistent with their message, get this information to the press either directly or in letters to the editor. You want to have a game plan—and a "hammer"—ready should your opposition take the hook. For example, you are running against an incumbent who claims to be a clean-air advocate. You point out how his voting record is inconsistent with that claim, knowing full well that his record contains other, favorable clean-air votes that he will pull out to make you look silly. That is OK; the hook has been taken. If he doesn't respond, your accusation stands, but if he does, you have a hammer. In this case, you hook him with his clean-air voting record and then hammer him with a history of contributions from polluting companies and other non-air-quality votes of his that would suggest that he is bought and owned by these

> "You smile discreetly, you look like you're enjoying yourself, like you're getting ready to get down to serious business. You've got to be careful what you say."
> **DAN QUAYLE**, on how to act with the press

companies. This is where your homework pays off. Hold the opposing campaign accountable to his or her voting record and message.

If you find ten inconsistencies with the opposing campaign, use them for ten press releases or press conferences, not one press conference with a list of ten. Use supporters to point out your strengths as well as the problems with the opposition. For example, the Board of Realtors endorses you, an antigrowth candidate. Call a press conference for this announcement, and help the Realtors with a reason. In their endorsement they should include not only why they are endorsing you, but also why they are not endorsing your opposition. Campaigning from a third party is often better because it appears less self-serving.

> "All reformers, however strict their social conscience, live in houses just as big as they can pay for."
> —————— **LOGAN PEARSALL SMITH**

Take advantage of events that are already happening, like a Fourth of July parade. Plan to attend events that are likely to get media coverage, and let the press know that you will be there. When considering what these events might be, look to your persuadable vote and not your base. Sending a candidate to events that reinforce his or her stand on a particular issue or to an event that is already largely supported by the base takes precious time and energy from the candidate.

It is also important to look at a possible downside of attending an event: Who will be influenced to vote for the candidate because of his or her participation, and at what cost? One great example of this occurred in 1994, when George W. Bush was running for governor of Texas. He decided to attend the opening day of dove-hunting season to show that he was one of the boys and supportive of a liberal gun policy. Of course, the press was invited by Bush's team. When Bush finally did pull down a bird, however, it was not a dove but a bird under protection. This did not play well, and he was fined on top of it. One must question whether this was an appropriate outing for this candidate in the first place. Was this a group of persuadable voters or part of his base? At what cost did he participate?

Fielding Questions from the Press

If the press calls with a question you have not considered or feel unprepared to answer, don't answer on the spot. Explain that you're busy, and ask if you can call back in a couple of minutes. Be sure to ask for their deadline, and don't end up crowding it. If the question asked is about a complicated issue and the story will not appear for a couple of days, take the time and do some research before calling back. If the reporter says he or she is on deadline and needs something right away, ask for five minutes. Even a short amount of time can be enough to get your bearings on the issue. Call your media adviser, your campaign manager, your partner, or a supporter with specific expertise, and come up with an answer. Be creative. Recently, a state representative from upstate called because a wastewater pipe had broken in her district and was dumping sewage into a nearby stream. Uncertain about what to say to the press, she called me because she knew that Ashland has its own wastewater treatment system, and she correctly assumed that I had dealt with such problems while I was mayor.

> "If there's more than one person—including yourself—in a room, consider anything said to be on the record and a probable headline in the morning paper."
> **JOHN F. KENNEDY**

It's a good idea to write down specific points you want to touch upon before returning the call. Make these short and quotable, but deliver them with spontaneity. For example, even though the answer is in front of you, pause from time to time as though you're thinking. It's OK here to throw in a few "uhs" and "you knows."

One important note: If you ask a reporter to "go off the record," he or she must agree, or you are not officially off the record. It does not work to say something and then tell the reporter, "And, by the way, that was off the record," or "Please do not print that." Sometimes, after the interview is over, reporters will engage a candidate or a representative of the ballot issue in small talk. You may be thinking that the interview is over, but it's not, so watch what you say. Some argue that nothing is off the record and that a good rule of thumb is to say nothing that you do not want to see in print at the breakfast table. Unless you know the reporter pretty well, that's a good rule to follow.

> "Speak when you are angry and you will make the best speech you will ever regret."
> **AMBROSE BIERCE**, 1842–1914

If you're upset about an issue, cool down before you head out to face the press. I cannot stress how important this is. Because tempers can flare when you're in the midst of a political campaign, think about how what you say or do will read the next day in the paper, and choose your words carefully. I hear people say that the papers took their comments out of context or distorted what they said, but I have rarely found that to be the case. More often, I have wished I had been misquoted.

Top Ten Media Tips

1. As the candidate, you want to project the image of a credible community leader. You must remember that reporters do many interviews and

miss very little. What kind of clues are you giving that speak louder than your words? Avoid nervous behavior. Don't click your pen repeatedly, jingle change in your pocket, or twist your hair. Avoid verbal ticks, like "um," "if you will," "quite frankly," "you know," and "to be honest." Toeing the ground—looking down and moving your foot in a half moon with your toe—signals insecurity. So does crossing your feet while standing. Stand with your feet no farther apart than shoulder width. Don't cross your arms. Don't put your hands on your hips. Stand with arms at your sides, or use your hands as a way to emphasize what you're saying. Speak in a clear, firm voice, and look directly at the reporter. Keep your hands away from your face at all times.

> "This is now in general the great art of legislation at this place. To *do* a thing by assuming the appearance of *preventing* it. To *prevent* a thing by assuming that of *doing* it."
> — JOHN QUINCY ADAMS

2. Be sure you know your subject well. Practice with family members or campaign supporters. Discuss talking points around the campaign table, and repeat these to yourself until they come out in short, concise sound bites. Reporters do much better if you're to the point and they don't have to do a lot of work to figure out what you're saying.

3. Although you may have the reporter in front of you at that moment, it is the voter who will be reading what you say the next day. Think about your audience, and talk to your base and swing voters.

4. I try to keep a positive spin on everything. Reporters like to print controversy, but if that will hurt your cause, do not go there. Remember, you do not have to answer the question being asked, you just have to sound as if you're answering it.

5. Even so, unless it's your intention, don't answer a question that hasn't been asked. Candidates, especially new ones to the arena, tend to talk on and on. They often will hear one question when another is asked or want to offer up more information than is necessary. Shorter is better, always. Keep on your message, and do not let a reporter pull you off.

6. When the press calls, take a moment to think about what you will say, call someone for help if you need it, jot down some notes, and then return the call.

7. In general, return all calls promptly. As a rule, the earlier you're interviewed, the higher up you will appear in an article.

8. Avoid going "off the record."

9. Never speak when angry. Calm down, and then do the interview.

10. You get to select where the interview takes place. Think about the backdrop and whether its visual effect can further your message.

Paid Print Media

Although television is huge, the legitimizing effect of newspaper advertising for a political campaign should not be underestimated. In 2000, the Center for Congressional and Presidential Studies at American University looked at ways voters get their election information. Of the 35 percent readership of newspapers, 86 percent of those surveyed saw print media as a very important source for election information, with television close behind at 84 percent.

> "It's better to recall something you wish you'd said than something you wish you hadn't."
> **FRANK A. CLARK**

In general, three advertising formats work well in newspapers: emotional, informational, and testimonial (endorsement). None of these ads are mutually exclusive.

- Emotional ads are just that: ads that use pictures or other images and copy that will elicit emotion in the voters. Children at school, a couple talking privately, a child drinking clean water from a hose bib, a river, backdrops of your city, congested streets, historic buildings, kids engaged in school activities, seniors, and so forth.
- Informational ads are generally used with issue-based campaigns and are designed to let the voters know some bit of important information, such as the impact a tax measure will have on their yearly debt load.
- Finally, testimonials or endorsement ads use a third person to speak on behalf of a candidate or ballot issue. While those listed or quoted may be movers and shakers in a community, testimonials and endorsement ads can also feature the average person. The testimonial approach is especially effective in a candidate race, as it is both more effective and more believable if someone else says you're smart and hardworking than if you say you're smart and hardworking.

Advertising Formats for Newspapers

Between literature drops, lawn signs, direct mail, and advertising, political campaigns have a tendency to look like clutter, a sort of strip mall of democracy. Whenever possible, organize your efforts, and give a sense of continuity and neatness to your campaign. Use your logo in all campaign literature, or bring some thread from one medium to another to create continuity for your campaign. If your lawn sign is an especially good design, use it as an identifier in print ads, television spots, direct mail, and badges for canvassers. It's your trademark, and it should be used just as a major corporation would use its trademark.

> "Poor ads disengage consumers from the category. They make you feel like the category is not worth entering. Consumers ask, 'Is that all the category of government is?'"
>
> **JOEL DRUCKER,** marketing and communications consultant

Although there are many formats for newspaper ads, here are a few examples that have helped move campaigns forward in the print media.

Create newspaper ads that mimic a news story in layout. Place the candidate's picture as a fairly prominent part of the ad, with the logo underneath. Select and place a headline with copy alongside the candidate picture. Ad copy should be no more than three paragraphs long, should cover only one subject, and should include the campaign logo and slogan. Figure 8.4 is an example.

This format can be rotated with five or six different headings and copy. So the voter does not become immune to your ads, change out the candidate picture in each. This format works well as a *two-by-four*—two columns wide by four inches high. Smaller ads like this are cheap and tend to be placed on top of other ads and directly under newspaper copy. I have seen local races effectively

> "There are two times in a man's life when he should not speculate: when he can't afford it and when he can."
>
> **MARK TWAIN**

place ads half this size, daily, on each page of the paper. If you have lots of money, you can make the ad any size you want.

A two-by-four lends itself well to informational and endorsement ads. Informational ads for issue-based campaigns should also adopt a uniform look that is recognizable to the public. Figure 8.5 is an example of an ad used in an issue-based campaign for school funding. The font, layout, and design intentionally lead the voter to connect the ad with schools. Similarly, the endorsement ad shown in figure 8.6 uses the same two-by-four format and visually links itself to other ads advocating for the same school tax measure.

> "Only those who will risk going too far can possibly find out how far one can go."
>
> **T. S. ELIOT**

Testimonial or endorsement ads are among the most effective you can use anywhere in a campaign, but they lend themselves especially well to newspaper advertising. Unfortunately, too many campaigns attempt to cram too much into this

CATHY GOLDEN ON INDEPENDENT MANAGEMENT AUDITS

Cathy
GOLDEN
FOR MAYOR

"Ashland city government is long overdue for a management audit by an outside professional firm. It just makes good economic sense.

Management audits consistently pay for themselves in money saved, improved service, and higher staff morale. And they let taxpayers know exactly what they're getting for their money."

Building a Better Community

FIGURE 8.4 Example of Candidate Ad Made to Look Like a Newspaper Article (Crystal Castle Graphics)

JuSt The Facts
Cultural and Recreational Levy 15-3

If the levy passes, will my property taxes go up?

No. They will continue still downward, as mandated by Measure 5, but just not as much. Each of the next two years, they will drop by $1.53 per thousand, instead of $2.50 per thousand.

Authorized by United Ashland Committee, Linda & Joe Windsor, Treasurers, PO Box 2000, Ashland, OR 97520

FIGURE 8.5 Example of an Information Ad

This ad uses graphical cues that we typically associate with schools to help the reader identify the ad with the tax measure. (Crystal Castle Graphics)

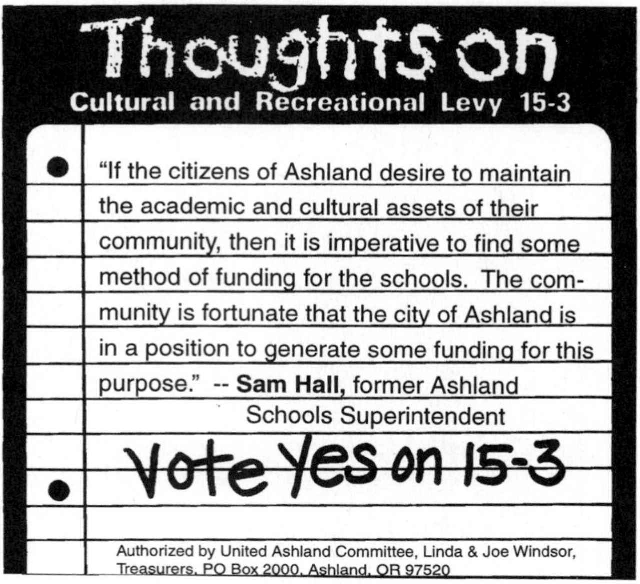

FIGURE 8.6
Example of a
2-by-4 Newspaper
Endorsement Ad for
an Issue-Based
Campaign

By design, this ad links
itself to schools and
other ads for the same
tax measure. (Crystal
Castle Graphics)

Thoughts on
Cultural and Recreational Levy 15-3

● "If the citizens of Ashland desire to maintain the academic and cultural assets of their community, then it is imperative to find some method of funding for the schools. The community is fortunate that the city of Ashland is in a position to generate some funding for this purpose." -- **Sam Hall,** former Ashland Schools Superintendent

● ## Vote Yes on 15-3

Authorized by United Ashland Committee, Linda & Joe Windsor, Treasurers, PO Box 2000, Ashland, OR 97520

format. Remember, newspapers are inherently cluttered, so do all you can to help your ads breathe. Keep the pictures simple and memorable. Pictures in small-format ads are difficult to see and work best with a close-up of only one person. Resist the temptation to show the candidate shaking hands with the person lending the quote. Keep all ads as clean and simple as possible.

"Victory goes to the player who makes the next-to-last mistake."
—— **SAVIELLY GRIGORIEVITCH TARTAKOWER**

This format can also be set up with text of a community leader or prominent citizen endorsing the candidate. Be sure to use a picture of the candidate and not that of the person who gave the quote: It's important to get the candidate's face in front of the public at every opportunity.

As the campaign progresses and the candidate gains endorsements, some of these candidate ads can be recycled to emphasize a point. For example, in my first run for mayor, I was characterized as a no-growth candidate. My feeling was that growth itself wasn't the problem, but rather the effects it had on our quality of life. Some would say it is too fine a distinction, but I argued that if we did all we could to mitigate the negative effects of growth, we would probably be OK. One of my small candidate-information ads referred to building moratoria resulting from inadequate planning for growth. Later, when I was endorsed by the Board of Realtors, I enlarged the building mora-

TIME IS RUNNING OUT!

OR

YOU
DECIDE

The revenues generated
by Measure 15-1 will
help preserve the land
that gives Ashland its
unique character.

Paid for & authorized by the *Good for Ashland!*
Committee, Hal Cloer, Treasurer, PO Box 0, Ashland. OR

IT'S GOOD FOR ASHLAND! VOTE YES ON 15-1

FIGURE 8.7
Example of an
Emotional Ad

(TAO Productions
and Crystal Castle
Graphics)

torium ad and included a banner highlighting the Board of Realtors endorsement. By coupling this endorsement with my advocacy of planning for
growth, I took the bite out of my opponent's "no-growth" charge and replaced it with a responsible-growth view. Remember, you do not want to get
on your opponent's message. Instead lead the voter to your message.

Issue-based campaigns generally do best with ads that tug at emotion. You
can and should run some information ads, but in general, information ads
tend to be off message. Expanding a library, adding curriculum options for
a school, and acquiring parkland are not about how cheap the projects are
but rather about what the projects will do for your community, society, and
future generations. There is no price for that. Stay on message: You are not
selling fifty cents a pound; you are selling apples, and if voters want apples,
they'll buy apples. Your job is to keep people focused on what they're buying, not on how much it will cost.

For example, in Ashland's open-space campaign, we ran ads that juxtaposed pictures of open fields filled with grazing sheep with more recent photos showing the same fields filled with housing. The caption urged the voter
to help leave some of the community open space untouched by voting yes.
Similarly, we ran other ads comparing pictures of wooded hillsides before and
after development (figure 8.7).

150,000 VISITORS TO ASHLAND A YEAR:

- **FLUSH TOILETS**

- **TAKE SHOWERS**

- **HAVE THEIR SHEETS AND TOWELS LAUNDERED**

This creates considerable sewage flow.

Visitors should share in the sewage solution.

The revenues from Measure 15-1 will come from a good blend of locals AND visitors.

Paid for and authorized by the Good For Ashland! Committee, Hal Cloer, Treasurer, PO Box 0, Ashland, OR.

Photo by Christopher Briscoe

IT'S GOOD FOR ASHLAND! VOTE YES ON 15-1

FIGURE 8.8
Another Example of an Emotional Ad

Whenever possible, use what is coming at your campaign and redirect it to the opposition.

Ashland's Youth Activities Levy was designed to pick up dropped extracurricular and co-curricular activities, and we needed to convey the importance of these programs to the future success of our students. To do this, we had one ad that juxtaposed two transcripts of the same student. One transcript had fine grades and an excellent GPA; the other had the same grades and GPA, plus a list of all the student's ancillary activities, showing involvement and leadership. The caption read: "Which student would you rather hire?" Another ad was identical except for the caption, which said: "Which student is more likely to get into a great college?" In these ads, without a lot of print, we were able to get to the heart of the challenges facing students if they are to get ahead.

> "Diplomacy is the art of saying 'Nice doggie' until you can find a rock."
> — **WILL ROGERS**

When local restaurants opposed a food and beverage tax for funding parkland acquisition and upgrades to the wastewater treatment plant, they argued that the tax was on the tourists who visited our city each year to enjoy the Shakespeare Festival. We agreed. They then said it was a tax on locals. We agreed again. To say this dramatically, we ran an ad with a picture of the city's central plaza on the Fourth of July, when more than 30,000 people drop in for the day. The caption pointed out that 150,000 visitors each year use our parks, have their bedding laundered, and flush toilets (figure 8.8). We took what was coming at us and redirected it back at the opposition, implying that tourists, like residents, should help pay for the systems they use.

Endorsements and Endorsement Ads

Endorsements from support groups, editorial boards, and business and community leaders can mean both money and votes for your campaign. As you get endorsements, incorporate them into your brochure and direct mail, and newspaper, television, and radio ads. Craft them into press releases, and send them to the local papers and newsrooms.

Endorsement ads or testimonials can take many forms. You can list the names of hundreds of people who support you, hopefully showing a broad cross-section of your community; you can pull quotations and names from letters to the editor; or you can have a page of logos from businesses that endorse you, with a caption identifying you. Figure 8.9 is an example of an actual ad that included the endorsement of a newspaper's editorial board.

Endorsement ads listing hundreds of names are routinely postponed by campaigns, forcing everyone to scramble in the eleventh hour to amass a list long enough to impress the voters. Whether or not you intend to run this type of ad, you should prepare for one from the beginning. Ask everyone you talk to if his or her name can be used in an endorsement ad. This not only will make producing an endorsement ad much easier, but also tells you whether the person you are contacting is in fact a supporter and how public he or she wants to go with that support. Some campaigners believe that endorsement ads are ineffective. But when you "hear" that your opponent is doing one, suddenly everything gets dropped while your volunteers start calling lists of people who might be willing to lend their name to an ad. This leaves your workers with the impression that the campaign is disorganized. It also

> "Political advertising ought to be stopped. It's the only really dishonest kind of advertising that's left."
> **DAVID M. OGILVY**

takes time away from other campaign activities at the end of the campaign, when volunteers are stretched to the limit. The last hours of a campaign are precious, so don't needlessly burden yourself: Take care of this as you go.

Ages ago, I worked on a campaign in which the candidate said early on that he thought endorsement ads were silly and ineffective and that he did not want to do one. Accordingly, we never collected names. Then, at the end of the campaign, his opponent came out with one of the best endorsement ads I have ever seen. The ad had great pictures of the candidate, a few tasteful

FIGURE 8.9
Example of an
Endorsement Ad

This ad was made
more striking by adding
shading and placing it
at an angle in a box.
(Crystal Castle Graphics)

lines about America and community, and a full newspaper page of names. And as if that weren't enough, he bought the back page of the paper for his ad. Even if we had the time and started calling then and there, we couldn't have pulled together an ad that would even have approximated what our opposition had done. The ad went unanswered. We lost that election.

When preparing an endorsement ad, keep a separate list of names in a computer, or create a field in your campaign database for an endorsement-ad sort. Use the computer to sort names alphabetically to help you find duplicates. However, when it comes time to run the endorsement ad, do not put the names in alphabetical order. A random listing of names pushes people to read through more of them, looking for familiar names. Also, random order allows you to put your big names in prominent locations, like at the top of columns or just above a prominent quote. If you know you are going to do an endorsement ad and you are not using a computer, periodically give names to someone who will enter them in a usable format in preparation of the endorsement ad.

In my first mayoral campaign, we ran the endorsement ad on bright yellow paper with a die-cut (a hole at the top) so it could hang from doorknobs. On the front at the top was the candidate's logo and the phrase "Join us in voting for Cathy Golden." Below this was a list of hundreds of names, which continued on the back to cover both sides of the door hanger. The Saturday before the election, about sixty volunteers covered the city in two hours. No matter where voters traveled in the city that day, these yellow endorsement door hangers could be seen hanging from door knobs.

After the food and beverage tax passed, funding parkland and wastewater treatment plant upgrades, restaurant owners began placing a postcard on every table in every restaurant in town. On one side, it asked patrons to let the city know what they thought about the meals tax, and on the other side of the card was my name and address at city hall. Obviously, the idea was to have patrons tell me that they hated the tax. Naturally, some postcards said just that; however, many came in with glowing remarks about Ashland and how happy the visitors were to contribute in some small way to the beauty of our community. I saved all these cards. Eventually, the people who opposed the tax pulled a petition and referred it back out to the voters through the initiative process. Once the referral qualified for the ballot and it was clear that we would have to run another campaign, I took the postcards supporting the tax and printed them verbatim in an endorsement ad (figure 8.10). Because I had not asked permission to use the names of the people who sent me postcards, I just used the initials.

With the growing number of people who read their news online, don't forget to check with your local paper about an advertising spot on its Web page. Be sure to secure this location early. In our county, there's room for only one banner ad across the top of each day's online newspaper.

The avenues with which campaigns communicate with the voters are fairly standard. Lawn signs, advertising, debates, voters' pamphlets, brochures, walking pieces, Web pages, and direct mail are standards used in a political campaign, whether it is issue-based or candidate-based. However, the difference between a winning campaign and a losing one is really how the campaign communicates

We *LIKE* the Meals Tax

We've been coming to Ashland since 1970. OSF is the impetus, but we've come to love the charm of your city/area. We make three trips a year into your economy. Since the ambience of the area attracts us, we don't object to contributing to ambience things like park areas, and mundane things like sewers. We're not paying the total cost with our 5% meal tax, just a contribution (maybe $25 a year). It's a small price to pay for the joy we get in return. How would the critics finance these things? And if you don't have them, folks like us wouldn't come. Don't be foolish, there's no free lunch – and we had a picnic in the park last night. 5% was only $1.50.
– R.S.
Eugene, OR

I applaud the wisdom of your voters in implementing this tax. I hope it continues.
– B.C.
Edmonds, WA

As frequent summer vacation visitors to Ashland, my wife and I are pleased to make a small contribution to the well being of your beautiful city through the tax. We feel it to be a good idea, not unreasonable.
– J.R.M.
Portland, OR

Paying 5% on our meals is a small price to pay to help keep Ashland the lovely city it is.
– T.W. **Talent, OR**

As a frequent visitor to Ashland, I welcome the opportunity to help pay for parks, open space and water treatment. The 5% tax seems appropriate to me.
– K.R.D. **Corvallis, OR**

I think you would be CRAZY NOT to collect this tax. These services benefit tourists, like us, therefore we should pay for them. This tax should focus more on visitors who put demands on your open space and utilities. Restaurant oriented taxation does that.
– J.H.J.
Winters, CA

I think the restaurants are foolish to oppose this tax. I support it and think we should have one in Eugene.
– G.S.
Eugene, OR

Good for you! Deal with your real problems ... I'm glad to chip in my share.
– M.P.
San Luis Obispo, CA

Although I work at a local coffee shop and am surrounded by opposition to the meals tax, I still support it. Please stick with your aims and goals no matter what pressure the restaurant owners put on you. 'Good Job!'.
– **Ashland, OR**

We have been annual visitors to Ashland for the past 16 years, and we do not feel burdened to support this sales tax for Ashland's parks and sewers (both of which we USE).
– R.K.
Los Altos, CA

Save our funding for park acquisition
VOTE NO ON 15-1 and YES ON 15-2
Paid & authorized by the Good for Ashland Committee, Jean Crawford, Treasurer

FIGURE 8.10 Another Example of an Endorsement Ad

Again, whenever possible, redirect back to the opposition what they send your way. (TAO Productions and Crystal Castle Graphics) through these different instruments. In product advertising, there seems to be little concern about whether someone remembers the product because the ad was irritating or because the ad was clever. This is not true in politics. In politics, where the period during which you must attract the voters' attention and move them to support you—and vote for you—is so short, irritating ads can hurt more than help. You want to create ads that have people saying to their family and friends, "Hey, check this ad out; it's really good." Your campaign must "pop" in a memorable way to break out of the clutter.

Years ago, I was involved in a campaign for a circuit judge. In the campaign war room was a local newspaper columnist who had been riding me and city hall for years. From time to time, I had responded to his missives with editorials that were as hard-hitting as those he had aimed at me. We happened to sit directly across the table from each other one evening in the war room. Everyone in the room who read the local paper knew the history, and I'm sure the tension was palpable. While we were discussing possible newspaper advertising, I suggested that the columnist and I be photographed back to back, arms crossed, looking directly at the camera. The caption would read: "They can only agree on one thing: Phil Arnold should be elected circuit court judge." We ran the ad. People in our community loved it and commented on it for weeks.

> "The significant problems we have cannot be solved at the same level of thinking with which we created them."
> **ALBERT EINSTEIN**

Brochures that breathe with pictures that have movement and that elicit emotion will distinguish yours over the opposition's. Lawn signs should be works of art, and slogans clever and memorable. A creative and memorable political campaign costs no more than one that is indistinct in every way.

Campaigns are the most fluid segment of the advertising market, and nowhere is it more important for your campaign to adapt to changing circumstances and new information than in advertising. One easy way to differentiate your campaign from others is in timing.

Timing Your Ads

Campaigns typically continue with advertising once they've begun, gradually increasing the number, size, and frequency of ads as the election draws near. However, for challengers there is a strong argument to begin advertising well in advance of the immediate preelection period, when the market is saturated. Early ads allow candidates time to introduce themselves without the distraction of competition with the opponent. Early ads also give a candidate an initial bump in the polls.

This does not mean your campaign should begin advertising in March and keep going until the May 18 primary. Rather, you would do ads one week at the end of March and then none until three or four weeks before the election. Television and newspapers may have specials in the spring to encourage people to spend money on advertising. Take advantage of this and jump in.

Your first ads can make the biggest impression, so choose them carefully. If you start and then stop in the final days, it gives the appearance that the campaign is faltering or lacks funds—that is, lacks support, which will make it harder to raise the necessary funds to get to Election Day. While an early advertising splash helps establish a challenger, if it will seriously cut into your media budget for the final push, you must consider this decision very carefully. Once you hit the final days, your campaign needs to maintain a presence until the end. Generally, I ask campaigns to buy the time closest to the election first and to work backward from there.

Although timing for a mail-in election is slightly different, for all others a media campaign should work like the fireworks on the Fourth of July. Start with a little at first, then add more and more, climaxing with the finale just before the election. Your money determines when you can start advertising, not when you will end. You always end a day out from the election.

Placing Your Buys

For newspaper advertising, talk to the person who sells display ads for your local papers. Although newspapers often include ad layout as part of the package and typically do a pretty good job, it is best to have your ad designed by a professional outside the newspaper. It is also worth paying extra to choose where in the paper the ad will be placed. Requesting placement typically adds 15 to 25 percent to the cost of the ad. Salespeople will tell you that it is not necessary to request placement and that they will do all they can to get you what you want for no extra money. This works about half the time. I have found that the personal bias of the editorial team, at least on small papers, gets your ad placed where they want it, not where you want it. If you can afford it, pay for placement.

The best spot for ad placement is opposite the editorial page. Pages 2 and 3 are also good choices. Stick to the outside of the page, not the fold. Much farther back in the paper, and your ad is at risk of disappearing. Don't forget the television listings section. In many papers, this section is tabloid-sized, and a full-page ad there costs a third as much as a full-page ad in the regular paper. Plus, people keep the TV section around all week. In my first run for mayor, I ran a full-page ad in the TV section. The ad contained the logos of all the businesses that were supporting my candidacy; naturally, the businesses loved the free publicity. My overarching theme was planned, thoughtful growth, so the headline read: "Planning for Ashland's Growth Is Good for Ashland's Businesses."

Don't forget the sports section, local high school newspapers, and college newspapers. Also, consider placing an ad in the help-wanted section: "Hardworking, energetic businesswoman seeks position with the County Commission. Willing to work long hours in community service. Vote [the candidate]." Finally, if you have the money and the space is available, a full-page or half-page ad on the back of the newspaper can work wonders. Ten years ago, a woman running for state representative bought the top half of the back page. Most of it was a color reproduction of a watercolor by a local artist of the hills surrounding our city. It was the best newspaper ad I had ever seen. She won by a handful of votes.

> "True compassion is more than flinging a coin at a beggar; it comes to see that an edifice which produces beggars needs restructuring."
>
> **MARTIN LUTHER KING, JR.**

With all this said about newspaper advertising, it is also important to look at the trends: In 1996, newspapers accounted for 48 percent of where voters received election news, and broadcast networks accounted for 39 percent. In 2000, however, newspapers accounted for 31 percent of where voters got their election news, broadcast networks 24 percent, and cable news 31 percent.[3]

By December 2008, Pew reported that those receiving national and international news online (40 percent) had passed those receiving the same from a daily (35 percent). More problematic for the health and longevity of newspapers in America is that more "traditionalist" voters, that is, those who receive a vast majority of their information from newspapers, tend to be older. Of the thirty-and-younger crowd, Pew reported in 2008 that 59 percent were receiving national and international news online. So the future of newspaper readership rests with those who are declining in numbers while those coming up through the ranks are not conditioned to receive news in a daily.[4]

Further, classifieds, which have contributed to newspaper income, have moved online, where people can sell their wares for free. Couple this with the struggling economy and a depressed ad market, where there are fewer businesses and fewer still with the ability to expend large amounts of money for print advertising, and the picture for newspapers becomes even more bleak. The income to support newspapers must come from someplace, and that appears to be from the remainder of those still advertising in the paper along with subscribers. But as rates climb, both subscribers and advertising dollars drop off. Further, as outlined above, newspapers hold less sway with Republicans and tend to speak to the base for Democrats. Given the sharp increase in costs of display ads in print media, campaigns must decide if this is a good expenditure of scarce campaign dollars.

One way to mitigate the high cost of media advertising yet still reach newspaper readers is to pay your daily to place an insert in its paper for your campaign. Given that newspaper readers are more likely to vote and are better educated, older, and more inclined to support schools, parks, and civic endeavors, this may be the happy compromise for getting the word out for a candidate or an issue-based campaign at a reasonable cost. Note, however, that inserts are often treated like clutter by the subscriber and come with a cost that could bump up against the cost of a display ad. For example, an insert may run one hundred dollars, versus five hundred dollars for the same-size ad within the newspaper pages. However, your campaign is responsible for layout and printing with an insert.

Miscellaneous Print Ads

A few years back, a local attorney bought the back cover of the phone book for "business" purposes. The cost was twenty-five thousand dollars. That spring (about the time the phone book came out), he declared his candidacy for the state legislature. Every day, a hundred thousand people look at his picture, sometimes dozens of times a day—all for just two thousand dollars a month. He further reinforced his candidacy by using the same picture that filled the back cover of the phone book in all his print ads.

Radio and Television

To be successful in a campaign, it's important to have a mix of media. When you first sit down to assess your preliminary budget, research the cost of radio and television, and consider what it can do for your campaign. Generally speaking, candidates for an office in a small town might be well advised to discard radio and television, focusing on mixes of the other media discussed above. On the other hand, candidates

> "The difference between genius and stupidity is that genius has its limits."
> —— **ALBERT EINSTEIN**

running for a countywide seat, state senate, state representative, mayor of the county's largest city, or further up the food chain should consider television and radio.

According to the study "Americans Speak Out About the 2000 Campaign," conducted by the Center for Congressional and Presidential Studies at American University, 74 percent of those surveyed felt that radio was an important source of political information. Although radio does not have the same presence it once did, many people listen to radio while traveling to and from work, and talk radio is everywhere. Stations know their audience numbers and their ratings, so reaching certain segments of the population through radio is pretty easy.

In some areas, the cost of radio production and air time is comparable to television production and air time, but that is not true everywhere. Because radio paints a picture with words and sounds whereas television paints a picture with images, radio should be treated differently than television. Nevertheless, in the 2002 general election, one of my clients ran a 60-second radio spot from two 30-second television ads we had produced. Because the ads were rich with Foley work (background sound) and had strong scripts that could stand alone without the TV images, it completely worked. As a side benefit, the ads playing in two media reinforced each other.

Radio spots are generally 60 seconds long, which allows the campaign plenty of time to tell a story. In the 2002 primary, a candidate running for circuit court judge ran a very effective radio campaign. He had inadvertently missed the voters' pamphlet deadline in the primary and was facing a well-heeled opponent who was everywhere, including on television. To overcome his opponent's money and organization, the candidate saturated radio stations with a great ad reminding voters that he was the one who wasn't in the voters' pamphlet. It was enough to help him barely survive the primary and eventually win in a runoff in the general election.

But let's be clear: Radio is not for everyone. In southern Oregon, for example, radio is exclusively on the extremes of the spectrum. The choices are a local public radio station, which takes no political commercials, and talk radio with local, statewide, and national hosts who spew vitriolic commentary, often about the very candidates who are paying their salaries through ad buys.

In August 2008, the Pew Research Center for the People & the Press conducted an extensive poll to determine where the public gets its news in a computer-savvy society.[5] The poll revealed that radio has mirrored the same decline as newspaper since 1991, when 55 percent of Americans got their news in some form from radio, to today's 35 percent who reported listening to radio news. This study also noted that of the 5 percent who listen to Rush Limbaugh regularly and the other 9 percent who listen occasionally, 80 percent describe their political views as conservative. Of the remaining listeners,

Talk Radio Listeners: Conservatives, Middle-Aged Males	
	Listen to talk radio regularly %
Total	17
Party/Ideology:	
Conservative Reps	**28**
Moderate/Liberal Reps	13
Conservative/Moderate Dems	15
Liberal Dems	20
Sex/Age:	
Men <30	17
Women <30	19
Men 30-49	**26**
Women 30-49	13
Men 50+	16
Women 50+	13

FIGURE 8.11

Who Listens to Talk Radio?

(Source: The Pew Research Center for the People & the Press, "Key News Audiences Now Blend Online and Traditional Sources," August 17, 2008)

Figures show the percent within each group who report regularly listening to radio shows that invite listeners to call in to discuss current events, public issues and politics.

10 percent claimed to be liberals and 7 percent moderates. This compares to the general public, which is 35 percent conservative, 35 percent moderate, and 20 percent liberal (figure 8.11).

As with newspapers, the campaign should determine to whom it needs to speak and spend dollars accordingly.

Television has a vast reach, especially in rural areas, which often have access to only a few local stations and limited cable penetration. In my county, we have four local stations, and although anyone living within a city has the option of hooking into cable, only about 60 percent do. More and more residents in the unincorporated areas where cable is not available have satellite dishes, limiting the effectiveness of local ads. Still, the primary access to local news is through the local stations, not cable or satellite.

> "Mixing buys of TV ads allows more types of voters to view it—you're looking for connectors, salesmen, mavens"
>
> — **MALCOLM GLADWELL**

Television can legitimize a candidate or campaign issue more quickly and effectively than any other medium. Although the costs for television ads near major media markets can be prohibitively expensive, that is not necessarily true in more rural areas. For example, in my market production for a 30-

second TV spot runs from $500 to $1,500 and anywhere from $8 per spot on cable to $3,300 for a 30-second ad on a network, top-ranked program. Spending $3,300 for a 30-second spot is completely unnecessary for the down-ballot race, as any campaign can get equal reach with increased frequency on cable or on network television during the day or

> "Rumps in, horns out."
> **COW PUNCHER'S CREED**

close to prime time. Still, raising enough money to have an effective television campaign, whether you're in an urban or a rural area, can be difficult. Also, although you could have friends who are professional photographers volunteering their talents, a sister doing the graphics for lawn signs and newspaper ads, and hundreds of volunteers going door-to-door, television is not something you can leave to people without skill and experience in the medium. Every step, from the creation of the storyboard and script, to production, editing, and airing, costs money.

The advantage of television, like radio, is that the market has been thoroughly researched. There are many sources you can use to research where your swing voters spend their viewing hours. Among these sources are Cabletelevision Advertising Bureau, Rocky Mountain Media Watch, Simmons' National Consumer Study, Nielsen, and Doublebase Mediamark Research. Industry tracking firms know who is watching what according to age, education, voting history, income, location, and gender—such as which programs are watched by voters who care about health care and who voted within the last twelve months.

> "Politics is short, very focused. To compete with all the commercial advertising you have to punch through."
> **LEO MCCARTHY,**
> former lieutenant governor

What is helpful for the campaign is that by using industry resources, you can develop and run ads that speak to an audience that is more likely to vote and one with highly specific demographics. Knowing who watches what helps a campaign avoid overtargeting a particular demographic group as well as reach the kind of voters who will support your efforts if given some information. Indeed, if your campaign can get great TV ads for around five hundred dollars, why not run a different ad on different cable stations at the same time? After all, the air time is the same, so the campaign is only out the production costs.

Cable Television: A Better Buy

In larger media markets where network television is prohibitively expensive for local campaigns, cable remains affordable. And in small markets, it can be the cheapest tool in your media tool box.

In southern Oregon, a campaign can buy a 30-second spot on cable for about ten dollars. In the Portland media market, where house races could not afford to advertise on network television, nearly all of the close house races in the 2002 general election advertised exclusively on cable. While ten dollars sounds cheap—and it is—remember, you're typically buying six spots per day on six to seven cable channels for three weeks. It adds up, and you haven't even bought network.

> "Placing TV ads based on cost and running them as often as possible may build voter-immunity."
> — **MALCOLM GLADWELL**

Campaigns buy six spots per cable station because cable advertising is often available only on rotators. That means you buy six spots, and the station will rotate your 30-second ad through a time slot, like 24 hours or (for a little more) from 6 p.m. to midnight. I've never found this to be a problem and do research for my buys with that in mind. People watch at all times of the day and night; the trick is to line up your buys on a daytime rotator with shows that people watch during the day and an evening rotator for cable networks and programs that tend to get watched more at night.

Finally, be sure to check out the Television Bureau of Advertising (www.tvb.org) Web site for demographics on cable network viewing. Also, Nielsen Online (nielsen-online.com) has examined Web audiences by site, size, demographic profile, and behavior. Once a campaign knows its audience, a small amount of time in research can help target both Internet advertising and television audiences and save money.

Fat-Free TV

In smaller media markets, television is a relatively affordable asset in your media budget. In the 2002 general election, we advertised on four daytime network stations, nearly every hour for one week, for the same price as developing and sending one direct-mail piece. That was still true in 2008. But to keep television affordable, attention to detail must be practiced at every level.

Although production for television should be left in the hands of a professional, the more you know about the process, the more input you'll be able to have in creating the finished product. There are a number of ways to stretch your campaign dollars if you decide to use television advertising.

> "The press always has the last word."
> **TOM OLBRICH,**
> campaign media adviser

It's important to do as much front-end work as possible. Research the candidate and the opposition. Anyone creating your ads should know both the strengths and the weaknesses of your candidate. While the strengths may be accentuated in ads that establish a candidate, your media specialist should also have a clear idea of where the candidate may be vulnerable. Once attacked, the media consultant may have to respond by delivering a finished product to the television stations within hours. Knowing your candidate's weaknesses allows you to begin the groundwork for response ads before they are necessary. If the need never materializes, all the better.

Your campaign should also research the strengths and weaknesses of the opposition. Even if you do not intend to run negative ads, by researching the opposition's flaws, you can juxtapose your candidate's strengths with your opponent's weaknesses and never mention them. They become implied. "Jane Doe will not miss important votes" implies that her opponent has (figure 8.12).

It's a good idea at this time to gather as much background information about your candidate as possible in the form of newspaper articles, childhood and current family photos (especially ones that help underscore an image you want to project), career history, and a list of names and phone numbers of close family and friends whom the media consultant can contact. To give a producer as many options as possible, collect newspaper clippings for the opposing candidate, as they can often be used in ads. Your efforts to gather information saves the campaign time and money and usually results in a better product. In the 2002 general election, we were called late in the cycle to do a few television spots for a local race. Although we had some footage of the candidate from a forum we attended, it wasn't enough, so an appeal was put out in the community for any video on the candidate. One local resident had video of all the candidates in the Ashland Fourth of July parade. Although the quality was marginal, converting it to black and white and slowing the motion gave it a timeless quality, and it added a great deal to the ad (figure 8.13).

Choosing Your Media Specialist or Team

Before you begin to interview producers for your ads, check to see what level of expertise already exists within your campaign team. With the advent of digital video, there are a lot more consumer-savvy hobbyists who may speak the same language as the producer you hire. Your team might have people with the skills and equipment to shoot your own ads—but a word of caution: Making television-quality video is not the same as shooting home video. Look at samples from whomever you use, whether it's someone you hire or a volunteer, before you commit your hard-earned media dollars. Volunteer producers can also be found at local cable access stations, where fledgling

242

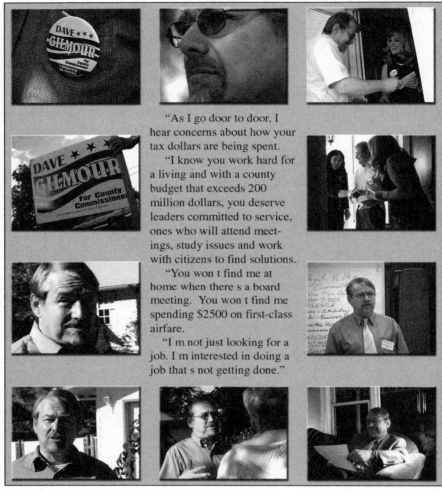

"As I go door to door, I hear concerns about how your tax dollars are being spent.

"I know you work hard for a living and with a county budget that exceeds 200 million dollars, you deserve leaders committed to service, ones who will attend meetings, study issues and work with citizens to find solutions.

"You won t find me at home when there s a board meeting. You won t find me spending $2500 on first-class airfare.

"I m not just looking for a job. I m interested in doing a job that s not getting done."

FIGURE 8.12 Example of a Comparison TV Ad

County Commission candidate Dave Gilmour was running with an eight-point registration disadvantage against a popular incumbent. The incumbent had been somewhat remiss in the use of public funds and had received damaging press regarding drug and alcohol abuse and marital problems. We felt that going straight after the incumbent's personal problems would be needlessly unkind and could backfire. Instead, as shown in these stills from the TV spots, we used images to portray the two candidates' differences: Gilmour projected a healthful image (walking door-to-door) and a sound family relationship (his daughter and his son narrated two of the three ads). And the ads spoke to integrity, referencing only his opponent's indiscretion with use of tax dollars. (rickshaw productions)

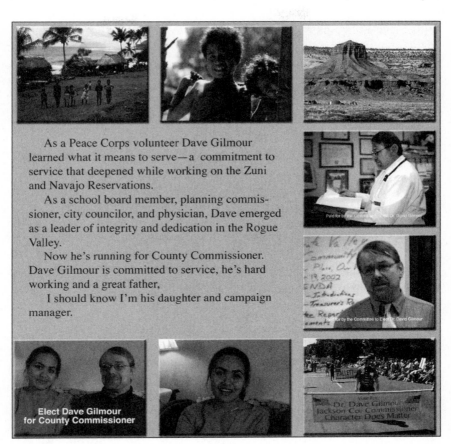

FIGURE 8.13 Example of an Establishing TV Ad

All ads should tell a story, but your first one should tell a story of the candidate. Effective ones reveal who the candidate is and not only touch on history but also tug at emotions. (rickshaw productions)

producers may be willing to work for the experience and exposure. Again, with television, free is great, but quality is more important. A bad or poorly crafted television spot can hurt your cause.

As an aside, the local community access station is often hungry for programming and may be willing to produce shows with a candidate at little or no charge. Such productions can provide some outstanding material for your producer to use in an ad or a portion of an ad.

In small markets, political campaigns are sometimes forced to go to ad agencies for television production, but remember, an ad for a sale at a clothing store is very different from a political spot.

So, what do you look for? First check around from the last campaign and look at locally produced spots. You can usually find out who produced particular ads by simply asking the candidates or their teams. Second, watch local commercials that are currently airing. Do any of them stand out? Check for the use of graphics, logos, and type of ad. Has the producer layered the ad with rich visuals and Foley (sound) work? Can you see a difference in quality? By simply calling or visiting local stations, you can find out the names of producers whose ads stand out. Third, ask for copies or demos of a local production team's work. Give preference to agencies that specialize or have experience in campaign ads, but don't ignore new talent in the form of some of those local commercials you liked. New producers are like new restaurants: They keep their prices down and give excellent service. Just make sure the food is good. That new producer may bend over backward to give your project all the attention it needs, but he or she still needs the skill and equipment to give it broadcast quality.

> "If Hitler invaded Hell, I think I would find a good word to say about the Devil in the House of Commons."
>
> **WINSTON CHURCHILL**
> (in response to criticism for siding with Stalin during World War II)

Spend some time looking at other political spots online. There is no reason an agency cannot model your ad after another campaign somewhere else in the country. Stanford University has more ads than you can watch at http://pcl.stanford.edu/campaigns/2008/. Check it out.

Television, like brochures, must breathe. Be sure that whoever you hire does not use clever swirls and bizarre dissolves or a voice-over that is trying to cram in as many words in as humanly possible. On-screen type should reinforce what's being said rather than introduce new thoughts.

Judge all demos on style, quality, and overall look. At this point, you're looking more for a feeling than content. When it comes to content, hopefully you'll be very involved in writing the script. Look for filmlike softness, lighting, and movement. Do the demos include subjects in motion? A car ad may look great, but that doesn't mean the same agency can shoot a candidate going door-to-door. Look for producers who like to shoot outdoors and use natural lighting. You will pay more for on-location shoots than studio shoots, but it is worth it.

Next, interview the top three to five producers on your list. Before you get to the nitty-gritty of production schedules and rates, spend some time talking about your candidate or cause. Can the producer understand why this is important to you? Why this candidate or issue-based campaign needs to win? Make sure the producer thoroughly understands your message and theme.

Leave plenty of room for discussion, brainstorming, and give-and-take. A good producer has probably been thinking in images the whole time and should have some immediate ideas for you. However, don't commit to anything just yet. The most important decision for you is whether this is a person who can work for and with your candidate or cause. This is especially important given that shooting film and video is stressful, expensive, and deadline driven.

Next, share all the possible materials you have (photos, newspaper clippings, and so forth), and ask the producer to send you a proposal with a budget breakdown. Ask for treatments and pricing for one, two, and three ads. You may later use this information for negotiating prices. If the budget includes crew, find out if the producer can or is willing to make use of your volunteers to reduce costs.

> "Wisdom oftentimes consists of knowing what to do next."
> **HERBERT HOOVER**

Local stations may also pitch you their own studio production at a fraction of the cost of local producers. Buyers beware, though: These ads are usually in a cookie-cutter, talking-head format with a studio backdrop. This format is best reserved for a candidate who is responding to an attack or for featuring local stars or incumbents with clout who are willing to publicly endorse a candidate or cause. If the talking-head format can stand on its own for your particular application, it can be a very effective and an inexpensive ad to produce. In 2000, I worked on a local campaign in which the candidate had the backing of Governor John Kitzhaber, who has an excellent television presence. Although the governor said he would cut some ads for us, it was difficult to get everyone's schedules lined up for a shoot in southern Oregon. Eventually, the scripts were written in Ashland and e-mailed to the governor in Salem, where we had arranged for a shoot in a studio that was located close to his home. A member of our campaign committee met the governor at the studio, and they did two or three takes on each of the scripts for about two hundred dollars for the cameraman. The video was then brought to a local production company in southern Oregon, where music, a logo, and a disclaimer were added to complete the ads for another hundred dollars.

There are plenty of occasions for the media team to attend events that include both candidates, providing a venue to capture footage of each. Seizing opportunities of this nature allows your campaign to study both candidates and pick up material for additional ads. Anytime a candidate attends a debate, send a video camera, and if a local station or public access channel has a debate or candidate forum, purchase the CD of the recorded show. After all, they do have professionals lighting the stage and working the cameras. We have cut a number of 30-second spots from pre-recorded candidate forums.

Streamline Production:
Ten Tips to Save Money and Improve Your Television Spots

Many producers don't press for multiple takes or worry much about mistakes made during filming out in the field, because most can be fixed in production. However, minimizing the amount of time the editor spends on your ads saves money.

1. As a candidate, if you're delivering a speaking part, know your part, and be fully prepared. TelePrompTers can be tricky. Look at the difference between John McCain and Barack Obama when it came to using a TelePrompTer in 2008. The TelePrompTer is not for everyone. If a candidate appears to be reading from one, it will be apparent to the viewer. It makes the candidate seem insincere and the message contrived. It also suggests that the candidate can't be trusted to speak well without a prepared text.
2. Bring a change of clothes. If your ad creates or re-creates events and settings that are quite different and supposedly took place over time such as a shot with the candidate at a day care center, another at a business, and another with seniors, audiences will notice if the candidate is wearing the same outfit in each shot. Recently, I saw an ad for a congressional candidate in Washington State. The ad began with her talking to the camera while walking through a hilly outdoor area in a skirt, a pink silk blouse, and white pearls. It was bizarre. My first thought was that she was out for the day to make ads and this was what she wore. Sure enough, in nearly every subsequent shot, she had the same pink blouse and white pearls. How much trouble can it be to bring a change of clothes? If you are going from woods to senate chamber, dress appropriately for the settings.
3. If the ad involves testimonials, impress upon those involved that they need to know what they will say, and provide them the lines. E-mail the scripts to people well before the shoot to provide enough time for them to learn the lines. When it comes to a shoot with testimonials, schedule all the people at a location that can take on many different looks. Be sure you do not have to deal with traffic noise. And remember, there's a reason advertisers use actors for testimonials. It is more effort than you can imagine to get an average person to sound plausible in advertising.
4. Find locations that convey message and image. Think about these ahead of time, and share your thoughts with the media specialists.
5. Consider using photos with a voice-over. Still photographs of the candidate as a child, at work, as a parent, as a spouse, fly-fishing, and so

forth, can be a very effective way to evoke a feeling of intimacy with a candidate. Don't forget to add newspaper stories to increase the credibility of the accomplishments mentioned.

6. Get enough baseline footage so that more ads can be cut without sending the crew out again.

7. Try using just music and no voice-over. Because TV is so noisy, if a 30-second ad appears with only music, everyone looks.

8. Consider using stock photos and film clips. For a relatively small cost, your campaign can purchase stock images to convey a message or create an emotion. This is especially important when your ad covers delicate issues such as domestic violence. Rather than send a professional photographer to an old-growth forest or a wastewater treatment plant that uses wetlands for polishing, why not purchase this footage? Images of the great halls of government, people shaking hands, crowds, a child with the American flag, piles of money, orchestras, you name it, are already available and professionally done. The Image Bank is one source, but there are others.

9. Send a professional photographer or talented amateur to early campaign events. Use these images for ads.

10. The script should be written for a 29-second read. Although you are buying a 30-second spot, the spots are actually 29.5 seconds. Too often, campaigns compensate for long scripts by having the narrator read faster. Remember the quip, "I would have written you a shorter letter if I had the time"? Take the time. This is a little like backpacking. Lay out everything you're going to take, and then reduce it by half, and then half again.

Great Ads Don't Just Happen: Be Creative, Organized, Focused

In television and radio campaign advertising, there are generally three types of ads: establishing, comparison, and response/attack. Whatever the format of your ad, certain overriding principles apply to all.

1. A good ad begins with a good script. The fewer spoken words the better; aim for eighty. It is not enough to simply have a presence on television. Television ads must have an objective. The first question to be asked and answered before a script is drafted is, "What is our objective with this ad?"

If your objective is to establish the candidate, that is, to tell a story about who he or she is, your ad must stay focused on that aspect of the candidate. An establishing ad, for example, should really tug at emotion; it's a voyeuristic

FIGURE 8.14 Another Example of a Comparison TV Ad

In the Maxwell for the House campaign, the Democrats drafted Shayne Maxwell after the primary, setting her considerably behind schedule. With this late start, with little money in a conservative district, and with a seventeen-point registration disadvantage, we knew the first ad had to be bold. It also had to establish the candidate and draw comparisons with her and her well-heeled opponent. (rickshaw productions)

glimpse into the candidate's personal life, past and present. It's a time capsule of what this potential community leader will bring to the table in terms of experience and core values. Is she a fighter? Has he volunteered for country or community? Has the candidate had unique challenges in life that have shaped who he or she is?

The media team must look at the candidate's bio and decide what should stay and what should go. An establishing ad is a good place for the old photos you had the candidate dig up; it is also an excellent venue for stock photos (figure 8.14).

2. Use language that reflects that of your voters. Don't talk over people's heads, and don't talk down to them. Talk about issues the way real people would talk about them.

3. Show clear comparisons between the candidates. This can be implied, as shown in figure 8.12, or it can be more direct, as in figure 8.14.

4. Make the ads believable. Whether you are attacking your opponent or promoting your objectives, be both specific and realistic about promises and programs you want to bring to the voters once you are elected. Be sure your goals are achievable. Making unrealistic claims or promises insults people's intelligence.

> "Endeavor to speak truth in every instance; to give nobody expectations that are not likely to be answered, but aim at sincerity in every word and action—the most amiable excellence in a rational being."
>
> **BENJAMIN FRANKLIN**

5. Look at other political ads—lots of them. Political ads are available on many university Web sites, as well as candidate Web pages. An excellent site can be found at the Political Communication Lab at Stanford University; it has hundreds of ads dating back to 1994.[6]

6. Let others do your bidding. Using family or prominent, respected community leaders can be an effective tool for an outsider to establish authenticity and credibility of a candidate. Using on-the-street people can show that an incumbent is still connected to everyday people.

7. Use black-and-white. What color does for direct mail, black-and-white does for TV. It's an effective tool to get noticed and to create mood, intimacy, and a sense of history for the candidate or issue-based campaign.

8. Ads should be easily distinguishable from one another. In a recent election cycle, a local ad firm cut four ads, each with the candidate sitting in a large leather chair talking directly to the camera. Other than the script, they were identical. Given that the opposition was making age an issue, the candidate could have met that criticism without actually acknowledging it by showing

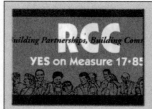

Hundreds of men and women found that Rogue Community College allowed them to pursue their dream and prosper in a now very uncertain economy.

RCC's expansion plans provide exactly what we need at the right time: a technical training center so our workers can learn new skills without relocating.

By voting for Measure 17-85 you support the economy of this region.

Support RCC. Vote yes on Measure 17-85.

It's a vote for all of us.

FIGURE 8.15 Example of an Issue-Based TV Ad Using Still Photos

This ad juxtaposed still, black-and-white photos with the brilliant red field sign used in the campaign. The producer brought the field sign to life in the last frames of the ad by cutting out each of the characters in the still photos and layering them on top of the silhouettes featured in the field sign. Using captivating music, the ad ran for ten days with no voice-over, to pull the viewer in and to pop the ad from all the other political clutter. We then came back with the identical ad and a voice-over. Because of the nature of the community-college-bond measure, we chose for the voice-over a student who had a great deal of experience in public speaking and an engaging voice that, although deep, had a youthful quality to it. (rickshaw productions)

images of him fly-fishing knee-deep in a river. Instead, what he got were four ads that looked same to the viewer.

9. Use still photography and create motion by zooming in or panning pictures. By mixing childhood photos with more current images, you can tell a story about the candidate in a controlled, evocative way. Still photos work well for issue-based campaigns (figure 8.15).

10. Carefully select the ad's music. Although an abundance of copyright-free music is available, most of it, unfortunately, is pretty bad. The Music Bakery has the best selection, but many online services are available. Most do not expect payment for a piece until you download it for use. Selecting music takes a lot longer than you can imagine, so allow yourself plenty of time.

In a spot we made for a campaign in 2008, the candidate wanted different music, so we sent him to Stanford Media's Web site to view other political ads and find something he liked better, which he did. We were then able to very closely match what he liked. You want to be involved in your production; you should always feel you can tweak an ad so it is more to your liking.

> "The consumer is not a moron, she is your wife. Never write an advertisement you would not want your own family to read. You would not tell lies to your wife. Don't tell them to mine."
> **DAVID M. OGILVY**

11. Use professional equipment, good camera operators, proper lighting, and thoughtful settings. The settings should all have a purpose. You're spending a lot of money and time, so don't cut corners here (figure 8.16).

12. Make video look like film. Many in the industry prefer to use film because it creates a more reflective feel. Few campaigns, especially local ones, can afford this. However, lighting can go a long way toward softening images and creating a filmlike look. Ask your production company what techniques they can use to soften video.

13. Use motion. When a candidate speaks directly to the camera, have him or her moving forward, either to a stationary camera or to one that moves with the speaker. This conveys the message that the candidate is someone who is going places, moving forward.

14. Defend on television; attack in direct mail. In the 2002 general election, we were helping a Democratic candidate who was being outspent seven to one, had very little money, and had a huge registration disadvantage. However, tracking polls showed her closing in on her opponent, and as his double-digit lead dwindled to the margin of error, he went on the attack through a direct-mail piece sent by Oregon Right to Life. With only a few thousand dollars in the bank, the campaign could not respond through direct mail, so we generated a television ad that brought back to the forefront the unprecedented nasty primary the Republican had run against the incumbent he unseated. "He's at It Again" aired for a week in closely targeted television markets (figure 8.17). In airing the ad, however, we made a couple of mistakes. First,

252

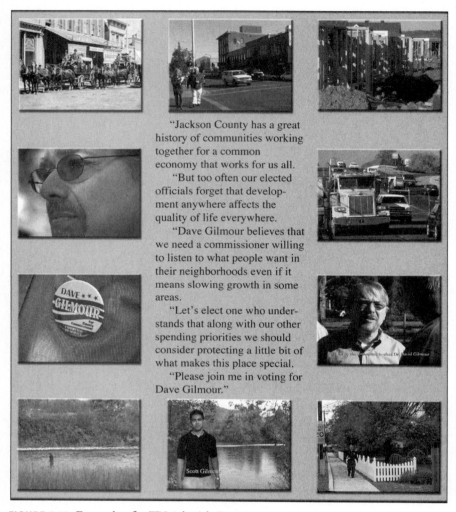

"Jackson County has a great history of communities working together for a common economy that works for us all.

"But too often our elected officials forget that development anywhere affects the quality of life everywhere.

"Dave Gilmour believes that we need a commissioner willing to listen to what people want in their neighborhoods even if it means slowing growth in some areas.

"Let's elect one who understands that along with our other spending priorities we should consider protecting a little bit of what makes this place special.

"Please join me in voting for Dave Gilmour."

FIGURE 8.16 Example of a TV Ad with Purpose

Late in the Gilmour for Commissioner race, canvassers reported that voters still did not know Dave Gilmour. We knew we had to go back in and lock his base without losing any swing voters. To do this, we took an issue that was problematic across all communities in southern Oregon—development—and used it as the anchor for the ad. By incorporating progressive environmental images embraced by Gilmour's base with countywide concerns about development, we accomplished our objective. The voice-over was done by the candidate's son. (rickshaw productions)

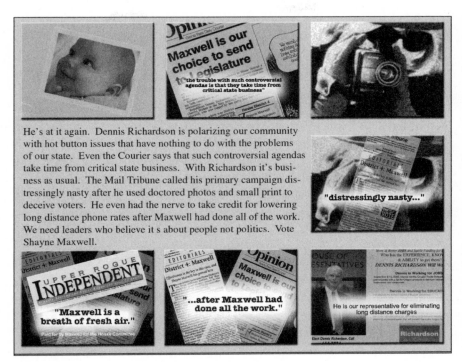

FIGURE 8.17 Example of a Response/Attack TV Ad

(rickshaw productions)

Oregon Right to Life had used a mailing list targeting the house district as well as a select group of Republican voters. The television ad, however, went out to a much broader audience and gave our opponent a reason to use TV ads and automated phone calls to defend himself in a very believable way. Because most people in the district had not seen his hit piece, it looked as though we had gone negative on him rather than the other way around. Second, attacks should be answered in the same medium in which they were made, which we could not do because of financial constraints. We would have served the client better in this case by leaving the charge unanswered.

15. Remember, television is about emotion, not information.

Placing Your Buys on Television: Research, Research, Research

Production companies that make your ads will often do the buy air time for them as well. The time is sold to them at a 15 percent discount, and then the agency charges the campaign full freight, which is where the real money is made. Buying is not a complicated prospect, especially if you're willing to do some research and have a good sales rep at the local station. Campaigns that directly buy their air time will save a lot of money.

> "It's the responsibility of the media to look at the president with a microscope, but they go too far when they use a proctoscope."
> — RICHARD M. NIXON

Do not fall victim to agencies that make your television spot for free knowing they will make their money, and then some, on the buys. Most advertising agencies are not adept at making political spots, and once an ad is made and given to you "free of charge," a campaign feels obligated to use it. Especially in a small market where agencies are headed up by friends or acquaintances.

In 2008, I received a call from a candidate who was working with a local advertising agency. The candidate had gone heavily into debt in the primary, outspending the opponents nearly three to one. He wanted to know how to get to a win for the general election. After looking over all his materials, which were rather rudimentary, I looked at his TV spot. It was awful. I told him he had to ask the agency to make a new one. He said, "But it was done at no charge to my campaign." I pointed out how much money the agency made placing the buys at his expense; still he could not bring himself to ask for a better ad. He lost the general as well. A bad ad—free or otherwise—is just that: a bad ad.

Political candidates must be offered the lowest unit rate. However, be aware that if you come in at this rate, your time is "preemptable" by other buyers. This means you can be bumped by someone who is willing to pay the full price. Usually you will be moved to a "compara-

> "The suspense is terrible. I hope it will last."
> — OSCAR WILDE

ble," that is, a spot with similar demographics. A second tier, at a slightly higher rate, is "preemptable with notice." At this rate, the ad rep must let you know you're about to be bumped so that you can pay more to secure the spot. Finally, the most expensive rate is nonpreemptable. You pay for this rate, and you're gold: No one moves you.

If you're working on an issue-based campaign, there may not be any break for TV ads. If that is the case, add at least 20 to 50 percent to your television budget buys. Even so, when I was helping a school tax measure in 2002, I talked to a sales rep of one of our three local stations and argued that "local" issue-based campaigns were quite different from statewide initiatives, which often came fortified with millions in special-interest money. Convinced, the station gave us the same break that candidates received. I then called the other stations and told them what their competition was doing for the community and got similar breaks across the board.

Because most campaigns run their media with greater frequency as the election approaches, open time slots for media buys become scarce. In television programming, as with radio, there are just so many available seconds in the hour. Unlike a newspaper, which can add more pages, television and radio have limited amounts of time to sell. Depending on the popularity of the show, the time when you might consider a buy can be even more restricted. If you do not secure your media buys early, there could be nothing available as the election deadline draws near.

That does not mean you have to deliver finished products the day you buy ad time. All the production work can be done later. But it does mean that in August or September, if you're going to buy 30 seconds on *60 Minutes* for November, you must have the cash in hand. This is where early endorsements and early money pay off.

Make your buys in August, and make them at non-preemptable rates. This is done for two reasons: First, you lock in the time so no one can bump you, and second, you also lock in the rate. As an election approaches and demand increases, so do rates. One local sales representative told me that during the 2008 season, a statewide issue-based campaign called from Portland with sixty-four thousand dollars to spend in three days. She said that by then, our region was commanding Portland metro rates. Buy early if you know you're going to do television. And even if you end up changing your mind, you can always sell the time back to the station down the road.

> "Television allows you to be entertained in your home by people you wouldn't have in your home."
>
> **DAVID FROST**

If you know which voters your campaign needs to target and exactly what message you want to deliver to which age group and income, one of the most predictable highways is television. Local station sales reps know their programming and will lead you to the best reach and frequency. So if your targeting turns up a specific demographic profile as likely to support you, your television ad rep will tell you where to place your ads and how many times they will need to air for the targeted voter to see them; the rep will also know how many times a viewer will see the ad, given the number of gross rating points (GRPs) you buy. For example, a purchase of six hundred GRPs, a typical buy for political campaigns in October, means that 89.6 percent of television viewers will see the ad 6.7 times each, according to David Townsend, who heads Townsend, Raimundo, Besler & Usher, a political consulting and public affairs firm in Sacramento.

A thousand GRPs, a typical purchase the week before an election for a hotly contested seat, means that 94 percent of the people watching will see the spot about 11 times each. If you're running a campaign in Nebraska, which is a relatively inexpensive television market, you will pay about $110 per GRP in a statewide race. That translates to $100,000-plus for the final week of the campaign. If you live in California, however, the same one thousand GRPs will cost you better than $2 million. Compare these with a local campaign in a rural area where viewing is restricted to a few stations. For example, in southern Oregon and comparable small communities across the nation, a thousand GRPs will cost less than $40,000. Since one thousand GRPs in a small market would be overkill, a fraction of that buy may be all you need to achieve a presence and establish credibility. This means in small markets, television becomes a very affordable tool.

> "Political ads are giving Americans a choice between bad and awful, distorting and undermining debate, increasing campaign costs and driving voters from the polls."
>
> **CURTIS GANS,**
> Committee for the Study of the American Electorate

In any television market, as GRPs increase, so does the number of times a viewer might see the ad. Obviously, the more GRPs, the greater the number of people reached and the greater the frequency with which they are reached. For example, according to the Television Bureau of Advertising, "a total of 100 GRPs in one week, placed in all time periods, can reach 56.7 percent of all people or homes an average of 1.8 times. Raise the figure to 200 GRPs and reach can go to 73.5 percent for an average frequency of 2.7 times."

Buy Smart

There are a few ways to reach your targeted audience and hit that critical mass if dollars are short. Television costs are based on the size of the audience: The bigger the audience, the higher the cost. However, purchasing less expensive time slots, when the audience is smaller (smaller-rated), may allow your campaign to air your ads more frequently for less money and still meet the reach and frequency you desire.

> "We all learn by experience but some of us have to go to summer school."
>
> **PETER DE VRIES**

If you know you will be advertising on television, but really don't have the funds to keep a critical presence for more than a week, buy your television time starting with election eve and work your way back. As money becomes available, you can buy ads for more and more days preceding the election. Also, by purchasing the time closest to the election first, you don't run the risk that this highly coveted time will be unavailable later. Smaller-rated "avails" (available time) are usually the last to go, so there may even be some opportunity for in-fill close to Election Day, but don't count on it. Buy early. However, the timing of ad placement changes dramatically when elections are run entirely or almost entirely with vote by mail (VBM). Although this is covered more thoroughly in the VBM section of this manual, ad timing for television, like everything else, moves up with VBM.

Rules and Regulations

The following are general rules and regulations as they apply to political advertising. Nevertheless, be sure to get media packets from your local stations and familiarize yourself with individual station requirements.

- You must be a qualified candidate for public office or an authorized campaign organization to promote a person's candidacy for office. Political action committees and noncandidate campaigns (issue campaigns) do not fall under the political advertising guidelines.
- Reasonable access for political "use" will be provided to all legally qualified federal candidates during the forty-five-day period before a primary or primary runoff election and the sixty-day period before a general or special election.
- While candidates may request specific programming, the station reserves the right to make reasonable good-faith judgments about the amount of time and program availability to provide to particular candidates.

> "Man is the only animal that laughs and has a state legislature."
> **SAMUEL BUTLER**

- All ads must comply with the visual sponsorship identification requirements of the Communications Act. In other words, they must all have a disclaimer. The disclaimer ("paid for by . . . ") must last at least four seconds and be at least 4 percent of screen height. Who or what follows the disclaimer depends on who paid for the ad and whether the candidate authorized it or not.
- Any spot for a political candidate or on behalf of an announced candidate must include video or audio use of the candidate's image or voice, or both. In many areas, political ads may not be placed just before, during, or just after news programs.

Web Page and YouTube

All campaigns, no matter how far down the ballot, must have a Web page. It should be user-friendly and have a method for supporters to contribute (like

PayPal), opportunities for volunteering, and plenty of information on your issue or candidate. Be sure to visit other Web sites and borrow ideas to share with your webmaster.

Here are ten additional things you can do for a great Web site:

1. Provide a table of contents with links for each page. This not only lets people know what is on a page without scrolling down, but also helps the user move faster to a particular topic he or she may want to read. Check out any Wikipedia page to see what I mean (en.wikipedia.org).

2. Include on your home page some tabs that will take the visitor to other parts of the Web site. Do not expect people to scroll endlessly on one page.

3. Place all campaign materials on your Web site—television ads, radio spots, direct mail, brochure, voters' pamphlet, newspaper endorsements, everything.

4. Place all your opponent's campaign materials on your Web site, and include commentary of where the person has not been forthcoming, contradicted himself or herself, or unfairly hit you. Be creative. In 2004, an opponent attacked (in direct mail) our candidate for supporting a statewide sales tax. In Oregon, a sales tax is considered the third rail for candidates. The truth was that my candidate did support a sales tax, but then so did our opponent. And we actually had video of our opponent saying so. While we did not want to scold him for supporting a sales tax, we certainly wanted to point out that he could not have it both ways. The Web page was the best place to juxtapose the direct-mail attack piece and the video.

5. Set the record straight. In the above sales tax example, the opponent had actually left eight words out of our candidate's quote about a sales tax, fundamentally changing what he said. Although we set the record straight with direct mail, we also did on our Web page.

6. If debates were videotaped, extrapolate some of the more brilliant moments and place those on your Web page. Similarly, place anything your opponent may have said that could be damaging to him or her. These should be kept brief (three to five minutes).

7. Spend some time with a videographer covering important issues in the campaign, and place these on your Web site. In 2006, one of our candidates talked extemporaneously on twenty-three subjects he felt were important in the county. Besides imparting his depth of knowledge of county business, the clips were incredibly informative for the average person. Each of the topics was under five minutes, and to make them

more interesting and reinforce what he was saying, we shot footage of locations of which he was speaking—intersections, bridges, waterways, buildings, and such—and cut away to these while the candidate spoke. His site received sixty-five thousand hits, an incredible number for our small market.

8. Have the names of individuals, civic groups, and other organizations that have endorsed the candidate or issue continuously scroll up the left side of the home page, and update the list regularly.

9. If you're running against an incumbent and the official government meetings are taped, go through them to pull out some of the more damaging things your opponent has said, and place them on your Web site.

10. Be sure to include a bio and lots of pictures.

While I advise campaigns to resist negative campaigning, there are exceptions. If your opponent is especially thick-headed on the business of the school district, county, city, or whatever office he or she is seeking, create videos of the opponent speaking about topics important to the community, and post them on YouTube for the world to see. This does not require any editing— just rope. If the opponent is an incumbent, send the videographer to meetings to capture the action. When incumbents are discussing hot topics that the local paper is also covering, you can send the YouTube link to the paper (remember, it isn't doctored in any way), which may post it for you on its own Web site.

If it is difficult to hear your subject, be sure to transcribe the portion that you want to place on YouTube, and have subtitles for the viewer to read while watching.

9

The Candidate

Once you declare your intention to run for office, you become part of the public domain. You are fair game for just about any criticism people might feel inclined to level at you. Should someone write a letter to the editor with an outright lie in it, you essentially have little recourse. You can defend yourself, but unless you can prove malice, you cannot sue. Some political analysts think candidates should ignore attacks and lies.

> "A candidate does not always need party infrastructure and a lot of campaign money to win—if he or she can get the public's attention. Regardless of economic conditions, people want government to regard *them* as the boss, not some party chief or big contributor."
>
> **DAVID BEILER**

Far more, however, think that unanswered allegations imply truth. Either way, it's a problem. You can defend yourself, but when you decide to run, you give up your right to whine. It is great preparation for holding elective office.

This chapter is about projecting a positive image before the voters and thereby minimizing the potential nit-picking that the public might do. You will also find suggestions on how to redirect negative questions at your opponent, turning the ammunition back on him or her. For a candidate, this is not a time to be defensive. Take criticism as a gift and an opportunity.

> "A mayor does not create a new vision of a city from the inner workings of his own mind. Rather, he collects it from scattered hopes and buried dreams of people he has listened to in the course of his own political journey."
>
> **RAY FLYNN**, former mayor of Boston, 1984 inaugural speech

Before declaring my intention to run for mayor, I was at a picnic with my family in a nearby city. The local historical society was sponsoring the event on a glorious summer evening on the lawn in front of a historic museum situated in a turn-of-the-century gold-rush town. The speaker was the Oregon secretary of state, who within a few years would be our first woman governor. I remember being wowed by her speech and filled with pride at the prospect of joining ranks in the elected arena with women of her capability.

As I was eating, a friend shared a comment she had just heard about me. A woman had said, "How can Cathy ever hope to run a city if she can't leave her children at home?" I was stunned, enraged, offended, and more. But once I calmed down, I thought about her criticism. If she felt this way at an outdoor picnic, imagine the criticism having my children at a more formal event

> "If you get to be a really big headliner, you have to be prepared for people throwing bottles at you in the night."
>
> **MICK JAGGER**

might draw. Rather than react defensively, I realized that my actions were more potent than my words. If I were elected, I could lead by example and thereby serve as a role model for young women in the community. However, if I moved off my campaign message to beat up potential voters on the double standards that exist in society, I might never hold a position of leadership, serve as a role model, or accomplish the programs that prompted me to run in the first place. I did not let the criticism distract me. I also chose not to drag my children with me through the political process. I would add that children need a family life of their own and are better off not serving as political props.

The Lay of the Land

Each elective office has specific powers and duties associated with it. For example, the Ashland City Charter says that the mayor is the chief executive of the municipal corporation and will closely oversee the workings of city government. Laced throughout the document are other stipulated duties associated with the office, such as appointment of department heads and duties in relation to the city council. The charter sets up a strong-mayor form of government.

Before running for mayor of Ashland, I spent a great deal of time familiarizing myself with council business and city documents, but I never actually read the powers of the office of mayor. Then, within my first six months in office, the city council members set about stripping the powers of the office. Their intention was to do it through a simple resolution, which, unlike an ordinance, does not need a public hearing and cannot be subject to a mayoral veto. As they put it, they didn't want to "take" the powers; they merely wanted to "share" them with me and to "help" me do a better job. I was young, just thirty-five, and felt both attacked and betrayed. No help came from the administrator, who was probably equally concerned about my ability and wanted the power to appoint department heads to fall under the jurisdiction of his office. Furthermore, no support came from fellow councilors, who in fact had initiated the coup and wanted equal say on city board and commission appointments.

Many department heads, who did not want to work for a woman, especially one as young and inexperienced as I was, aligned with the administrator even though they technically worked for the mayor. Word came back that many at city hall were saying disparaging things about me, including name calling—my favorite was "the meddling housewife." I represented an upset and a change of the status quo. The problem wasn't necessarily that I would wreak havoc on the city or that the existing system wasn't working all that well. There is just a general suspicion, especially in government, when moves are made from the known to the unknown. The overall proposed action would result in moving Ashland from a strong-mayor form of government to a weak-mayor form of government, all without going to a vote of the people.

Things heated up quickly. I did not want to go down in history as the mayor who lost the powers of the office. I floundered in meetings as I tried to find footing. I simply could not figure out how to stop the train. Then, another southern Oregon mayor told me he thought his city's charter was modeled after Ashland's, and if they were the same, what the city council was doing was illegal. He said, "Read your charter." Simple, obvious, good advice. I did just that.

At the next meeting, armed with information, I held my ground, recited the powers of my office, and threatened to take the council's actions to a vote through the initiative process if the council members persisted. They backed off. Four tumultuous years followed, during which time three department heads and the city attorney went. By the time I left office, twelve years later, there had been a complete changeover in all department heads and the administrator and I had moved from a relationship of suspicion to one of trust, understanding, and mutual respect.

Before you run for office, know the powers and duties of that office; attend meetings and familiarize yourself with the lay of the land. Wouldn't you prefer to know before you run whether you're suited for the kind of work that goes with the office? You should also know something about the system: how land-use laws work, how property and other taxes are distributed, the revenue stream, the expenditure stream, and which follows which.

In the 1998 California primary, gubernatorial candidate Al Checchi gave a speech to the Democratic Leadership Council; the speech was followed by a question-and-answer period. At some point, he stated that all property taxes went to the state. Knowing this to be false, reporters followed up, asking Checchi to explain. Again he said that the state claims all real estate taxes. Two more follow-up questions, and Checchi did not change his assertion. He did not know something as basic as how property taxes were distributed, and yet he wanted to be governor. Details such as this are not missed by the press or the voters.

> "There is no conversation so sweet as that of former political enemies."
> — **HARRY TRUMAN**

It's also important to know the lay of the land of your community. Recently, an Ashland candidate appeared in a debate at the Rotary Club. Prior to making a point, he asked if there were any businesspeople in the room. He was not joking.

So what do you do if you make a mistake? Own up to it. A while ago, the Southern Pacific Railroad divested some very important real estate in the heart of our city. We had hoped for a portion of it to create a pocket park, but the option to buy was quickly secured by a developer. The neighborhood was upset. After many calls from the city trying to cut in line without success, I gave up. I explained to the neighbors that it was hopeless and that we needed to look elsewhere for a park. But they would not give up. Finally, somehow, they got the parcel for the park. Sometime later, at a council meeting, I was chastised by this group for giving up and calling the situation hopeless. I had to admit it was the best crow I ever ate, and I acknowledged the group for its success where I had failed.

More recently, former Mayor Willie Brown of San Francisco attacked a *San Francisco Chronicle* reporter for exaggerating a problem regarding vandalism and drug abuse on the part of homeless people. When later reports corroborated the reporter's allegations, the mayor apologized and said he wished he could retract his words.

Many people are propelled into the public arena as a spokesperson for an issue that has the electorate enraged. Often, in the heat of the fight, these individuals decide to take on public office to further champion the cause. A word of caution for such individuals: Single-issue candidates generally make bad elected officials. Government has become a complex business that needs office holders who are engaged and attentive to the many facets of the public corporation. Too often, single-issue candidates have trouble with the wide array of duties of a given office and, once elected, sit disengaged until the governing body hits a topic that connects with their issue. It can be unsatisfying and frustrating for the office holder, fellow office holders, and the community.

Finally, another thing to keep in mind is that while you are a candidate, you should never work on other campaigns, either issue or candidate based. Voters are suspicious of candidates who appear to be manipulating an outcome in too many arenas. Your only task is to get yourself elected; once in office, work on as many campaigns as you please.

Packaging the Candidate

A political candidate is selling a lot more than political views. People are looking for an individual who will represent their community, city, school, or county in a professional way. Elected officials fulfill the role of continually answering to the public trust. If the community believes in the candidate, then it will believe that its money is in good hands.

To meet voter expectations, the candidate must always look the part. If you have a spot on your clothing, no matter how

> "Politics is supposed to be the second-oldest profession. I have come to realize that it bears a very close resemblance to the first."
> **RONALD REAGAN**

small, change clothes. You should not have any holes in your clothes; your shoes should be polished, and your clothes buttoned, and the buttons should not be pulling or strained from a poor fit.

Because people associate weight loss with happiness and success, an overweight candidate may choose to diet and lose weight during the campaign. It's actually helpful to be disciplined in all things while campaigning, and a good diet helps keep stress levels down and appearance at an optimum. Canvassing can really help in this area. Whatever improvements can be made in your appearance and dress, make them. Attention to appearance will project a positive image, and you will look and feel the part. You and your campaign cannot afford to cut corners on your personal appearance and dress. A crumpled look may be endearing at home, but not on someone running for public office. Inattention to personal appearance translates into inattention to detail and incompetence.

Dress in a consistent style. This gives the community the impression that you are stable and know who you are. Do not do things out of character. We all remember the picture of Michael Dukakis in the military tank. Cowboy hat and boots worked for Ronald Reagan but not for Bill Clinton. When Bob Dole began dressing in khakis and running shoes in an effort to appeal to younger voters in his 1996 bid for the presidency, he looked silly. Somebody got to Bill Clinton, who began his first term in office jogging in shorts and a T-shirt that hung below the bottom of the shorts. By his second run, he had moved to the golf course, a more presidential activity. While off the course, he was rarely seen in anything other than a black suit. He was *the* president and looked the part of a president. One candidate in eastern Oregon who wore Pendleton shirts changed to three-piece suits midway through the campaign because his numbers were sagging at the polls. After his makeover, the numbers dropped further. Behave and dress in a way that is consistent with who you are.

> "The Constitution gives every American the inalienable right to make a damn fool of himself."
> — JOHN CIARDI

Recently, a mayoral candidate in San Francisco countered accusations that he was uptight by jumping into the shower with a couple of radio disc jockeys. It backfired. Voters want stability in office and are apt to run from candidates who act out of character or unpredictably. If someone accuses you of being uptight, say, "Maybe I am, but might I suggest that is exactly the kind of person we need right now." Then move back to your message, redefining *uptight* in terms of your strengths and with specific examples of what the city needs and how you will meet the challenge.

Image Over Ideology

The uninterested, undecided, and persuadable voters will decide on a candidate according to who they think the candidate is (image) over what the candidate says (ideology). In 1984, polls indicated that more Americans embraced the ideology of Walter Mondale over that of Ronald Reagan, and yet they voted for Reagan in overwhelming numbers. People in

> "If you look good and dress well, you don't need a purpose in life."
> — ROBERT PANTE

this important and elusive group are making their decision on the basis of a feeling they have about each of the two candidates.

Ideology comes into play with your base support. While a candidate may craft theme and message to get at the persuadable voter, he or she must not forget the base and what issues are important to this group. If there is any hesitancy on the part of the base to support the candidate, it must be addressed quickly and within the parameters of your theme and message. So in creating theme and message, leave room for this possibility. For example, again, in the 1996 presidential race, California's environmentalists were upset with Clinton's policies on the issues they cared about most—so much so, that many were threatening a move toward the Green Party candidate, Ralph Nader. To lock these voters in, Clinton set aside 1.7 million acres of southern Utah, the Grand Staircase–Escalante National Monument, under the Antiquities Act. For Clinton, Utah was a lock for the GOP. Nothing that he was going to do or say would move that voter base to him, so the giveaway cost him nothing there while locking in his electoral-rich California base and drawing in much-needed campaign workers from the environmental community.

"I Yam What I Yam"

People running for office often are embarrassed about their résumés and anxious to beef them up in an effort to present a more credible image as a community leader. What may feel like a painful biographical note to the candidate can actually be an asset. For example, if a candidate is embarrassed because she dropped out of high school, she is overlooking the possibility that having earned her GED followed by working her way through college carries more weight because of her early struggles.

Candidates and campaigns committees who are tempted to embellish personal history should think long and hard before doing so. It's a crime to place any false statement into the voters' pamphlet and takes only an accusation by the opposition to activate an investigation.

In 1994, Wes Cooley was elected to the Second Congressional District of Oregon. During the campaign, he had claimed in the voters' pamphlet that he was a member of Phi Beta Kappa. When that statement was found to be false, the secretary of state gave Cooley the benefit of the doubt and let it go. However, in Cooley's reelection bid two years later, he made more claims. He listed "Army Special Forces, Korea," among his qualifications, although he was never in Korea. During the investigation, he claimed that it was a top-secret mission and all very hush-hush.

> "What shall it profit a man, if he should gain the whole world and lose his own soul?"
>
> **MARK 8:36**

It didn't let up. Because of his constant denials, the press took on the investigation and in so doing turned up far more than the Korea fabrication. He failed to get building permits for home improvements, the contractor had not been paid, and he and his wife were secretive about their marriage date so that she could continue to collect benefits as a marine's widow. Cooley backed out of the race and later was indicted.

What is particularly instructive about this story is that more voters could probably relate to someone who was simply drafted and never went anywhere than to someone who claimed to be part of a secret special mission. More people do average things than the opposite. More have attended state-owned universities than private and graduated without honors than have, and most never made the football team. Don't miss the opportunity to build relationships with the average citizen by instead trying to make yourself look "more qualified."

> "Voters want fraud they can believe in."
> — **WILL DURST**

Manners Matter

As important as dress and appearance are, there is more to looking the part of a serious public servant than that. The candidate must adopt the kind of manners a mother would be proud of. Do not chew with your mouth open, pick your nose, clean your ears, or floss in public. Most people remember George W. Bush chewing with his mouth open. Cover your mouth when you yawn. A few years back, a candidate running for office called and asked to meet with me to "touch bases." During our forty-five-minute meeting, he must have yawned five times, and not once did he cover his mouth. I cannot remember what we talked about, but I remember his uvula.

When appearing as a dinner speaker, you should eat only moderately at the event or, better yet, have a light meal beforehand. When people are nervous, digestion slows down. You cannot afford to have a stomach upset from nervous energy and certainly can't afford to burp through the speech. One candidate I worked for who had atrocious eating manners would eat a full meal at the head table before rising to give his speech. During the speech, he would need to burp, but for some reason, this guy always burped by turning his head sideways. I watched as he did this a couple of times and noticed the audience turning their heads with the candidate's. In general, eating and greeting don't mix well for candidates, which is ironic, given that food and drink are often the bait used to pull potential supporters to a political event.

Avoid drinking alcohol while running for public office. Besides the fact that alcohol adds empty calories and affects one's ability to deal with stress, people have tons of issues around alcohol and it's not worth the grief or uncertainty of how drinking, even as little as one glass of wine, will play. Similarly, if you're a smoker, keep it closeted.

Bring along a sweater or light jacket to cover up possible nervous perspiration. Wear deodorant and clean shirts. Previously worn clothes can carry body odor that might be activated with nervous perspiration. Go light on perfume and aftershave. Do not chew gum. Place a few breath mints in your pocket for easy and unnoticed retrieval; don't be a candidate who pulls out the little bottle of breath freshener and squirts it midsentence. In fact, avoid all public grooming: hair combing, lipstick, and the like. Also, you can avoid problems if you think ahead. For instance, when I get nervous, my mouth gets dry, so I always go to the podium with a glass of water.

As I said before, a woman candidate should leave her children at home. Not only does that enable her to be more focused, but it also meets the voters' need to see her in a professional role. It is difficult for many people to accept a woman as a leader if the only image they have of her includes children clinging to her. This is absolutely not true for men. In fact, men are given bonus points for being seen with their children. Society assumes that men are professional, and seeing a man with his children gives the voters the idea that they are getting a glimpse into his private life. He seems warmer (figure 9.1).

Groomers

Given the importance of image, it's a good idea to have a "groomer" for the campaign. As a candidate, I generally recruited a friend whose only campaign job was to let me know how I looked and to make suggestions on what I should wear and how to better project my image. In all three of my campaigns for mayor, I had a groomer who proved to be invaluable. In my second run for mayor, I was to be on television in a debate with my two male opponents, and my groomer advised me to dress conservatively. Both of my opponents showed up dressed very casually and looked less than professional to the television audience. The show repeated seven or eight times throughout the campaign cycle.

> "You'd be surprised how much it costs to look this cheap."
> DOLLY PARTON

The next campaign debate was covered by the media but not broadcast live. My groomer predicted that my principal opponent, having looked casual for

Photo courtesy of SOHS

While Jeff Golden chats with supporters, daughter Sarah Beth gets an eyeful of photographer.

Golden celebrates win

New commisioner's daughter accompanies him

Candidates each bring their own style and special approach to politics, sometimes they carry a lot of political baggage.

But only Jeff Golden carries a baby on his back.

For much of Tuesday evening – ev live TV interview – the Ashland D wore a baby backpack that held hi daughter, Sarah Beth, born a year giving.

FIGURE 9.1 A Candidate with a Baby

When it comes to children, there is a double standard in society, and the standard carries over into campaigning. Whereas women are penalized for campaigning with their children, men are rewarded.

the televised debate, would try to make up for that mistake by dressing conservatively for this one. He advised me to wear my hair differently and dress in a brightly colored dress that I had rarely been seen in. The idea was that I should stand out to the live audience.

I did as I was told. My opponent, as predicted, wore a three-piece black suit and appeared quite intense, severe, even funereal. I had time before the debate to say hello and chat with members of the audience and to enjoy myself. My appearance was friendly, and I was clearly having a good time. My opponent did not smile and seemed out of place, strapped in his television armor. The difference between us was dramatic, and the debate proved to be a turning point in the campaign.

When I work for other candidates, I usually assign a groomer as well. I look for a man or woman with an eye for fashion and detail. If my candidate needs a haircut, I encourage him or her to get the best one available. Have the campaign pick up the cost of a studio photo shoot. The groomer and I will often discuss the kind of look we want out of the shoot and share those ideas with the candidate and the photographer. For example, if I have a candidate who smiles very little and is somewhat hesitant, I look for a photo where he or she leans into the lens. Whatever may be a weakness of your candidate in personality or appearance, your photo shoot is an opportunity to make it look otherwise. Many believe that a photo starting low, looking up at the candidate, projects power and one from above angled down, the opposite. Personally, I think nostril shots are unflattering and don't use them. I like the photographer to work with the camera coming straight on. Chapter 3 presents examples of candidate photos that work well.

> "Non-verbal cues are as [important as] or more important than verbal cues."
> **MALCOLM GLADWELL**

A groomer must be willing to attend debates and observe the candidate's behavior. I usually like to talk with the groomer after an event to discuss how delivery can be improved; we then talk to the candidate and discuss adjustments. All such suggestions, however, should be cushioned with lots of praise. Candidates' egos can be fragile, and you don't want them to be self-conscious at the next event.

Pick and choose your events carefully. Do not say yes to every coffee or speaking-engagement offer that comes your way. As campaign manager, think ahead about where you intend to spend time and energy, and go where the votes (and the money) are. Take into consideration your candidate's personality. For example, minimize the amount of time in public for the candidate who is awkward in a crowd. Also, remember that candidates who go to events of strong supporters often get in trouble. This is especially true late in the campaign cycle, when candidates are tired and let their guard down. Part of your job is to keep your candidate from saying something stupid, and sometimes the easiest way to do that is to keep him or her away from gatherings where it is more apt to happen.

> "Enlightenment will be extinguished . . . unless applied . . . to the machinery of political and legislative action."
> **MARGARET SANGER**

Stay on Your Message

Don't let your opponent pull you off message. Ever.

The candidate's image is important, because voters need to be able to identify with him or her. However, the candidate and the campaign team must

"No man ever listened himself out of a job."

_____ CALVIN COOLIDGE

know who will support the candidate and why. The reason that people vote a specific way will become the basis for your campaign message. Develop that message to build relationships between the candidate and the voters. A benchmark poll can really help here.

List all of the candidate's positives and why the team feels that voters will support this individual. The list might include programs the candidate has been involved with, stands on controversial issues, votes in previous offices, vision, character, and experience. It might be nothing more than a clear list of issues and beliefs that the candidate embraces.

You must also develop a list of issues and concerns that might hurt the candidate's support. (There should be a fair amount of overlap between the lists of positives and negatives.) It is this list that you will use in preparing the candidate for negative questions and in formulating strategies to defuse negative perceptions. For example, if the candidate has an image of being slick, the team sends him to neighborhood meetings, where he can be seen as one of the crowd. This requires a candidate who is open to observation and criticism, and a close campaign team to develop the campaign message.

Once you have developed your campaign message and strategy, stick to it. When your opponent hits you, respond and move the discussion right back to your message. When appropriate, go after your opponent's campaign inconsistencies and weaknesses.

The campaign team will work only as hard as the candidate or campaign leader. So work hard. Keep in mind that the public, besides looking for a

"My center is collapsing, my right flank retreats . . . situation excellent! I shall attack!"

FRENCH FIELD MARSHAL FOCH
_____ at the Battle of the Marne

community representative and leader, is observing everything during the campaign: your stand on issues, your presence and composure, your appearance, how you handle stress, and your ability to answer their questions. In particular the public is looking for how well you react under pressure and how hard you work to get into office. That will tell them something about whether they can expect you to keep your head and work hard once you are in office.

Staying on message can be particularly hard for candidates under attack. It's important to respond to attacks, but how you do translates into whether you're on your campaign theme and message or have moved over to that of your opponent. In a recent local campaign for district attorney, the incumbent's opponent was accusing him of running an inefficient office. The incumbent had an increasing caseload with a stagnant tax base. The challenger had left the DA's office a few years before to go into private practice and now wanted back in as boss.

The incumbent, being the first to speak at the debate, stood and said, "I would take issue with anyone who says I'm not running my office efficiently." Boom, he was on his opponent's message. The following day, the debate was covered in the local paper. The headline: "DA denies allegations of mismanagement."

How could this have been handled differently? First, the DA could have laid out to the audience the dramatic increase in caseload, decrease in staff, and marginalized tax base that, with inflation, translated to less, not more, real dollars. He could have suggested that his opponent left his job at the DA's office because of a workload that pales in comparison to the current one. He could have compared tax dollars expended per case today and in the past. He could have talked about the increasing complexity of some crimes being committed and how these cases required additional court time, legal process, and resources. In short, he could have promoted his achievements while preempting any criticism that his opponent might be tempted to wage, and he could have done it all without sounding defensive. He would be safe under the umbrella of disclosure.

While looking professional, minding your manners, working hard, and being on message, you must find some way to minimize stress. One way is to listen to your campaign manager. Another is to do nothing that, once done, will lead you to tell a lie.

One dramatic example of a lie gone bad occurred a few years back, when a county commissioner was undergoing a recall in another part of the state. The recall looked dead, even though its proponents were able to gather the signatures and actually get it to a vote. It was a vote-by-mail election, and as is often the case in vote by mail, the computer spit out a few ballots whose signatures did not quite line up. One of these was the wife of the county commissioner targeted in the recall. The local elections office, in conjunction with the secretary of state's office, asked the county commissioner if the ballot had, in fact, been signed by his wife or someone else. The commissioner said his wife did indeed sign it. They checked again, and it still came out as a no-match. They asked the commissioner and his wife again. Both said she signed it. The secretary of state's office continued to press. Finally, the commissioner confessed to signing his wife's ballot because she was in the hospital and had directed him to do so. While the commissioner had easily beaten the recall, he now had to resign and was charged with and convicted of a Class C felony. Obviously, he shouldn't have signed the ballot to begin with, but had he said from the get-go, "My wife asked me to take care of it for her while she was in the hospital; isn't that OK?" the secretary of state told me he would very likely have said, "No, don't do it again" and dropped the matter.

If a candidate is caught in a lie while on the campaign trail, it is sudden death. As one of the ten commandments of campaigning and one of the cardinal sins, being caught in a provable lie is about the worst thing that can happen to a candidate.

In the 2002 general election in Oregon, a Democratic candidate for the house was to attend and speak at a Coalition for School Funding Now meeting. The campaign between the Democratic challenger and the Republican incumbent had been very friendly, and in fact it had been the incumbent who had suggested that his opponent jump in the race and run against him. As a candidate, the Democrat was a dream: She was involved in schools, church, and other community groups. She was well organized, articulate, and hardworking. She had a supportive extended family and a great campaign team. She was such a good candidate that in a poll conducted in the last days of the campaign, she was ahead of the incumbent by twenty points.

Consequently, the campaign was confident of the election. So when the coalition meeting was in conflict with another gathering, the candidate and her campaign manager split the duties, with the manager attending one while the candidate attended the coalition meeting. Unfortunately, the candidate, who had a full work and volunteer schedule in addition to her campaign, got away a little late. She then misread the directions, got lost on the way to the meeting, and arrived later than comfortable for all concerned. As a result, the candidate was flustered and off center, and the coalition group was irritated.

After the meeting, the state Republican Party sent a direct-mail piece to the district, saying that the Democrat was in favor of a sales tax to resolve Oregon's budget shortfall. Since the allegation was attributed to the Coalition for School Funding Now meeting, the campaign committee asked the candidate if she had said anything that would lead the other party to believe that she supported a statewide sales tax. The candidate, who had been repeatedly schooled by her committee never to talk about a sales tax, said no. Just to be sure, the campaign manager called a couple of people who she knew had attended the coalition meeting and asked them if the candidate had said she supported a sales tax during any part of the meeting. They said no.

The candidate and her campaign committee were outraged at the attack and so, along with the Democratic campaign office, registered a complaint with the secretary of state's office. The investigation uncovered an audiotape made by a staff member of the Republican Majority Office who had attended the coalition meeting. On the tape, the candidate could clearly be heard saying that she would support a sales tax if all other avenues were exhausted and if it included a reduction in the state income tax. The comment was made after an audience member and school advocate repeatedly pressed the candidate to make a stand on a sales tax. The twenty-point lead disappeared after the tape hit the airwaves, and the Democrat lost the election by 92 votes, out of 11,418 votes cast.

Set aside the whole sales tax issue: If the voters do not understand a lie, they will not forgive it. Being caught in a provable lie is a cardinal sin; it's death to a campaign. While the general response would be to focus in on the mistake made by the candidate, many mistakes leading up to the original mistake should not be overlooked, either.

First, it is not enough for a campaign committee to tell a candidate never to discuss a topic. While that can be the directive, there should also be a what-if scenario that the committee works out with the candidate. In the above example, a red flag for the committee would be that the candidate personally was not against a sales tax. If the candidate holds an opinion that could cost support if openly expressed, the issue must be addressed in the war room. The team and the candidate should have covered all appropriate responses should this occasion ever arise, such as: "Once elected, I will look at every revenue stream just as I will look at every expenditure. Without the opportunity to first examine where we are spending money, it would be premature for me to talk about revenue streams to remedy the budget deficit." Further, I have sat in many war rooms where a difficult issue was brought up for discussion and had the candidate say, "We don't need to go over that; I have an answer." Whenever a candidate says this, ask to hear the answer.

Second, there should always be a committee member present at public forums. Even if it cannot be the campaign manager, someone must go with the candidate or meet the candidate at an event. What typically happens in the final days of a campaign is that good candidates who are really very trustworthy are left to cover ground on their own. But things happen, and you need someone from the committee to help communicate with the war room.

Third, candidates must allow enough time to get to an event. It is the responsibility of the campaign to get clear directions and a phone number to call should any mishaps occur en route. Ask a volunteer to drive the route if it is new to the candidate and report directions and distances. Print out a map and directions from a program such as MapQuest for the candidate. Whatever it takes, getting to an event should not be stressful for the candidate. I had one candidate who always ran late and would almost always get lost on his way to anything, no matter how many maps we gave him. Whenever he was in route, there had to be someone near the phone to talk him into his destination because he would completely freak out when he got lost. Finally, I assigned a staffer to pick up the candidate from work and drive him to his events. After the election, when I no longer had someone to "get him to the church on time," I found that reviewing the map with him, prior to departure, really helped. Eventually, we got him a global positioning system for his car. It saved everyone time and aggravation.

Fourth, once the candidate is late, he or she should still take some time to gather composure and acknowledge to the group that she has made them wait. In other words, "center the audience." Start with a personal and warm story. Something that happened on the campaign trail that the group would love to hear. If I know the candidate is running late, I will call the host with a heads-up and a reason that can be shared. Either way, someone must get the room centered. If you don't, you run the risk of having hecklers—especially among your saints. In politics, teams love to eat their own.

Fifth, a candidate must be aware of what he or she says and not hang the committee out to dry. In this example, if the candidate had remembered what she said, she could have brought this back to the committee, and damage control would have been implemented. Unfortunately, candidates are so overloaded that their memories cannot be trusted. (See the second item above.)

Sixth, supportive groups need to cut a candidate some slack. People running for office are spending insane amounts of time to secure positions that typically result in a pay reduction while they serve—not to mention huge amounts of time away from family. For a member of a group supportive of a candidate to choose to press and press and press an inflammatory issue is both stupid and counterproductive.

Finally, one must question why a candidate who, as a school official, was loved throughout the education community accepted an invitation to speak at a Coalition for School Funding Now meeting in the first place. Going to the saints pulls time and energy from other activities—and might even cost you the election. Even so, candidates love to speak to groups who are supportive. So much of campaign work is difficult and stressful, and attending a meeting of "friends" feels good. The flip side is that when candidates go to a supportive group in the final days, they are often very tired, they let down their guard, and they say something they shouldn't. It happens all the time.

A follow-up on this last point: I have found that support groups can be some of the hardest on a candidate. They still want "their" time with the candidate and frequently make requests for the candidate to attend non-fundraising events put on by their saints. For example, toward the end of the 2002 general election cycle, our district office received a call from the campaign of the Democratic gubernatorial candidate. The campaign wanted to know if the state representative I worked with could attend a Jackson County Democratic Central Committee meeting in place of the gubernatorial candidate.

> "The question, 'who ought to be boss?' is like asking 'who ought to be the tenor in the quartet?' Obviously, the man who can sing tenor."
> **HENRY FORD**

Similarly, when I was dining at a senior center during the 2008 general election cycle, one of the residents, a former reporter, came up to me and complained that Obama was not intending to visit southern Oregon. Further, she did not like that lawn signs, buttons, and bumper stickers were hard to come by and had to be purchased from the campaign. She concluded by saying that even though she was a strong supporter, she intended to write an op-ed piece scolding the campaign for these failings. I asked her if, as a supporter, she thought it was a good use of his time to visit a state he would win anyway and would she still feel that way if he did so at the expense of another state he had to win.

Folks, if you're a member of the "team," give candidates a break; make as few demands on their time as possible. Your job is to give money, write letters, volunteer, deliver the votes, and help the candidate woo the savables by spending time where it is most beneficial to a win.

Outsider Campaign Versus Incumbent Campaign

If you are in government already, you are an insider; if not, you're an outsider. Insiders and outsiders typically run very different campaigns, because the voters expect the insider to defend what government is doing and the outsider to challenge it with a fresh outlook. In reality, however, skillful politicians who have been in office for years have, when the need arises, waged outsider cam-

> "People that are really very weird can get into sensitive positions and have a tremendous impact on history."
> **DAN QUAYLE**

paigns against first-time candidates. Insider or outsider status is as much a state of mind as a fact. Whatever the actual status of the candidate, insider and outsider campaigns require distinctly different strategies.

Whether you are the incumbent or the challenger, you should list all personality characteristics of both the office holder and the challenger, both strengths and weaknesses. Your objective is to contrast your strengths with your opponent's weaknesses.

Outsiders

To run an outsider's campaign, you must first legitimize yourself through establishment endorsement (no matter how tangential the endorsement might be). The public record the incumbent has amassed while in office actually defines that person—but in terms of image, not specifics. If you're an outsider, it's important for your team to define the test the voters will apply. Obviously, you want to stay away from experience, since an incumbent would easily pass that test. Your best hope is to define the test the voters will apply as that of "time for a change." Ultimately, as an outsider, you will find that it is more important to present sound reasons for why an incumbent should be cast out of office than to explain why you should be elected.

Attacks on the system are effective if they plant seeds of doubt about how things are being done or where attention and public money are being focused. You cannot just throw complaints against a wall to see what sticks. You have to know what you're talking about. Research how things have worked or not worked, and explain them to the voters. Remember, you must sound like a potential office holder rather than a malcontent. That requires offering solutions, not just criticizing. This is where your homework really pays off.

Before my first run for mayor, I went to the local college library, checked out ten years of city council minutes, and read them all. I also checked out every current report on every system in which the city had hired a consultant. I read the city's comprehensive plan and the downtown plan. This put me at a decided advantage: Because it was so fresh in my mind, I could recall the information more quickly than my opponent, who had been a sitting city councilor for ten years. Incumbents who live through the events compiled in such reports while in office will find it difficult to recall the details, and they make matters worse by believing they can. Typically, an incumbent will underprepare for an election.

Incumbents

If you are an incumbent, you must show that the average citizen still supports you and show how, working cooperatively with other elected officials, you have made a positive contribution. In other words, your campaign should make the test applied by the voters that of experience and accomplishment. This is a strong theme when voters have a grasp of the complexities of government. Again, your public record defines who you are. But avoid looking at each vote individually. This definition is more about image than specifics. Although you may not actually use the word, stick close to a theme of "proven" leadership. Make your record the focal point of the campaign by using examples that the average person will understand and that apply to the day-to-day lives of those being served. Avoid speaking in governmentalese— that is, using acronyms and jargon that only those in government would know.

Your Opponent

You may breathe a sigh of relief when you discover that you are unopposed in your election or groan when you find that at the last minute, someone has filed to run against you. However, an opponent in any campaign is a blessing. Without an opponent, your race will be ignored by the press, and the programs and issues you want to get before the voters will be that much more difficult and expensive to get there. If you are involved in a hotly contested race, the press will more likely provide front-page coverage, which greatly reduces the amount of advertising you will have to buy. Just compare the Republican presidential primary of 2008 with the Democratic presidential primary. Barack Obama

> "What is noble can be said in any language, and what is mean should be said in none."
>
> MAIMONIDES

and Hillary Clinton were lead stories every day, whereas John McCain could not get the attention of the press. This inattention contributed to McCain's loss just as Obama's primary momentum contributed to his win.

If you have a primary race in which you are unopposed, you may never build the momentum and party support that are necessary to win the general election. Do not lament if someone declares against you. Thank your lucky stars, and organize a great campaign. Bring forward programs you want to begin or to maintain, and use the election as a mandate to muscle these into place. Use the campaign as a reminder of who you are and what you stand for and as a rallying point to get people behind your efforts.

Some voters need something to vote for, while others need something to vote against. Voters who are more motivated by one candidate's negatives than the opposition's positives lie at the heart of negative campaigning. Average voters watch the debate unfold in the paper and on the news and listen to see who makes sense and who doesn't. Others get outraged by a candidate's track record or by inane arguments from the opposition and decide to vote for your cause although they normally would not. Without the missteps and misstatements of your opposition, you might never get the necessary support to push your campaign over the top.

Debates

Don't use debates to attack your opponent; rather, use them to share what you know and would do once elected. Keep on the sunny side.

Debates can be turning points for a campaign or amount to nothing. I've seen amazing mistakes made during debates that had little or no effect on the campaign and seen other items that should have gone unnoticed blow up. There are a number of ways you and your campaign committee can minimize the risk factor and make a debate work in your favor. Small precautions include familiarizing yourself with the room before the event and making sure that some friendly faces are in the audience. However, preparation is your best tool for positioning yourself. When you are well prepared, political debates are surprisingly easy

> "Sometimes when you look in his eyes you get the feeling that someone else is driving."
> — **DAVID LETTERMAN**

and great fun. As a political candidate, you should welcome the showiness of debates, the pressure, and the opportunity to get your opinions in front of voters. When you have successfully positioned yourself as a candidate, people recognize who you are and what you do. You make sense to them.

The central rule of debating is that the voters should know more after the debate than they did before. Come armed with lots of information. In my third run for mayor, I had the advantage of being well versed in city matters—and even though I was the incumbent, I studied like crazy to prepare for all six of my debates. In the first debate, I was shocked at how uninformed my opponent was in city matters. He had seemingly done little or nothing to prepare for the event. I thought, boy, this is going to be easy. But with each debate that followed, my opponent took, verbatim, statistics and anecdotal examples that I had used in previous debates and presented them to each new audience as though they were his thoughts and his research. It really threw me. I couldn't say, "Hey, you sound just like me," or "That's exactly what I said last week," without sounding like I was petty, whining, accusatory, or on the attack. Every debate was before a new audience who had never heard either of us, so they assumed he was delivering his spiel, not mine. In hindsight, I should have had a campaign supporter who would, as the pattern unfolded at each event, call him on it.

To get ready for a political debate, choose eight to ten subjects that are important to you or the community. You should include among them issues that are part of your campaign platform. For each of the subjects you have chosen, list on one side of a 5-by-8-inch index card the information and points that you feel are relevant. Use only one card per subject and only one side of the card.

For example, development in the forest interface is of great concern in my community. As an incumbent, I would list on a card all that government (with my help) has done to limit development in these fire-prone areas as well as fire mitigation implemented on existing structures. On the right side, I would list remaining concerns of fire danger and what government still needs to do to make the forest and the community safer. If I were running an outsider's campaign, for the same subject I would list all that is being done, how this is not enough, what has gone wrong (being specific), and exactly what I would do to correct the course. This information is just listed on the card, not written out. The idea is to be very familiar with the information before the debate and to use the cards to focus what you want to talk about, not exactly what you will say.

> "I will never apologize for the United States of America—
> I don't care what the facts are."
> **GEORGE H. W. BUSH**

Once you have the subject cards filled out, choose a separate color for each card, and color a single stripe along the top of each card in a particular color. For example, your card for budget issues might be red; for forest interface, brown; for park issues, green; for recycling, yellow; for air quality, blue; for transportation, black; and so on. Once the cards are color-coded, the appropriate card can be found at a glance. By color-coding in advance, you can avoid disorienting yourself looking through all the cards to find the one you want. Once you have the card you need for a particular subject on top of the stack, you can glance at it while looking around the audience. When looking at the cards, you should appear to be collecting your thoughts rather than reading.

Do not kid yourself that you can guess all the subjects or questions that will be asked in a debate. You will undoubtedly prepare for areas that are never addressed and have nothing for areas that are covered. Even so, with the preparation done ahead of time, you will be much more relaxed and "on" during the debate. Be sure to bring extra blank cards to jot down thoughts during the debate. This will help you remember on rebuttal what you want to say.

Familiarize yourself with any ballot measures coming before the voters or any initiative petitions being circulated. Either the press or your opponent may ask you about your position on these issues, so have a clear idea of where you stand and why.

The importance of your image and how you present yourself cannot be overstated. Smiling and speaking clearly and slowly enough so those in the audience can hear and understand is very important. A certain amount of tension surrounds a campaign in general and a debate in particular, and people will notice how you deal with that tension. Be aware that your image gets projected in a hundred ways.

What follows are some of the more famous examples of debate situations in which one candidate appeared to greater advantage than his opponent— either by chance or design.

Before a 1960 Kennedy-Nixon televised debate, John F. Kennedy's team checked out the studio location for the debate a few days earlier and found it set up with a drab, gray background. To contrast with the background, Kennedy was told to wear a dark blue suit and spend some time under a sun lamp. The hope was that he would project an image of youth and vigor. Kennedy was also told to look directly at Richard Nixon when Nixon spoke and to look directly at the cameras (his audience) when he himself spoke. This would show that Kennedy had respect for what people had to say, even his opponent, and that he could communicate with the nation. Kennedy's advisers also found out that Nixon had hurt his leg while campaigning, so they requested that the two candidates stand. During the debate, Nixon looked tired. He was poorly made up, and he was sick. He shifted about because of his leg pain, and he perspired under the hot lights of the studio.

> "There was a gap between what went on in his mind and what came out of his mouth."
> — JAMES M. CAIN

In the second debate between Gerald Ford and Jimmy Carter, Ford was asked about the Soviet sphere of influence in Eastern Europe. He responded saying there was no Soviet domination in Eastern Europe.

In the Reagan-Carter debate in 1980, President Carter said he asked Amy, his daughter, what she thought was the most pressing issue facing the world, and her response was nuclear weapons. The opposition assumed correctly that Americans would be uncomfortable with teenager Amy Carter as a presidential political adviser and made it a campaign issue. In the same debate, Ronald Reagan scored big points by crossing the stage to shake hands with the president.

In the Reagan-Mondale debate, President Reagan said, "The nation's poverty rate has begun to decline, but it is still going up." Comments like this brought the factor of his age to the race, but only briefly.

In the Bush-Dukakis debate, Michael Dukakis was asked whether he would change his mind about capital punishment if someone raped and killed his wife, Kitty. Dukakis's response lacked passion and emotion. Some said he framed his answer no differently than if he were asked whether he preferred a dill pickle to relish.

A defining moment in the Gore-Bush race had to be the first debate in which Al Gore harrumphed and rolled his eyes at responses given by George W. Bush. Just as looking respectfully at Nixon while he spoke gave Kennedy an advantage, the inverse caused Gore to falter and ultimately struggle for the remainder of the campaign.

In one of the Obama-McCain debates, while Obama spoke, McCain wandered around the stage and eventually wandered between the camera and the moderator. This brought his age and mental acuity further into question.

Fielding Negative Questions

Think of everything as a gift or opportunity.

You will very likely get nasty questions and innuendos during a debate. Look at such questions as an opportunity to show how well you respond under fire. People know that being subjected to negativity is part of serving in public office, and they will want to see how you handle it. Never be defensive. If possible, be humble and self-effacing; if you can come up with a little joke that turns the attack to your advantage, so much the better. Find anything that uses the ammunition of the opposition and redirects it at them. If you redirect attacks, it is important to do so with class, without sounding defensive, and with poise. This is your opportunity to sound smart. Being quick on your feet is not a function of IQ but of preparedness, confidence, and poise.

Grace Under Pressure

Your campaign committee members should help you list everything that is a weakness: every vote, every misstatement, every missed meeting—all of it. They should also list everything on which your candidate may appear vulnerable: past voting records, who is paying for the campaign, special-interest support, inconsistencies in statements and personal deeds, such as missed child-support payments. Once this level of homework is done, you will be much more comfortable.

In general, there are four options for responding to an attack:

1. I did not do it.
2. I did it, but it's not how you think.

3. I did it, I'm sorry, I won't do it again.
4. Attack the source.

If you are attacked and do not respond, you are presumed guilty, especially if the attack is considered fair. When you do respond, you should do so on the same level as the attack. For example, if you were attacked in direct mail, respond with direct mail.

Fatal Flaws

One way to prepare yourself for attacks is to sit with your campaign team and brainstorm on every possible negative question that might come your way. Practice responding to questions concerning your weaknesses. Listing the "fatal flaws" of a candidate or measure allows your support group to deliberate on the best possible responses. These responses may be placed according to topic on your 5-by-8-inch cards for handy reference during the debate. Even if the attack is not exactly what your team predicted, this level of preparation lends comfort, poise, and organization to the candidate, resulting in better responses in high-pressure situations.

Here are examples of how to capitalize on negative questions. In my second bid for mayor, I responded to criticism of city budget increases by explaining that I was the only member of the budget committee who voted no on the last budget. Later in the campaign, my opponent pointed out (during a debate) that when this same budget came before the city council for final approval, the council vote was split. He went on to point out that I failed to cast the tie-breaking no vote and instead voted yes. Why, he asked, if I was so opposed to the budget during the budget process, was I unwilling to vote no at the council level?

> "I really didn't say everything I said."
> — YOGI BERRA

Until that moment, I had forgotten that the budget had come before the council when two members (who would have voted yes) were away and two (for odd reasons) had voted no. That had left only two voting yes. As mayor, I had been obligated to cast the deciding vote. As I went to the podium to respond, I pulled out my color-coded budget card.

From the card, I was able to outline the exact issues on which I had concern as a budget committee member. After relating those concerns to the audience, I explained that I had lost my appeal to the budget committee to delve into those issues further and explained that the committee ultimately had adopted the budget. Having been outvoted at the committee level, I suggested to the audience that it would have been disingenuous to veto, in effect, the budget by casting a no vote in a tiebreaker. I had therefore voted to put in place the will of the majority of the committee and council, even if I personally disagreed with some budget provisions.

Because I was prepared, my opponent gave me what I could not get on my own: the opportunity to show that I had good reasons to vote against the budget during the budget process and that once outvoted, I was able to set aside my differences with the budget committee. As an incumbent, I was able to demonstrate that I was still willing to challenge the process and yet be a team player.

At another debate, one opponent brought up a program that I had initiated to use volunteers to clear fuel (dead and dying brush) from the forest interface. He cited how the program had been a miserable failure and had placed the city at risk of potential litigation because of possible worker (volunteer) injury. I picked up my forest card and took the microphone. I said that while the outcome of the program had been different from what was first envisioned, it raised community awareness of the need to mitigate fire danger. Moreover, the voters needed to make a decision for the future: Did they want leadership that never tried anything out of fear of failure or leadership that solved problems creatively at the risk of an occasional partial success?

> "Earlier today the senator called a spade a spade. He later issued a retraction."
> JOE MIRACHI

By using this attack as a gift, I was able to direct attention to the limited success of the program and then shift back to my message, which was strong, creative leadership: leadership willing to take risks.

Another approach to leading or negative questions is the "Yeah, so?" response. For example, the opposition might say, "Since you became mayor, the city has acquired more and more programs that should be run by the private sector." Your "Yeah, so?" response might be, "I'm sorry. How is this a problem? The proof is in the pudding. We are extraordinarily successful at providing a broad range of outstanding programs, programs that our community may never have enjoyed if left to the private sector. And we do so while saving the taxpayers money." While you may not use these exact words, this is the tone: "Yeah, so? What's your point?"

In Debates, Attacks Can Backfire

Hitting your opponent with a negative during a debate is somewhat unpredictable. Do it carefully. Here is an example of how it can backfire: I worked for a candidate whose opponent, an incumbent, was receiving lots of PAC money. My candidate wanted to hit the incumbent for taking special-interest money. Because the campaign team had heard rumors that the incumbent had a story to die for whenever he was hit on PAC money, the campaign team felt that an attack was dangerous.

At the next debate, however, our candidate went after the credibility of the incumbent, because of the PAC money coming in. Our candidate implied that the incumbent was bought and owned because so much of his money came from PACs and so little from citizens. True to the rumors, the opponent stood up and said that when he was first elected, a supporter who had given a three-thousand-dollar campaign contribution visited his office at the capitol. According to the story, the contributor was looking for a particular vote on a bill and felt that the size of the campaign contribution warranted this vote. Our opponent went on to say that after hearing the demand, he went to the bank, took out a personal loan, and returned the money to the contributor. He concluded by saying that no one owned his vote.

In about thirty seconds, our opponent not only killed the whole PAC money attack, but also showed that he was poor like everyone else in the room—he had to take out a personal loan to pay off the contributor—and that he had integrity. In hindsight, this attack would have taken on new meaning if our campaign had been able to point out exact figures on campaign contributions and accompanying votes that appeared to follow PAC money.

In debates, you just never know how your opponent will turn an attack around. So, unless you are armed with concrete information, avoid rehearsed attacks. If, however, your opponent leaves himself or herself open, seize the opportunity. For example, a few years back, a Democrat and a Republican were facing off for a U.S. Senate seat. The Democrat had been criticizing the Republican for using federal superfund money for the cleanup of industrial waste in his family-owned business. During a debate, the Republican, who was worth millions, was challenged by the Democrat to pay back the money to the taxpayers. The Republican stood and said, "I'll pay it back just as soon as you pay back the honoraria you said you would never take when you ran for Congress." The Democrat in a very flustered voice said, "Why . . . why, you've insulted my integrity!"

This is an opportunity that doesn't come along very often. The Democrat should have seen this coming and been ready. He missed an opportunity to reach into his pocket to pull out a checkbook and say, "Deal! I'll pay back all the money I received for giving speeches. You get out your checkbook and do the same for the federal cleanups, which amounts to $XYZ. And while you're at it, make it out to the federal deficit, because the only way we're going to get our arms around it is if those who have, stop taking from those who don't." While the Democrat had received thousands in honoraria, the Republican had received millions—an easy exchange.

Developing Your Public Speaking Skills

Before my very first debate as a candidate, I was genuinely excited about what was ahead of me. I was charged up and armed with enough information to handle any question thrown at me. Afterward, I thought I'd done a great job. So when someone from the audience handed me a slip of paper, I was certain it would be the name and address of a potential campaign volunteer. The note said: "You said 'um' 48 times during your speech and the question and answer period that followed. Why don't you join us at Toastmasters?"

Unless you're a top-notch public speaker—either a natural or an actor, you need to get some skills and you need to get them quickly. Even after three campaigns and twelve years in public office, I still got nervous before a speech; it didn't matter how perfunctory it was or how young the audience. But remember, it isn't what you say that's important but rather how you say it. Given how quickly people form opinions of candidates, the candidate who gets some early help in giving speeches will have a longer shelf life than the candidate who receives none. Training in public speaking does not need to take a whole lot of time and can ultimately make the journey much more enjoyable.

> "This amendment does more damage than it does harm."
> **LOUISIANA STATE LEGISLATOR** during a floor debate

The following describe three simple things the candidate and team can do to improve speech-giving, debates, and public appearances.

1. The On-Camera Interview. Have a friend or campaign worker with a video camera, ideally one that approximates those used by newspeople, ask the candidate questions that might come up in the campaign. The team can go over questions ahead of time, but the candidate should not know them. In any case, do not spend a lot of time worrying about the questions; the objective of this exercise is not to see how well your candidate answers but rather how well the person handles himself or herself. In addition to general questions, ask some that are personal and a little borderline, like, "How do your children feel about you running for office?" and "Do you think being Hispanic will help or hurt your chances?" The interview can run, say, fifteen to twenty minutes.

After the interview, the candidate and someone with experience in public speaking should go over the video. Ask the debate coach at the high school, a newsperson, a friend who will be honest, or someone else involved in public speaking. Look at everything:

- What's behind the candidate? Remember, for interviews, the candidate can almost always choose the backdrop and setting. If reporters want to interview a candidate, they generally come to the person. Always look around and see what will be behind the candidate. If the candidate is to be seated, choose the chair carefully; avoid overstuffed chairs, which can affect delivery and make a candidate look slouchy. You want a setting that will further the image you want to project. Choose the wicker furniture on the front porch, the horse corral, a park, a garden, or the living room. If the interview will be outside, remember that the sun must be in the candidate's face, so orient him or her accordingly.

> "The Republican Party stands for: 'Anti-bigotry, anti-Semitism, anti-racism.'"
> — GEORGE H. W. BUSH

- Look at the candidate's clothes, mannerisms, eyes, hair—everything. Does the candidate have verbal tics, scratch his chest, toe the ground, stroke his chin, fluff his hair, or jut the chin? Does she hold her hand to her cheek when seated? Does she do a nervous yawn? Tap her foot? Click a pen?
- Finally, does the candidate answer the questions in a direct manner?

In this exercise, it does not matter if the interviewer is in the picture, so the person behind the camera can be the one asking the questions. When we do this for candidates, the camera is set on a tripod with the interviewer asking questions while running the camera.

2. Mock Debates. Mock debates are really fun and very helpful for a candidate. To do a successful one, you must have a moderator, an opponent, and an audience. High school government teachers, newspaper reporters (though not those who will be covering the campaign), and people who are politically active and involved make the best audience. Your objective is to have seven or eight people who are well versed in public speaking and politics, are smart, and can communicate suggestions without offending

> "Well, I would—if they realized that we—again if—if we led them back to that stalemate only because that our retaliatory power, our seconds, or strike at them after our first strike, would be so destructive that they couldn't afford it, that would hold them off."
> **RONALD REAGAN**, when asked if nuclear war could be limited to tactical weapons

the candidate. Rearrange the furniture in the living room so that it looks more like a classroom. Use bar stools for the real and the pretend opponent to perch on. The moderator should be armed with questions that most certainly will come up in a campaign. This is the time to focus on your questions. Let all involved know that everyone will be in character throughout the mock debate. The moderator should be dressed up, and whoever is playing the opposition candidate should study how that candidate dresses, moves, answers questions, and attacks in real life. This does not take long: Read the literature, and watch him or her on a commercial, interview, or public appearance, and you're there.

Have everything in place when the real candidate and the pretend opponent arrive. Establish guidelines and time the answers, just as they would be in a real debate.

After the debate, questions are taken from the audience and answered by both the real candidate and the pretend opponent. If the campaign is concerned about how the candidate will respond to a question, this would be the time to have someone in the audience persist in asking it.

This is followed by a frank discussion of the candidate's performance, which questions posed problems, and what made the candidate defensive. Cover body language, the brevity and clarity of answers, hairstyle, and clothes: everything.

Most public speakers are best when they have a command of the material and can talk off the top of their head. However, if you are working with a candidate whom you have told time and again not to read speeches because he or she is horrible at it, be sure to send the debate questions ahead of time. In general, candidates read because they feel uncertain of their ability. If you provide the questions ahead of time and

> "He can compress the most words into the smallest idea of any man I ever met."
> **ABRAHAM LINCOLN**

a clear directive that reading is not a choice, the candidate will prepare content and fret only about delivery. Helping a candidate gain confidence works best if specific aspects of a debate or speech are isolated and worked on one at a time. You don't teach someone to swim by throwing the person in the deep end.

As you did for the mock interview, be sure to have someone videotape the mock debate. This way, the candidate and team can review it later.

Recently, we set up a mock debate for a novice candidate. The candidate was given questions ahead of time, and the audience was also prepped. I served as the moderator, and my husband, Rick Shaw, who headed up the television media team, volunteered to role-play the opponent. In preparation for his part, Rick read direct mail, white papers, the brochure, and newspaper ads and studied the mannerisms and dress of the opponent. Rick was the opposition in nearly every way—vaguely answering questions and subtly going after our client as we had seen the opponent do in real debates. The reporter who attended was smart and direct with questions, as were a U.S. history teacher from the high school, a teacher from the middle school, and an assortment of people from the war room.

The whole debate took over two hours, including the question-and-answer period that followed. It was very successful except for one thing: The candidate was furious with Rick after the debate, in much the same way opposing candidates are in real elections—so much so that she never watched the video of the mock debate.

At the next debate, however, when the real opponent (who, by the way, was dressed identically to my husband, right down to the American flag on the lapel of his cheap suit) seemingly reenacted what had occurred at the mock debate, our candidate was brilliant. Her response to a demeaning comment made by her opponent brought the conservative crowd to a round of boisterous applause. She was so good and her opponent so bad that we cut an ad of that debate by simply juxtaposing the two for thirty seconds.

> "I would feel that most of the conversations that took place in those areas of the White House that did have the recording system would in almost their entirety be in existence but the special prosecutor, the court, and I think, the American people are sufficiently familiar with the recording system to know where the recording devices existed and to know the situation in terms of the recording process but I feel, although the process has not been undertaken yet in preparation of the material to abide by the court order, really, what the answer to that question is."
>
> **RON ZIEGLER,**
> former White House press secretary, answering a question about the Nixon White House taping system

3. *Attend Public Appearances with the Candidate.* One way to help candidates find their feet is to start with coffees before they head out on the debate trail. A coffee can be well attended with lots of unknown faces, but it will almost always be a forgiving crowd.

Have at least two committee members attend the first coffee, and let them know you want feedback. I will often ask the groomer to attend the first coffee, and if I am the campaign manager, I will make notes as my candidate is speaking. Here are some things to watch for:

- Are responses to questions clear and brief?
- Does the candidate scan the room, or fixate on just a few faces?

- Does the candidate toe the ground or look at his or her shoes?
- Does the person play with change or keys in his or her pocket?
- Does the candidate's voice drop so that those in the back cannot hear?
- Does he or she ramble?
- Given an answer, is it clear that the candidate does not know a certain subject area?
- Do verbal ticks distract from content of answers?
- Does he or she lean against the wall?
- Where are the candidate's hands? They should be used to reinforce what is being said, not stuffed in pockets or laced behind the back.
- Does the candidate cross his or her feet while standing? This is a sign of insecurity and an attempt to make oneself smaller. It reveals inadequacy.

A few years back, I was running a campaign for a very capable, well-educated, professionally successful candidate. However, after a debate, I was called by the groomer whom I had asked to attend to observe the candidate in action. She did not have much to say about his dress, but told me that his answers were rambling, that he continually said he agreed with his opponent, and that his opening and closing statements were weak.

I immediately called the candidate on his cell phone and asked if he could exit the freeway and return to my home. Although the candidate and I had previously gone over all issues and discussed possible answers, he had not yet made debate cards as he had been instructed. So for two hours we revisited the issues and made debate cards together. (Note: This is not something you can do for the candidate on your own; the candidate needs to be in on this task.) In addition to issue cards, we discussed how no candidate should ever say he agrees with his opponent and why. Finally, we prepared opening and closing statements. No matter how great your candidate is, this kind of coaching is invaluable to his or her success. For the campaign manager, getting the candidate's speaking and debating skills in order is every bit as important as printed materials, ads, lawn signs, and letters to the editor. As the candidate left my home, he said it was the best two hours he had spent since the beginning of the campaign. After that, he became focused and had a level of comfort I had not seen before.

> "Experience is a hard teacher. She gives the test first, the lesson afterwards."
> **ANONYMOUS**

Below are a few things the candidate can do to make speeches and debates more effective.

1. Arrive a few minutes early, but before leaving your car, go over your speech one last time. You will neither have the time nor the inclination to do it once inside.
2. Arrive in the room a little early to get a feel for the audience and the setting.
3. When asked a question, answer it (or appear to be answering it). I have an unfortunate tendency to drift into a stream-of-consciousness thing. One thing reminds me of another and another and another. Avoid that.
4. Have fun. Remember you are on stage. This is your moment. Enjoy it. Smile a lot.
5. Lose the verbal tics: *Um, you know, basically, if you will, quite frankly, to tell you the truth,* and *like* all can distract from your presentation. For the campaign manager, just calling attention to a candidate's verbal tics or an inclination to use certain words or phrases is usually enough to change the candidate's behavior. Every moment does not have to be filled. Silence can be a time to gather power. Never underestimate its force.

> "From you. And let me say something about the tenor of that question. I look around this room and I see privileged people. It's easy to sit back and criticize government efforts to help ordinary people, but helping them is our responsibility."
>
> **ROBERT F. KENNEDY,** at an elite medical school, responding to a student who asked him where he was going to get the money for the solutions he proposed to fix a deeply troubled country

6. Have some notes about what you are going to say, even if it is a short speech and one you have given a million times. I was once asked to speak at the local outdoor Shakespearean Theater, which had a standing-room capacity of around a thousand. I had never spoken to such a large group, under lights, or on a stage like that. I walked out and could not remember one line of my two-minute, memorized speech. Not one. I stood there for what seemed like an hour waiting for it to come to me. Nothing. Finally, with no hope of it coming back, I looked down at my notes. The first line triggered the speech, and out it came. Even if you think you won't need them, bring along some notes.
7. Make your speech fun for others to hear. Include something in it to make them feel proud or appreciated. Throw in some self-deprecating humor. I once watched a candidate give a speech at a Rotary Club meeting. She got up bemoaning the fact that one more lumber mill had closed. It would have been much more effective if she had stood up and said, "In Jackson County, small business is big business." She could have followed that up with examples, using members sitting in the room—all testimo-

nials of our economic strength. She also could have pointed out how the success of communities like ours is dependent on the volunteerism and commitment of organizations such as the Rotary Club. Again, give examples. People really hate to hear candidates whine. Avoid it.

One speech I gave as mayor was to the Annual Conference of the Engineers of Oregon. I am the daughter of an engineer, and although my son graduated from Pomona College in economics, he only now has faced his genetic code and is in a postbaccalaureate program in engineering. Anyway, one night, when I got home from work quite late, my son, six at the time, called me to his bed, I thought, for a kiss goodnight. Instead, he pulled out from under his bed one of the most bizarre contraptions I'd ever seen and said, "If I could just have a little piece of electrical tape . . . ." I told this story to the engineers with the tone of "You don't know how your mothers suffered," and then pulled three or four examples of my son's handiwork from a bag. It was great fun. It was a room full of people who grew up with contraptions under their beds waiting for a piece of electrical tape.

> Failed in business, 1831.
> Defeated for legislature, 1832.
> Fiancée died, 1835.
> Nervous breakdown, 1836.
> Defeated in election, 1836.
> Defeated for U.S. Congress, 1843, 1846, and 1848.
> Defeated for U.S. Senate, 1855 and 1858.
> Defeated for U.S. vice presidency, 1856.
> Elected president of the United States, 1860.

8. Add history to speeches. Some people know the background of their town, but many don't. Call seniors or local historians for ideas.

9. Focus on friends in the audience. I gave a speech once while I was in the middle of a really horrible campaign for a city money measure with which I was personally aligned. In the audience was one of the opponents of the tax, making faces and otherwise distracting me. It had to be the worst speech of my career. Now I look for friendly faces and focus on them.

10. Use quotations, jokes, and anecdotes. Although there are exceptions, I usually do not tell jokes but rather incorporate jokes as funny stories within a speech. This is where self-deprecating humor works.

For example, at a speech to the Oregon Nurses Association, I came on after two women who were not nurses but rather children of nurses. Although I had not thought of this while I wrote my speech, I said that I too was the daughter of a nurse: an operating room nurse. I told them that OR nurses are the only people I know who wash their hands before and after they go to the bathroom. Even my mom laughs at this, because it's true. Give people something of yourself.

Collect quotations, and incorporate them wherever possible. There are many books available that offer food for thought in quotations. I have included about three hundred short quotations in this book. Look for them, and incorporate applicable ones in your speeches. Modify these sayings, so that they are your own words or fit the moment.

11. Share experiences that happened to you on the campaign trail. "The other day, while I was canvassing . . . " can be an effective way to make known that you canvass and care what voters think; plus, it provides an opportunity to communicate an important idea that is part of your platform.
12. Save correspondence that is entertaining, and incorporate it in your speech. My favorite was a letter from a supporter telling me I needed to wear more makeup. I never reveal the author's name in this situation.
13. Target your audience with the campaign message.
14. Give your speech to yourself in the mirror, or have a supporter videotape a speech and have the campaign team watch and critique it.
15. Avoid "word stir-fry"—that is, avoid confusing people with unprepared, incoherent speeches or answers to questions. It makes those listening think you do not know what you're talking about.

Speaking Engagements

Look for opportunities to speak before groups. You need to get your name and face known to the public if you are a candidate, and you need to get your cause before the public if you are working for an issue-based campaign. On the other hand, it is just as important to protect the candidate's time from too many activities with marginal returns. Look for speaking opportunities

> "If you think gun control, abortion and gay and lesbian civil rights are controversial issues, try a stop sign, a speed bump or a tree that needs trimming."
> **ANTONIO VILLARAIGOSA,** mayor of Los Angeles

where the audience should be receptive to your campaign message, and focus on the savables.

Write-In, Third-Party, and Nonpartisan Candidates

In some circumstances, you may be running at a distinct disadvantage as a write-in or third-party candidate. In other situations, depending on the laws of the area, the first election the candidates face might be the deciding election. All these situations require some unique approaches.

The Write-in Candidate

After the sudden death of a city councilor just weeks before the general election of 1998, a few of us got together to help a write-in candidate. This turned out to be a great campaign. There were lots of volunteers, plenty of money, great ads, well-placed lawn signs, an excellent brochure, and a solid candidate—one who was both hardworking and willing to do anything her campaign committee asked, from walking districts to modifying her "look." She had been actively involved in city politics and had served on volunteer boards and commissions, she was smart and well spoken, and she did her homework. She got strong endorsements from both local newspapers. She was also a very progressive Democrat.

> "[They] leave the impression of an army of pompous phrases moving over the landscape in search of an idea; sometimes these meandering words would actually capture a straggling thought and bear it triumphantly, a prisoner in their midst, until it died of servitude and overwork."
> **WILLIAM MCADOO,**
> regarding President Harding's speeches

The opposition really ran no campaign other than two or three ads and about as many lawn signs. The opponent was a conservative Republican, a political category that in terms of registration in the city, comes in third behind Democrats and nonaffiliated voters. We made no mistakes during the campaign, and still we lost.

Write-in campaigns, under the best of circumstances, are tough to win. Can it be done? Absolutely. There are examples everywhere of people pulling it off. Washington State elected a congresswoman on a write-in ticket. Write-ins are really no more work than a regular election. However, depending on the ballot type, voting for a write-in is more complicated for the voter. In the case of this write-in candidate, our county was using a punch-card ballot, requiring voters to do more than just write a name next to a position.

> "I have always found paranoia to be a perfectly defensible position."
> **PAT CONROY**

First things first:

1. You must know the ballot type used by your county and what it looks like.
2. Find out precisely how a write-in vote must be cast at the ballot box. Does the voter have to pull down the full name and the position of the office?

3. Know the law. Laws for financial disclosure are the same for a write-in as for a candidate on the ballot.

4. Know when the absentee ballots are mailed. You must both identify support and turn out your absentees on or before Election Day. This is crucial for a win.

5. Know what percentage the absentees are of those who vote—not the registered voters, but of those who actually vote. For example, although 25 percent of all registered voters may request and vote absentee, on Election Day, they may represent 50 percent or more of the voter turnout.

6. Run two campaigns: one for absentees and one for walk-ins.

7. In your campaign literature and advertising, even on the lawn signs, illustrate and reinforce what voters will see on their ballot.

8. Get your candidate on the speaking circuit with the opponent(s).

9. Conduct all other business as you would for any other campaign, keeping in mind item 7 above.

10. If your state has one, get in the voters' pamphlet.

You might think this sounds convoluted, but write-in campaigns are actually more fun than running a regular campaign. No one really expects a write-in to win, so everyone is rooting for you. Also, because write-in campaigns are so rare, the media gives the campaign more attention with feel-good stories during the news, especially if the candidate is working his or her tail off in an obviously well-organized effort. This kind of campaign creates a sense of urgency that brings out the best in volunteers, so they really go the extra distance for the campaign.

> "I don't care if he did it or not, just get him to deny it."
> — **LYNDON JOHNSON**

It is usually difficult to raise money for a candidate who appears to be losing. With a write-in, however, people don't perceive being behind as the fault of the candidate but rather of circumstances beyond the candidate's control. As a result, if you have a strong write-in candidate, it is surprisingly easy to raise money.

Finally, because people know the odds are long on a write-in winning, when you lose, your efforts get far more attention than they would in a more traditional race. Depending on the kind of campaign you run, the candidate ends the race with more stature, power, and respect in the community than before the campaign and, ironically, is not portrayed as the loser. Next election cycle, get on the ballot and you will win.

In our write-in race, we had a punch-card ballot, perhaps the most difficult type for a write-in. On the punch-card ballot, now made famous by

Florida, our voters had to write "city council," the actual position number of the council seat, and the candidate's name in an area completely separate from where the actual punch position was on the ballot. They also had to remember not to punch the corresponding number of the opponent on the ballot itself. The name had to be the same on all write-ins. For example, my name is Cathy, but if someone wrote in Kathy, Cathie, or even Catherine, our clerk would not accept it.

To visually reinforce what was required of the voter, we re-created a ballot to use as our campaign logo and put it on everything: lawn signs, the brochure, and direct mail. Still, according to the county clerk, the voters made so many mistakes—such as failing to put the proper council position or any position on the ballot, writing only the position number without specifying "city council," and so on—that hundreds of write-in votes did not count.

Third-Party Candidates

As in all campaign activities, a third-party candidate can be a blessing or a curse. If you're a third-party candidate, you will benefit most by presenting the Republican and the Democrat as one and the same. You and you alone provide an alternative. To win as a third-party candidate, you must be able to pull votes from both major parties, all age groups, and all income levels.

Most often, third-party candidates act as spoilers by splitting the vote of one party and thereby increasing the likelihood of a win by the other. Voters registered as independents will track the party of greatest registration within their precinct, so the candidate running as an independent has little claim to any voter and will pull votes from either the Democrats or the Republicans, depending on how he or she stands on the issues. In 1990 a very conservative independent went on the gubernatorial ticket in Oregon. He ran on an anti-choice, anti-sales-tax, anti-land-use-planning platform and successfully pulled conservative votes from a very popular moderate Republican and, as a consequence, effectively gave the Democrat the win.

In New Mexico, Republican Bill Redmond won a congressional seat in 1996 in a district registered heavily Democratic by using a third-party candidate to pull support from his Democratic opponent. Redmond's win was due primarily to three strategies: Target the Democrat with negative ads, boost the Green Party candidate to split the Democratic vote, and turn out the Republican base. Redmond's campaign even sent literature to registered Democrats for the Green Party candidate.

In 1999, in California, Audie Bock became the first Green Party candidate elected to state office in the United States. Her rise began with the resignation of Congressman Ron Dellums (D-Calif.), who left office in the middle of his fourteenth term. A special election was held to fill his seat in the U.S. House for the remainder of his term, and another to fill that of Barbara Lee, the California state senator who won Dellums's seat. Yet another special election was held to fill the Sixteenth District Assembly seat of Don Perata, the successor to Lee's senate seat. It was dominoes, with everyone in office moving up the food chain.

Two Democrats weighed in for the Sixteenth District: former Oakland mayor, Elihu Harris, who had also served twelve years in the California State Assembly, and Frank Russo, who also had a long list of party credentials behind his name. No Republican entered the fray, as this district had a Democratic registration advantage of fifty-one points. Because California law forced the top vote-getters of each party into a runoff if no one received a majority of total votes cast in an open primary, either Russo or Harris had to pull in more than 50 percent of the votes to lock the win.

Seeing a potential opportunity for a runoff, the Green Party recruited Audie Bock and hoped that neither Democrat would garner the necessary votes for an outright win, thereby forcing a runoff between the Democrat and Green Party candidate. That is exactly what happened. Harris beat Russo, but attained only 49 percent of the vote.

In the runoff, Bock ran on a platform that focused on the Democratic Party machine and suggested that the machine was responsible for the series of special elections, beginning with the midterm resignation of Congressman Dellums. While the Harris campaign packed up the headquarters in Oakland and Harris went to Sacramento to select furniture for his new office, Audie Bock hit the streets. Her team of forty primary volunteers grew to one hundred; they walked, phoned, and targeted voters. She had five hundred lawn signs and enough money for one mailer—a postcard.

Harris's consultant ran a late poll and became so concerned that he dropped a dozen mail pieces in the last two weeks. But it was too much and too late, and the last-minute flurry served only to reinforce the Bock campaign theme urging voters to shun big-party politics. Having spent only $40,000 against Harris's $600,000, Bock won by 327 votes with 30,000 cast.[1]

Nonpartisan Races

There are typically two kinds of nonpartisan races: The first matches all candidates in a primary and only requires a runoff of the top two if no one receives 50 percent or more of the votes cast. The other is when all the candidates face each other in a single election, usually the general, and whoever receives the majority of votes cast wins.

If your election is the first animal, that is, you must get 50 percent or have a runoff, you first must accurately predict voter turnout for each of the parties in the primary and employ strategy accordingly. Not all primaries are the same. Depending on what is on the ballot, there could be more Democrats or Republicans weighing in. Therefore, predicted voter turnout is a function of other ballot noise. The goal is to lock in the party that will perform the best in the primary, and then come back and get the other in the general. Even if the campaign does not garner the requisite 50 percent, the general will be more winnable with this strategy.

Let me give you an example: By the time the 2008 Oregon primary rolled around in May, John McCain already had a lock on the Republican nomination, but Hillary Clinton and Barack Obama were still in full tilt. That presented an unusual opportunity for nonpartisan primary races in our county, where the Republicans, who held a three-point registration advantage (3,400) underreported for their civic duty with a 53 percent primary turnout. Meanwhile, a whopping 75 percent of the Democrats turned out to vote. The net result was 7,400 more Democrats who voted in the primary than Republicans. That translates into nearly an 11,000-vote advantage the Democrats would *not* have in the general. With 7,400 more Democrats casting a ballot in the primary than Republicans, any Democrat looking to garner the 50 percent vote in a nonpartisan race should have been able to pull off a win—as long as the voters "sort of" knew which candidate was which. Although nonpartisan races are just that, voters generally know which candidate is the Democrat and which candidate is the Republican. If they don't, it's the campaign's duty to provide the clues.

In judicial races, where it's prohibited for candidates to announce their party registration or use it in campaigning, a campaign can still give voters clues through endorsements. Further, after conducting a precinct analysis, any candidate should be able to predict where the bulk of the votes will be cast, in light of who and what is on the ballot.

Here is another example from 2008. A judicial race in our county featured three candidates in the primary: two Republicans and one Democrat. One of the Republican candidates had a Democratic strategist who correctly assessed who would vote in the primary, and he sent his candidate out to lock in the Democratic vote. The other Republican in the race had no strategist. The Democrat hired a local Republican strategist who sent him after the Republican vote through direct mail and canvassing.

After the votes were counted, the Democrat with the Republican strategist had substantially outspent the other two candidates, and although he came in first in ballot returns, he did not garner the requisite 50 percent to avoid a general election runoff. The Republican, who courted the Democrats in the primary, came in second. The other Republican with no strategist came in third and immediately endorsed his fellow Republican in the race.

Now the two top vote-getters marched off to the general. For the general, the Republican candidate moved over to Republican areas of the county, and the Democrat, who underperformed in the primary, moved over to woo Democrats who were not locked in during the primary. Both used endorsements to give clues about who was the Democrat and who was the Republican.

However, Democrats who had already voted in the primary for the Republican either continued with him or, confused over which was which, undervoted the category. The undervote topped out at 25 percent. This undervote, coupled with a veritable tsunami of Republican votes in the general, half of whom had not even voted in the primary, gave the election to the Republican. The Democrat with the Republican strategist again outspent his opponent in the general by two to one and lost by two points. Brutal.

Nonpartisan races that are decided by a simple majority with no runoff can have their own challenges. Typically, these races lie outside judicial races, so letting people know your party is fair game. If you are a Republican running in a heavily registered Democratic area or a Democrat running in a highly partisan Republican area, it's time to re-register as a nonaffiliated voter.

That done, your next challenge centers on the number of candidates in your race and how the vote will split. If there are more than three, you have your work cut out for you. Further, if one of the candidates in the field previously ran for office, he or she has a tremendous advantage irrespective of whether the previous race was won or lost. Typically in down-ballot races, a candidate loses not because people do not support that candidacy but rather because they prefer one over the other. Therefore, there often is no "against" vote in the prior election bid. This means that anyone running and losing a clean race can at least count on the same votes he or she received in the previous run. Of course, the rest of the votes will be divided among the rest of the contestants in the field—including the candidate who ran before.

Although I always encourage people to run for office, if you are considering a run in a race with multiple candidates and one of them has run once before and lost, consider sitting it out. Unless something is terribly, terribly wrong with the person who ran previously, he or she will win. Why? Two reasons: First, voters like to be fair; they tend to give the loser the nod in a second attempt. Second, he or she will have name recognition that is tough to catch in a nonprimary, winner-take-all election. However, should a candidate be running for a third or fourth time with no wins, all bets are off.

Media and the Candidate

You and your campaign team may suspect bias on the part of the local media, and you may even have those suspicions confirmed, but there is no way to use something like this while campaigning. Complaining about the press makes a candidate look weak—and it's political suicide. The best revenge is to win.

> "You never get ahead of anyone as long as you try to get even with him."
>
> **LOU HOLTZ,**
> Arkansas football coach

Although I'm amazed when I see candidates go after the media, especially presidential candidates, who should know better, it's understandable why they do. In recent years, the media, especially in talk radio, have become more vicious and combative. They can be merciless in their treatment of elected officials—who have volunteered time to serve the community—and then wonder, editorially, why so few throw their hat in the ring for the next election cycle.

Although candidates should respond to attacks from the opposition, they would do best to ignore any bait that the press floats on the pond. Even so, if the editor of your local paper is coming after you, call supporters to come to your defense in letters to the editor.

Blogs

Blogs are a very real part of promoting and attacking political candidates and causes, and because the Web sites of local papers often allow bloggers to be anonymous, people really have at it. Any time a print article comes out on your race, your team must be prepared to respond to the "online comments section" that immediately follows the article. The team should defend the candidate on any attacks, and even if there are none, the team should weigh in with positive comments. "Great to see Willie in the race; I volunteered with him at the school and he's an excellent man." Whatever. Someone must be on top of this medium and protect and promote the candidate.

Negative Campaigning

Negative campaigning is inherent in the process. After all, you are running because you embrace issues or values that differ from those of your opponent.

You are working on a campaign—whether for a candidate or an issue—for a reason, and as you define that reason, you define both your campaign and that of your opposition. The inverse is true also.

Although the thought of being attacked in public can cause panic for a candidate or campaign team, remember that it is yet another opportunity to get your message out and to show how you comport yourself under pressure. Do it with grace, and an attack can actually help.

> "Whatever else there may be in our nature, responsibility toward truth is one of its attributes."
> — **ARTHUR EDDINGTON**

In listing the strengths and weaknesses of a candidate or an issue-based campaign, you are preparing for the inevitable attack. Candidates who have reviewed all the possibilities with the committee and drafted responses will have confidence and strength under fire. By preparing, the committee and the candidate can deal with attacks immediately, succinctly, and deftly. If no response comes from your side, an attack often gains credibility.

If your campaign goes negative, keep in mind that numerous studies conducted on the impacts of negative campaigning indicate that only four areas consistently fall in fair territory when it comes to attacks: actual voting records, current ethical problems, business practices, and money received from special-interest groups. Finally, do not think you can win in a direct-mail war; your campaign must be smarter and have scores of volunteers assisting your efforts.

> "In politics as in sport, you take a grave risk when, instead of playing to win, you play not to lose. Running not to lose (means) running on your resume rather than your vision. . . . people don't elect resumes. They elect candidates with an agenda."
> **LES AUCOIN,**
> former U.S. congressman, in a letter to Democratic gubernatorial candidate Ted Kulingoski

So what do you do if you are attacked? In 1999, the University of Maryland conducted a study, the Campaign Assessment and Candidate Outreach Project, that looked at the impacts of negative campaigning on voters. Charges that voters considered unfair placed the attacking candidate in serious trouble, whether the opposition responded or not and regardless of whether the voters considered the counterattack fair. Charges that were deemed fair (such as a voting record) caused problems for the candidate being attacked, especially if he or she did not respond or did so in an unfair manner. The best outcome for the candidate under attack is to counter with a "fair charge" in return.[2]

> "You better start swimmin' or you'll sink like a stone."
> — **BOB DYLAN**

Unfair Attacks Can Backfire

Let me repeat: It is mandatory that a candidate come clean about anything ugly that might pop up during a heated campaign. This becomes more important as candidates move up the ballot, where outside consultants often call the shots with little regard to their client's reputation in their communities.

In 2000, I ran a campaign for a candidate for the Oregon House and as always hired a firm to do opposition research on both our candidate and the opponent. As mentioned before, I like to do opposition research on my candidate to see what the other side might dig up. After the research was concluded, the candidate alerted us to one thing that was not uncovered.

Apparently, twenty years before in another state, our candidate was summoned into court on a bench warrant for failure to pay child support. At the time, he felt his children were at risk and therefore wanted custody. His attorney advised him the only way to get his former wife into court was if she summoned him, not the other way around. And so the attorney advised a cessation of child-support payments, anticipating the ex would come after the deadbeat dad. Once the parties were in court, the custody issue could be revisited. My client reported to me that he followed his attorney's advice and indeed did end up with custody of the children. After hearing this, I decided to hold this information in confidence and share it with the committee only should it become an issue, which it didn't. But that all changed in 2004, when my client ran for higher office.

In 2004, three weeks before ballots were due, a friend and lobbyist called the candidate saying he had seen a direct mail-flyer regarding the custody battle and the bench warrant for back child support. The lobbyist reported seeing it in the office of a Republican strategist, and after chastising the strategist for the piece, the lobbyist told the Republican that he (the lobbyist) would be telling our campaign about it. The strategist said that the piece would be dropped (mailed) in a week—two weeks before ballots were due. Because my candidate had revealed this situation to me previously, I already had had four years to think about how to respond to this issue, and we went into action.

First, you never want your committee to get this kind of information through the grapevine or in the morning news, so calling a meeting of committee members was the first order of business. Then, the editor of the local paper was called and given our side of the story. He told us that the former wife had already dropped all of the court documents at the paper's door, but he said he would hold the story and cover the issue only if and when our opposition went public.

The candidate and I suspected that our opponent knew nothing of the piece, so I talked with our opponent's campaign manager, and my candidate called his opponent, urging that the piece be pulled. Our worry was that it would hurt our opponent's reputation. He was a good man who held a great deal of respect within our community.

I then got the media team together, and we drafted a 60-second spot to counter the attack and flew in one of the candidate's daughters to do the ad. We cut the new ad, paid for the additional time, but did not take the ad to the stations, as we did not want it to accidentally air before the direct-mail piece was distributed.

The following week, volunteers and staff began "Dumpster diving" post offices in the district. In rural parts of the country, many people can get their mail only through the post office and often do not have trash pickup at home, so junk mail is thrown away at the post office. Dumpster diving for direct mail is actually very useful.

Serendipitously, a well-respected, very conservative businessman called me, dismayed with other nasty pieces our opponent had sent. I shared with him what was about to happen and asked if he would cut a radio spot for us; I knew that radio in this region speaks almost entirely to conservative men. My hope was to drive up an undervote. The radio spot was cut and began with the validator identifying himself as conservative and a Christian who had had enough.

Finally, with only a week remaining before Election Day, I received confirmation that the deadbeat dad piece was in mailboxes. We released the response ad, and I called the editor of the paper and told him that the hit piece landed, so he could get the paper's story in.

As expected, the front-page article that gave the full story, coupled with the radio spot and television ad in which the daughter gave a compelling and heart-wrenching account of the personal events that led up to the children's living with their father, decimated the effectiveness of the hit piece and, sadly, the reputation of the man we were running against. Game over.[3]

Ten Dos and Don'ts of Attacks

1. Resist starting a campaign with an attack.
2. Define yourself before going on the attack, especially if you're running against an incumbent who is respected by the voters.
3. Have a focused message.
4. Avoid mixing a lot of unnecessary arguments together.
5. Avoid mixing positive and negative issues within the same ad or directional piece.

6. Avoid misleading or unconvincing arguments.
7. Avoid inconsistent claims: Anything questionable will lead the voter to doubt everything.
8. Do your homework so that you can back up any charges you make, and be prepared for a counterattack.
9. Be sure that any attacks are believable and fair.
10. Time your attack carefully. An attack launched too early in a campaign may not have the intended impact, and one launched too late may not have enough time to sink in with the voters.

Campaign committees must prepare the candidate for the possibility of negative attacks. Just as a team prepares the candidate for debates, the team also anticipates anything that may come at the candidate. It can do this by listing all possible scenarios and then preparing responses for the candidate and committee, should they come under fire.

A Word of Caution

In 2000, a friend of mine was running for office. One night, she was on her cordless phone talking with her campaign manager when suddenly her next-door neighbor and the campaign manager of her opponent came on the line. Their voices were as clear as if she were on a conference call; she easily recognized both men, and they called each other by name. Amazingly, they were talking about her race and in the conversation revealed some very damaging information they had dug up about her. Apparently, someone had come forward and relayed some ancient history to the opposing campaign; the conversation included who came forward and a detailed account as related by the informant. The discussion revolved around whether and how to drop the dirt, so that the voters would know before casting a ballot.

My friend's neighbor, an unhappy man in general, had been actively opposing her candidacy and was desperate to break the news. He strongly urged the campaign manager to leak it. From the tenor of the voices and what was said, my friend believed that her neighbor was more interested in personally hurting her than in winning the race for her opponent. The opposition's manager was reluctant to move forward with a hit piece. My friend hung up before hearing the decision on what to do with the information.

It was the wildest story I had ever heard. When campaign committee people are talking strategy on the phone, urge them to stick to land lines and avoid cordless phones. You just never know who will be listening.

Thank-You Notes

With the introduction of computers and desktop publishing, a printed thank-you note does not carry the same weight as a handwritten note from the candidate. Most people know that computers not only can generate a personalized thank-you note but can also print the candidate's signature. While a campaign should send a thank-you note or receipt for a contributor's tax records, if you are working with a candidate who is willing to scratch a few lines in his or her own handwriting, it really goes a long way. Besides thank-you notes for contributions, it is important to send notes to volunteers who have gone above and beyond the call of duty and to anyone who hosts a coffee or facilitates a campaign event.

Because thank-you notes are fairly expensive to send, I look at them as an opportunity to strengthen a relationship between the donor and the candidate. To do this, I put together a printed, personalized thank-you note for the candidate to sign but will look for some small thing that the candidate can add to the note after it is printed. I will go through the lists of contributors with the candidate to identify those he or she knows personally. This doesn't take long and can be done over the phone. I make a note on the photocopied checks of contributors the candidate knows so that I can keep those notes apart from the rest. If I personally know the contributor because of his or her involvement with the campaign, I attach a Post-it to the thank-you note, indicating what I want the candidate to jot on the bottom. For example, if the campaign receives a contribution from someone who also baked all the cookies for a coffee earlier in the campaign, I instruct the candidate to acknowledge that effort one more time in the contribution thank-you note: "Still thinking about those great desserts you brought to the coffee last month. Hope all is well, and thanks again." In the 2008 general election, Obama called the parents of one of his workers to thank them for her efforts. Very classy.

When responding to contributors from a targeted mailing such as doctors, teachers, dentists, lawyers and such, I will include in the body of the thank-you letter information that the contributor may want to know because it pertains to his or her field of interest. I also try to make these a little gossipy, so the contributor feels more a part of the inner circle. In other words, acknowledge the contribution, but give the donor a little more. This is especially important with anyone who gives more than a hundred dollars. Only a small portion of a thank-you note is about the gift. The real power of a thank-you note is to curry the donor for the next "give" so that subsequent contributions will increase. In local elections, personal communication with donors is about investing them in the campaign in more ways than just money.

FIGURE 9.2 Example of Stationery for the Candidate's Personalized Notes

(Design by Crystal Castle Graphics)

In all preprinted thank-you notes, be sure to have the candidate sign in an off-color pen. Because blue and black ink are often used in computer-generated signatures, green is best. You can get away with blue, however, if you use a pen with a slightly thicker point. Avoid colors like pink, red, or purple.

For thank-you notes that do not need a contribution receipt, I have special stationery that I print from my computer. On the front is a picture of the candidate on the campaign trail or a collage of the candidate in different settings. I usually ask my graphic designer to put together the layout and then e-mail it to me so that I can print out the letters as needed. However, if your design will use just one photo, it is pretty easy to drop it in yourself (figure 9.2).

To generate this stationery, lay it out in landscape format so that each sheet of paper will make two note cards, and use paper that is slightly heavier, such as 80-pound vellum Bristol, with matching preprinted envelopes (the ones you used for your world's smallest brochure mailing work well). To help the candidate, it is a good idea for the campaign manager or someone from the committee to make a short list of who might receive a personalized thank-you note. Have the envelopes preaddressed and stamped so that the candidate need only jot a note before the notes are stuffed, sealed, and mailed.

The Issue-Based Campaign

IN THIS CHAPTER
- Initiative and Referendum
- Local Preemption
- Polling and the Issue-Based Campaign
- Speakers' Bureau
- Recall
- A Petition Is Pulled!
- Saving Our Libraries
- Investing in Education
- Packaging the Issue-Based Campaign
- Flies in the Ointment: The Double Majority, Independents, and the Super Majority
- The State Initiative and Referendum Process

Initiative and Referendum

The initiative and referendum process arose out of the fundamental controversy about whether government should come directly from the people or through representatives to the various levels of government. Although some direct democracy existed in the early years of U.S. government, during the first hundred years, it was almost exclusively representative. It wasn't until the late 1800s, when dissatisfaction with government and distrust of the state legislatures became prevalent, that citizens enacted the initiative process. Primarily a western-state phenomenon, the initiative process began in reaction to laws that benefited a few powerful interests rather than the body electorate. Its effect was to enlarge the role people have in policy decision making.

Ironically, today it has become a tool for special-interest groups with agendas related to natural resources, morality, minority rights, taxation, and so forth.

As Oregon's former secretary of state Phil Keisling said, "At key moments in our history, the initiative has held up a mirror to who we are as [a society], reflecting our pettiness as well as grand visions, our mean-spiritedness as well as our generosity, our perils and possibilities as a political community."[1]

The state initiative process enables citizens to bypass the legislature and directly place proposed statutes and constitutional amendments on the ballot by gathering signatures. Each of the twenty-four states with citizens' initiative authority has different criteria to activate the process (see table 10.1, at the end of the chapter). Before you begin an initiative campaign, contact your local elections office or secretary of state's office to learn all the necessary details.

> "To be successful, grow to the point where one completely forgets himself; that is, to lose himself in a great cause."
>
> — BOOKER T. WASHINGTON

The referendum process, by contrast, serves as a check on the governing body by forcing adopted legislation to a vote of the people, allowing them to accept or reject it. The signature requirement for referring legislation out to a vote is usually less than the initiative process.

Increasingly, the initiative process is being used to amend state constitutions in an effort to keep legislative bodies from tinkering with a voter-approved initiative. The result is that state constitutions and city and county charters are needlessly cluttered. However, in defense of this practice, in the 2003 legislative session alone, Oregon Republicans tried to undo a number of voter mandates. One mandate, a measure to increase the minimum wage in the state, had received voter approval just three months before the house majority advocated undoing the law at the behest of the business interests that funded their campaigns. Another mandate attempted to undo a ban on the use of bait and traps for cougars and bears; the mandate had previously been affirmed by voters on two occasions. Also, during each session, legislators revisit voter directives related to reproductive rights.

> "I pay my taxes gladly. Taxes are the price of civilization."
>
> — OLIVER WENDELL HOLMES

Initiative and referendum processes are also available in many local jurisdictions, and their requirements and scope usually mirror state requirements. Local initiatives can be very useful tools for school districts, libraries, and municipal and county government.

In a local initiative, although most of the guidelines are established by state statutes, the percentage of signatures that need to be gathered varies by locale. Voters may also refer (through referendum) any legislation passed by the local governing body to the voters. As with the state, the number of signatures required is some percentage of the number of people who voted in a specific election—for example, 10 percent of those who voted in the last mayoral election.

The local referendum process differs from the initiative process only in the number of signatures required for qualification and in a time limit; that is, the referendum must be referred within a certain number of days after adoption by the governing body. However, if enough people are opposed to a law, it can, in essence, be repealed through the initiative process at any time. Because both the initiative and the referendum process circumvent the legislative body, they have some inherent problems. If you're not working in conjunction with the local elected officials, be prepared: They have more tricks in their bag.

Who drafts the ballot title may have a decided advantage. Some titles are prepared in such a way that you cannot tell whether a yes vote is actually a yes or a no (for example, "yes, repeal it" versus "yes, don't repeal it").

Also, some states have limitations, such as allowing only a single subject to be covered in a measure. Meeting this limitation can be a little more difficult than it sounds. Often, citizens are anxious to throw in a couple of ideas, each of which may strengthen the other and are quite related, and then, after collecting the signatures or running the winning campaign, the participants find that their wording covered more than one subject. It really isn't for the local governing body to determine whether you have more than one question. If you intend to do all this work, hire an attorney—a good attorney.

> "It is the same story here as in every state, people for it, corporations against it, politicians trying to straddle the issue and save their scalps."
> **GEORGE JUDSON KING,** National Initiative and Referendum leader after initiative provision was dropped from New Mexico constitution, 1910

There are many restrictions on initiatives and referenda. In Oregon, for example, local government cannot put land-use matters to a vote, only legislative matters. So before spending a lot of time and money, learn what your parameters are.

Another caution: Those signing the petition must be registered within the jurisdiction of the area that will be affected by the proposed legislation. For example, if your school measure is to be voted on by those within your school district, then only those registered within the school district will qualify as signers on the petition. Similarly, if your proposed legislation affects your city, then only those registered within the city limits would qualify. In this way, only those affected get to weigh in on the discussion.

Also, in a statewide initiative or referral, the people whose signatures are on the petition must be registered in the county in which they signed the petition. This requirement stems from the fact that signatures are verified at the county level where voters are registered.

Be sure to get at least 10 percent more signatures than is required for qualification.

Of the states with no initiative process, many have provisions for initiatives and referenda at the local level. The following states do not allow statewide initiatives or referenda, but have some form of direct democracy.[2]

Alabama: Voters must approve constitutional amendments proposed by the legislature, and voters in major municipalities have the right of referendum on ordinances.

Connecticut: A number of cities, including Bristol, East Hartford, Enfield, Manchester, Middletown, Southington, Stratford, and West Hartford, allow initiatives on ordinances or charters.

Georgia: The state requires popular approval for constitutional amendments proposed by the legislature, but does not allow statewide initiatives or referendums. At the local level, all home-rule cities are required to allow citizens to propose and approve ordinances and charter amendments by initiative.

Hawaii: The county of Honolulu allows both initiative charter amendments and ordinances.

Kansas and Louisiana: Both states provide for recall of statewide elected officers and municipal initiatives and referenda.

Maryland and New Mexico: Both states allow for the referendum process.

New York: Only Buffalo has a referendum provision. There is limited initiative and referendum provision in local jurisdictions, including New York City; the provision allows voters to propose charter amendments by petition of fifty thousand voters (about 2 percent of the city population).

North Carolina: Nine cities have initiative and referendum powers.

Pennsylvania: The commonwealth allows for initiatives and referenda in most major cities except Philadelphia and Pittsburgh.

South Carolina: All municipalities can initiate and approve ordinances.

Competing Measures

Competing measures have two forms. The first, which results from a legislative body's responding to a qualifying initiative, is designed to give voters an alternative to the citizen-drafted law. In this case, the governing body places before the voters legislation that is linked in some way to an initiative or a referral generated by the public. A competing measure is a powerful tool that can be used effectively. For example, in 1993, Ashland voters approved a prepared-food and beverage tax to fund an open-space land-acquisition program and state-mandated upgrades on its wastewater treatment plant. It was a divisive campaign that had local restaurants, Realtors, and the state food and beverage industry on one side and the parks commission, environmentalists, and citizens buckling under potentially astronomical utility bills on the other. Although the proponents were outspent five to one, the voters approved the tax by a narrow margin. Opponents decided to immediately refer it back to the voters.

In the meantime, the state legislature decided to place a statewide sales tax for school funding before the voters. The timing was such that the referral of the meals tax would appear on the same ballot as the sales tax proposal. I assumed the proponents of the food and beverage tax repeal would use the scare tactic of suggesting that the food and beverage tax would be added to a statewide sales tax. Although a statewide sales tax was unlikely to pass, given that it had been defeated at the polls eight times already, Ashland had always been supportive of such a tax. While the voters might approve a 5 percent local food and beverage tax, few would stand still for a 10 percent tax that would result from the two combined. To head off this predicament, the city placed a competing measure on the ballot along with the food and beverage tax referral. The competing measure said that (1) if the state sales tax passed, Ashland's food and beverage tax would be repealed, and (2) if people voted in larger numbers for the competing measure than for the repeal of the tax, it would override the referendum on the food and beverage tax. Citizens chose the competing measure over an outright repeal of the tax. The statewide sales tax was defeated three to one, with Ashland supporting it two to one.

Just a note: Measures approved by voters, no matter how narrow the margin, are rarely overturned when re-referred. Voters historically come back on the referral and reaffirm previous intentions by even larger margins.

The other type of competing measure occurs when two or more unrelated money measures appear on the same ballot. They can come from the same governing body, such as two county measures requesting funding through the property tax, one for juvenile services, the other for adult detention, or from different governing bodies placing money measures on the same ballot, such as a county, city, school, or special district.

> "A life spent making mistakes is not only more honorable but more useful than a life spent doing nothing."
> **GEORGE BERNARD SHAW**

These days, counties and cities often place competing measures on ballots, because so many needs are falling by the wayside. However, doing this increases the likelihood that all will fail. For example, in November 1998, our county placed three bond measures before the voters, and all went down. The reason is fairly simple. Among voters, some will vote no on any new taxes, and others will vote yes on some. Of the yes voters, some will vote for more than one money measure, and some will choose between the measures, effectively splitting the yes vote. They compete with each other.

> "It doesn't make sense to talk about successful corporations in a society whose schools, hospitals, churches, symphonies, or libraries are deteriorating or closing."
> —— **CLIFTON C. GARVIN, JR.**

That counties and cities would place two measures on the ballot at the same time might suggest that some muddled thinking was involved. In some situations, however, it cannot be helped. For example, your school district is trying to pass a bond measure for a new gym, the city needs money for new fire stations, and the county needs the library system upgraded. Three governing bodies, all with the right to place items on the ballot, separately create a competing-ballot-measure scenario. Ideally, they would be talking to one another and work together to spread these items out, but that doesn't always happen.

The survival rate of competing measures is further complicated when statewide initiative-driven legislation is placed on the ballot and inflames one group over another, such as legislation dealing with gun control, reproductive rights, or sexual orientation. Issues of this sort will bring out a voter who might otherwise stay home, and as long as they're at the voting booth, they'll weigh in on your issue-based campaign.

Despite these problems, there are times when a competing measure can actually help. If one of the money issues on the ballot is poorly constructed, the campaign is poorly conducted, or fatal flaws have been committed right out of the gate, voters may choose to overwhelmingly dump it. When they do, there is a fairness doctrine that kicks in, and other measures get a little more of the swing vote than they might normally receive.

Local Preemption

State legislatures love to preempt local government. Having served twelve years as a mayor and witnessing two Oregon legislative sessions as chief of staff for a state representative, I find it remarkable that an assembly that could not organize a sock drawer would have the cheek to prevent local governments from solving issues within their jurisdiction. However, moneyed interests have discovered that fighting targeted taxation and legislation is much easier in a state capital, where money is king, than in a hundred municipalities. For example, in 2002, two statewide grassroots initiatives on the Oregon ballot went down in flames. One, a proposal for universal health care, was outspent 32 to 1, and the other, which would have required labels on genetically modified foods, was outspent 61 to 1. The latter prompted the agricultural industry, which dumped five million dollars into defeating the food labeling measure, to get legislators to introduce a bill prohibiting local government from implementing any food labeling laws.

During my last term in office, the city of Ashland, which owns the electric utility, brought in high-speed data services and cable television as part of the electric utility system upgrade. By doing so, the city was able to provide high-speed, direct-connect Internet access to schools, libraries, and the university for pennies. It was also a boon for our software industry and graphic design businesses. Although the private sector had no intention of providing high-speed data services until the city stepped up, businesses urged the Oregon legislature to introduce legislation prohibiting other cities from doing what Ashland had done—and tried to make the law retroactive in an effort to undo Ashland's system. Government participation in the creation of this kind of infrastructure is no different from when it participated in state highway systems or rural electric development in days gone by, and it may be one of the best tools for strengthening local economic development. However, when moneyed interests knock on legislators' doors, those answering are often willing to do the bidding for special interests on the house or senate floor.

> "The spirit of resistance to government is so valuable on certain occasions, that I wish it always to be kept alive."
> **THOMAS JEFFERSON**

Polling and the Issue-Based Campaign

Political consultants and pollsters generally agree that to make it through the campaign process, an issue-based campaign must begin with polled support of at least 60 to 70 percent of voters. While this is certainly the case for any issue in which something is requested of the citizens, such as a tax increase or restrictions on where cows can graze, issues that restrict government, such as term-limit legislation or mandatory sentencing for certain crimes, track a different polling pattern.

In my experience, legislation proposing to restrict government, such as disallowing parkland divestment without a vote of the people, restricting city-owned water sales outside the city limits, or imposing term limits, need only show a voter preference in initial polls to successfully pass on Election Day. Typically, issues that appear on the ballot through the initiative process stem from angry voters who have been poked in some way. When this happens, the issue need only cross the finish line to win.

Further, there are other considerations in reading polls than a simple majority in favor of or opposed to the polled issue. For example, a statewide poll looking at proposed legislation to reintroduce term limits in Oregon showed voter support at 56 percent and opposition at 30 percent. At first glance, it looks as if this proposal does not meet the 60 to 70 percent threshold for passage following a heated campaign. But comparing the support and opposition numbers shows almost a two-to-one voter preference for term limits. The other thing to consider is the "hard" support and "hard" opposition of the proposed issue-based campaign. In this term-limit example, the hard numbers in favor (definitely for) came in at 35 percent, and the hard numbers in opposition (definitely against) came in at only 20 percent. These numbers suggest that term-limit legislation would be approved by a proportion similar to the Oregon 1992 constitutional amendment, which passed with 69.6 percent.

Here are some things to consider before embarking on an issue-based campaign:

1. It must be simple and straightforward.
2. It must have voter appeal and speak to emotion. Remember, you are selling an idea, not a person, so there are some inherent challenges. Issue-based campaigns that sell hope and opportunity tend to do best.
3. It must be self-serving. The voter must feel that he or she will personally get something upon passage: a park, better schools, a library, reduced taxes, or a shifted tax burden (e.g., to tourists, business, or the wealthy).
4. For fund-raising purposes, it must have populist appeal. Remember: Money is thy savior.
5. Timing is everything. Will you be in a midterm or off-year election, when turnout is lower, or in a presidential cycle, when everyone participates? Will the election be a primary or a general?
6. What else will be on the ballot? Has government or a citizens group placed on the ballot legislation that will induce one segment of the population to turn out more than another?
7. Will your issue-based campaign hurt or help candidates you want to support or need to keep in office by turning out an "against" vote?
8. Is there enough time to make your case to the voters, and do you have people willing to head up the campaign?
9. Who will be drafting the ballot title and summary—a friend or a foe?

10. What are the polling numbers? If you're working on a losing campaign from the beginning, you will finish the race exhausted and will have actually set your cause back.
11. Who will carry the measure? Who will carry the opposition? The chair, speakers' bureau, endorsers, and opponents of an issue-based campaign are often the biggest clues the voters have for supporting or rejecting an idea.
12. Have mistakes been made that could sink your efforts even before a decision to place the issue campaign on the ballot?
13. Finally, an issue-based campaign designed to raise taxes must answer four questions: (1) How high will (can) the tax go? (2) Where will it be spent? (dedicate the funds) (3) When will it go away? (sunset clause) (4) Is there a nexus between what is being taxed and where the revenue will be spent? An example would be a cigarette tax to fund health care. If there is not a logical connection, your campaign must make one. For example, in the prepared-food and beverage tax, we pointed out that tourists and residents alike use city parks and flush toilets, so both groups of people should help improve these systems.

Speakers' Bureau

When organizing campaigns for ballot measures, set up a committee of supporters whose sole job is to serve as speakers; collectively, they are the speakers' bureau. If it is a countywide proposition or measure, the speakers' bureau might be quite large. In an individual city, it may be as small as two. Whatever the size, the group's job is to seek opportunities to speak and to make sure someone is there from the committee to explain the ballot measure and answer questions in a knowledgeable way. These should be people with little political baggage.

A speakers' bureau is a terrific way of publicly involving big-name people who want to be aligned with a campaign. It is also good for the ballot proposal. Whereas an election with a candidate depends on that candidate and his or her ability to build relationships with the voters through political stands and ideology, ballot measures typically encompass only one idea. Often with a ballot measure, the people who attach their name to it create the relationship. You might have the president of the college, the president of the

> "I should have dropped the Math and English Departments and study hall. Then no one would have known about it."
> **JAMES TAYLOR,** College of Southern Idaho president, reacting to outcries against his dropping three sports and five coaches to solve a financial crisis

Rotary Club, the mayor, the leaders of every church, and so on. Each will bring a following. Their names have come to represent something in the community, and it is their reputations that help draw attention to the vote.

Recall

As with the initiative and referendum process, recalls require a number of signatures of registered voters equal to a specific percentage of those who voted in a specific election. For example, the number of signatures for a recall for a state office might be equal to 8 percent of the number who voted in the last election for governor, whereas a recall of a city official might be 10 percent of those who voted in the last mayor's election. Once a petition is pulled, it must be filed within a specific time (depending on the state or local statutes), and a special election must be held within a specific number of days after verification of the signatures. In Oregon, the whole process can last no more than 140 days: 90 to gather the signatures, 10 to have them verified, and 40 to organize the special election. You cannot begin a recall until someone has been in office for six months after his or her last election. This goes for those who are in their second or third term of office as well.

From my experience, recall attempts are often prompted by one specific action that coupled with the personality of the office holder, means trouble. The recall attempts often focus on strong, smart, outspoken women and strong, smart, soft-spoken men with an overriding theme that the office holder doesn't know who butters his or her bread. If you find that you are the subject of a recall, remember: You only need to survive; they need to conquer. A failed recall attempt generally leaves the office holder in a politically stronger position than before. Whether you believe enough signatures will be gathered is really not the point. Once the attempt has begun, do not hang your head: Fight back. There are lots of people who do not believe in recalls— 76 percent of black voters in California, for example, according to data from the 2003 recall of Governor Gray Davis.

Fighting a recall is no different from running a regular campaign. As soon as you hear of an attempt being waged against you, organize a campaign committee. If the organizers of the effort against you claim that you are supported by only one segment of the population, or one community in the county, then be sure that you have representatives from every city and people from all walks of life. If you're being thrown out because of your connection with special-interest groups, then be sure they are nowhere to be seen in the campaign; show broad-based support.

Begin by fund-raising. You want to amass a war chest that will scare the opponents before they file the papers. Depending on the circumstances, fund-raising events for office holders subjected to a recall are often surprisingly easy and raise lots and lots of money. A bonus is that because you're undergoing a recall while serving in office, no one expects you to do more in the campaign than just show up. So enjoy: Raise money, support, and marginalize your opposition as the small-minded, self-serving people they are. If you cannot find a way to say this yourself, have it said by others in blogs and letters to the editor, and do it again and again and again.

The campaign defending an office holder is actually made easier because the recall communication is all negative. Obviously, little is positive about a recall—all communication, TV, direct mail, and radio will be on the attack. After all, the recall proponents must make the case of why someone should be thrown out of office in the middle of a term. Negative campaigning tends to both disengage voter participation and create support for the person subjected to the public execution. Further, if voters feel the attack is unfair, you're gold. Unfair recall attempts can generate a lot of money for the subject of the recall. Use the opportunity to raise money for your next run.

If you're thinking about recalling an elected official, stop and reconsider. Recalls are almost never warranted. They generally take on the atmosphere of a public flogging. Recalls also scare off other qualified, honest, hardworking people, the kind of people we need, from serving public office. If you're mad enough to want to recall an office holder, get over it and run a candidate or run yourself in the next election.

A Petition Is Pulled!

Whether you are fighting a recall, an initiative, or a referendum, once a petition has been pulled, there are lots of things you can do to prepare for the inevitability that the petitioners will get the required signatures. Do not make the mistake of waiting to see if it actually happens. If you do, the momentum will be with the petitioners, and you will not have enough time to mount a viable campaign. Remember, the best way to prevent signatures from getting collected is to organize, fund-raise, and line everything up for a full-on frontal assault. You want petitioners to believe that you're really enthused, delighted, and looking forward to the possibility of going toe-to-toe with them.

Here's what you do:

1. Organize a campaign committee.
2. Send at least one mailing to your house list explaining what is going on.

3. Set up phone banks, and begin voter identification work immediately in all swing precincts. Know who is opposed to the recall or referendum, as getting them out on Election Day, will be critical to survival.

4. While you're on the phone, secure lawn sign locations and names for an endorsement ad. It will be important to show broad community support for your side. Secure field sign locations as well.

5. Whether the movement is local or statewide, when it comes to referrals and recalls, voters are hugely influenced by their neighbors and community. The best way to fight a recall or referendum is to focus in close. The battle is waged neighborhood by neighborhood. Show individual support if you're facing a recall, and show individual opposition (rebellion) if your tax measure is being targeted.

6. Establish a speakers' bureau, and put the speakers on the circuit immediately.

7. Do not let petitioners define you. If your efforts are backed by unions, they should stay in the closet. If your efforts are backed by big business, keep it at a distance.

8. You must go on the offensive; define the opposition, and communicate that those referring the tax measure are self-serving, outsiders, or supported by special interests. Have proof.

9. As soon as a petition is pulled, start fund-raising, especially if the opposition's campaign is being bankrolled by special-interest groups. If the law does not allow fund-raising until petitions are verified, then ask for pledges you can call in the moment the opposition qualifies for the ballot. But remember, if you have kept your campaign bank account open, you do not need to wait until your opposition gets the signatures. Supporters can give to your existing committee. If you closed your campaign account, simply reopen it under your same committee name. Since committees are often called "Committee to Support Whoever," you can continue to use that committee name to fight the recall.

10. Line up letters to the editor and supporters to monitor and respond to blogs. Remember, while your opponents are gathering signatures, you are, too—signatures for letters, contributions, endorsement ads, and the get-out-the-vote effort. As a campaign, review these letters and decide when they go to the paper(s). Letters need a mix of emotion, pragmatism, and ridicule of the petitioners. Keep 'em short.

11. Get TV and radio ads made.

12. If you're fighting a recall, sing long and hard on accomplishments and service, but make the messenger the average person. If you're fighting a referendum, do not fight the actual referral, but rather promote and

protect what is being referred. If it's about taxes for schools or the disabled, you are selling hope, opportunity, independence, and investments in our future. Don't get on their message.

13. Know your audience, and ask sales reps in both television and radio to set up schedules for air time. You don't actually have to buy, but you want to know the cost, penetration, reach, and frequency that will get you what you need. The nice thing about recalls is that they happen at a time when other campaigns are not competing for air time, so you can purchase time up to the last minute.

14. Design your lawn signs and brochures, and have the camera-ready art at the respective printers with a directive to wait for your phone call.

15. The moment the petitions are filed and certified, you want to be able to make five calls and quickly move the whole process into high gear.

Saving Our Libraries

In the age of technology, voters often look at libraries as a throwback and consider funding them a frill. Unlike new wastewater treatment plants or water pipelines, both of which can be funded through revenue bonds, libraries have suffered under taxpayer revolts and a lack of understanding. If your mission is to get money to build a new library or to remodel and expand an existing one, there's plenty of hope.

> "To develop the drop of compassion in our own heart is the only effective spiritual response to hatred and violence."
> **THICH NHAT HANH**

Library campaigns must be set up a little differently from other bond measures, in part because it is more difficult to convince some of their importance. There are basically three steps involved in setting up a library bond campaign and a number of choices within each of those steps.

1. Establish a committee to examine needs, opportunities, and direction. Your first step is to get a select group of community members together to usher your project through. Although some may end up working on the campaign, that is not the purpose of this committee. Its members' job is to serve as liaisons with the community and the project. Assemble people who represent the many sides of your community and are well respected in their circle. You may select an individual from the immediate neighborhood, a businessperson, representatives of influential city boards or commissions (such as planning and historic), a builder, a librarian, a member of the Friends of the Library group, and a liaison

to the city council. It is also important to have city or county staff there for guidance and administrative support. It doesn't matter if all the committee members are not 100 percent on board for the project at the beginning; it's actually better if opinions are spread. Don't worry, people will come around or the project won't fly, anyway.

2. Once you have the committee in place, working with the local government, hopefully municipal, you will need to select an architectural team. The architectural team should be committed to community process and inclusivity. You want architects who are interested in what the community wants, not what they think is best for the community. Through community visioning, in which citizens are invited to attend a half-day workshop, a clear idea of what people want will emerge. From this the architects can draft architectural renderings and come up with a money figure to place before the voters (figures 10.1A and 10.1B).

> "We shape our buildings; thereafter our buildings shape us."
> — WINSTON CHURCHILL

3. Obviously, you want your governing body to place this on the ballot for you. If they don't, see the section above on the initiative process, and consider running for office next time someone in the governing body is up for reelection. Using the money figure generated by the architectural team and backed by your committee, the council should place the matter before the voters. You now have to convince the voters.

Here you might consider who gets to vote on this issue. In my area, those who live in the unincorporated areas—that is, outside city limits—tend to vote no on such things, so I prefer to leave them out of the district and limit the vote to the city. It's also much easier to turn out the vote if it's just city-wide. Don't forget, those who use the library the most live closest to it.

If you think you'll have trouble convincing the city council to place the measure on the ballot or you want additional public input and direction, consider having your Friends of the Library group print flyers with questionnaires and canvass the city. One part of the flyer can be dedicated to what the community proposed in the visioning process, and another part could invite community members to join the Friends of the Library. You would be surprised at how much money you can bring in with this small effort. Keep in mind, however, that this money and effort can never touch your campaign. It must be kept separate and distinct.

> "This nation cannot afford to maintain its military power and neglect its brainpower."
> — JOHN F. KENNEDY

FIGURE 10.1A Historical Photograph of Ashland's Carnegie Library

This photo was used on the front of the "Campaign for the Carnegie" brochure. (Photo courtesy of Terry Skibby, Ashland Historian)

FIGURE 10.1B Inside the "Campaign for the Carnegie" brochure, we used this image to show voters what they were buying. In issue-based campaigns, use a mix of the old with the new. Civic buildings reflect who we were as well as who we are. As Winston Churchill said: "We shape our buildings; thereafter they shape us."

If the cost estimate of your library project comes in on the high side and sticker shock among voters is a concern, here are some suggestions to get the price down:

1. Have local donors or organizations financially sponsor different rooms, fixtures, floors, rugs, and so forth. Determine how much the children's section, the young adult section, and reference area will cost, and ask civic groups to fund a room with a promise of having their name placed over the door. Go to likely organizations that might pick up the computer component.
2. Have either local organizations or the historical society consider funding and placing all the artwork for the library. Have the walls tell the story of your library or town through pictures.
3. If it's a historic structure, are there local, state, or federal historic renovation grants available for some portion of the remodeling?
4. Consider writing grants for some portion of the expansion, such as community meeting rooms or a kitchen.

Typically, there are two kinds of issue-based campaigns when it comes to libraries, schools, or government efforts: operating and maintenance, and facility upgrades (capital improvements).

If your initiative is for operation and maintenance, it will typically be supported by a property tax levy, which goes out for voter approval. When it comes to "selling" operations and maintenance to the community, the test placed before the voters is one of hope and opportunity. When asking voters to fund facility upgrades, the test is one of need. Are books being damaged by a leaky roof? Is overcrowding so bad that for every new book brought into the collection, an old one must exit the shelves to make room? How many people a day use the facility? You are basically making the case that improving the facility is good way to spend taxpayer money and that it will save money in the long run.

There are two ways that facility upgrades can be funded: One is through revenue bonds; the other is general obligation bonds (GO bonds). With revenue bonds, the government entity guarantees payment of the bond through a reliable revenue stream. For example, you want to upgrade your water treatment facility, so you sell bonds on the bond market and the repayment of those bonds is guaranteed through the revenue stream of water rates. The government may raise water rates to pay these loans back.

If you intend to fund your project through GO bonds, then the repayment of those bonds comes from the property tax. Depending upon your state and local guidelines, GO bonds require voter approval whereas revenue bonds do not. Also of note is that GO bonds typically get a better interest rate because property tax is seen as more stable than a revenue bond's income stream. Obviously, some publicly held interests—like schools and libraries— make no revenue so they must go to the voters for approval as a GO bond.

Investing in Education

The biggest obstacle that public school districts have in passing measures for operation and maintenance money or construction bonds is that schooling has evolved beyond the kind of education much of the electorate received. As a result, many voters see computers in the classroom as a luxury, extracurricular activities such as debate and business programs as unnecessary, and connection to the World Wide Web as a frill. I can't tell you how many times I have heard how we need to get back to the basics of reading, writing, and 'rithmetic. The reality our students face has to do with screen-based literacy, collaborative learning, and critical thinking.

> "All who have meditated on the art of governing mankind have been convinced that the fate of empires depends on the education of youth."
> **ARISTOTLE**

In order for voters to support the changes needed in our schools, we must educate the populace to understand that our schools are no longer training students for trades and specific jobs. Instead, students are trained, and need to be trained, to work with people, to be flexible in an ever-changing job market, and to think creatively and freely with access to data. Most of the jobs for today's elementary school students do not yet exist.

The bulk of America's schools were built in the early 1950s or earlier and either are falling apart or are inadequate for the electronic demands of the computer age. The task of rebuilding them or constructing new ones, on top of all the other costs of public education, is almost overwhelming to taxpayers, leaving them immobilized. In Ashland, however, we have had great luck in this sphere. Here are some tips that we found useful from our experience:

> "Education makes a people easy to lead, but difficult to drive; easy to govern but impossible to enslave."
> **BARON HENRY PETER BROUGHAM**

1. Again, set up a committee that represents a good cross-section of the community. The last time we proposed major improvements to our schools, we started out with about forty citizens, all invited, who then worked in focus groups to design a plan and figure out a dollar amount

that would work for our community. However you decide to do it, just remember to start broad and continue to widen involvement all the way to the campaign.

2. An architect will need to be selected. Obviously, you can't use a large group to select this individual or team, but this is a really important step and needs the right people. Too often, in an effort to save money and make public buildings salable at an election, we cut corners. We should construct civic buildings with materials that suggest permanence, are compatible with the community, and will be objects of civic pride. It costs no more to build a beautiful building than an ugly one. Look closely at what the architect has designed before. Do the buildings all look the same? Have past contractors had trouble working with the architect? Do a lot of research and homework here, or you'll be sorry.

> "We are continually faced with a series of great opportunities brilliantly disguised as insoluble problems."
> — JOHN W. GARDNER

3. If you think you'll have trouble getting this sort of thing to pass districtwide, ask the council to float it to city residents.

Packaging the Issue-Based Campaign

In an issue-based campaign, the message is the messenger. You want those in your community who have broad support and leadership standing to usher your project through. I have touched on issue-based campaigns throughout this handbook, but there are many specifics that bear emphasis.

1. Set up a "committee to support" of movers and shakers. This committee is separate from your campaign committee and comprises people whose name will appear on ads, in direct mail, and on the brochure.

2. Find the right chair (or co-chairs) for this committee: someone who embraces the many sides of your community. This is an opportunity to use an individual who will bring along the savables, not the saints.

3. Remember, with schools' and libraries' operating and maintenance, you are selling opportunity. You are not asking people to fund needs. This means you must educate the electorate on the changing world. The aforementioned idea of contrasting the high school transcripts of two straight-A students, only one of whose transcripts lists extracurricular activities, resonates with voters. It asks voters to ensure the success of their children and grandchildren in the future. There is also an element

of self-interest to consider. As an aging society, we must position ourselves to improve the education of those who will take care of us in our old age.

4. With facility upgrades, you are making the case for need. Failing roofs, time wasted mopping up after rain, exploding boilers, poorly heated classrooms, unsafe water, meeting federal requirements for in-stream dumping, books ruined by mildew or moisture from leaks—these concrete images can influence voters in ways that they can easily grasp.

5. Talk about reinstating libraries as information hubs. Our libraries have become as historic on the inside as on the outside, and the pathways and opportunities they can open to a community, young and old, are often overlooked, even by librarians.

6. In designing libraries, be sure to have areas that can be used after hours for community needs apart from the books. These areas might include meeting, reading, and study rooms as well as computer labs that members of the community can use to become more computer literate.

7. Conduct a precinct analysis that closely tracks who has voted for similar measures. If you are looking for funding for a library, look at census data to determine who has school-age children, and then target them. Remember, schools are moving more toward training our students to work in groups, and these groups need to gather somewhere to do projects and research. What better place than the public library?

8. Acknowledge the changing face of libraries and schools. For example, because of the Web and CD-ROMs, reference sections are actually getting smaller.

9. Use teachers, PTAs, and parents to volunteer for this effort.

10. Pay close attention to any fatal flaws. For example, in a nearby school district, a bond measure for schools failed because voters discovered that it included money to pave the parking lot. At no time did the committee tell the voters that federal track-out laws require paving if remodeling occurs.

11. Have a speakers' bureau of people who can speak to civic groups. This should not be teachers or librarians, who have a vested interest in the bond's passage.

12. Create a strong theme and message, and stick to them. Remember, a theme is strategic, not tactical. Aim at the souls that can be saved, and use the theme as a focus point for your campaign team and committee to support.

13. In campaigns, timing and context are everything. In general, the further away from a presidential election, the more conservative the vote. However, distance from a presidential election means a lower voter turnout and fewer competing measures which typically get placed in a presidential general election. A low voter turnout offers more weight to the campaign with a strong voter identification and GOTV effort and thus can translate into a win, which otherwise could not happen with a higher voter turnout. There's a case to be made for both. Find out if there will be other issue-based campaigns that will compete with yours. To have a ballot on which only one money issue is presented to the voter allows that single issue to get lots of light, air, dialogue, debate, and media attention. Plus, it gives those working for them a chance to turn out the support without another election poking a sleeping dog somewhere else.

In 2006, I was hired to help pass an $189,000,000 school facilities bond for the largest school district in southern Oregon. The city of Medford, where the bulk of the schools needing repairs and the majority of the voters in the district lived, had not passed a money measure in a midterm cycle in the twenty-five years I'd been working elections in our area.

By the time I was called in, the lawn signs had been ordered, the logo was done, the Web page was up, a poll had been conducted, and the committee had a number of white papers with different campaign messages that were distributed to parent-teacher organizations. Problematic was that their literature felt defensive and even a little scolding. On the up side, the committee was full of smart, hardworking, energetic community leaders, businesspeople, school board members, and teachers. Although they had little campaign experience, there was enormous talent in the well-balanced group.

In a facility bond, the voters must be made aware of the needs and convinced that money should be spent to meet these needs. It cannot be something that would be "nice" to have, like smaller classrooms or computer labs, but rather more fundamental. As it turned out, that was not so difficult to convey. In this school district, boiler rooms were exploding; wiring was old and dangerous; water pipes were breaking under playgrounds, causing unexpected geysers; some of the buildings—over one hundred years old—lacked proper insulation and had antiquated heating and cooling systems that were stealing education dollars from the classroom. Some classrooms were forced into closets because of space issues. At one elementary school, the well failed and water had to be brought in by truck, or the children were without bathroom facilities and drinking fountains. Although the city water was within feet of the school, there were no resources to hook into it. We weren't talking about bringing district buildings into the twenty-first century or frills of any sort; we needed to bring them into the nineteenth century.

The committee essentially had six weeks, in which time the message needed to get focused, decisions had to be made on advertising on TV and radio, spots cut, and a precinct analysis conducted to focus canvassing and GOTV efforts. The team also needed to be convinced to leave the lawn signs in the boxes; untargeted activities in such a difficult race could hurt more than help.

Harnessing the team and moving it in the right direction was surprisingly easy. Although money was short, we did put together a television spot. To give the ad intimacy, we used the high school chamber choir for background music and did the first ads with no voice-over; after a week or so, we brought in the same ad with a voice-over. Nearly every image used on television was provided by the committee, although some video was beefed up with stock purchases.[3]

Essentially, no mistakes were made. Everyone on the committee was disciplined, focused, and hard working. We put together a killer GOTV effort, in which forty volunteers per night called for eight nights straight. And although we went to bed behind by 150 votes, by morning the campaign prevailed with a landslide margin of 315 out of 31,000 votes cast. How cool is that?

Flies in the Ointment: The Double Majority, Independents, and the Super Majority

The Double Majority

In November 1996, Oregon passed an initiative that included, among other things, criteria requiring at least a 50 percent turnout of the registered voters for money measures affecting the property tax. This requirement that both a majority of voters must turn out and that, of this turnout, a majority must vote for the initiative, is call a *double-majority* vote. The author of this initiative felt that too many money measures were placed on the ballot during obscure special elections, when officials knew turnout would be low. The only exception to this rule was during even-year general elections, when the double majority would not apply.

Under the double majority, the challenge becomes one of turning out at least 50 percent of the vote, not just a majority of support. However, opponents quickly figured out that if they stayed home, their no-show status worked more in their favor than if they actually cast a no vote. Their challenge became one of not voting and urging their friends to stay home as well, so the tax measure would be defeated before votes were even counted. An added bonus was that people who had not been purged from the voter rolls after they moved or died got, suddenly, a de facto vote.

In March 1997, the city of Ashland needed to pass a flood restoration bond after the New Year's Day flood to raise the necessary local matching dollars for Federal Emergency Management Agency funds. Having never run a campaign under the double-majority rule, the GOTV campaign was set up as outlined in Chapter 11, except that phone banks were run for six nights instead of seven. Still, it was the longest and most ambitious GOTV campaign we had conducted in the city.

> "Human history becomes more and more a race between education and catastrophe."
> — H. G. WELLS

During the six nights of calling, we easily made it through 80 percent of the registered voters. At that time, retrieving phone numbers from the Internet was prohibitively slow, so huge clerical teams were assembled to look up phone numbers of registered voters. Throughout the calling, volunteers hit scores of nonvoting college students, people who had moved, local kids away at college, and the residences of about ten dead people still on the voter rolls. (One vote, one person . . . for eternity.) All in all, about 10 percent of the voter rolls were unavailable to vote. That meant we needed to turn out between 55 and 60 percent to meet the 50 percent requirement under the double-majority rule.

The final numbers showed the bond passing by 55 percent; however, the turnout ultimately fell short by 150 voters to make the necessary 50 percent requirement. In May, after working with the county to purge deadwood from the registration rolls, we returned to the voters with beefed-up phone banks and an additional night of calling. This GOTV formula has worked for six out of seven double-majority elections I've worked on since that time. The one in which it did not work added one more piece of information about double-majority elections: independents or nonaffiliated voters.

Independents

In the 2002 midterm primary, we failed to meet the 50 percent turnout threshold on a countywide college bond levy. This campaign had a great GOTV component, and for seven nights, eighty-five volunteers called registered voters. Approximately one-third of the 100,000 registered voters in the county were contacted and reminded to vote. With each night of calling, the Republicans and Democrats tracked turnout numbers similar to those of previous elections. However, independents did not. Independents turned out in such low numbers that it was impossible to make up their poor showing with party loyalists to get to the 50 percent mark.

In nonpresidential primary elections, when even party loyalists under-perform, independents stay home in huge numbers. They do so because they are often not allowed to participate in the primary elections of either party. If you are working an issue-based campaign under double-majority constraints, there is little you can do to meet the required 50 percent turnout in a midterm election unless the campaign covers a small area (city or school district) with an active electorate. Save your money. You will win the vote but lose the election because of turnout. Ironically, these same campaigns, coming back for a second shot in the midterm general election, often lose because of support. It is almost as though everyone who stayed home in the primary voted no in the general. A postmortem on the primary will not give you solid predictors for the general, because the primary support numbers simply do not carry over. To predict these elections, you must take another general midterm election for an issue-based campaign that lost in a primary.

> "The absence of alternatives clears the mind marvelously."
> **HENRY KISSINGER**

The upside of a double-majority election is that if 50 percent turn out, it almost always results in a win. Apparently, protax voters are simply less motivated to vote than antitax voters. The introduction of a double-majority requirement was great: It created a sense of urgency on the part of the protax voter as well as the volunteers needed to prod them, and it had the added benefit of scaring away competing measures. One small caveat is that double-majority elections work best in cities.

Although Oregon voters rescinded the double-majority requirement in 2008, many states labor under them. However, some states require that the majority turnout carry over to all those casting a vote within the specific issue. In this way, even though 50 percent may turn out to vote, if they do not all weigh in on the ballot issue requiring a 50 percent turnout—that is, if there is a large undervote—then the ballot issue fails.

Keep the Vote Within City Limits

Those living in the unincorporated areas can be the most conservative of American voters and often want little or nothing to do with what government has to offer. They have wells and septic drain fields, and many heat exclusively with wood or some other fuel shipped directly to their homes. Oh, they love to drive on paved roads, use libraries, have the sheriff and fire patrol appear promptly, and have their kids attend great public schools, but when it comes to being taxed, they're a loud and strong no vote. People living in cities, however, tend to want what government offers and are willing to tax themselves to get it. If you have an opportunity to run an election under the double-majority rule without the unincorporated vote, do it.

The resounding no vote of the unincorporated voter can keep city residents from getting what they want. There's a disparity in how we pay taxes: County residents pay only for county services; city residents pay for both. If you want programs for your school district or library system and can keep the vote within the city limits, your chances of passage increase significantly. Here are five reasons to keep the vote within city limits for programs benefiting both those in and out of town:

1. The assessed valuation (per acre) is greatest within the city, so even if you include county residents in the overall funding scheme, it won't have a huge impact on the cost per thousand dollars of the property tax.
2. People within city limits have a higher voter turnout than those in the county, so you're already ahead if you have to meet a double-majority rule.
3. It's easier to run an election and bring in votes within city limits because of the population density.
4. The percentage of people favoring taxes for anything is higher within city limits than in the county.
5. By holding your voting district to the city limits, you eliminate a greater proportion of nonsupporters because of the voting tendencies of those living in unincorporated areas.

Think Creatively

There are all kinds of things that have to go to a countywide vote or a vote larger than the city, but schools and libraries aren't among them. Be creative. If you're an elected official, you are in a unique position to help constituencies realize programs that they want in the community. When roadblocks are placed in your way, keeping your community from having great schools, open spaces, and libraries, don't take that road. Find another path.

For years, community leaders in our county had been advocating for upgrades to the county library system. Each library had unique challenges for meeting long-overdue improvements to the point that a systemwide upgrade would easily run tens of millions of dollars. The county commissioners were reluctant to put it to a vote prior to other county improvements they felt were more important. The county Friends of the Library group also seemed hesitant, as a countywide vote could ultimately be turned down by the voters, leaving them with dilapidated buildings that no longer could house the incoming books or the volume of patrons availing themselves of the system.

The Ashland Friends of the Library was dogging the county to move forward, but to no avail. Finally, they came to me and asked if the city could help. As the Ashland branch of the library was actually owned by the city, we were in a unique position to help. After the first meeting with the Ashland Friends of the Library, it was clear that a general mistrust existed between the Ashland group and the county. There were concerns that Ashland would not get from the county the quality of renovation that the local community wanted and that Ashland would be put on the end of the list after areas that were walking in lockstep with the county.

I proposed that the Ashland renovation move ahead of the countywide upgrades, but the county wanted no part of this proposal. It believed that Ashland voters would not support county system upgrades on top of the Ashland branch renovation and expansion. The county also felt that without a strong Ashland vote, the countywide tax measure would have more difficulty surviving an election. Those in the Ashland contingent were concerned about a countywide measure passing, period, with or without Ashland, and were further concerned about meeting a countywide double-majority requirement, which would be very difficult. Meanwhile, county election officials were not moving.

To get all the parties what they wanted, we moved Ashland's city library upgrades to be voted on ahead of the county vote. How-

> "Experience is not what happens to a person, it is what a person does with what happens."
> **ALDOUS HUXLEY**

ever, should the bond measure pass in the city, we agreed to hold off on issuing bonds to pay for the project until the county had an opportunity at the polls. This approach had many benefits. First, it got us off our knees begging the county to do something; a citywide initiative required only the Ashland city council to vote to place the tax measure before the voters—an easy prospect. Second, it would guarantee Ashland voters that a specific amount would be spent on our branch and that the renovation outcome would reflect what citizens had agreed upon in the community visioning process. Finally, for those who did not want to pay twice, holding off on issuance of bonds for the project negated those concerns. To underscore this, we agreed to communicate with the voters that a vote for the county system upgrades would result in lowering the debt load for the Ashland improvements with our taxpayers. The latter is important because the first vote held in the city would mean that only city residents would pay for upgrades, while folding our improvements into the county bond would mean that those surrounding the city would also share in the tax burden. In this way, we locked in how much money would be spent in Ashland and exactly what the upgrades would look like. The countywide vote simply became reaffirming what Ashland wanted but for less money.

In the spring, the city bond measure passed easily and with an ample double-majority turnout. In the fall, when the county put the whole system before the voters, it was approved and the double-majority requirements were also met. Eighty-five percent of those casting a ballot in Ashland voted for the countywide upgrades, more than twenty points higher than typically vote for county library measures. Given that the second vote actually lowered Ashland's tax on the library upgrade, one would have to wonder what the 15 percent who voted no were thinking.

The worst thing we could have done would be to place an Ashland library upgrade before the voters at the same time as a countywide library upgrade, where the two would become competing measures. Although these two sides had plenty of history and suspicion of each other, we were ultimately able to craft an agreement that met all concerns. And given that the city would hold off on floating the voter-approved bonds only until the next election, it pushed the county commissioners into action.

The Super Majority

The super-majority rule, applied to tax measures, requires that either two-thirds or 60 percent of those voting approve the measure before it may take effect. Here your objective is dramatically different from when your constraint is a double majority. The best defense you have to pass anything with a super majority is to place your money measure on an election with the lowest voter turnout possible and no competing measures. Then you must identify your supporters and have a top-notch GOTV effort to get them to the polls or to mail their absentee ballots.

A few years back, in Marin County, California, supporters of a school facility plan used an interesting tactic to pass their bond measure under the super-majority rule. The supporters of the measure determined that those sixty-five and older were both a no vote and likely voters. To move this age group over to the yes column, the bond measure excluded them from having to pay, but did not exclude them from the vote. The campaign then worked hard to turn out the sixty-five-and-over age group, who had nothing to lose by voting yes. The facility plan passed. Given that many seniors are two generations away from having children in public education and have probably already paid enough, this seems like a happy compromise.

The State Initiative and Referendum Process

There are three types of initiatives:

1. *Direct initiative:* The completed petition places a proposed law or amendment directly on the ballot, bypassing the legislative process.
2. *Indirect initiative:* The completed petition is submitted to the legislature, which then may enact the proposed measure or one substantially similar to it. If the legislature fails to act within a specified time, the proposal is placed on the ballot.
3. *Advisory initiative:* The outcome provides the legislature with a nonbinding indication of public opinion.

There are four kinds of referenda:

1. *Mandatory referendum:* Requires the legislature to refer all proposed amendments to the constitution as well as measures regarding tax levies, bond issues, and movement of state capitals or county seats.
2. *Optional referendum:* The legislature may refer to the citizens any measure that it has passed. This is often called a referral.
3. *Petition referendum:* Measures passed by the legislature go into effect after a specified time unless an emergency clause is attached. During that interval, citizens may circulate a petition requiring that the statute be referred to the people either at a special election or at the next general election. If enough signatures are collected, the law is not implemented, pending the outcome of the election. The signature requirement is usually lower and the time allowed to gather signatures less than for a straight initiative.

> "Here may the youth of this extensive country forever look up without disappointment, not only to the monuments and memorials of the dead, but to the examples of the living."
> **JOHN ADAMS,** of the nation's new Capitol

4. *Advisory referendum:* The legislature may refer a proposed statute to the voters for a nonbinding reflection of public opinion.

Initiative and Referendum Procedures

1. *Preparing the petition:* Preparing the initiative petition and organizing the collection of signatures is the responsibility of the chief petitioner(s). The text of the proposed measure is drafted by the chief petitioner(s), with legal assistance if desired, and filed with the secretary of state for state initiatives and the local election office for local initiatives.

2. *Filing the petition:* Any prospective petition must include the names, addresses, and signatures of the chief petitioner(s), a statement of sponsorship signed by a certain number of registered voters and verified by county election officials, a form stating whether the circulators of the petition will receive payment, and the complete text of the proposed measure.

3. *Obtaining the ballot title:* State statutes usually provide strict timelines for moving a filed petition through the process to obtain a ballot title. For statewide initiatives, all petitions are filed with the secretary of state, and two additional copies are sent to the attorney general, who prepares a draft of the ballot title.

4. *Preparing the cover and signature sheets:* The chief petitioner(s) must submit a printed copy of the cover and signature sheets for approval prior to circulation. The cover sheet must include names and addresses of the chief petitioner(s), the proposal itself, the ballot title, and instructions to circulators and signers. The cover sheet must be printed on the reverse of the signature sheet and contain instructions to signature gatherers. Notice of paid circulators must be included. Signature sheets must never be separated from the cover sheet and the measure's text.

5. *Circulating the petition:* As soon as approval is obtained from the election officer, the ballot is certified and may be circulated for signatures. Usually, you can withdraw the petition at any time. Any registered voter may sign an initiative or a referendum petition for any measure being circulated in a district where the registered voter resides. All signers on a single sheet must be registered voters residing in the same county.

6. *Filing the petition for signature verification:* There's a deadline for signature verification statewide (usually four months) and locally (usually less time).

7. *Filing campaign and expenditure information:* Within a specified period after filing petition signatures for verification, the chief petitioner(s) must file a statement of contributions received and expended by the petitioner(s) or on their behalf.

Before a political committee receives or expends any funds on a measure or proposition that has reached the ballot, the committee treasurer must file a statement of organization with the secretary of state, and subsequent contributions and expenditures must be reported. Sometimes this must be done even if a petition is withdrawn.

TABLE 10.1 States with Citizens' Initiative Authority for Constitutional Amendments and Statutes

This table highlights the requirements for the initiative process in states allowing direct democracy.

State & Date Adopted	Constitution Signature Basis	Statutes Signature Basis	Amend or Repeal by Legislature	Restrictions
Alaska 1959	Not allowed	10% votes in general election from 2/3 election districts	After two years can repeal or amend	No revenue measures, appropriations, acts affecting judiciary, local or special legislation. No laws affecting peace, health, or safety
Arizona 1910	15% of vote for governor	10% of vote for governor	Yes	One subject only, legislative branch only
Arkansas 1909	10% of eligible voters	8% of eligible voters	2/3 vote each house	Limited to legislative measures
California 1911	8% of vote for governor	5% of vote for governor	With voter approval	One subject only
Colorado 1910	5% of votes for secretary of state	5% of votes for secretary of state	Statutes, yes Constitution, no	One subject only
Florida 1972	8% presidential election; 8% from _ congressional district	Not allowed	Amend, yes Repeal, no	One subject only
Idaho 1912	Not allowed	10% of vote for governor	Yes	No provisions
Illinois 1970	8% of vote for governor	Not allowed	No provisions	Limited to legislative branch; structural & procedural subjects only
Maine 1908	Not allowed	10% of vote for governor	Yes	Any expenditure in excess of appropriations void 45 days after legislature convenes
Massachusetts 1918	3% of vote for governor, no more than 25% from one county	3% of vote for governor, no more than 25% from one county	Yes	Not for religion & judiciary, local, special legislation or specific appropriations
Michigan 1908	10% of vote for governor	8% of vote for governor	Yes, by 3/4 each house	Applicable to statues that legislature may enact
Mississippi 1992	Qualified elector 12% of vote for governor, 1/5 from each congressional district	Not allowed	Yes, with voters' approval	No modification of bill of rights, modification of public employees' retirement, or labor-related items

Missouri 1906	8% of vote for governor 8% each of 2/3 congressional district	5% of vote for governor 5% each from 2/3 congressional district	Yes	One subject; not for appropriations without new revenue; not if prohibited by constitution
Montana 1904	10% of vote for governor 10% from 2/5 state leg. districts	5% of vote for governor 5% from 1/3 state leg. districts	Yes	One subject; not for appropriations; not for local and special laws.
Nebraska 1912	10% eligible voters, 5% each from 2/5 counties	7% of vote for governor 5% each from 2/5 counties	Yes	Limited to matters that can be enacted by legislature; no more often than every three years
North Dakota 1914	4% resident population	2% resident population	After 7 years except by 2/3 vote each house	Not for emergency measures, appropriation for support & maintenance of state departments and institutions
Ohio 1912	10% of vote for governor 1.5% each from 1/2 counties	3% of vote for governor 1.5% each from 1/2 counties	Yes	One subject; not for property taxes; legislation only
Oklahoma 1907	15% of votes cast for office with highest no. of votes	8% of votes cast for office with highest no. of votes	Yes	Single subject; legislative matters only
Oregon 1906	8% of vote for governor	6% of vote for governor	Amend and repeal, yes	Single subject; legislative measures only
South Dakota 1898	10% of vote for governor	5% of vote for governor	Yes	Except laws as necessary for immediate preservation of public peace, health, or safety support of state government and existing public instruction
Utah 1900	Not allowed	10% of vote for governor 10% each from 1/2 counties	Amend, yes	Legislative matters only
Washington 1912	Not allowed	8% of vote for governor	After 2 years, 2/3 each house	Legislative matters only
Wyoming 1968	Not allowed		Amend, yes Repeal, after 2 years	No earmarking, make or repeal appropriation create courts, define jurisdiction of courts or court rules, local or spec. legislation defeated initiative within 5 years, or legislation prohibited by constitution

(Source: Oregon League of Women Voters, 1996, updated 2008; Initiative & Referendum Institute at University Southern California, www.IandRinstitute.org)

11

Getting Out the Vote (GOTV)

IN THIS CHAPTER
- The Essentials
- Identifying Your Voters
- Last-Minute Efforts to Persuade Voters
- Poll Watching
- Phoning
- The Absentee Ballot and Early Vote
- Vote by Mail
- Organizing the GOTV Phone Banks

Make no mistake; everything you have done up to this point is about the get-out-the-vote (GOTV) effort. Everything. You've canvassed, mailed, advertised, phoned, raised money, and delivered your message again and again and again. Why? To move voters and activate your base for support on Election Day. But voters get busy: Kids get sick, cars break down, food boils over, an old friend calls. . . . In short, life gets in the way, and somehow, 8:00 p.m. rolls around and best intentions to vote are out the window. Now, after months of campaigning, your job, your one and only job, is to remind your supporters, remove obstacles for them, and motivate them to do their civic duty.

> "The final days are the longest."
> **BILL MEULEMANS**

While canvassing is about activating the people who you think will vote favorably, a GOTV effort is about activating voters who you know will support your cause. With your base, you know its voting potential because of registration, neighborhood, and historical voting patterns. With everyone else, you know because your campaign has personally contacted these voters and has been told. As explained earlier in the book, the identification of how the swing and undecided voter will vote is called voter ID, and getting your support out on Election Day is called GOTV. Whether voter ID is conducted while canvassing or during phone bank calling, the campaign must keep track of voter intentions (supportive, somewhat supportive, undecided, somewhat opposed, opposed) and secure a current phone number for election night.

The Essentials

Activating Your Base

Regardless of whether your campaign conducts voter ID, you must activate your base to increase voter turnout among the saints. Although your base vote, that is, party loyalists, has not received the same level of attention as potential swing voters have received, it has not been neglected, either. Your base has received some direct mail, has been given lawn signs, and has seen and heard your ads. In some cases, it has even been canvassed. When it comes to the GOTV, this group is extraordinarily important. Your precinct analysis has told you who among your base will vote with very little effort from the campaign and who needs to be reminded before Election Day.

> "Persistence in the face of adversity is what wins an election."
>
> **PATRICIA SCHIFFERLE,**
> former assistant to the Speaker, California; principal, Pacific Advocates

Those who need a little prodding can actually be quite different, depending upon their context. With these voters there are generally two groups. The first are those who live in areas of equal or slight registration advantage (up to ten points) but are disengaged. The second group is also disengaged, but these voters are embedded in neighborhoods where their party (and that of the candidate) is greatly outnumbered.

For our purposes, you will have three strategies for your base:

1. Your hard-core voters, those who traditionally have high turnout rates, will need little effort from the campaign. Although it is a good idea to canvass them with a drop piece on Election Day, if time, money, volunteers, and logistics are a problem, this activity could be dropped. It will be important, however, to track the returns from these precincts, because you are really counting on them. If it looks as though their turnout will be down, the campaign should be ready to activate them with GOTV phone calls.

2. For your lazy yet loyal voters (high support and low to medium turnout), your campaign has canvassed, mailed, called, and canvassed

them again. Now you need to stay on them like a fly on compost. If you're in a state that doesn't use vote by mail, your GOTV team will closely watch the polls and absentee lists to make sure these voters do their duty. If they don't, you will need to call them. These are the voters you must continue to activate in the days leading up to the election; remind them that voting early helps your volunteer efforts, and emphasize that their vote and their vote alone will make the difference in a win. For the precincts that are loaded with lazy voters, organize canvass teams to go in and rattle their cage on Election Day. In vote-by-mail elections, send canvassers in to pick up ballots and return them to the drop boxes for the voter.

3. The third group is a little trickier. Voters registered in your party but who live behind enemy lines will need very specific attention, as they are often the most difficult to activate. These voters should be treated like swing voters: They must get direct mail from the campaign, and they should be canvassed by the candidate. It is critical that these voters be part of your voter ID effort, as they are the least predictable of your entire party. Your swing analysis will tell you what percentage will always vote party. Voter ID will tell you, by name, whom you can count upon. I recently worked on a campaign for a Democrat for whom nearly all the support was in areas of heavy Republican registration. During the GOTV, all party voters were called, but more than a third of them said, "Why are you calling me? I'm a registered Republican and always vote Republican." Since we were working from county registration lists that clearly indicated that their registration was Democratic, it was a little disorienting. The good thing about this group is that if you identify them as supporting your opponent and then do not contact them again, they tend to be nonvoters.

Swing Voters

The next group of voters your campaign will identify are those who live in precincts with high numbers of swing voters. Recall that the precinct analysis has told you exactly which precincts they live in and how many of the voters you need to win. Because the campaign must have a clear reading of who will be supporting you, who is undecided, and who will not move, use the candidate, volunteers registered in the opposing party (validators), and your best canvassers to knock doors in these areas. Your campaign must keep track of the voters who say they will support you, and it must send persuasion mail to the undecideds. After the persuasion piece has been mailed, the campaign should follow up with a phone call to determine whether the voter's support can be counted on. If the answer is yes, two questions are asked: (1) Will you take a lawn sign? and (2) Can we use your name on an endorsement ad?

You want the swing voter to go public. These two simple and inexpensive "public" contributions to the campaign will guarantee a vote. Depending on the reason, if the voter says no to both of these questions, you should assume that on the issue of support, you have been told what you want to hear rather than given a guarantee.

The Pleasure of Your Company

It's always a good idea to be aware of other ballot issues that may affect your turnout or that of the opposition. If no other campaign is conducting a strong GOTV that will help you, do not let anything keep you from running a comprehensive one for your campaign. In a close election, a GOTV is the difference between winning and losing.

If you're involved in an election in which a controversial measure is also on the ballot, there may be a high voter turnout that significantly affects your efforts. For example, a few years back I was working for a progressive Democrat who was on the ballot with two ballot measures intended to limit the rights of a targeted minority. Our campaign had a well-organized GOTV, and we had conducted voter ID from September through November. The committee working in opposition to the two ballot measures also had a great GOTV effort, which helped ours even more. The state Democratic caucus was running tracking polls, and we knew we were neck and neck with our opponent. We also knew from polling that the two ballot measures were going down statewide. What we had not anticipated was the huge turnout of the sinners' precincts to vote yes on these ballot measures, and as long as they were there, they voted against our candidate as well.

Unfortunately, we realized too late that we spent far too much time identifying and getting out the vote where the proponents of the two ballot measures were also working. Had we left this portion of the electorate to the other campaign, more volunteer time and energy could have been freed up for voter ID and GOTV of our persuadables.

Disorganized and uncoordinated GOTV efforts can enrage hard-core voters. In Ashland, largely because of the statewide passage of the double-majority requirement in 1996, we have had a GOTV machine that rivals any in the state. Voters are conditioned to vote early if they do not want to be bothered with activation calls during the week leading up to the election. However, in the 2000 general election, other well-meaning campaigns, specifically those working for candidates running for state and federal office, duplicated the efforts of hundreds of volunteers working on our campaign. Making matters worse, a local teacher, anxious to involve students in the electoral process, conducted yet another GOTV effort. As a result, voters were called three or more times in a single evening. It was ugly.

This kind of voter harassment must be minimized if at all possible. To avoid it, conduct cooperative GOTV efforts with other campaigns, or at the very least, call and see what other campaigns intend to do. Call all campaigns that may inadvertently duplicate your efforts, and carve up the county so that there is no overlap in calling areas. Contact high schools, and let leadership and government teachers know how, when, and where their students can help.

Identifying Your Voters

Whether identifying voters by phone or by canvassing, you will need walking lists. Walking lists are used because your precinct analysis indicated communities, neighborhoods, and precincts where the base, swing, and opposition support lives; in other words, where attention should be focused, as a result of social context. These lists can be generated from the registered-voters disk you bought from the county, from a voter contact service, or from an organization that is endorsing your efforts.

Since you do not want to waste time on households where registered voters do not participate, prepare your lists so that only the two out of four voters—those who voted in two (or more) of the past four elections—or better are listed. These lists will need to be organized by precinct and then by street and street number.

The lists should be prepared so that streets are separated by page. Across the top of each page have columns labeled "Supporting," "Leaning support," "Undecided," "Leaning no support," and "Not supporting," or use a 1-to-5 number rating system that corresponds to the categories from "Supporting" to "Not supporting." Once you have the walking lists, you will ID voters by canvassing, phoning, or both.

Canvassing for Voter ID

If you intend to ID voters while canvassing, you need to organize the walking lists to match your canvassing maps. This is a lot more work than you might imagine. Do not let just anyone help you with this task! If you do, you might spend days undoing and redoing. Once you match a walking list to a canvassing map, place the list inside the canvassing envelope. If you're using a voter activation service, linking registered voters with maps is part of the package and will save a great deal of time.

If you are canvassing to ID voters, you will need twice the number of canvassers normally required, or more. At the door, each of your canvassers must ascertain whether the house will be in favor, opposed, undecided, or leaning in some way. If voters are leaning toward support or undecided, your campaign should be ready to follow up with literature or a phone call to bring them into your camp. If no one is home, you must have clean-up teams going out to reknock or do the voter ID at phone banks to determine how people intend to vote.

> "There is no knowledge that is not power."
> — RALPH WALDO EMERSON

The idea here is to identify individual voters who support your candidate or cause and to compile a list of these supporters. In this way, your campaign can track them on Election Day and remind them to vote if it looks as if they might be a no-show.

Voter ID by Phone

Although it puts a heavy burden on the phone bank team, I tend to prefer voter ID by phone, for a number of reasons:

1. For some canvassed areas, only 40 percent of the households have anyone at home during the canvass. That means that the remaining homes have to be recanvassed or called, anyway.
2. It is generally easier to get phone volunteers than canvass volunteers, and canvassing for voter ID eats up people.
3. Although canvassers can read body language and facial expressions to determine voter intent, voters are often more forthcoming on the phone about their support, especially if they support your candidate or issue-based campaign. It's sometimes hard for voters to tell candidates or volunteers face-to-face that they will be supporting the opposition.
4. Voter ID by canvass will sometimes net individuals who are not registered to vote.
5. The closer a campaign is to Election Day, the less inclined a voter is to reveal intent. Therefore, a campaign must get to voters in a narrow period, when the voters have enough information to make a decision but are still willing to reveal intent. More voters can be reached by phone in this important window than by canvassing.

Whether your voter ID is by phone or canvass, your goal should be to target 10 to 15 percent of the total number of votes you need to win. As the area and voting population increases, your voter ID efforts must also expand. Always start with the precincts that will give you the most return for the effort. For voter ID, that means going into swing voter precincts to look for swing voters and calling your embedded party registration living behind enemy lines.

If you are conducting voter ID by phone, you can use walking lists. Be sure to include phone numbers if you intend to use the same lists for both types of voter ID. Should you decide to identify all voters by phone and use canvassing only for activation and persuasion, you might as well prepare your calling lists in a format that will work best at the phone banks.

> "Winners never quit and quitters never win."
> **VINCE LOMBARDI,** NFL football coach

Pull precincts where you want to ID voters, and sort by last name alphabetically and by phone number. If you sort only alphabetically, you risk repeating calls to households where people have different last names. If you sort by name and phone number, you improve your chances of catching and organizing duplicates in a way to prevent repeat calls.

To identify your supporters, systematically call every registered voter in the identified precincts. Remember, you are first calling areas that have a high swing voter tendency, so you will be calling as many voters as you can reach. Often, county lists do not have all phone numbers listed, so plan ahead and get these from a voter activation network, the party, or a supporting political action committee. If none of these options are available to you, you may need to set up clerical sessions to look up phone numbers before your phone banks begin. Don't forget to check Web directory services. Phone banking to identify supporters goes much quicker than canvassing.

In your first round of phone calls, your campaign has a couple of choices: You can conduct blind calls or persuasion calls. In a blind call, volunteers ask questions about the candidates or issues but do not reveal for whom they are working. In a persuasion call, the caller immediately lets the voter know which organization is behind the calling effort. I prefer the persuasion call simply because it saves time by eliminating one step. If you start with a blind call and the voter is undecided or has a question about one of the candidates, your volunteer cannot field the question or attempt to persuade.

> "To do great and important tasks, two things are necessary: a plan and not quite enough time."
> **ANONYMOUS**

Your campaign must be ready to follow that call with direct mail or another call from the campaign to try to persuade the voter.

If the first call is a persuasion call and your volunteer finds an undecided voter, he or she can immediately provide information that may help move the voter to support your candidate or cause. A campaign can also use an endorsement group, such as the National Rifle Association, a clean-air coalition, teachers' associations, nurses' groups, and so forth, to draw voters in a persuasion call. You can also use people from within a particular precinct to call their neighbors: "Hello, is this George? Hi, I'm Shirley Smith, I live just down the street from you. . . . " Indirect supporters can be very persuasive.

Last-Minute Efforts to Persuade Voters

1. Mail or walk a door hanger to your high-priority precincts reminding them to vote.
2. To swing precincts, mail or walk a persuasion piece that features an individual or a group that normally would not support your cause or candidate (validators) to encourage voters to split their ballots.
3. Mail pieces designed to give the voters useful information such as polling places, how to mark a ballot for your write-in candidate, whom to call if a ballot needs to be picked up, or whom to call for a ride to the polls. These are very effective and often rise above other direct mail clogging mailboxes in the last week.
4. While mail is easier, showing that your campaign is rich with volunteers can be far more effective, especially given the huge amounts of political mail seen in the last days of a campaign. Any big canvassing effort is bound to draw positive attention.
5. The night before Election Day, move lawn signs from one location to another. People get desensitized to lawn signs, but if a new one goes up in a neighborhood or, better yet, ten new ones appear, voters will notice.
6. Attach helium-filled balloons to lawn signs located on busy streets.
7. Hand-paint specialty signs for a specific neighborhood, and place them the day before the election. "Elect Mayor Daniels for a central bike path." "For more parks, elect Daniels." You want a personalized message for just that neighborhood that will present the look of an upwelling of new support. (I have used the reverse side of old lawn sign stock for this.)
8. Have the local paper place a 3-by-5-inch Post-it note on the front page of the paper reminding people to vote for your candidate or cause. Use a yellow Post-it, red ink, and a style and size of font that looks like handwriting yet is very easy to read. Our local paper has done this from time to time for local businesses—usually for oil changes. The first time

I saw one, I could not believe how it popped out at me as I unfolded the paper in the morning. So we did one for a GOTV on a double-majority issue-based campaign in the 2003 primary. Although the Post-it notes must be printed somewhere else, our local paper did the insert for $142 per thousand. It was very effective.

9. Some local papers that place the daily in a plastic bag will sell advertising space on the bags. Like the Post-it note inside the folded paper, this "message on a bag" goes to people who subscribe to and presumably read the newspaper—some of the more likely voters. Check with the newspaper to see if it can use different messages for different cities or areas within your voting district.

Avoid Untargeted Activities

A GOTV effort is most effective in elections where there is voter apathy and low voter turnout is expected. Through the GOTV, you bring up the turnout of one segment of the population while leaving the support for the opposing camp alone. Still, every candidate I have worked for has wanted to stand at the entrance of the county fair, set up a table on the plaza in the heart of the community, wave signs at commuters, or hand out flyers in front of a grocery store. Do not confuse motion with progress. Unless you live in Hawaii, where there is a time-honored tradition for candidates to wave to drivers from the edge of the highway on Election Day, avoid untargeted activities. With the exception of areas with overwhelming support, untargeted activities can actually work against your GOTV effort. Remember, GOTV is about getting *your* voters to the polls, not all voters.

> "When they call the roll in the Senate, the Senators do not know whether to answer 'Present' or 'Not guilty.'"
> **THEODORE ROOSEVELT**

One might also argue that there are far better ways to use the candidate's time during the GOTV than standing on a corner during rush hour, waving a lawn sign. For example, it's a great time to have him or her on the phone for the GOTV or to call and thank supporters for their donations and volunteers for their time.

The GOTV: A Raft in a Hurricane

There comes a point in a campaign where you and your team have done everything you could possibly do. You have run a tight, well-organized campaign and raised enough money to get a clear, resonating message across to the voters. You may have been outspent by an opposition that had better television ads, brochures, press, and direct mail. But as the election draws near and you prepare for the GOTV, remember that both your campaign and your opponent's are headed into the same storm. If your efforts have placed you within striking distance, the GOTV is a great equalizer, often making the difference between a win and a loss. In the end, the odds are best for the team that is better prepared.

> "Let me tell you the secret that has led me to my goal. My strength lies solely in my tenacity."
> — LOUIS PASTEUR

Although there are many who would disagree, I have found that by the final three weeks of a campaign, most voters have made up their minds. While campaigns send copious amounts of direct mail, especially toward the end, if you have not made your case three weeks prior to Election Day, no amount of money or direct mail is going to change that. Don't misunderstand: There will still be voters struggling with the decision of whom to vote for, which is one reason a comparative piece is best left until last. But they are few and far between. By the end of a campaign, the effort is really about who can rally the most troops out of the bunker, regardless of how many happen to be in there. Effective last-minute direct-mail pieces are more about relocking your base and rallying your troops to get out and vote than about moving voters from one bunker to another. Although there may be last-minute revelations that will swing campaigns twenty points, those are the exception, not the rule.

After the recall of Governor Gray Davis in California, voters were surveyed and asked (among other things) what impact the last-minute allegations of sexual harassment charges had on their support of Arnold Schwarzenegger. The surveys "showed that more than two-thirds of the voters had made up their minds more than a month before the election. As a result, the intense publicity in the last week of the campaign about accusations of Mr. Schwarzenegger's unwanted sexual advances appeared to have had little effect on how women—and others—voted."[1]

In the last month before the 2000 presidential election, polling numbers showed Al Gore and George Bush bouncing into and out of the lead. At the time, this was attributed to voter whim. However, after analyzing fifty-two polls conducted by seven polling firms, Donald Green and Alan Gerber found that the "preferences toward the candidates changed little" and that "the failure of certain polls to predict the closeness of the actual vote reflects sampling bias, not the electorate's capricious preferences."[2]

After the 2002 general election in Oregon, one political consultant attributed Democratic losses in house seats with close registration numbers to insufficient direct mail and a general unwillingness among Democrats to send hit pieces. But on closer examination of the eleven close house races, only four of the winning races sent more direct-mail pieces, and only five of the winning races sent more negative pieces than the opposition did.[3]

After the 2008 general election, Rasmussen Reports polled voters and found that 70 percent of those polled said they made up their minds a month before Election Day, with another 14 percent deciding within the month leading up to Election Day. Of the 5 percent still undecided in the week prior to the vote, they were evenly divided among McCain and Obama.[4]

While each race has its unique signature requiring specific action, the overriding features of losing campaigns are that they (1) did not communicate a clear message and (2) did not give due attention to the GOTV among last-minute campaign demands.

From day one, all communication with the voter should be about getting your base to care enough to vote and moving swing voters and undecided voters to your camp. Keeping track of who moves (voter ID) and getting your base, plus those who have moved, to the polls (GOTV) is what wins elections, not copious direct mail.

As the final week before the election approaches, everything about the campaign should shift so that attention can be directed to the GOTV effort. That does not mean media, direct mail, or solicitation stop, but everyone on the team must be focused on filling the phone banks. Like fund-raising, GOTV should have its own team leader and timeline. To run a successful GOTV, a campaign must accomplish a few tasks:

1. Have 10 to 15 percent of the registered voters identified, including, hopefully, most of those outside the party base in identified precincts of swing voters.
2. Have enough volunteers and phone lines to contact both identified voters and base party voters living in precincts with high support and low and medium turnout.
3. Have a well-organized data system, and have someone other than either the GOTV coordinator or the campaign manager supply the campaign with calling lists generated from registration rolls. In vote-by-mail states, this person would also be responsible for getting daily updates from the clerk's office of inactive voters (those who have not yet returned a ballot) for the week leading up to the election. Typically, county clerk offices keep track of ballots that have been received, or active voters. To get a list of inactive voters, those whose ballots have been received are removed from voter registration lists and the difference is

the inactive voter. It is the same process for absentee—the county keeps track of the absentee ballot return and your campaign is keeping track of that list.

Once you have identified your supporters, your campaign must track them to see if they've voted. Tracking for vote-by-mail elections, early voting, or absentees can be done electronically. However, if you are tracking voters at the polls, you have a couple of choices: One is poll watching, and the other is working your list by phone and asking voters if they have cast a ballot.

Poll Watching

Poll watching is a labor-intensive campaign activity that requires plenty of preparation. It cannot be put together at the last minute, so prepare ahead of time. Find someone who will oversee this activity, and support that person with your volunteer base. Each poll watcher will need lists of people who have been identified as supporters sorted alphabetically and by polling station. Ideally, you would use a list of all members of the candidate's party, with supporters highlighted, although a list that includes only your identified supporters is fine.

> "I wanted to look nice if we won, and if we lost this would be nice to be buried in."
>
> **BOB BORKOWSKI**, assistant coach, on why he showed up for a game in a black, pinstriped suit

Things to Do for a Successful Poll Watching Effort

1. Before the election, ask your county clerk or election official what is required of poll watchers. Are there forms that must be filled out and returned? Does the clerk require training conducted by his or her staff? In my area, before the introduction of vote by mail, it was legal for poll watchers to review the poll book, as long as they didn't interfere with the work of the election board. In some areas, however, poll watchers can only listen for names as they are being called out.

> "It's not so important who starts the game, but who finishes it."
>
> **JOHN WOODEN**, former basketball coach at UCLA

2. Provide poll watchers with an alphabetical list, a clipboard, pencils with good erasers, and a cell phone. It is also a nice touch to send them out with a folding chair or stool. We used to provide each poll watcher with more than one list so that when volunteers come to retrieve the list to

start calling no-shows, time wasn't burned transferring names, but with the advent of cell phones, names can be called in.

3. Place your poll watchers in high-priority precincts (that is, where high numbers of your supporters have been identified), and direct them to note which of your identified supporters have voted throughout the day.

4. As the name of the voter is called out, the poll watcher will check the list of supporters to see whether that individual is among those who have been positively identified.

5. Relay this information back to phone banks, and approximately four hours before the polls close, supporters who have not yet voted get a call from a volunteer urging them to get down to the polls.

6. Regardless of what you think about the outcome of the election, tell the phone bank volunteers to impress upon the voters how important it is that they get to the polls, that you predict a very close election, and that every vote will count. The supporter who hasn't yet voted must feel from the caller a sense of urgency to get to the polls and vote.

7. Offer rides to get supporters to and from the polls. With the poll watcher, the phone bank, and the transportation effort, you will have a lot of people involved, and you may find that the best hope for pulling it off is to combine efforts with other campaigns.

Precinct Captains

Each precinct where poll watching is to take place must have a precinct captain who is responsible for the precinct team. Each captain has three specific duties:

1. Before Election Day, your identified voters must be highlighted or somehow noted on the lists as supporters. It is best to do this as IDs come in rather than waiting until the end. One thing that has helped speed up data input is that some counties and voter activation networks include bar codes for the voters. The campaign can take advantage of this by renting a bar code scanner, which usually runs around $125 for the entire campaign. As IDs roll in from phone banks and canvassing, your data-input team can simply scan bar codes

> "The important thing in life is not the triumph but the struggle."
> **PIERRE DE COUBERTIN**

to link the information into your database of voters. Note: If the voters' phone numbers did not come with your lists and cannot be found, run a line through their names as though they had already voted.

If your campaign has not identified supporters before Election Day and the intent of your poll watching is to call all supporters in your highest-priority precincts, then be sure to put a line through the names of those who have voted absentee.

2. The captain is responsible for recruiting four poll watchers and one standby. These five people need to be certified, trained, and supervised. Poll watchers should meet with their team captain the weekend before the election. Signed certificates for each poll watcher should be provided to the precinct captains at that time. Your county clerk or county elections office will supply you with all the information and forms you may need.

3. The captain must be present at his or her precinct when it opens at 8:00 a.m. and supervise the precinct on and off throughout the day.

Poll Watcher Responsibilities

1. Arrive a few minutes early at the polling place.
2. Give your signed certificate to the election judge, who is a member of the polling board.
3. Do not engage in conversation with the election board. You may, of course, answer questions, but do not discuss other topics with the board.
4. As voters arrive and give their names to the board, listen for the name and then cross it out on your list as they are voting.
5. Two hours before polls close, the final poll watcher should start calling in names to the phone banks.

The Importance of Poll Watchers

In close elections, the work of the poll watchers and the phone banks that follow is often what supplies the margin of votes needed for a win on Election Day. However, because of the amount of organization required and the labor-intensive demands of this activity, few campaigns conduct poll watching anymore. If at all possible, do it. Voter ID, poll watching, and GOTV make the difference between winning and losing in a close race.

> "Anything worth doing is worth doing frantically."
> —— **JANE TOWER**

Regulation of Persons at the Polls

As in all aspects of a campaign, it is important to know the law, but in poll watching, it is imperative. The polling place has special regulations that cover everything from how close individuals may stand to the polls if they are not voting and are not certified poll watchers to what topics may be discussed by those present. The campaign manager should contact the county clerk well beforehand and get the regulatory information to the precinct captains in written form.

Authorized poll watchers are allowed in the polling place and must sign a specific section of the front cover of the poll book. Only as many poll watchers are allowed as will not interfere with the work of the election board.

Poll watchers must have written authorization from one of the following:

1. For the purpose of challenging electors at the polling place, either from the county clerk or a political party
2. For the purpose of observing the receiving and counting of votes, from a candidate

Poll watchers *may*

- Take notes
- Have access to poll books, so long as it does not interfere with the work of the board
- Challenge persons offering to vote at the poll
- Challenge entries in the poll book
- Wear campaign buttons
- Distribute sample ballots as long as there is no campaigning involved (We did this in Ohio in 2008. As people stood in long lines, they were given sample ballots to familiarize themselves for what lay ahead.)

> "The only thing that hasn't changed is our ability to think differently."
> **ALBERT EINSTEIN**

Poll watchers *may not*

- Campaign in any way
- Circulate any cards, handbills, questionnaires, or petitions
- Fail to follow the instructions of the election board
- Take poll books off tables

ELECTION DAY PHONE SCRIPT

Hello, this is _____ .

I am a volunteer worker for *(name of the campaign).*

I am calling to remind you that the polls will remain open until 8 P.M., and also to encourage you to vote. This will be a very close election, and we really need your support for *(name of person or ballot measure)* to win.

Your polling place is located at _____ .

Will you need transportation to the polls?

> ## If transportation is needed, they can call the following numbers:
>
> _____
>
> _____
>
> _____
>
> _____

FIGURE 11.1 Election Day Phone Script

All members of the poll-watching effort should familiarize themselves with the specific election law violations.

Phoning

Let's suppose that you do not have enough people to watch the polling places all day. Don't worry. I recently worked on a campaign in which we came up with an approach that was very effective and less labor intensive than poll watching.

For this process, you will need a good precinct analysis. Remember, your precinct analysis will tell you where your support is and show you where people have voted for candidates or causes similar to yours in the past. Your precinct analysis will also tell you where people live who will never vote for your cause or candidate. If it is clear that a precinct has traditionally voted against campaigns such as the one you are working on, don't canvass it, don't call people in that precinct, don't activate them. Forget them for the GOTV effort. Instead, look for precincts that have been split: those that have narrowly supported or narrowly defeated past campaigns similar to yours. These are the precincts you should call to ID voters. Then on Election Day, call only the identified yes voters, even though they may have already voted (figure 11.1).

> "Democracy is a contact sport."
> **RAY MCNALLY**, McNally Temple Associates, Sacramento

As for those remaining precincts that have overwhelmingly supported past campaigns similar to yours, it is not so necessary to ID the voters. You know they will tend to vote your way.

On Election Day, while your people are going down the list of supporters in the marginal precincts and calling the identified yes votes, they can call all of the voters in the high-priority precincts for an issue-based campaign, and for a candidate race, all who are registered in your party. If your campaign has time before Election Day, you may want to ID the voters in the high-priority precincts as well, but this is not as important. Look at the phone calling on the day of the election as your one last canvass in high-priority precincts. If your precinct

> "This 'telephone' has too many shortcomings to be seriously considered as a means of communication. The device is inherently of no value to us."
> **WESTERN UNION**, internal memo, 1876

analysis is accurate, you will turn out strong support that might have stayed home otherwise. *Remember, here you are not changing minds, just the turnout.*

When a caller reaches someone who has already voted, that person's name should be crossed off the list so that he or she will not be called again. For those who have not voted, it is up to you to decide whether you want to call them again later. If the election is close, you may want to urge them *one more time* to get down to the polls.

One important note: *Don't duplicate calling lists for phone banks.* Each phone bank caller or phone station needs a separate and unique calling list.

The Absentee Ballot and Early Vote

Voting absentee used to be a service to the voter who was temporarily out of the area or unable to get to the polls. However, with thirty-one states now allowing for early voting and twenty-nine of those allowing no-excuse absentee voting, more and more voters are electing to do just that.

For instance in Ohio, 11 percent voted absentee in 2004, versus 17 percent in 2006. By 2008, the percentage of those voting by mail in Ohio nearly doubled again to 30 percent. In California, 42 percent of the 13.7 million 2008 general election voters voted by mail. In Washington State, all but two counties (King and Pierce) conduct all vote-by-mail elections (88 percent of the voters), and for the last fifteen years, Oregon has conducted all elections by mail.

Although early voting and absentee voting have become the vote of convenience, there are other factors behind the growing lines for early voting—not the least of which is that a voter, turned away at the polls, still has time to fix whatever problem precipitated the dismissal. In this way, voters are insuring themselves against the debacles that unfolded in battleground states in 2000, when so many voters were turned away at the polls for nefarious reasons.

> "If the only tool you have is a hammer, you tend to see every problem as a nail."
> — ABRAHAM MASLOW

Further, as ballots become longer and more complex, the busy and conscientious voter is choosing to vote absentee so as to have time to vote on the entire ballot in the comfort of his or her home. In a recent California election, it took some voters more than an hour to complete their twelve-card ballot.

With long, complicated ballots, you run the risk of voter fatigue. Voter fatigue occurs when voters actually lose interest in voting as they spend more and more time working through their ballot. Once fatigued, they simply turn in their ballot with everything below left blank. This is called *ballot roll-off.* While roll-off is technically an undervote, it happens to everyone and everything at the bottom of the ballot, whereas undervoting on a mail-in or an absentee ballot happens randomly throughout the ballot. Because local elections are at the end of ballots, down-ballot candidates and issues are often overlooked. If your candidate or measure is way down on a ballot, encouraging voters to register and vote absentee at home may help minimize the undervote for those races.

There are a number of reasons it is to your advantage to register as many of your supporters as possible to vote absentee or early:

1. Often campaigns don't heat up and get nasty until the final three weeks. As voters are becoming more and more disillusioned with negative campaigning, their response is to stay home on Election Day rather than voting for or against the candidate slinging mud. If a candidate or party has a huge percentage of the turnout locked in before things get nasty, it's at a decided advantage.

2. If you know who will vote absentee, then your campaign can concentrate on these voters well before Election Day, closer to when they actually will vote.
3. Nasty weather can affect voter turnout on Election Day.

In the 1998 midterm election, nearly half of the registered voters in Oregon requested absentee ballots. Of those who requested them, 73 percent returned them. Of those who did not request absentee ballots, only 41 percent turned out to vote. The absentee ballot represented over 58 percent of the total voter turnout.

Although in the 1998 general election Oregon voters approved vote by mail for all elections, they could already register as permanent absentee voters in 1997. The lists of absentee voters were available from the county clerk for a small charge, and about 40 percent of the names also had phone numbers listed. Having lists of those who will make up nearly 60 percent of the overall voter turnout is very helpful and means that with a little effort, any campaign can reach a large group of likely votes, ID whom they intend to support in the election, send persuasion mail to the undecideds, and make sure that those supporting your efforts return their ballots by Election Day.

"Vote early and vote often."

AL CAPONE

In many states the option to register absentee is open to anyone for the asking, up to the day before the election. Those who request absentee ballots within the three weeks before an election are the most likely to actually vote. Your county elections office may be able to provide updated lists of those requesting absentee ballots as the election draws near. When someone makes the request, that voter should be immediately contacted by the campaign. The local election office may also keep data as these absentee ballots are returned and for a price will provide a campaign with updated activity lists.

Some states have *early vote*. With early vote, the registered voter may go to a designated polling place between certain hours and vote just as though it were Election Day. Depending on the state, it can take place anywhere from four to forty days before an election. As with absentee voting, early vote gives a campaign an opportunity to lock in votes before the election. However, it does require that a campaign peak twice: once for the early vote and absentees and once for Election Day. Direct mail, advertising, canvassing, and everything else must happen earlier for these voters.

Voters love the convenience of absentee and early vote, and those who use these options tend to be among the most likely of the likely voters. Whether your state or county has early vote or absentee voting, the following steps can help you reach as many of these voters as possible:

1. Check past elections to determine the number who requested or took advantage of this option.
2. See whether a list of those who requested absentee ballots is available to your campaign through the county clerk or election office.
3. Inquire about updated lists of those who actually vote absentee or early as the election draws near. That way, you will not be continually contacting those who have already returned their ballots, burning up campaign money and time.
4. If the lists of absentee voters do not include phone numbers, get them.
5. If you are in a state that offers early vote, hound your supporters to vote early.

"Poll Watching" for Absentee Ballot Requests

Absentee ballots present some unique challenges to the grassroots campaign. Here is an inexpensive way to deal with absentee ballots if lists are not available from the county elections official.

Assign the task of the absentee voters to a team. One person must be willing to go to the county clerk's office daily to find out who has requested absentee ballots. This person keeps a running list. The requests must be checked regularly because voters who request absentee ballots will often fill it out and return it very quickly. Once you know which voters requested an absentee ballot, you must try to persuade them to vote for your candidate or cause. Forget the precinct analysis for absentee voters. For this group, you are not hoping that those who don't support you will not be voting. You know that nearly all of them will vote. To persuade these voters, you have a number of choices:

> "You may be disappointed if you fail, but you are doomed if you don't try."
> — BEVERLY SILLS

1. Use direct mail to persuade—this is most effective if it is a comparison piece rather than an advocacy piece or an attack piece, according to Kathleen Hall Jamieson, in *Everything You Think You Know About Politics . . . and Why You're Wrong.*[5]
2. Send volunteers or the candidate out to canvass these voters at home.
3. Have the candidate, a friend, or a prominent citizen call.

4. Send a personalized letter from the candidate or from a well-known, well-respected local leader of the same party affiliation as the voter.
5. Use some combination of all these techniques.

Vote by Mail

Currently, twenty-eight states are either using or considering using vote-by-mail elections. Vote by mail (VBM) was originally introduced to Oregonians in 1981, and by 1987, most counties in Oregon conducted VBM elections for local elections. The cost savings to taxpayers and the increased voter turnout are the two most tangible benefits of vote by mail. According to the Oregon secretary of state's office, the cost savings of the 2000 VBM primary election over the 1998 primary precinct election was nearly $600,000: "In general, the cost of conducting all-mail elections is one-third to one-half of the amount required for polling place elections."[6]

A Brief History

The genesis of voting by mail dates back to the 1700s, when landowners, whose homes were vulnerable to attack from Native Americans, were allowed to vote absentee. In 1857, only Oregon made it possible for men away from home to vote. However, it was not until the Civil War, when nineteen of the twenty-five Union states and seven of the eleven Confederate states enacted legislation to provide soldiers an opportunity to vote absentee. After the Civil War, nearly all states discontinued military absentee voting.

During World War I, when three million Americans were inducted, there was renewed pressure to provide military personnel the opportunity to vote absentee. By 1917, most of the forty-eight states provided absentee voting for the military, and twenty-four states had enacted some form of absentee voting laws.

At the close of World War II, work-related reasons were accepted by over twenty states for absentee balloting. Today, all

> "Trust in Allah, but tie your camel."
> **ARAB PROVERB**

states permit absentee voting, with eight states offering voters permanent absentee-ballot status out of the twenty-nine that allow no-excuse absentee balloting.

With vote by mail (VBM), all registered voters receive ballots through the mail. Although VBM began as a Western-state phenomenon, it is now conducted in some form in fifteen states, from New Jersey to Hawaii. In 1977, California was the first to hold a VBM election.

All states, except for Oregon, provide hybrid voting, or poll voting in conjunction with absentee balloting. Oregon has no poll voting.

Oregon

In 1981, the Oregon Legislature approved a test of VBM for local elections. By 1987, VBM was made permanent for local and special elections, and a majority of counties used it. In 1993 and 1995, the first and second statewide special elections were conducted using VBM.

In the summer of 1995, the Republican-controlled legislature passed a bill expanding VBM to primary and general elections. Under pressure from both the Democratic legislator minority, who were concerned that VBM could reduce the power of the state Democratic machine, and Clinton operatives, who were concerned about the president's reelection bid in Oregon, Governor John Kitzhaber vetoed the bill, declaring that more study of the issue was the prudent course. This veto came despite calls from Democratic operatives who tracked local VBM elections and determined it was party-neutral, saved taxpayer dollars, and was easier for campaign organizations than hybrid voting. Both Republican and Democratic leaders believed that VBM would perform like absentee voting, which historically favored candidates who were more conservative.

In 1995, after the resignation of Senator Bob Packwood, Oregon's Democratic secretary of state, Phil Keisling, exercised the option to run the December primary and January general special elections using VBM. After Democrat Ron Wyden defeated Republican Gordon Smith, both caucuses in the legislature reconsidered their previous positions. In the 1997 legislative session, Democrats, realizing their error, supported legislation to pass VBM.

> "You know, back in 2000 a Republican friend of mine warned me that if I voted for Al Gore and he won, the stock market would tank, we'd lose millions of jobs, and our military would be totally overstretched. You know what? I did vote for Al Gore, he did win, and I'll be damned if all those things didn't come true."
> — **JAMES CARVILLE**

Although it passed the House, the Republican majority in the Senate allowed the bill to die. The option for statewide VBM never revisited the desk of Governor Kitzhaber, who said that he would have signed the bill into law, given the second chance. When legislation allowing voters to register for permanent absentee status passed, 41 percent took advantage of this option.

In the 1998 primary election, with a record-low turnout, absentee voters accounted for nearly two-thirds of all ballots cast. This election represented the first in the nation where absentee voters, with a 53 percent turnout, cast more ballots than poll voters, who turned out at 22 percent.

In June 1998, Secretary Keisling spearheaded an initiative drive to circumvent the Oregon Legislature and, using no paid signature gatherers—only volunteers—successfully garnered the number of signatures required to qualify for the November ballot. Oregon voters approved the initiative to expand VBM to primary and general elections by nearly 70 percent.

Implications of VBM

VBM is credited with increasing voter turnout and saving taxpayer dollars. Indeed, the hybrid voting process (both poll voting and absentee balloting) used in every state but Oregon requires election officials to run two elections: one for absentee voters and one for poll voters.

Curtis Gans, director of the Committee for the Study of the American Electorate, contends that no-excuse absentee and early voting actually hurts voter turnout. To make his case, he uses eligible voters rather than registered voters. He attributes lower turnout to diffused mobilization of voters that extends over many weeks rather than one single day.[7]

In 2000, Michael Hanmer and Michael Traugott conducted a survey of voters in Oregon before and after VBM. They found only modest changes in turnout and composition of the electorate after VBM.[8] Rather than mobilizing new voters, VBM ultimately affected those who generally voted but who might have difficulty participating in any given election. This finding is corroborated by a 2003 study by Pricilla Southwell from University of Oregon, which found that a majority of respondents (two-thirds) indicated no change in their turnout. Of the one-third of the respondents who reported voting more often since the introduction of VBM, the increase came primarily from women, the disabled, homemakers, and 26- to 38-year-olds.[9]

As with other studies, Hanmer and Traugott and Southwell indicated VBM is party-neutral. Further, the Hanmer and Traugott study showed an absence of ballot roll-off with VBM.

Arguments that VBM hurts the poor and minorities who cannot afford a stamp were dispelled by another Southwell survey in 1996 after the special statewide VBM election to replace Senator Packwood. Her study revealed that VBM increased participation of minorities, single parents, younger, those who had moved within two years, students, and registered independent. This same group was also less likely to be retired and more likely to be paid by the hour than traditional voters.[10]

Fraud

Much of the hesitancy to implement full-scale VBM in other states centers on existing voter fraud with absentee balloting. However, election officials consistently cite the difficulty in supervising hybrid elections, in which the volume of absentee-ballot requests and processing competes for time with managing poll sites and poll workers.

> "Those who cast the votes decide nothing. Those who count the votes decide everything."
> — JOSEF STALIN

Project Vote, a national nonprofit organization focused on mobilizing marginalized and underrepresented voters, associates four forms of ballot fraud with absentee ballots: signature forging or using fictitious names, coercion, vote buying, and siphoning absentee ballots. Despite these problems, Oregon election officials who managed elections both before and after VBM underscore that managing only one type of election, vote by mail, allows closer scrutiny of the integrity of the ballot. Comparison of optically scanned signatures on the ballot and voter-registration form has all but eliminated voter fraud.

After two decades of VBM, Oregon has had only four cases of fraud resulting in prosecution. One, discussed earlier in this book, occurred when a husband signed his wife's ballot because she was in the hospital.

Real voter fraud, the kind that can have tangible results, is far more effective when placed in the hands of those who know what they're doing; a husband signing a ballot for his hospitalized wife is not in this category. The 2000 general election in Florida, where impediments seemed to have been contrived to prevent voter participation, represents the kind of election that needs attention more than vote by mail.

Black voters in Florida and around the country turned out in record numbers on November 7. Since then, many have complained that Florida election officials removed large numbers of minorities from state voting rolls, wrongly classifying them as convicted felons—and accused Florida officials of using police to intimidate voters in some areas. [Jesse] Jackson cited the reports of students from historically black colleges in Florida, who have said they went to the polls carrying voter identification cards and were told they were not on the voter rolls.

The Florida Supreme Court had ordered a hand recount of all ballots where mechanical counts had registered no vote for president. Many of those "undervotes" came from majority-black precincts, heavily Democratic, where aging punch-card ballots failed to record votes for president in mechanical counts.[11]

One area of concern remains with Oregon's VBM: the unregulated collection of ballots by volunteers or party operatives, who then deliver them to election departments for voters. Coincidentally, this was the same concern of Civil War soldiers. They relinquished their ballots to commanding officers, who became responsible for getting the ballots to the soldiers' hometown election authorities.

Higher turnout and dramatic savings to the taxpayer are strong endorsements for VBM. What's more, this way of voting increases voter turnout among all segments of society. These segments include those who have been underrepresented for various reasons: minorities, single parents, students, people who are paid by the hour, nonaffiliated voters, young voters, and people who have moved within the last two years.[12]

With little evidence of fraud, opponents are now claiming that VBM represents one more step in the progression of isolation in American society. Although this view is certainly understandable, and isolation is indeed cause for concern, a better solution might be to ban drive-up windows (as we did in Ashland for the same reason) than to sanction barriers that, once removed, facilitate voter participation.

Campaigning with VBM

Campaign managers, party operatives, candidates, and strategists outside Oregon insist that VBM increases the cost of running a campaign because ballots are mailed to voters about eighteen days prior to the election. During this period, ballots are returned by voters in two surges, the first week, followed by a lull and then another surge just prior to Election Day. It is argued that both surges must be met with mail, radio, television, and other campaign activities.

The hybrid election, however, requires two separate campaign structures as well: one to communicate with and track absentee voters and another for poll voters. Whether a state allows no-fault absentee voting or not, absentee voters remain the most likely of likely voters; they tend to be Republican, women, and over sixty-five years old. Further, they represent a far greater percentage of the voter turnout. No campaign can afford to ignore them. Communicating with precinct voters requires media, mail, and phoning—paid or volunteer—up to and including Election Day. Tracking identified supporters who vote at the polls is also a massive organizational enterprise for a campaign.

Although VBM has shown only modest improvement in voter participation, there are other advantages. The level of voter enthusiasm, the dramatically reduced administrative costs over hybrid elections, and a more manageable campaign structure suggest that this simple, low-tech approach should be considered throughout the nation.

The difference between a mail-in and a hybrid campaign isn't money, but rather timing. In a conventional election, canvassing continues up until Election Day, and nearly all of your ads appear in the three weeks before the election. The all-mail-in election must be front-end loaded, so the campaign peaks when the ballots are mailed, not the day they are due back.

This means that all canvassing should be completed by the weekend after the Friday that ballots are mailed. Ads must start to run at least a week before the ballots leave the county clerk, and television should peak the first week voters receive their ballot. Even though many voters will return their ballots immediately, your campaign should maintain a presence in the media until the day before the ballots are due, or until a critical mass of ballots have been returned. In VBM, a campaign can actually taper off advertising as Election Day draws closer.

> "It's far easier to start something than to finish it."
> — AMELIA EARHART

GOTV and Voter ID

A GOTV effort for a VBM election is remarkably easy and painless. With VBM, counties keep track of who has returned ballots as they're received, and for a nominal charge, the county will print or e-mail a list of those who have voted (activity list) or those who haven't voted (inactivity list). For a GOTV effort, you want to know who has not voted, so if you're only able to get the activity list, then delete those names from the full registration lists that you got from the county earlier in the month, after the registration deadline passed.

Although you want to conduct voter ID throughout the campaign, as the election draws near, your team will have to buckle down and make sure that all supporters within targeted precincts are identified. Here is what you do:

1. Print a list of registered voters in your high-priority and swing precincts (you determined these when you did your precinct analysis) with phone numbers.

2. Find phone bank locations, and set up phone banks to begin calling the voters in your favorable precincts to ID them for support of your candidate or ballot measure.
3. If the voter is undecided and needs persuasion, this is the time to do it.
4. Follow up all undecided voters with direct mail and phone calls from friends, colleagues, co-workers, the candidate, or prominent citizens. Stay on the undecided voters until you know where they stand.
5. ID the voters who should be supportive of your candidate or cause in lower-priority precincts. Do this by looking at party affiliation, age, income, and education. Be sure to keep track of whether their support is yes, no, or maybe.
6. Follow up maybes in the lower-priority precincts, and leave the no voters alone everywhere.

It's in the Mail

Once ballots are mailed, all campaign efforts shift to the GOTV. Hopefully, the GOTV coordinator and the field director or volunteer coordinator has a pretty full roster for each night of the phone banks. If not, it is now the campaign committee's responsibility to help get people to the phones. All of my committee members work at least one evening of phone banks, and I train them to supervise the activity. Although some believe that phone banks should begin as soon as ballots are mailed to voters, I like to give early voters a chance to get their ballot in without a phone call. Although calling during the first week after ballots have been mailed will give the campaign an initial spike of ballots received, any benefits realized by phoning early are equalized by Election Day.

> "The people who win elections are those with the guts to keep on running when nobody else gives them a prayer."
> **CHRISTOPHER MATTHEWS,**
> *San Francisco Examiner*

Calling the first week after ballots are mailed, however, puts a campaign at risk of running out of volunteers and steam when they're needed most—in the last week. This can be disastrous in a double-majority election, in which 50 percent of all registered voters must return a ballot before the ballots are counted. In terms of a GOTV effort, the last week is the most important, so fill those volunteer seats first.

> "The wise don't expect to find life worth living; they make it that way."
> **ANONYMOUS**

If you are not working with a voter activation network that updates ballot returns, you can work directly with the clerk's office: Ten days before the ballots are due to the clerk, order an inactivity list (alphabetically by precinct). Again, if your county does not separate those who have and have not voted, and no one on your team can remove those who have voted from the lists, line up a clerical team to highlight who has not yet voted; this will make calling a little easier for your phone bank team.

Set up another clerical team to look for voters who have said they will be supporting your candidate or cause, but who have not yet returned their ballot. Then set up phone banks to call and activate these supporters.

At this point, your GOTV effort is two-pronged; not only will you call voters who have been identified as supporting you, but you will also make the calls to turn out your base. To do this, print out lists of the voters in precincts whose base is supporting but not reliable on turnout. These voters will be called first. Precincts with a voting history of high support and high turnout are called next, to give them a chance to get their ballot in, thereby saving your campaign time. Finally, come back in for a second pass on the lazy base voters.

The other option is to simply call all voters in targeted precincts according to their voting history. For example, your voter activation network tells you who is a four (voted four times out of four), a three, and a two. So start with the twos, and work your way back, calling the threes and fours second, and then make another pass on the twos. Calling in this order provides more time for the high performer to get his or her ballot in before the campaign rattles the cage. And this means more time for your team to harass the poor performer.

Each caller can contact fifty voters in a ninety-minute shift. Because you know how many callers you have for each night and how many inactive voters are in each precinct, it is not necessary to print all inactive voters in all precincts—you will need just enough of them to keep your banks busy each night. The next night, you can print out lists for new precincts with that day's active voters already removed. Remember, call only base and identified supporters.

> "Spend the time to make the foundation right or you will pay in time and money all the way to the roof."
>
> —— **TONY NUNES**, builder

In an Oregon House race I worked on in 2000, forty volunteers called two thousand registered voters each night for seven nights straight. Still, those fourteen thousand phone calls did not reflect even half of the thirty-five thousand registered voters, and many voters were called two and three times. While a GOTV effort in a state without VBM will focus primarily on support that has been identified, VBM allows your campaign to begin its efforts in precincts where your party historically underperforms and to continue all the way to those precincts of high support and high turnout before going back in to work the high-support and low-to-medium-turnout precincts. By working through precincts, campaign work is really cut to an efficient level.

For your base voters who are located in low-support and low-turnout precincts, if you have not identified them before the GOTV, you can sometimes conduct GOTV and voter ID in the same phone call. Be aware, however, that voters are very reluctant to indicate their voting proclivities once their ballot is in their hand.

Nevertheless, for those wanting to try to ID voters on the GOTV call here is what you do: First, you must determine whether the voter on the other end of the phone is supportive. I do this by simply asking. If the voter is not supporting, get off the phone. Don't worry about activating no votes. For those called who say they are supporting your cause but, for whatever reason, still have their ballots, offer to pick up their ballots. In this case, ask the voter to tape the ballot to the screen door or tuck it into the doorjamb, so a volunteer can quickly pick it up without knocking. I've found that most people don't want you to pick up their ballot. Nearly three-quarters of the people we

"Out of the strain of the Doing / Into the peace of the Done."
JULIA LOUISE WOODRUFF

call who are supportive and still have their ballots instead say that they'll drive it immediately to a drop-off box—usually located at the nearest public library. Because I can never be sure that a voter's good intentions will be enough, I push the voter just a bit more and say, "Hey, we have someone driving right by your house to get another ballot, let us save you the trip." If they say, "No, I'll do it," then I let it go.

For the final two nights, Monday until 9:00 p.m. and election night until 6:00 p.m., have phone banks going full tilt, and have runners lined up. More runners are needed for Tuesday than for Monday night. Runners are people whose sole job is to go out and pick up ballots as phone banks turn them up. It's best to use two runners per car so that the driver doesn't have to park. The driver stops, the passenger hops out and retrieves the ballot from the screen door or the doorjamb, and off they go. Use runners efficiently: Divide the voting district into logical areas so that runners don't wind up spending an hour to pick up four ballots. As soon as a phone volunteer has a ballot to pick up, put the address and name on a card or piece of paper, and route them. Continue to do this until a driver returns and there are enough ballots to pick up in another area. It is best for runners to have cell phones so that ballot locations can be called to the car as they come in.

On election night, with the polls closing at 8:00, pack it in at 6:00 or 7:00, depending on how many ballots need to be picked up. At this time, all callers become runners. The phones shut down, and everyone goes out to pick up the last of the ballots.

Organizing the GOTV Phone Banks

Although phone-bank systems are described in Chapter 4, some repetition might be helpful here. The importance of having fully staffed phone banks on a GOTV effort cannot be overemphasized. In the earlier example, in which forty volunteers for a 2000 Oregon House race called two thousand registered voters each night for seven straight nights, if each shift were short just one caller each night, that would amount to two hundred calls per night, or fourteen hundred calls over the course of the GOTV effort. To give you an idea of the impact this can have on the outcome of a race, consider that of seven close House races in Oregon's 2002 general election, all were won or lost by 2,700 *combined*, out of 280,000 voters. Even if you think you will win big, organize a strong GOTV effort.

> "One thing the world needs is popular government at popular prices."
> — GEORGE BARKER

Remember, it is not enough to win; you want to shove the win down the opposition's throat. While George W. Bush proved you do not need a voter mandate to do what you want to do once you are in office, that is not the case for down-ballot candidates. For these candidates, a big win means power after the oath and the potential to scare away opponents in the next election. For issue-based campaigns, a decisive win will tend to dissuade opposition from referring the measure back to the voters.

Make a spreadsheet listing all volunteers for the GOTV phone bank. The first column contains their names, and the next, their phone numbers. Then have a smaller column with "CB?" (for "called back?") as the column header; later, a check mark is placed in this column on the printout after a volunteer has been called back and confirmed that he or she will be there for the next day's phone bank. Next are seven columns with dates, one for each night of phone banking. Each phone bank will have its own spreadsheet, listing only the volunteers who will be calling from that location.

Below the dates, I list the starting times of the phone banks. For example, the first bank usually runs from 6:00 to 7:30 p.m., and the second from 7:30 to 9:00 p.m. (figure 11.2).

The names on the spreadsheet are kept in alphabetical order. If your lists are short, this detail is less important, but in the example of the phone bank with two shifts of ten for seven nights, the campaign will have 140 volunteers working the GOTV in one location alone. As volunteers let the campaign know if

NAME	NAME (LAST)	Place lead names here for each night PHONE #	CB?	LEAD NAME Wed. 11/1		Thur. 11/2		Fri. 11/3		Sat. 11/4		Sun. 11/5		Mon. 11/6	
				6:00	7:30	6:00	7:30	6:00	7:30	6:00	7:30	6:00	7:30	6:00	7:30
				6:00	7:30	6:00	7:30	6:00	7:30	6:00	7:30	6:00	7:30	6:00	7:30
				6:00	7:30	6:00	7:30	6:00	7:30	6:00	7:30	6:00	7:30	6:00	7:30

FIGURE 11.2 Example of a GOTV Phone Bank Spreadsheet

they can do the early or late shift, the time slot is circled in red so that the lead or supervisor can easily see it. It is a good idea to attach a blank sheet for people who volunteer to call after the GOTV begins. Each night of calling must have a lead person or a supervisor. The lead's duties are as follows:

1. Arrive a few minutes early and open the phone banks.
2. Have paper cups for water and red pens for marking precinct lists.
3. Bring enough phone bank instructions so that each caller in each shift will have a set.
4. Bring targeted precinct lists with inactive voters—this is provided by the campaign.
5. Have the master copy of all volunteers participating in the GOTV. (I have a satchel with cups, pens, and the GOTV master calling list inside. I secure the precinct calling lists before the phone banks start and either deliver the lists to the leads or have the leads pick them up, at which time the satchel is passed off as well. In outlying phone banks, I have the GOTV coordinator organize everything except the voter lists to call. These are e-mailed to the coordinator early enough for him or her to print them before the phone banks start.)
6. Welcome the volunteers and give instructions (provided by the campaign).
7. Have callers begin, and then circulate among the callers and answer questions.
8. Fill water cups and distribute one to each volunteer, refilling if necessary.
9. Once questions subside, call *all* volunteers for the next evening's phone banks, using the master lists for the GOTV phone bank and checking off the call-back column for each confirmation. Afterward, look over the call-back column; any last-minute cancellations must be communicated to the campaign as soon as possible so the spot can be filled.
10. The next shift arrives fifteen minutes early for training. Begin anew, providing instructions to the next team.
11. At exactly 7:30, the next crew pulls the first shift off the phones and takes over at their desk, continuing to call down the sheets provided for the first shift.

12. Again, circulate, answer questions, pick up old water cups and distribute new ones, and be available for as long as necessary.
13. Once questions subside, get on the phone and make GOTV calls until 9:00 p.m., when the banks close.
14. Clean up all remnants of the work crews: cups, pens, lists, and so on. The pens and the master call list are returned to the satchel along with any unused cups.
15. Lock up and get the satchel to the next lead or back to campaign headquarters.

A couple of years back, I ran a GOTV effort for an issue-based campaign in which the system was set up as outlined above. On the third night of phone banks, my lead called and told me that three callers had not shown up for the first shift, and four for the second. As this had never happened before, I contacted the lead from the previous night's phone banks and found that she had become busy with personal business and had never made the calls to remind the next evening's volunteers as instructed. GOTV calling—especially on a double-majority election—is so tight that we had to set up a separate phone bank to make up for the seven callers we lost on that one evening. It is important always to call your volunteers and remind them of the location and time; if a lead does not get to the job, he or she must let the campaign know so that someone else can do it in time to ensure a full contingent at the next day's phone banks.

One other GOTV war story: In 2000, I was running a campaign for a candidate for the Oregon House. We had phone banks set up at a real estate office we had used for many campaigns. But just before the GOTV, we were informed that the campaign needed to find another location. It turned out that the local Board of Realtors had endorsed our opponent, and we were out. It's always a good idea to have a backup location just in case.

Finally . . . When word gets out that you're running an organized, well-staffed GOTV, every campaign you can imagine will call requesting other names be added to the script. Do not do this. An effective GOTV mentions no more than two names. Remember: GOTV calls are about *activation*, not persuasion. Besides, anyone who thinks a voter can be moved from the dark side by simply mentioning a name on a GOTV call is clueless. It would be better to say no names than to slog through a long list of candidates.

12

The Campaign Flowchart

IN THIS CHAPTER
- Setting Up a Preliminary Flowchart
- Finalizing the Flowchart
- The Campaign Calendar

You are almost all the way through this handbook and can now decide, given your time, resources, and volunteer base, what campaign activities you are capable of doing well. It is now time to put together your campaign plan or the campaign flowchart, which actually marks the beginning of your campaign. For our purposes, a campaign flowchart is identical to a campaign plan except that the flowchart is a linear model that is placed on a wall rather than in a three-ring binder. If you are working on a state campaign where political action committees and party members are unfamiliar with a campaign flowchart and instead want a campaign plan, you can convert your completed flowchart to a campaign plan by simply writing down each of the activities and accompanying date, beginning with the election and working backward to the first day of your campaign.

> "Simply reacting to the present demand or scrambling because of tensions is the opposite of thoughtful planning. Planning emphasizes conscious, disciplined choice."
>
> **VAUGHN KELLER**

To make a campaign flowchart, start by listing the tasks you need to complete before the election. These might include canvassing, brochure development, media, phone banks, fund-raising, and lawn signs. Your choices, of course, are dictated by your resources and the type of campaign you are running. Obviously, you will not place anything in the flow chart that you have no intention of doing. For instance, you may not be able to afford direct mail or you may have decided you do not want to do lawn signs.

Once you have the list of campaign tasks, all you need to do is transfer them onto your campaign flowchart in the proper sequence. A mock-up of a campaign flowchart is included in this chapter.

Setting Up a Preliminary Flowchart

A campaign flowchart (or plan or calendar) is an essential tool in any successful campaign. Flowcharts keep the campaign organized and provide you and the rest of your team with a visual plan of the whole campaign. I have also found that the chart can have a calming effect on the candidate and staff because it clearly outlines exactly what needs to be done and when. Dedicate a specific color for each activity so it can be easily traced throughout the campaigning process.

To construct your flowchart, you will need a long, unbroken wall and the following items:

- Five or more Post-it pads in assorted colors
- A long roll of paper, like butcher or freezer paper
- At least six different-colored marking pens
- A yardstick
- Masking tape
- One or two key campaign people (no more) to help you think

If possible, pull in someone who has worked on other campaigns to help you. Although an experienced campaigner is an invaluable aid in building the flowchart, you can also use the table of contents of this book. That's what I do, and I've done dozens of flow charts.

To begin your chart, unroll about ten feet of paper, and tape it up to a wall. On the far right-hand bottom of the chart, place the date of the day after the election. On the far left bottom, place the date of the beginning of your campaign. It may be the date that you start your flowchart or the date of your first "formal" campaign activity, such as your announcement. Draw a single line along the bottom between the two dates (this is your x-axis). Divide the line into fairly equal monthly or weekly parts by drawing in all the dates between the day your campaign begins and the day it will end.

On the y-axis, there will be a list of all the things you intend to do in your campaign: lawn signs, brochure, canvassing, media, fund-raising, and so on. I draw a horizontal line straight across using different-colored markers for each of the activities. So, for example, clerical is blue; media, red; lawn signs, green; and so on. You now have on your butcher paper a line across the bottom with dates on it, and parallel to this line are a series of different-colored lines that coordinate with a specific campaign activity on the y-axis.

Next, using a Post-it of a different color for each campaign function, begin brainstorming with your helpers. Slap up on the butcher paper the appropriately colored Post-it on the corresponding line. Place the note above the date that you want to do that particular campaign function. For example, if lawn signs are represented by green Post-its, put a note that says "Take down lawn signs" on the day after the election, because you know that your crew will have to take down lawn signs on that day.

Work your way backward from the end of the campaign, making decisions as you go. Continuing with the lawn sign example, you know you will need to repair lawn signs the day after Halloween, so place a green Post-it reading "Repair lawn signs" above November 1. Lawn signs usually go up one month before the election, so put that up next: Above the date of October 8 will be a Post-it on your green horizontal line: "Lawn signs go up 10/8."

You'll need a work party to get the signs stapled if you're using poly tag; if you're using corrugated, you'll need a team that will actually attach the sign to the stake. This is a clerical function, so choose a different color that will be used for all clerical work. Write on the Post-it "Staple lawn signs," and put it up somewhere in the week before the signs are to go up.

But wait: Before you can attach lawn signs to stakes, you need to buy stakes, so that goes up on a note the week before you assemble your signs.

You also need to get them printed, which takes about ten days, so on a line two weeks before the date that your team comes to assemble signs, you place a Post-it that says: "Lawn sign design goes to printer."

But before the design can go to the printer, your graphic designer must create the lawn sign. So give him or her a week to get that done. Place another Post-it note saying "Develop lawn sign design" above that date.

Also, before you can put up lawn signs, you need locations. Finding locations is a phone bank activity, so you place a phone-bank-colored Post-it that says "Call for lawn sign locations" on your phone bank line. This may take two weeks, so you are showing this activity on your phone bank line with an arrow down to your lawn sign line.

But before your volunteers can call, you need lists of people they can call. So you make a post-it that says "Secure lists for calling for lawn signs." Also, before you can call, you need to secure a location for the phone banks. That goes on a Post-it that is placed on a line representing the week before the phone bank team begins to call.

Keep working your way back, thinking through each of the campaign activities you have on your list. Review the chapters and headings in this manual. Think in terms of the progression of an activity and all the subactivities needed to support it.

Spread Out the Activities

With this method, time periods with too much campaign activity become immediately apparent. For example, if you find by the concentration of multicolored Post-its that brochure development, two direct-mail pieces, and a phone bank for an event are all happening at the same time, you may consider moving something to another time slot. Brochure development could move up and be done sooner, and the direct-mail pieces may be handled (just this once) by a mailing house, or they may be prepared earlier or later. Your Post-its are mobile for a reason, and you want to take advantage of this during this campaign planning activity. Spread out the activities so that you and the volunteers do not get overworked or burned out. If nothing can move, you will know to line up extra help to organize the work.

> "A perfection of means and a confusion of aims seem to be our main problem."
> — ALBERT EINSTEIN

By using colored Post-its for every function in a campaign on the chart, you build a visual representation of the campaign. The process is simple: Just take whatever it is that you want to do, give it a color, and work your way back from the date that you want to see that function completed to the point where that task must start in order to be completed on time. Some of the functions will end when others begin. For example, your brochure must be ready in time for canvassing. If canvassing will take you two months, working each day after work plus weekends, then your brochure must be back from the printer by this time. Therefore, the Post-its for "Brochure development" and "Printing" will end on the flowchart before canvassing activities start (figure 12.1).

Here is a partial list of activities that should be represented on your flowchart:

- Ads—print, radio, and television
- Lawn signs, field signs
- Web page design and upkeep

- Coffees, fund-raisers, special events
- Letters to the editor
- Direct mail
- Brochure development
- Canvassing and precinct analysis
- Phone banks

Finalizing the Flowchart

Once all your Post-its are up and are located where you want them, you are ready to put together your permanent campaign flowchart. Take another ten feet of paper, your colored marking pens, and a yardstick. Lay the paper on the floor in front of the Post-it flowchart. If there is room, you can hang the new chart on the wall directly below the old one. Now, all you have to do is write in and make permanent your campaign commitments on the dates listed.

> "Time is nature's way of keeping everything from happening at once."
> **WOODY ALLEN**

Follow your color scheme. For example, if lawn signs were in green Post-its, use a green marking pen for lawn signs on the flowchart.

Above the various dates, write the activity that is on the Post-it for that date, and then draw a line in the same color to the next date or activity, and so on, until you have transferred everything from the Post-it chart. By using colored lines, you will be able to follow a particular activity at a glance across the whole campaign. Figure 12.1 presents an example of a typical general election race.

The Campaign Calendar

As noted earlier, many campaigns lay out the activities and duties of the process in a campaign plan. Nearly every book on campaigning makes reference to campaign plans and provides examples of how to set them up. Because I prefer a campaign flowchart, I write campaign plans only when I'm forced to as a way to get money from lobbyists who otherwise would not give to my candidate.

I have, however, had great results using a campaign calendar (figure 12.2). This tool has a decided advantage: Smaller, monthly versions can go into your campaign committee packets for your team to use on an ongoing basis.

Although you can keep a wall-size calendar at campaign headquarters, I generally set one up on Excel so that it can be e-mailed to committee members

378

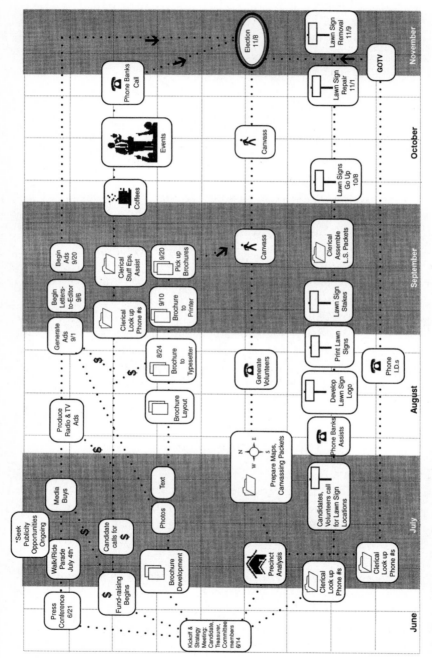

FIGURE 12.1 Example of a Campaign Flowchart

Sunday	Monday	Tuesday	Wednesday	Thursday	Friday	Saturday
15	**16** Committee working on Brochure wording Lawn Sign to Graphic Designer	**17**	**18**	**19**	**20** → Lawn Sign to Printer	**21**
22 8PM Campaign Team Meets	**23** Brochure copy to Graphic Designer Call for Volunteers to put up Lawn Signs	**24**	**25** Review Brochure with Committee	**26**	**27** Pick-up Brochure from Graphic Designer	**28**
29 8PM Campaign Team	**30** Brochure to Printer	**1** 11AM Ground breaking for Senior Center 4PM Opponent on Ken Linbloom Show KCMX Call for $	**2** 10AM Temple Emek Shalom Ribbon Cutting Golden Class: Meet the Candidates Candidate call for $	**3** Pick-up Lawn Signs fromPrinter Organize Lawn Sign Cards	**4** Clerical Party to Staple Lawn Signs - Bundle Stakes	**5** 8-10AM Lawn Signs Go up 12 - firefighters 2 - Carole, Ken 2 - Bill Street Canvass?
6 Canvass 8PM Campaign Team Meets	**7** Candidate Calls for $	**8** 5:30-7PM Chamber of Commerce - Meet the Candidates, AHI	**9** 12 noon LWV Lunch at the Mark 5-6 Canvass $ Calls	**10** Canvass Ashland Mine 6:30-10PM Kathleen Brown Dinner SOWAK, Red Lion	**11** 12 Noon Welcome Leadership Conference 4-6 Canvass	**12** 10AM Canvass 3-6PM Make informercial SOU for Cable Access $ Calls
13 Canvass 12-3 3-5 Canvass 8PM Campaign	**14** 5-6 Canvass $ Calls	**15** 7AM Lithia Springs Rotary Debate 5 min. + Q&A $ Calls	**16** 4 PM Office Hours 5-6 Canvass $ Calls	**17** 10AM Meet the Candidates 1023 Morton St. DEBATE - AAUW/LWV	**18** Letter-to-Voters Ad to Graphic Designer 4-6 Canvass Kennedy Roosevelt Dinner	**19** 10-1 Canvass 4-6 Ribbon Cutting of Environmental Center Design and Write Experience Ad
20 10AM Crop Walk 12-3 Canvass 3-5 Canvass 8PM Campaign	**21** Experience Ad to Graphic Designer Camera-ready Letter-to-Voters Ad to paper 4PM Ken Linbloom Radio Show	**22** 7PM Cable Access Debate	**23** 5-6 Canvass	**24** Camera-ready Experience Ad to paper Run Letter-to-Voters Ad Noon Rotary Debate	**25** Run Letter-to-Voters Ad again 4-6 Canvass	**26** Bob Miller 2-1001 Welcome Lions Club AHI 10-1 Canvass 3-5:30 Canvass Letter-to-Voters Ad again Call for EndorsementAd
27 12-3 Canvass 3-5 Canvass 8PM Campaign Meeting	**28** Run Experience Ad Layout Endorsement Ad Canvass	**29** Run Experience Ad Camera-ready Endorsement Ad to paper Canvass	**30**	**31** Run Experience Ad	**1** Run Endorsement Ad Lawn Sign Team Clean-up 4-6 Canvass	**2** Run Endorsement Ad Canvass 10-1 3-5:30 Canvass
3 12-3 Canvass 3-5 Canvass 8PM Campaign Meeting	**4** Run Endorsement Ad	**5** - ELECTION DAY -	**6** Lawn Signs come down			

FIGURE 12.2 Example of a Campaign Calendar for a Nonpartisan General Election

and updated daily. Each tab at the bottom of the Excel file is marked with the month. So if you're doing a primary election in May, you will have a tab for February, another for March, and one for May within the file. In general, I assign one person to do all scheduling; this is the same person who maintains and e-mails the calendar to committee members. You can also simply transfer data from your campaign flowchart to a calendar.

13

After the Ball

IN THIS CHAPTER
- Facing Election Night
- Retiring a Campaign Debt

There are many things you must do to put your campaign to bed, win or lose. However, before taking down your lawn signs, bundling your stakes, paying your bills, finishing reports for the state, closing out bank accounts, and reassembling your house, you must first face election night.

> "In every thing one must consider the end."
>
> *THE FABLES OF LA FONTAINE*

Facing Election Night

On election night, if you are not in a well-known location with other candidates and their volunteer teams, you should let the press know where they can find you. I have held campaign parties in restaurants and at my home. I prefer the latter. In the last days of the campaign, I let my volunteers know that I will be home and throwing a party in honor of them and a great campaign. I live in a small town, so people call and stop by all night. It is difficult to stay home and watch returns alone if you have been involved in a campaign, especially a winning one. Most people drop by to share the excitement, even if it is just for a few minutes. My home is open.

If your campaign was one that covered an area larger than one city, you need to go to a more central and public location. Again, tell all your volunteers where you will be, and invite them. Spend election day or even the weekend before the election calling and personally thanking volunteers; this is also a good time to remind them of the election-night gathering. Don't wait to thank them until after the election. If you lose, volunteers are anxious to talk and reflect and comfort, and you are anxious to sit alone on the floor of a dark closet with the door closed.

There is no preparing for a loss, and I'm not sure people *ever* get over it. It will change your life, just as winning will. But win or lose, you must be prepared to face the media and do it with class.

In one election on which I worked, I sat with the candidate as the first big returns came in. The shock that went through us as we realized we were losing is indescribable. I remember cameras pointing at our faces. There is something predatory and morose about our society when it comes to watching a leader fall.

> "Always let losers have their words."
> — **FRANCIS BACON**

We had expected a win and were not prepared for what was before us.

The next day, our pictures were in the paper. I looked for shock, disbelief, upset, disappointment. None of it was there. We just sat, stunned, looking at the huge TV screen in the restaurant. In the story that followed, the candidate thanked his volunteers, his campaign team, and his supporters. He thanked everyone for a chance to serve. The end.

Win or lose, that is the speech. You must be graceful and appreciative. If you win, you must be humble, acknowledge the efforts of your opponent, and immediately begin mending fences that might have been broken during the process. Win or lose, you thank your family, volunteers, supporters, and the community for support. If you lose, there is one more call you must make, and that is to your opponent. Congratulate that person, and say that you are on board to help make his or her time in office as successful as possible.

In my second bid for mayor, we won handily, by nearly two to one. On election night, my house was full of friends and volunteers. Well-wishers phoned. Everyone brought something to eat or drink. Then a reporter called and said that one of my opponents was convinced that he had lost because of a damaging letter to the editor that had accused him of criminal wrong-doing twenty years ago. The reporter said my opponent had suggested that I was responsible for the letter. Although I had nothing to do with the

> "When the fall is all there is, it matters."
> — **PRINCE RICHARD**, *Lion in Winter*

letter and the accusation was without merit, it made me feel as though the campaign wasn't over.

Have you ever watched a game where the coach for the losing team says basically it's no wonder we lost—we made mistakes or didn't play our best? While it may make that person feel better, it makes the losers feel guilty and the winning team feel slighted.

Be graceful. If you lost, say you put together a great effort but that your opponent put together a better one. Give your opponent a little of the limelight if you won and a lot of the limelight if you lost. Don't blame your loss on an insufficient campaign effort. That translates to "My volunteers are responsible for my loss." The most common feeling among volunteers of a losing campaign is, "What a waste of time that was." Say that you had a great campaign team that put in countless hours and that the whole thing was a ball—challenging, instructive, and fun from beginning to end. Take heart in the fact that you have come to know yourself and the democratic process better.

Should you ever run for office again, you will be glad you acted magnanimously.

Retiring a Campaign Debt

I counsel all candidates to spend within their means. Lending money to your own campaign sends the wrong message to the voting public. A campaign that is chronically short of funds is a sure sign of one that is in trouble. Nevertheless, it happens, and when it does, it is up to you, the candidate or the campaign manager, to retire the debt.

Never walk away from debt with businesses that have provided services to your campaign. Graphic designers, print shops, photographers, and such are trying to make a living, and generally they are very well connected with the community in which you live and hope to serve. In politics, nothing is more important than your reputation. But short of taking a second

> "The two happiest days of my life were the day we moved into the White House and the day we moved out."
> **BETTY FORD**

mortgage out on your home, there are a few things you can do to ease your debt. Win or lose, it is tough to retire a campaign debt. However, if you win, you tend to have more options.

1. If you have run for the state assembly and have won, go through the contributions and expenditures form for all those who gave to your opponent, but not to your campaign. Contact those representing "moderate" interests, and ask them to match the contribution given to your opponent. It should be obvious which among them will double dip, and it should be obvious which ones you do not want listed on your finance form.

2. Win or lose, you should be able to go to your most faithful donors. Send an appeal to your donor list, explain that you are doing all you can to retire your debt, and ask for some help.
3. Call major donors and ask for contributions. Set up a time each day to make these calls.
4. Reactivate your finance committee.

Afterword

You are now prepared to begin on that time-honored path of a political campaign. Campaigns are enormously fun and exhilarating. If you do everything right, you greatly improve your chances of winning. Just a few reminders before you begin:

1. Know the law.
2. Stay on your campaign theme and message, and you will be in control.
3. Deliver that message to your targeted voters: Aim at the souls that can be saved.

> "The great use of life is to spend it for something that outlasts it."
> **WILLIAM JAMES**

4. Redirect negative campaigning at your opponents, and use it as an opportunity to restate your message.
5. Work hard, and others will work hard for you.
6. Be humble, and listen more than you speak.
7. Know who you are before others find out.
8. Smile. Always look as though you're having a great time.

Win or lose, you will emerge from the process a different person, a leader within your community.

Notes

Chapter 1

1. Bill Bishop, "You Can't Compete with Voters' Feet," *Washington Post*, May 15, 2005, B2.

2. Alex Lundry, "Microtargeting: Knowing the Voter Intimately," *Winning Campaigns Magazine* 4, no. 1.

3. Rhodes Cook, "Moving On, More Voters Are Steering Away from Party Labels," *Washington Post*, June 27, 2004, B1.

Chapter 3

1. Karl G. Feld, "What are Push Polls, Anyway?" *Campaigns & Elections,* May 2000, 63.

2. Sam Stein, "Nasty Anti-Obama Push Poll Launched in Ohio," *Huffington Post*, September 11, 2008, available at www.huffingtonpost.com/2008/09/11/nasty-anti-obama-push-pol_n_125607.html.

3. For a general description of the Bradley effect, see "Bradley effect," *Wikipedia*, http://en.wikipedia.org/wiki/Bradley_effect; for the Confederate flag issue, see Sean Wilentz, "How the Confederate Flag Flap Helped the GOP," *Salon,* November 12, 2002, available at http://dir.salon.com/story/politics/feature/2002/11/12/confederate_flag/index.html.

4. John Ritter, "City Council Pays for Lessons in Civility," *USA Today*, October 4, 2007, available at www.usatoday.com/news/nation/2007-10-04-citycouncil-help_N.htm.

Chapter 5

1. Center for Responsive Politics, "Money Is the Victor in 2002 Midterm Elections," news advisory, November 7, 2002, www.opensecrets.org.

2. Center for Responsive Politics, "Big Picture: Winning vs. Spending," OpenSecrets.org Web chart, www.opensecrets.org/bigpicture/bigspenders.php?cycle=2006&Display=A&Sort=D&Memb=H.

3. Blue State Digital, "Case Study: MyBarackObama.com," Blue State Digital Web page, www.bluestatedigital.com/casestudies/client/obama_for_america_2008/.

4. Center for Responsive Politics Web page, www.opensecrets.org.

5. David Erickson, "Barack Obama's Online Fundraising Machine," January 1, 2009, http://e-strategyblog.com/2009/01/barack-obamas-online-fundraising-machine/.

6. Institute for Politics, Democracy and the Internet, "The Political Consultants' Online Fundraising Primer," www.ipdi.org/UploadedFiles/online_fundraising_primer.pdf.

7. Paul Pelletier, "Fundraising Direct Mail: A Success Story," Campaigns & Elections, April 1, 2000, 54.

Chapter 7

1. Alan Gerber, Donald Green, and Ron Shachar, "Voting May Be Habit-Forming," *American Journal of Political Science* 47 (2003): 540–550.

2. Wendy K. Tam Cho, James G. Gimpel, Joshua J. Dyck, "Residential Concentration, Political Socialization and Voter Turnout," *Journal of Politics* 68 (2006): 156–167.

3. Thomas S. Dee, "Are There Civic Returns to Education?" *Journal of Public Economics* 88 (2004): 1697–1720.

4. Center for Information on Civic Learning and Engagement, Tufts University, Web page, www.civicyouth.org.

5. Oregon Secretary of State, www.sos.state.or.us.

6. Mark DiCamillo and Mervin Field, "California's Turnout Increase Coincides with Growing Popularity of Mail Ballot Voting and Permanent Mail Ballot Registration," January 2009, Field Research Corporation Web page, http://field.com/fieldpollonline/subscribers/Rls2296.pdf.

7. U.S. Census Bureau, "Table 400: Voting-Age Population, Percent Reporting Registered, and Voted: 1994 to 2006."

8. Scott Keeter, Juliana Horowitz, and Alec Tyson, "Gen Dems: The Party's Advantage Among Young Voters Widens," Pew Research Center for the People & the Press, April 28, 2008, available at http://pewresearch.org/pubs/813/gen-dems.

9. Andrew Kohut, "Post-Election Perspectives," remarks at Pew Research Center 2nd Annual Warren J. Mitofsky Award Dinner, Washington, D.C., November 13, 2008, available at http://pewresearch.org/pubs/1039/post-election-perspectives.

10. U.S. Census Bureau, "Voting and Registration in the Election of November 2008."

11. Scott Keeter, Juliana Horowitz, and Alec Tyson, "Young Voters in the 2008 Election," *Pew Research Center Publications,* November 12, 2008, available at http://pewresearch.org/pubs/1031/young-voters-in-the-2008-election.

12. Donald P. Green and Alan S. Gerber, "Getting Out the Youth Vote: Results from Randomized Field Experiments," unpublished report, Yale University, New Haven, Conn., December 29, 2001, available at www.yale.edu/isps/publications/Youthvote.pdf.

13. George Washington University Graduate School of Political Management, *Young Voter Mobilization Tactics* (Washington, D.C.: George Washington University, 2006), available at www.civicyouth.org/PopUps/Young_Voters_Guide.pdf; and Center for Information and Research on Civic Learning and Engagement (CIRCLE), Tufts University, Web site www.civicyouth.org.

14. Russ Freyman, "The Deserted Group in American Politics," *Campaigns & Elections,* August 1, 2000, 63.

15. Green and Gerber, "Getting Out the Youth Vote," 19.

16. Ibid.

17. Public Opinion Strategies, "Understanding the Election: National Post Election Survey," November 2006, www.scribd.com/doc/7062016/November-2006-Poll.

18. Ronald Brownstein, "The Hidden History of the American Electorate," *National Journal Magazine,* October 18, 2008, www.nationaljournal.com/njmagazine/cs_20081018_7864.php.

19. *New York Times,* "Election Results 2008," November 5, 2008, http://elections.nytimes.com/2008/results/president/national-exit-polls.html.

20. Stochastic Democracy, "Assignment Desk: Black Turnout and Prop 8," November 23, 2008, stochasticdemocracy.blogspot.com.

21. Cho, Gimpel, and Dyck, "Residential Concentration."

22. Lake Research Partners, "How to Reach Unmarried Women: Edition II," memo by Lake Research Partners and sponsored by Women's Voices, Women Vote, available at www .wvwv.org/assets/2008/10/23/How_to_Reach_Unmarried_Women_2.pdf; Brownstein, "The Hidden History of the American Electorate."

23. Greenberg Quinlan Rosner Research, "Unmarried Women Play Critical Role in Historic Election," Women's Voices, Women Vote, www.wvwv.org.

24. Women's Voices; Women Vote, General Social Survey, 2006, www.wvwv.org.

25. Ibid.

26. Ibid.

27. Rose M. Kreider, "Marital Status in the 2004 American Community Survey," December 2006, Working Paper No. 83, U. S. Census Bureau, Population Division, Washington, D.C.

28. Women's Voices, Women vote, Current Population Survey, 2006, www.wvwv.org.

29. Rose M. Kreider, *Living Arrangements of Children: 2004,* Current Population Reports, P70-114 (Washington, D.C.: U.S. Census Bureau, 2007); and Rose M. Kreider and Jason Fields, *Living Arrangements of Children: 2001,* Current Population Reports, P70-104 (Washington, D.C.: U.S. Census Bureau, 2005).

30. Jessica Arons and Alexandra Cawthorne, "Fair Pay Is a Better Way," Center for American Progress Web page, April 25, 2008, www.americanprogress.org/issues/2008/04/why_ would.html; Page Gardner, "The Impact of a Declining Economy on Unmarried Women," April 6, 2009, Women's Voices, Women Vote, Web page, www.wvwv.org/research-items/the-impact-of-a-declining-economy-on-unmarried-women.

31. Women's Voices; Women Vote, www.wvwv.org; Priscilla L. Southwell and Justin Burchett, "Survey of Vote-by-Mail Senate Election in the State of Oregon," *PS: Political Science and Politics* 91 (1997): 53–57; Priscilla L. Southwell and Justin Burchett, "The Effect of All-Mail Elections on Voter Turnout," *American Politics Quarterly* 29 (2000): 72–80; Priscilla L. Southwell, "Five Years Later: A Re-assessment of Oregon's Vote by Mail Electoral Process," *PS: Political Science and Politics* (January 2004): 89–93; Adam J. Berinsky, Nancy Burns, and Michael W. Traugott, "Who Votes by Mail? A Dynamic Model of the Individual-Level Consequences of Voting-by-Mail," *Public Opinion Quarterly* 65 (2001): 178–197.

32. Jim Gimple, "Computer Technology and Getting Out the Vote: New Targeting Tools," *Campaigns & Elections,* August 2003, 40.

33. Kathleen Hall Jamieson, *Everything You Think You Know About Politics, and Why You're Wrong* (New York: Basic Books, 2000), 107–110.

34. Dan Romer, Kathleen Hall Jamieson, and Joseph Cappella, "Does Political Advertising Affect Turnout?" in *Everything You Think You Know About Politics, and Why You're Wrong,* by Kathleen Hall Jamieson (New York: Basic Books, 2000), 111–120.

35. CNN, "Black Democrats Angered by Supreme Court Ruling," December 13, 2000, available at http://archives.cnn.com/2000/ALLPOLITICS/stories/12/13/african.americans/index.html.

36. Crounse & Malchow Inc., "We've Got Mail! Use of Direct Mail in Political Campaigns," *Campaigns & Elections,* June 1999, 25.

Chapter 8

1. The Pew Center for the People & the Press, "Key News Audiences Now Blend Online and Traditional Sources," survey report, August 17, 2008, available at http://people-press.org/ report/444/news-media.

2. Ibid.

3. Pew Center for the People & the Press, *Campaigns & Elections,* June 2000, 75–80.

4. Pew Center for the People & the Press, "Key News Audiences."

5. Ibid.

6. Political Communications Lab, "Campaign 2008," http://pcl.stanford.edu/campaigns/2008/.

Chapter 9

1. David Beiler, "Green, Lean, and Keen," *Campaigns & Elections*, September 1999, 22–27.

2. Owen Abbe, Paul S. Herrnson, David Magleby, and Kelly Patterson, "Going Negative Does Not Always Mean Getting Ahead in Elections," *Campaigns & Elections,* February 2000.

3. To see the ad, go to www.youtube.com/user/oakstpress.

Chapter 10

1. Phil Keisling, quoted in City Club of Eugene, "Ballot Measure 79," 2005, available at www.cityclubofeugene.org/reports/79.html.

2. Information on state provisions is from the Initiative & Referendum Institute at the University of Southern California, www.iandrinstitute.org.

3. You can see the ad at www.youtube.com/user/oakstpress#play/uploads/8/zg0rPFmQ4Ugs.

Chapter 11

1. Katherine Seelye and Marjorie Connelly, "Signaling Voter Unrest, Schwarzenegger Cut Deep into the Democrats' Base," *New York Times,* October 9, 2003.

2. Donald Green and Alan Gerber, "What Causes Polls to Fluctuate?" Yale University, New Haven, CT, August 2001.

3. This observation comes from data gathered from the political consultants involved in house races for both Democrats and Republicans, and the Oregon secretary of state.

4. Rasmussen Reports, "Most Voters Made Up Their Minds Weeks Ago," November 5, 2008, www.rasmussenreports.com.

5. Kathleen Hall Jamieson, *Everything You Think You Know About Politics . . . and Why You're Wrong* (New York: Basic Books, 2000).

6. Priscilla Southwell, "Five Years Later: A Re-Assessment of Oregon's Vote by Mail Electoral Process," report, University of Oregon, Eugene, 2003.

7. Curtis Gans, "Making It Easier Doesn't Work: No Excuse Absentee and Early Voting Hurt Voter Turnout; Create Other Problems," press release, Committee for the Study of the American Electorate, Washington, DC, September 13, 2004, available at http://www1.american.edu/ia/cfer/research/csae_09132004.pdf.

8. Michael Hanmer and Michael Traugott, "The Impact of Voting by Mail on Voter Behavior," *American Politics Research* 32 (2004): 375–405.

9. Southwell, "Five Years Later."

10. Patricia Southwell, "Final Report: Survey of Vote by Mail Senate Election," report to Vote-by-Mail Citizen Commission, Oregon, April 3, 1996, available at https://scholarsbank.uoregon.edu/xmlui/bitstream/handle/1794/1268/VBM%20Full%20Report.pdf?sequence=5.

11. CNN, "Black Democrats Angered by Supreme Court Ruling," December 13, 2000, available at http://archives.cnn.com/2000/ALLPOLITICS/stories/12/13/african.americans/index.html.

12. Southwell, "Final Report."

Appendix

Conducting a Precinct Analysis

Gathering Data

What follows requires some proficiency in Excel. Indeed, other than amassing the data, none of the precinct analysis can be done without a computer. So if you do not have the skills, find someone who does. This is completely worth it.

A precinct analysis can be done on any kind of election, although some analyses are more illuminating than others. In areas of solid homogeneous populations, where races are typically decided in a partisan primary, an analysis reveals the gray tones rather than the black-and-white of mixed rural and urban populations. Typically in these areas, the candidate who works the hardest wins, but a precinct analysis will reveal subtleties that can give one candidate an advantage over another.

> "Every election is a sort of advance auction sale of stolen goods."
>
> **H. L. MENCKEN** (1880–1956)

In a primary, where candidates of the same party square off, the analysis involves looking at past voting records for candidates of that particular party in that cycle. In nonpartisan primaries, where all candidates run the field, with the two top vote-getters facing each other in the general, the analysis will look a lot like a regular general election analysis. The reason: Nonpartisan primaries typically have a Republican and Democrat in the race, or one candidate will lean left or right of the other, and voters know which is which.

If you're facing opponents in a nonpartisan race in which the winner is determined by the candidate who receives 50 percent of the vote or then faces an opponent in the general election, ways to get 50 percent are covered in Chapter 9.

If the analysis is for a candidate in a general election, compare the past voting trends of all parties in a similar cycle. If it is for an issue-based campaign, compare the voting histories for similar ballot measures or propositions using the same election cycle (presidential general, special election, midterm primary, etc.). Regardless of the type of election, the materials you need to conduct a precinct analysis are the same.

> "Everything should be made as simple as possible, but not simpler."
>
> — **ALBERT EINSTEIN**

My county keeps election results online for a couple of weeks after the election, but some counties keep them online indefinitely. If your county is of the latter category, download what you need row by row or page by page. Most counties use Excel or an Excel-compatible spreadsheet, but the online data is usually in PDF format. Getting the data online, on a CD, or e-mailed to you will save a lot of time. Online data in PDF format will need to be entered into your Excel spreadsheets by hand unless you have a program to convert the data.

For counties that do not have election results that you can obtain in some electronic form or that you can photocopy at the elections office, you will need to either enter the information into a spreadsheet on a laptop computer or write it down on paper at the election office. If you do not have a laptop, you may want to create an election data form using the spreadsheet categories provided in figures A.1 and A.2 to take with you. Be sure to create at least six blank sheets. Once you have the data recorded on paper, you must enter them into a spreadsheet. By the way, it saves a lot of time if a friend accompanies you to read the numbers off while you enter them into the laptop or spreadsheet.

> "The ax handle and the tree are made of the same wood."
>
> — **INDIAN PROVERB**

If your county does not break down results according to voter registration, you can approximate registration percentages using a primary election where only party registrants can vote to nominate someone within the party. Using the turnout percentage of a party in the primary will allow you to extrapolate an overall party registration to use in the analysis based on percentage of turnout. For example, 100 Republicans in Precinct 2 turned out in the primary and the county says this equals a 50 percent turnout, so you know there are 200 registered Republicans in Precinct 2. Once you have a number of reg-

2008 General		Total	Total Registration			Turnout			
Precinct	Description	Reg	Ds	Rs	Os	Ds	Rs	Os	Total

FIGURE A.1 Sample Spreadsheet Headings for Precinct Analysis

D = Democrat; R = Republican; O = Others (such as independents [NAVs], Green Party, Constitutional, and Libertarian). Eventually, all third-party and NAVs are combined.

President			U.S. Senate				Governor				New Race		
Obama	McCain	UV	D	R	O	UV	D	R	O	UV	D	R	UV

FIGURE A.2 Continued Headings for Sample Spreadsheet for Precinct Analysis

D = Democrat; R = Republican; O = Others; UV = Undervote.

istered Democrats and Republicans, you can calculate what percentage of the total registration they are owed.

Beginning the Analysis

First, you will create one master document that has all the necessary past voting information. In your Excel document, you will have many spreadsheets. Each spreadsheet tab should be labeled according to the election and year of the election. So, one tab may read "2002 General," and included in it will be the following data:

- Precinct number (be sure to put "pct" in front of each precinct number)
- A description of the precinct (e.g., South of Market, East of VanNess, north county; something to help you identify geographic location)
- Total registration for each precinct
- Registration of parties for each precinct
- Turnout
- Election results of candidates and some pertinent issue-based races, again all by precinct

Note that the precinct number and description can be copied and pasted on subsequent sheets.

The next tab or spreadsheet will have the same information but for another cycle, such as the 2004 primary election. The third might be for the 2006 primary or general, and then another for 2008. Although your election may be a midterm general, having all the years of voter performance and registration will assist in determining voter-registration trends, which is extremely helpful. Typically, counties purge deadwood from the voting roles prior to an election. For example, if a voter fails to participate in any election in a five-year period in Oregon, he or she will be dumped from the registration lists. Before the 2006 primary in my county, more than six thousand voters were purged, and another four thousand were dropped prior to the same year's general election; charting where people are purged will provide a fascinating glimpse into voter migration.

> "Nothing will ever be attempted if all possible objections must be first overcome."
> — SAMUEL JOHNSON

But for a particular analysis, you are looking for past elections that reflect the one you are about to dive into. So if you're running an election in a general election cycle, you may want to gather only general election data.

Issue-Based Analysis

If you are testing the waters for an issue campaign, again the idea is to look for similarities, especially if your campaign is about raising money. Issue-based campaigns dealing with revenue generally come in two varieties: capital improvements (bricks and mortar), and operation and maintenance. Within these two categories are police, fire, schools, cities, counties, libraries, parks, water systems, special districts, and so on. Issue campaigns that have to do with restricting the power of government, such as term limits, the right to die, abortion, and mandatory sentencing, are covered in Chapter 10. As with candidates, keep in mind that it is best to use identical election cycles, such as a nonpresidential primary, a presidential election year, special election, and so forth, for analyzing issue-based campaigns.

> "When we're elected, we'll take care of people like you! Okay, boys, throw him out!"
> — RICHARD NIXON, to a heckler

Election Data Form

You begin your analysis by going through the election data and transferring it to your spreadsheet (figure A.1). The election information may include the percentages of registration and turnout, but don't waste your time jotting that down as it is easy to calculate once you have all the information. After the data included in the headings of figure A.1, you will gather data for races you wish to compare (figure A.2).

Although the county printout includes more information than you may think you need, enter as much information as you can about previous elections and outcomes. The additional information can be helpful in identifying areas where certain issues may be more problematic or helpful than other areas. For example, money issues for public education and libraries can help define a voting area for candidate elections. Blowout elections are less helpful, except in predicting swing voters.

I've found the data from gubernatorial races to be extraordinarily useful in precinct analysis—unless, of course, your governor has attempted to sell a Senate seat or has done something equally damaging. While voters tend to retain congressional incumbents, swinging wildly from party to party to support him or her, this is not true with the governor, for whose elections they stick to party lines.

Create a Master Spreadsheet

Once you have created one complete Excel file of election data, labeled each of the tabs at the bottom by election and year such as general 2002 or primary 2008, then save this entire file and label it: Election Master 2002, 2004, 2006, 2008, or whatever years are included.

After saving your master, create an exact duplicate with which to work for your precinct analysis. Never make any alterations to your master data spreadsheets. Should anything go wrong with any of your spreadsheets while you are doing your analysis, you will need the original spreadsheet to rebuild scrambled information. Believe me, you do not want to go back to the elections office to reenter data halfway through a precinct analysis.

Expanding the Data

Once your master is safely tucked away in your files, you can begin the precinct analysis on your duplicate. First, between each of your headings after the Party Registration column, add the columns for the percentages for each of the registration columns (figure A.3). Note that in figure A.3, I have combined nonaffiliated voters (NAVs) and third-party registrants (and labeled them O for "Other") and determined a percentage of that total. If your county does not keep registration breakdown on all the parties, no worries; you really only need know the registration of the Democrats and Republicans, because everyone else will be collapsed into their registration percentages.

Total Registration			Percent of Registration			Turnout				Percent Turnout			
Ds	Rs	Os	Ds	Rs	Os	Ds	Rs	Os	Total	Ds	Rs	Os	Total

FIGURE A.3 Example of Expanded Spreadsheet for Precinct Analysis

D = Democrat; R = Republican; O = Other (third-party and NAVs)

Next, calculate all the percentages for registration, turnout, and percent candidates received. Don't forget that the formulas remain with cells where they are computed unless you copy a column and then click "values and number formats" within the "paste special" option. Personally, I like to leave formulas in my spreadsheets to help me remember how I came to a number. But should any original number in a column get fiddled with, it will change all subsequent numbers associated with that cell in a formula. This can be a bad thing and a good thing.

For example, what if you transposed a registration number when getting data from the county? This mistake may not be discovered until you go to calculate percentages and notice that the Democrats in some precinct are 150 percent of the registration. Not possible. So, after you call the county and get the correct value for that one item and replace the transposed number with the real number, the percentage will automatically be recalculated because the formula remains in the cell. Sometimes, mistakes are not discovered until days after you've begun your analysis and you have multiple formulas stretching across a spreadsheet. One change corrects everything if formulas are left within each of the cells, just as one change can mess up everything that follows. Simply remain aware that for your calculations to work, all the previous components of the formula must be present.

Pressing the Data

Once you've gathered all the information, entered it into Excel spreadsheets, saved a master document, created a duplicate, and calculated percentages, you're ready to press the data—that is, begin the precinct analysis.

The first thing to look at is registration. How a precinct trends in registration can offer great information. Look at registration as many ways as you can. I will typically assign one of my spreadsheets to registration, and line up all the registration by number and percentage of a given year and then compare one year with another. Are the percentages constant, or have they shifted toward or away from your party? If the precinct is even in registration, has it always been even? If it has actually been trending away from your party for years, you will want to take a closer look at that precinct in your swing analysis. Remember that when you move data, like registration percentages, to another spreadsheet, you must copy and "paste special" the "values and number formats," or you will end up with gobbledygook.

Precincts that have flipped registration within a census period can be a gold mine if the flip was toward your party and a warning if it moved away from you. Profoundly shifting registrations always make a statement at the ballot box.

Because precincts can range in size from four hundred to four thousand within the same voting area, it is important to look at registration shifts both by number and by percentage. Once you have compared years, subtracted the growth or fall-off of one party over another, and factored in county purging of inactive voters, you're ready to chart registration.

In the Zone

Unless you're working on a down-ballot race that covers just one small city, you will want to break the area being charted into zones. These are the same zones you will give your pollster should a poll be conducted by your campaign or on its behalf, so think this part though carefully.

Zones should make sense. For example, I break my county into nine zones: One is a city of twenty thousand plus surrounding precincts, another is two small adjacent cities and their surrounding precincts, I broke the largest city into two zones, and everything else is grouped into geographic areas. Some of my zones are larger than others, some by population and some by geography.

In another part of the state, I used state House districts for the zones. In another, I combined the small cities of the western part of a rural House district as one zone, treated the unincorporated areas of farmland as another, and worked my way across in similar fashion, going west to east and combining like with like, according to geography or cities.

If your county has organized the precincts in ascending order by geography, you're in luck and you will need to do very little to break your data in and out of zones. This means you can create charts along the way. I like to make charts as soon as I come across interesting data, so that I can study some nuance. However, if the county has a more hodgepodge approach to numbering precincts (often the case, because populations swell and precincts are divided and renumbered), it's best to keep your data together, that is, listed as it comes from the county, until everything is pressed; this will leave all your charts for last. Either way, once precincts are scrambled to make zones for charting purposes, you may need to put them back in the county order for

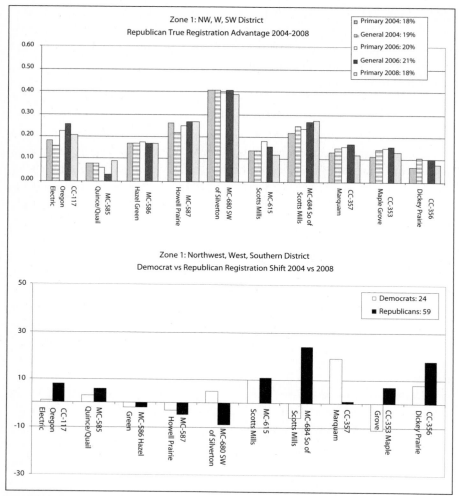

FIGURE A.4 Registration Comparisons

The top graph shows net registration advantage of Republicans, spanning five election cycles; the bottom compares net growth or loss of registration by number by party.

some unforeseen reason. To allow for this, I create a numbered column that is independent of my precinct numbers for quick reorganization.

Chart Your Data

There are many ways to chart your registration data; two examples are shown in figure A.4. The top graph simply charts the net advantage of Republicans within a zone (a group of precincts) and compares year after year of their net advantage by percentage. The bottom chart looks at the net shift of each party between two years comparing growth or loss of registration in number (not percentage).

Registration trends show where a precinct is headed. Since 1985, when I started tracking registration trends in my county, zones and precincts within those areas of the county have either flipped, gotten to be more of what they were, or stayed relatively constant. Those remaining relatively constant are the ones with the greatest swing.

As indicated above, you can do all sorts of mathematical computations within your Excel spreadsheet. But to chart, you must transpose the data from vertical to horizontal on the page. (Select the area to copy, then click Copy, Paste Special, Transpose, and paste in cells below data, where there are *no* data that might accidentally get erased with your pasted cells.)

In order for your precinct numbers to remain apart from the bars of the graph, there must be lettering prior to the precinct number. This is why you labeled them "pct 1," "pct 2," and so on. I also include the description of the precinct in my charts because most people don't know one precinct from another. The descriptions can simply be the name of the city the precinct falls in or a description of a portion of your city such as "hospital to university."

After you transpose the data, click on the Chart icon within Excel, and follow the steps—it's easy. Once you have your chart, you can change colors of the bars in the bar graph and change values on the x-axis and y-axis. I make Republicans red, Democrats blue, and undervotes light yellow and light green.

I like to make my charts right below the data and then copy, cut, and paste the charts to another spreadsheet labeled "Charts." *But* if you change anything in your transposed data, remember it is linked to the chart and will change your chart—no matter where it is in your computer. So heads up. Again, this is good and bad. If something is incorrect in the transposed data, you only need to correct it there for the chart to also get corrected. But if you decide you want a little more room below your spreadsheet and delete the transposed data, the next time you look at the chart, it will be empty.

Excel likes to set the scale for the y-axis but since I want to compare apples with apples, I make everything the same—chart after chart; for example, a scale of 800 to −800 in figures A.8, A.9, and A.10. To change anything within a chart, point and click, and the options become evident. Generally, I do all my graphs and then come back and do the scale on all the graphs at the same time. Some precincts need more room than other precincts and thus end up dictating the high or low points on the scale. Some of my precinct analyses have better than one hundred charts. I make lots of charts, because

I'm always looking for patterns and I find this the easiest and quickest way to see things.

Questions? E-mail me: cathyshaw@mind.net.

Votes Owed

Votes owed is simply a predicted percentage or number of votes that partisan candidates are owed determined only by the Republican and Democratic registration percentages. These percentages are determined apart from NAVs and third-party registrants.

Calculating Votes Owed Versus Received

To calculate votes owed against those received, you will again expand your Excel spreadsheet by adding more columns (figure A.5A). Remember that you're ignoring all third-party and nonaffiliated voters and will only determine the percentage of the Democratic and Republican registration.

> "Politics is more difficult than physics."
> — **ALBERT EINSTEIN**

Therefore, you will need a column labeled "D + R," which represents the registration of the Democrats added to the registration of the Republicans.

What is owed the Democrats is the Democratic registration total divided by the D + R column and, similarly what is owed the Republicans is the Republican registration divided by the D + R column. In other words, you're finding what percentage the Democrats and Republicans are of their combined total rather than of the total registration (figures A.5A and A.5B).

Next, determine if the partisan candidates actually received the votes owed. You do this by multiplying the percentage owed for each of the parties by the total voter turnout. This will yield a number of votes owed for each parties. Then subtract this number from the actual votes received by each of the candidates within each party (figure A.5C).

So, for example, in Precinct 2, Obama received 7 more votes than he was owed; McCain, 101 fewer than he was owed. The undervote is all those who voted for third-party candidates plus the actual undervote. Therefore, in this example, 94 votes were thrown into the undervote for Precinct 2, and 118 for Precinct 4. Votes for third-party candidates can be added to the undervote or subtracted from the voter turnout before subtracting votes owed from votes received.

Next, the data are charted. In figure A.6, the two aforementioned precincts are shown, but typically, all precincts within a zone would be charted.

Precinct No.	Description	Total Reg	Total Reg Ds	% Reg Ds	Total Reg Rs	% Reg Rs	Total Reg NAVs	% Reg NAVs	TO Total	TO % Total	D + R
2	Ashland	3,613	2,383	66	407	11	823	23	3,325	92	2,790
4	Ashland	3,454	2,237	65	437	13	780	23	3,122	90	2,674

FIGURE A.5A Example of a Spreadsheet with Actual Numbers, Presidential Election 2008

D = Democrat; R = Republican; NAV = nonaffiliated voter; TO = turnout.

Precinct	D + R	% Owed D	% Owed R	Votes Owed Ds	Votes Owed Rs
2	2,790	85	15	2,840	485
4	2,674	84	16	2,612	510
		(D + R) / D reg	(D + R) / R reg	(% owed D) × TO	(% owed R) × TO

FIGURE A.5B Expanded Spreadsheet That Includes Columns for Percentage of Votes Owed and Number of Votes Owed Both Democrats and Republicans, Presidential Election 2008

D = Democrats; R = Republicans; reg = registered; TO = turnout. Formulas for the calculation are shown in the bottom row of the spreadsheet.

Precinct	Votes Owed Ds	Votes Owed Rs	Votes Received Obama	Difference	Votes Received McCain	Difference	UV
2	2840	485	2847	7	384	-101	-94
4	2612	510	2606	-6	398	-112	-118
	(% owed D) × TO	(% owed R) × TO					

FIGURE A.5C Actual Votes Received, Followed by Votes Owed Versus Votes Received, Presidential Election 2008

D = Democrat; R = Republican; UV = undervote; TO = turnout.

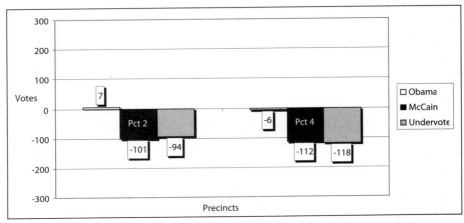

FIGURE A.6 Votes Owed Versus Votes Received, Precincts 2 and 4, Ashland, Oregon, 2008 Presidential Election

Nonpartisan Primaries

Within any general election, I have not found an appreciable difference between calculating the percentages of votes owed using total party registration and calculating the same percentages using party turnout totals. But this relationship does not hold when you are calculating the percentages of votes owed for a nonpartisan primary race.

To calculate the percentage of votes owed for a nonpartisan primary, you must use party turnout, because there can be dramatic variations of party performance in a primary, depending upon what is on each side of the ballot. In this case, rather than dividing party registrants by the combined Democratic and Republican registration totals, you will divide party turnout by the Democratic turnout plus the Republican turnout. For example, if the Democratic turnout is 100 votes and the Republican turnout is 75, to calculate votes owed, you would first add 100 and 75, to get 175 votes cast. In this example, the Democrats would be owed 100 out of 175, or 57 percent of the votes cast, and Republicans would be owed 75 out of 175, or 43 percent of the votes cast.

Assigning the Undervote

As mentioned in chapter 1, in 2004, State Representative Alan Bates (D-Ashland) ran against local businessman Jim Wright (R-Medford). In Precinct 2, Bates was "owed" 80 percent of the ballots cast, and Wright was "owed" 20 percent. However, Bates only received 79 percent and Wright only 17 percent. So where were the other 4 percent of the votes? If there is no third-party candidate—and there wasn't—you will find the missing votes in the undervote. That is, those who voted for neither candidate but who still participated in the election.

> "The seeds of political success are sown far in advance of any election day. . . . It is the sum total of the little things that happen which leads to eventual victory at the polls."
>
> **J. HOWARD MCGRATH**, former chairman, Democratic National Committee

The genius of this detail is that you now know who undervoted whom. So, again using our example, for Precinct 2 with a 2004 registration of 3,400 voters, Bates is attributed 1 percent of the undervote, or 34 votes, and Wright is attributed 3 percent of the undervote, or 102 votes. Figure this precinct by precinct for past elections to reveal which party consistently underperforms for the team in which precinct.

Being able to assign the undervote helps diagnose potential problem areas so they may be remedied. For example, in 2006, I was hired to determine why

Democrats, with a 6 percent registration advantage, were consistently losing a state House seat to Republicans in another part of the state. Charting votes owed against those received for previous state House elections revealed that the entire undervote came from the Democratic side of the ticket. This information allowed for a very simple fix. Knowing why past elections were lost provides critical information and opportunities to correct a course to reverse a trend in future elections; undervotes typically reside at the foundation of a loss.

Let me show you two zones in our county (figures A.7, A.8, and A.9). The precincts on the left are one zone, and the precincts on the right are another. Notice how the voters tend to vote like their neighbors in each of the two zones. Because of space limitations on figures A.7, A.8, and A.9, the undervotes (UV) are not marked as attributable to either of the candidates. However, most of the undervote was on the Republican side of the ticket. In the Bates versus Wright race (figure A.7), Bates did have a few undervotes, but the swing from Republicans countered that and then some, giving him 302 more votes than he was owed districtwide. Wright received 3,180 fewer than he was owed—of which 302 went to Bates and 2,878 Republican votes were left on the table. Bates won by 2,462 of 62,664 votes cast.

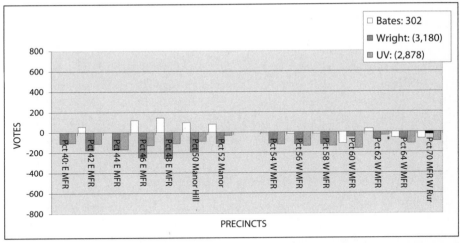

FIGURE A.7 Votes Owed Versus Votes Received, Bates versus Wright, 2004 Election

In 2004, Democrat Alan Bates and Republican Jim Wright ran for an open state senate seat previously held by a Republican for nearly three decades. This chart includes two of the five zones the senate seat was broken into for study of swing. The final analysis showed that 302 people moved across party lines to vote for Bates, and another 2,878 of Wright's votes were thrown into the undervote (UV). Nearly all campaign efforts focused on the four precincts left of center, which the swing analysis revealed as prime real estate for swing voters. In this 2004 race, the Democrat won by the undervote margin.

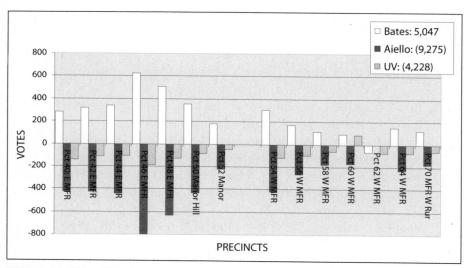

FIGURE A.8 Votes Owed Versus Votes Received, Bates Versus Aiello, 2006 Election

In 2006, Senator Alan Bates was challenged by Republican Lynn Aiello for his state senate seat. Aiello, an unknown and much weaker candidate than Jim Wright in 2004, was owed an additional 9,275 votes that she did not receive. Of those, 5,047 were given to Bates, and 4,228 were thrown in the undervote (UV). Clearly, swing is a function of the candidates; Bates easily overcame the 4 percent registration disadvantage. Again, the chart represents two of the five zones from the senate district.

On figures A.7, A.8, and A.9, anything above the x-axis represents how many more votes a candidate received than he or she was "owed," and anything below represents votes "owed" that were not received by a candidate. The undervote (always below the line) is the smaller bar.

Predicting Voter Turnout

Because turnout can vary dramatically, depending upon the election cycle and the strength of candidates, simply averaging the last three elections will not necessarily give you a clear prediction of voting behavior for your election. To determine the expected voter turnout, find a similar past election in the same season. For example, is your election in a presidential or nonpresidential primary or general election? Is it a special or an off-year election? Whatever it may be, use the same election cycle.

Next, compare what was on the earlier ballot with what will be on yours. If the referenced election had a hotly contested governor's race, this will influence the voter turnout. If you are running in a presidential primary and

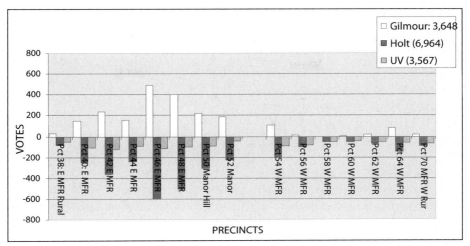

FIGURE A.9 Votes Owed Versus Votes Received, Gilmour Versus Holt, 2002 Election

When Democrat Dave Gilmour challenged incumbent Republican Ric Holt in 2002 for the county commission, Republicans held a countywide 11 percent registration advantage. In this election, Republicans gave Gilmour 3,648 votes owed to Holt and threw another 3,567 into the undervote (UV). Gilmour's win of 2,646 votes out of nearly 73,000 cast can be found entirely in the undervote. Much of the county swing lives in the precincts in the zone on the left side of the chart, where Republicans hold a 22 percent registration advantage.

the Republicans hold the White House and have only the president on the ballot, compared with two candidates in the Democratic field, you can safely assume that Democrats will turn out in larger numbers than Republicans in the primary. Take such information into consideration, and adjust expected turnout up or down accordingly by averaging three similar cycles.

In the election you are using for comparison purposes, look at the turnout, precinct by precinct, for each party. Let's say that in Precinct 1, turnout among Republicans was 65 percent, turnout among Democrats was 62 percent, and turnout among NAVs was 35 percent. However, in your election, because of controversial issues on the ballot, you predict that voter turnout will be at least 10 percent higher. So, in Precinct 1, you will multiply the current number of registered Republicans by 75 percent, the current number of Democrats by 72 percent, and the current number of NAVs by 45 percent. Add these numbers together, and you get your predicted turnout for Precinct 1. Do the same for all precincts.

If you are uncomfortable with predicting increases or decreases in voter participation based on ballot issues, you will be close if you simply multiply the percentage of voter turnout of the last identical election by the current number of registered voters. Even if turnout changes substantially in one direction or the other, the parties will track similarly, within a couple of points within any general election. In other words, in a given precinct, you will not see a substantial increase in turnout for one party without seeing a similar spike in the other parties.

> "There are only two tragedies in life: one is not getting what one wants, and the other is getting it."
>
> — OSCAR WILDE

The exception of this rule is a primary. Some primaries do not allow NAVs to participate and some primaries have candidates on one side of the aisle running unopposed while candidates on the other side have heated races. In the 2008 presidential primary in Oregon, where Democrats were slugging it out in both the U.S. Senate and the presidential campaigns, Democrats outperformed Republicans by ten points in the primary. Predicting this sort of turnout can be very useful in a nonpartisan race where the winner of the primary must secure 50 percent of the vote or head off to the general election. For example, if your nonpartisan candidate is running in a primary where all the action is on the democratic side of the ticket, he or she should lock that party's vote in the primary cycle and then come back and work Republicans in the general.

Base Party Vote

The base party vote is a useful number and is very easy to calculate. It tells you the number of voters in each precinct who will always vote with their party, regardless of how bad the candidate may be. Your base party vote is the number of votes you and your opponent will get, no matter what you do or say (figure A.10).

Here's how to find the base party vote:

1. You need election results in which a candidate in your party was pounded. Since you're going to translate these numbers precinct by precinct, it really doesn't matter if the poor outcome for your party was in the same election cycle. Although it can include more precincts, it must have all the precincts of your campaign area. For example, a heavily lopsided governor's race could be used for a house or senate seat.
2. List all the precincts in the area where you are running (column A).
3. For each of the precincts, list the percentage of votes the candidate in your party received (column B). Remember, this is a race where your party's candidate lost big.

A	B	C	D	E
Precinct Number	Worst % of Votes for Same-Party Candidate	Current Voter Registration	Percentage Expected Turnout	Number of Voters Who Won't Leave the Party (D _ C) _ B
58	35	655	67	153
59	37	916	73	247
60	38	707	72	193
61	37	676	76	191
62	42	424	66	118
64	45	822	74	274
65	46	693	72	230
66	43	703	67	202
67	37	756	62	173
68	41	740	72	218
69	38	949	70	252
70	36	723	65	169
71	35	1,038	71	258
TOTAL		9,802		2,678

FIGURE A.10 Sample Form for Determining Base Party Support

4. List, precinct by precinct, the current voter registration (column C).
5. List the percentage turnout you expect (column D).
6. Finally, multiply the expected percentage turnout by the current number of registered voters, and multiply the result by the percentage of votes the same party candidate got in the previous election (D C B). This will give you the number of people who will vote for your party, no matter what.

> "Under democracy, one party always devotes its chief energies to trying to prove that the other party is unfit to rule; both commonly succeed, and are right."
>
> **H. L. MENCKEN**

Repeat these steps with data from an election in which someone in the opposing party lost by huge numbers. The result of this tabulation will be the number of votes your opponent will receive simply because of party affiliation.

Alternatives for Finding Swing Voters

Swing voters are those who are registered in one party but who are willing to vote for someone from another party, and consistently do so. Swing voters are sometimes called "smart voters" because they vote according to issues and information rather than party. However, they also include voters who are persuaded solely by emotion and their impressions of the candidates. Your job is to find them and persuade them that they should vote for your candidate.

Although I exclusively calculate swing votes according to the votes-owed model, this is another approach to determine potential swing by precinct. First, calculate the base-party support for both your party and your opponent's (figure A.10). To find swing voters, add columns to your base-party vote spreadsheet and simply subtract the election percentage where your party destroyed the opposition from one where the opposition destroyed the candidate in your party. That will give you a percentage that will potentially swing. Multiply this by the predicted voter turnout, and you will have the predicted number of voters who will potentially swing (figure A.11). An alternative way to compute potential swing is outlined in Chapter 1.

> "You've got to be very careful if you don't know where you are going, because you might not get there."
>
> — YOGI BERRA

A	B	C	D	E	F	G
Precinct No.	Highest % Votes Cast	Lowest % Votes Cast	Percent of Swing (B – C)	Projected % Turnout	Current Voter Registration	Number of Voters Who Could Swing D (E _ F)
58	65	35	30	67	655	132

FIGURE A.11 Sample Form for Determining Swing Voters

Votes Needed to Win (VNW)

Once you have calculated the predicted turnout, base vote, and swing vote, you're ready to calculate the votes you will need to win. There are a couple of ways to estimate the number of votes you need to win. One is to simply divide the overall predicted voter turnout (number) in half, and add one more vote to your number. A second way, one that will provide a little more insight, is to calculate the predicted voter turnout by party and by precinct, add these up, and divide by two; again, add one more vote to your side.

So, to recap, you know:

1. Your base-party vote—that is, exactly how many people in your party will never stray from you, no matter what you say or do. Add these numbers up.
2. How many will never leave the opposing party—precinct by precinct, so add those up. What's the difference? At a deficit? Look for precincts with the greatest swing. Does the swing consistently go toward or away from your party? By how much? Add these to your column or your opponent's.
3. Generally, one-third of each party sticks with the base; this leaves 40 percent of the remaining voter turnout that's up for grabs. Some of these voters live in left-leaning precincts, and some in right-leaning; you know which is which, because you did a precinct analysis that told you so.
4. Clearly, it will be easier to get votes in the right-leaning precincts if you're a Republican and in the left-leaning if you're a Democrat.
5. If registration is skewed—that is, if you're at a fundamental disadvantage because more people are registered in a party other than yours, you need a higher undervote in precincts that will vote for the opposing party to help even the registration numbers. How far down can you drive the opposition support? Your precinct analysis will tell you if there are typically higher undervotes of one party over another, precinct by precinct. If the undervote is greater consistently in your party, then you will go into those precincts and put the fear of God in the voters to activate them to vote. Remember, you cannot activate voters with vacuous mail; it must make sense. Think you can do it? Add those underperformers to your list.

> "Democracy is the theory that the common people know what they want . . . and deserve to get it good and hard."
> **H. L. MENCKEN**

6. Look at the consistent undervote of the opposing party. If your registration disparity is great, then you need these voters to remain asleep. Where opposition undervote is consistently high election after election, avoid untargeted activities—like lawn signs. Subtract the number of voters who you think will not participate in this election if you quietly go about your business without pounding the ubiquitous drum. Subtract these from the opposition's abacus.
7. Hopefully, the bottom line has your team ahead. If not, work harder.

About the Author

Cathy Shaw served three terms (twelve years) as mayor of Ashland, Oregon. First elected in 1988, she was the youngest person and the first woman elected to her city's highest post. She also served as a member chief of staff in the Oregon legislature.

For over two decades, she has managed and consulted for scores of political campaigns, successfully passing innovative taxing measures for funding public education, recreation, parks, open-space programs, libraries, and civic buildings.

Outspent in every election, sometimes as much as five to one, Shaw developed and perfected techniques to combat big money and to engineer seemingly impossible wins. She has been a frequent guest speaker and instructor for political science classes and campaign schools.

Shaw currently works as a political consultant and is available for teaching at campaign schools as well as for telephone and on-site consultations.

For consultation or questions regarding any portion of this book, please contact her by e-mail: cathyshaw@mind.net.

Some of the television ads referenced in this work can be found on YouTube, www.youtube.com/user/oakstpress.

Index